Building Spring 2 Enterprise Applications

■ ■ ■

Interface 21

with Bram Smeets and Seth Ladd

Lead Editors: Matthew Moodie, Steve Anglin
Technical Reviewer: Rob Harrop
Editorial Board: Steve Anglin, Ewan Buckingham, Gary Cornell, Jonathan Gennick, Jason Gilmore,
    Jonathan Hassell, Chris Mills, Matthew Moodie, Jeffrey Pepper, Ben Renow-Clarke,
    Dominic Shakeshaft, Matt Wade, Tom Welsh
Project Manager: Kylie Johnston
Copy Edit Manager: Nicole Flores
Copy Editor: Marilyn Smith
Assistant Production Director: Kari Brooks-Copony
Production Editor: Laura Cheu
Compositors: Dina Quan, Linda Weidemann
Proofreader: April Eddy
Indexer: Becky Hornyak
Artist: Kinetic Publishing Services, LLC
Cover Designer: Kurt Krames
Manufacturing Director: Tom Debolski

Distributed to the book trade worldwide by Springer-Verlag New York, Inc., 233 Spring Street, 6th Floor, New York, NY 10013. Phone 1-800-SPRINGER, fax 201-348-4505, e-mail orders-ny@springer-sbm.com, or visit http://www.springeronline.com.

For information on translations, please contact Apress directly at 2855 Telegraph Avenue, Suite 600, Berkeley, CA 94705. Phone 510-549-5930, fax 510-549-5939, e-mail info@apress.com, or visit http://www.apress.com.

The source code for this book is available to readers at http://www.apress.com in the Source Code/ Download section.

Contents at a Glance

Contents

Introduction

This book covers the Spring Framework, the Java application framework of choice for tens of thousands of Java developers worldwide. We feel it is important to introduce you to the Spring Framework by showing you how to use it. So we wrote a book that uses a complex sample application to demonstrate how the Spring Framework is used in a typical business application. By exploring the code from the sample application, presented throughout this book, you will benefit from many insights in application development. This is important knowledge for any developer, no matter how many years of experience you have.

Ultimately, the goal of this book is to make you, the reader, more efficient as a Java developer by taking the things that are good about the Java platform and using them in the most efficient and reliable way.

In this book, we focus on how to be successful in two areas that are important in software development: simplicity and consistency. Both goals can be achieved with the Spring Framework, although creating a simple design requires effort from your side as well.

The concept of API consistency involves applying the same design and coding pattern where applicable. Clients of a consistent API feel at home when using it, and are able to concentrate on its logic instead of its semantics. The Spring Framework excels at bringing consistency to the Java platform. We're going to show you how to leverage this consistency to make your applications more consistent.

Simplicity in software development means four things:

- To implement only the functionality that is absolutely required and nothing more
- To write code that is as clean, readable, and simple as possible
- To write code that is easy to test and is tested only once
- To streamline the development process cycle to be as agile and rapid as possible (taking into account the settings of your projects)

The Spring Framework enables you to implement your applications in a simple way, but it does not stop you from writing overly complex software that is hard to test and doesn't deliver what is expected. This book will guide you in achieving simplicity in your code and show you how the Spring Framework helps to write simple code that is easy to test.

Who This Book Is For

This book is intended for Java developers who want to use the Spring Framework in their applications. You will learn not only what features the Spring Framework offers, but also when to use them and how to use them correctly.

How This Book Is Structured

This book is divided into ten chapters:

Chapter 1 introduces the Spring Framework and its core values. In this chapter, we will discuss the modules of the Spring Framework, introduce the sample application, and use the Spring Framework to solve an important problem that many applications face. This chapter also examines Spring's relationship with Java Enterprise Edition and Enterprise JavaBeans.

Chapter 2 details the core deployment model of the Spring Framework that you can use to configure and deploy your applications. It's the perfect start to bring consistency to your applications. Once you know how this deployment model works, you can reuse it every time you need to configure objects.

Chapter 3 explains how to *reuse* the most efficient and flexible solution to a problem everywhere you need it. The technical term for a solution that is required in multiple places is a *cross-cutting concern*. This chapter introduces Spring's aspect-oriented programming (AOP) framework.

Chapter 4 builds on the theme of AOP and shows how Spring 2.0 makes AOP more consistent and simpler to use.

Chapter 5 describes how data access—also called *persistence*—is simplified and made consistent by the Spring Framework. If you handle data access correctly, it will improve the simplicity of your applications significantly, and Chapter 5 explains how to do that.

Chapter 6 discusses the data-access layer of the sample application, which is implemented using Spring's JDBC framework.

Chapter 7 shows you how to move transaction management out of your application code by using Spring's transaction management framework.

Chapter 8 introduces Spring's web framework and discusses how the web layer of the sample application is implemented.

Chapter 9 demonstrates different ways of returning content to the browser window. This chapter also explores how to create and return Adobe PDF and Microsoft Excel files to the browser with ease.

Chapter 10 shows you how to do less work during development projects by testing applications before you write code. In economics, the standard way to reduce costs is to do less work and deliver to customers only what they really want, and nothing more. This chapter translates this principle to application development.

This book shows how the Spring Framework can make you more efficient as a developer and as a team member. The final chapter brings everything together and explains how you can start changing your development process so that you not only develop more efficient code, but also shorten the development life cycle.

Prerequisites

We assume that you have a good understanding of the Java programming language, preferably version 1.4 or later. For the first four chapters of this book and in Chapter 10, you are expected to understand classes, objects, inheritance, exception handling, and threads in Java.

For Chapters 5 to 7, you are expected to have a basic understanding of JDBC, relational databases, the SQL query language, and database transactions.

For Chapter 8, you are expected to have a basic understanding of HTML, JSP, and servlet containers such as Tomcat.

Chapter 9 discusses specific frameworks with which the Spring Framework integrates. If you are not familiar with any of these frameworks, but wish to use them, you are encouraged to first gain a basic understanding of how they work, and then return to this chapter to learn how to use them in combination with the Spring Framework.

Downloading the Code

The source code for this book is available to readers from the Apress website (`http://www.apress.com`), in the Source Code/Download section. Please feel free to visit the Apress website and download all the code there. You can also check for errata and find related titles from Apress.

■■■

CHAPTER 1

A Gentle Introduction to the Spring Framework

The Spring Framework is an open source application framework written in Java, which supports Java 1.3 and later. It makes building business applications with Java much easier compared with using the classic Java frameworks and application programming interfaces (APIs), such as Java Database Connectivity (JDBC) and JavaServer Pages (JSP). Since its introduction, the Spring Framework has significantly improved the way people design and implement business applications by incorporating best-practice methodologies and simplifying development.

As an introduction to the Spring Framework, this chapter will cover the following topics:

- The process of developing a typical business application and the role the Spring Framework can play

- An overview of the modules that make up the Spring Framework

- An introduction to the sample application that you'll be working with in this book

- An example that demonstrates one of the Spring Framework's core features: managing dependencies

- How the Spring Framework integrates with Java Enterprise Edition (Java EE)

- How to set up the Spring Framework in your applications

Building a Business Application

A modern business application typically consists of the following components:

- *Relational database*: Stores the data related to the problem domain. The database is not necessarily part of the application, but the data-access classes have been written for the specific schema of the database, so that the application is closely coupled with the database schema.

- *Graphical user interface (GUI)*: Lets users interact with the business processes that are implemented by the application. Since the days of the web revolution, many business applications are web-based.

- *Business logic*: Controls and monitors the execution of business processes. The business logic must work with the database and is called by the GUI.

Unfortunately, as tens of thousands of Java developers worldwide can testify, developing business applications in Java can be very hard and frustrating. This is especially, although not exclusively, true at the join points, where the business logic meets the database and the GUI meets the business logic.

Java Platform Hurdles

Java is one of the most powerful and easy-to-use programming languages for developing business applications, so it might seem strange to suggest that developing business applications in Java is difficult. The main hurdles involve its extensive set of libraries and frameworks, each of which adds a wide range of capabilities to Java.

The parts of the Java platform that are crucial for building typical business applications are as follows:

- The JDBC API allows Java applications to connect to a wide range of relational databases.

- The Servlet and JSP specifications are crucial for web-based business applications.

- Desktop applications rely heavily on the Swing or Standard Widget Toolkit (SWT) APIs.

Each of these APIs offers useful capabilities for developing business applications, but most of them are very difficult to use. For example, it's hard to use the JDBC API correctly for very basic queries on a database (see Chapter 5 for an example). JDBC is an *intrusive* API—it influences the design of an application in such a way that the focus of the design shifts away from its original goals toward trying to use the API in the application. In fact, because the JDBC API is so intrusive, application developers should not spend their time trying to use it correctly. The same can be said for many other APIs in the Java platform. This is where the Spring Framework steps in.

Enter the Spring Framework

A new open source application framework for Java was released on the first day of spring 2003. This release was based on the source code introduced in Rod Johnson's best-selling book, *Expert One-on-One J2EE Design and Development* (Wrox, 2002).

This 1.0 release offered the building blocks for business application development. Common tasks, such as connecting to and querying a database, managing transactions, and configuring applications, were made more accessible and easier to accomplish. These building blocks used the standard Java APIs behind the scenes and spared the developer from handling their complexity. The 1.1 and 1.2 releases consistently improved existing features and added new features and capabilities. The most recent release (2.0) takes the efficiency of the Spring Framework one step further by offering unparalleled improvements to ease of use and functionality.

The Spring Framework has started a revolution in the world of enterprise Java application development and set in motion a series of events that have forever changed the way applications are developed and deployed. A quick look at the modules that make up the framework should give you an idea of its scope.

Introducing the Spring Framework Modules

The Spring Framework is a collection of subframeworks that solve specific problems and are grouped together in modules. You are free to use any of these frameworks separately. Unless otherwise mentioned, these modules are part of the Spring Framework distribution.

Inversion of Control (IoC) Container: Also called the Core Container, creates and configures application objects and wires them together. This means that resources and collaborating objects are provided to objects, so the objects do not need to look them up. This moves an important responsibility out of your code and makes it easier to write and test code. Chapter 2 introduces the Core Container.

Aspect-Oriented Programming (AOP) framework: Works with *cross-cutting concerns*—one solution to a problem that's used in multiple places. The Spring AOP framework links cross-cutting concerns to the invocation of specific methods on specific objects (not classes) in such a way that your code is unaware of their presence. The Spring Framework uses cross-cutting concerns and AOP to let your application deal with transactions without having a single line of transaction management code in your code base. AOP and cross-cutting concerns are covered in Chapters 3 and 4.

Data Access framework: Hides the complexity of using persistence APIs such as JDBC, Hibernate, and many others. Spring solves problems that have been haunting data-access developers for years: how to get hold of a database connection, how to make sure that the connection is closed, how to deal with exceptions, and how to do transaction management. When using the Spring Framework, all these issues are taken care of by the framework. Chapters 5 and 6 cover data access with the Spring Framework.

Transaction Management framework: Provides a very efficient way to add transaction management to your applications without affecting your code base. Adding transaction management is a matter of configuration, and it makes the lives of application developers much easier. Transaction management is quite a complex subject, and in Chapter 7, you'll see how the Spring Framework simplifies it dramatically.

Resource Abstraction framework: Offers a wonderful feature for conveniently locating files when configuring your applications. Chapter 2 discusses resource abstraction.

Validation framework: Hides the details of validating objects in web applications or rich client applications. It also deals with internationalization (i18n) and localization (l10n). Chapter 8 discusses validation.

Spring Web MVC: Provides a Model-View-Controller (MVC) framework that lets you build powerful web applications with ease. It handles the mapping of requests to controllers and of controllers to views. It has excellent form-handling and form-validation capabilities, and integrates with all popular view technologies, including JSP, Velocity, FreeMarker, XSLT, JasperReports, Excel, and PDFs. Chapters 8 and 9 cover the Spring Web MVC and the view technologies.

Spring Web Flow: Makes implementing web-based wizards and complex workflow processes very easy and straightforward. Spring Web Flow is a conversation-based MVC framework. Your web applications will look much smarter once you learn how to use this framework. Spring Web Flow is distributed separately and can be downloaded via the Spring Framework website. *Expert Spring MVC and Spring Web Flow* (Apress, 2006) covers Spring Web Flow in detail.

Acegi Security System: Adds authentication and authorization to objects in your application using AOP. Acegi can secure any web application, even those that do not use the Spring Framework. It offers a wide range of authentication and authorization options that will fit your most exotic security needs. Adding security checks to your application is straightforward and a matter of configuration; you don't need to write any code, except in some special use cases. Acegi is distributed separately and can be downloaded from `http://acegisecurity.org/downloads.html`.

Remote Access framework: Adds client-server capabilities to applications through configuration. Objects on the server can be exported as remotely available services. On the client, you can call these services transparently, also through configuration. Remotely accessing services over the network thus becomes very easy. Spring's Remote Access framework supports HTTP-based protocols and remote method invocation (RMI), and can access Enterprise JavaBeans as a client. *Pro Spring* (Apress, 2005) covers Spring Remoting in detail.

Spring Web Services: Takes the complexity out of web services and separates the concerns into manageable units. Most web service frameworks generate web service end points and definitions based on Java classes, which get you going really fast, but become very hard to manage as your project evolves. To solve this problem, Spring Web Services takes a layered approach and separates the transport from the actual web service implementation by looking at web services as a messaging mechanism. Handling the XML message, executing business logic, and generating an XML response are all separate concerns that can be conveniently managed. Spring Web Services is distributed separately and can be downloaded via the Spring Framework website (http://www.springframework.org/download).

Spring JMX: Exports objects via Java Management Extensions (JMX) through configuration. Spring JMX is closely related to Spring's Remote Access framework. These objects can then be managed via JMX clients to change the value of properties, execute methods, or report statistics. JMX allows you to reconfigure application objects remotely and without needing to restart the application.

Introducing the Sample Application

The sample application that comes with this book is a complex business application that tracks the course of tennis tournaments and matches. The application consists of three modules that perform the following functions:

Manage tennis tournaments and players: The application creates tournaments and players in the database and handles player registration for tournaments. The application will automatically place players in tournament pools based on their Association of Tennis Professionals (ATP) ranking and will draw the matches for each pool. The application will also automatically create a calendar for each court that's available during the course of the tournament and manage the many other variables of a tournament.

Track the course of tennis matches played during tournaments: The application has a user interface that records each point and error during the course of a tennis match. The application knows when a set is over, who won it, and when the match is over. The business logic behind this can be easily ported to mobile devices such as cell phones to conveniently track the course of a match from the audience.

Report on historic data: Reports show the tournament history of individual players, the results of individual matches and pools, the consistency of the tennis game of individual players, a consistency comparison between players, and many other interesting pieces of data related to tennis matches.

One of the core functions of the sample application is to track the course of a tennis match. To better understand the domain of this application, you should have a basic understanding of the game of tennis. Tennis has many rules and statistics, but for the sample application, we'll keep the basic rules for the game as follows:

- A player is either the *server* of a game or the *receiver*. The application will automatically rotate the service when a game ends.

- A service that scores a point without the receiver being able to touch the ball is called an *ace*. The number of aces scored by each player in the course of a match is an important statistic to track.

- A server that makes an error during the service gets another chance. If the server fails at the second attempt, the point goes to the receiver. The number of single and double service errors is another important statistic.

- When the receiver handles the ball and returns the service, a *rally* begins. The point goes to the player who can force the opponent to make an error. Some errors cannot be attributed to any factor other than poor judgment by a player or lack of concentration and are called *unforced errors*. This is another important statistic.

To summarize, the application needs to track the following statistics:

- Who scores each point
- The number of aces per player
- The number of single and double service errors per player
- The number of unforced errors per player

The application will use the scores to calculate when a game is over, when a set is over, and when the match is over. The other statistics are stored for each player per each set.

The sample application is web-based and uses the Spring Framework throughout. Its implementation proves that the Spring Framework reduces the indirect costs of development projects by providing solutions to common problems out of the box. In other words, you don't have to reinvent the wheel. This book will use code from the sample application to illustrate how to use the different parts of the Spring Framework. By studying the implementation, you will be able to familiarize yourself with the most efficient usage of the Spring Framework in typical business applications. The sample application comes with extensive documentation that explains the design choices and the usage of the Spring Framework. You can download the sample application and all the examples used throughout the book from the Source Code/Download section of the Apress website (http://www.apress.com).

Now that you've seen the application we are going to build, let's look at an important component of application development—managing dependencies—and how the Spring Framework removes a lot of the complexity.

Managing Dependencies in Applications

To demonstrate how the Spring Framework manages dependencies, let's take a look at a use case from the sample application that needs a data-access object that is configured to connect to the database. We'll see how a plain Java application deals with this situation and contrast this with how Spring does it.

A Use Case That Has Dependencies

One of the requirements of the sample application is to start recording the course of a match during a tournament. Before a tournament starts, all players who have registered are divided into pools, depending on their ranking, age, and gender. For each pool, matches are created in the database. If a pool consists of 32 players, 5 rounds are created: 16 matches in the sixteenth final, 8 matches in the eighth final, 4 matches in the quarter final, 2 matches in the semifinal, and 1 final match. The matches of the sixteenth final are drawn at the start of the tournament.

When any match in the pool is started, the application will check in the database for the following information:

- Whether the match exists

- If the match hasn't finished yet

- If there are any previous matches

- If both previous matches have finished and who the winners are

Some matches are not played because one or both players don't show up, give up before they start, or are injured.

The TournamentMatchManager interface has a startMatch() method that takes the identifier of the match to start, as shown in Listing 1-1.

Listing 1-1. *The TournamentMatchManager Interface*

```
package com.apress.springbook.chapter01;

public interface TournamentMatchManager {
  Match startMatch(long matchId) throws
    UnknownMatchException,
    MatchIsFinishedException,
    PreviousMatchesNotFinishedException,
    MatchCannotBePlayedException;
}
```

This interface defines the contract of TournamentMatchManager. Classes that implement this interface must go through all the steps in the process of starting a tennis match, as shown in Listing 1-2.

Listing 1-2. *The DefaultTournamentMatchManager Class, Which Implements TournamentMatchManager*

```
package com.apress.springbook.chapter01;

public class DefaultTournamentMatchManager implements
        TournamentMatchManager {
  private MatchDao matchDao;

  public void setMatchDao(MatchDao matchDao) {
    this.matchDao = matchDao;
  }

  protected void verifyMatchExists(long matchId) throws
        UnknownMatchException {
    if (!this.matchDao.doesMatchExist(matchId)) {
      throw new UnknownMatchException();
    }
  }

  protected void verifyMatchIsNotFinished(long matchId) throws
        MatchIsFinishedException {
    if (this.matchDao.isMatchFinished(matchId)) {
      throw new MatchIsFinishedException();
    }
  }

  /* other methods omitted for brevity */
```

```
public Match startMatch(long matchId) throws
        UnknownMatchException, MatchIsFinishedException,
        PreviousMatchesNotFinishedException, MatchCannotBePlayedException {
  verifyMatchExists(matchId);
  verifyMatchIsNotFinished(matchId);
  Players players = null;
  if (doesMatchDependOnPreviousMatches(matchId)) {
    players = findWinnersFromPreviousMatchesElseHandle(matchId);
  } else {
    players = findPlayersForMatch(matchId);
  }
  return new Match(players.getPlayer1(), players.getPlayer2());
  }
}
```

Let's walk through what the startMatch() method in Listing 1-2 does:

1. The database is checked for a match with the given identifier (verifyMatchExists()).

2. The database is queried to verify that the match hasn't been played already
   (verifyMatchIsNotFinished()).

3. The database is queried again to check if the match that is about to start depends on the
   outcome of two previous matches (doesMatchDependOnPreviousMatches()).

   • If the match depends on previous matches, the winners are loaded from the database
     (findWinnersFromPreviousMatchesElseHandle()) if those matches have ended. If one or
     both previous matches have not been played, the match is not started and is marked in
     the database as over.

   • If the match is played in the first round of the tournament, the players who are drawn to
     play this match loaded from the database (findPlayersForMatch()).

4. When two players have been found and no exceptions have occurred, a Match object is
   returned to the caller. The Match object is used to track the course of this game, and when
   the match is over, the statistics are saved to the database.

The startMatch() method needs an implementation of the MatchDao interface that defines
the contract for working with the database. Implementation classes of the MatchDao interface are
responsible for informing the business logic about the current state of the match information in the
database. This information is vital to let the business process work correctly. (We use an interface
here to loosely couple the business logic to the data-access code, as explained in later sections.) The
MatchDao interface is shown in Listing 1-3.

Listing 1-3. *The MatchDao Interface That's Responsible for Querying the Database*

```
package com.apress.springbook.chapter01;

public interface MatchDao {
  boolean doesMatchExist(long matchId);

  boolean isMatchFinished(long matchId);

  boolean isMatchDependantOnPreviousMatches(long matchId);

  boolean arePreviousMatchesFinished(long matchId);

  Player findWinnerFromFirstPreviousMatch(long matchId);
```

```
    Player findWinnerFromSecondPreviousMatch(long matchId);

    void cancelMatchWithWinner(long matchId, Player player, String comment);

    void cancelMatchNoWinner(long matchId, String comment);

    Player findFirstPlayerForMatch(long matchId);

    Player findSecondPlayerForMatch(long matchId);
}
```

If you look at the course of a tournament as a workflow, you'll see that there's a start and an end. The methods that return Boolean values in Listing 1-3 provide the business logic with information about the current state of the tournament.

The methods that return Player objects use the information in the database to determine who won previous matches. The cancelMatchWithWinner() and cancelMatchNoWinner() methods update the state of the matches in the database.

Classes that implement the MatchDao interface need a connection to the database. For this purpose, a data source is used (the javax.sql.DataSource interface) that creates a connection to the database on demand. Data sources are discussed in more detail in Chapter 5; for now, you only need to know that the javax.sql.DataSource interface is used to create connections to the database.

Let's round up the dependencies in this use case. DefaultTournamentMatchManager objects need a collaborating object that implements the MatchDao interface to access the database. For the remainder of this chapter, we'll use the JdbcMatchDao class as an implementation class. The JdbcMatchDao class has a dependency on the javax.sql.DataSource interface, as shown in Listing 1-4. JdbcMatchDao objects need a DataSource object to get a connection to the database.

Listing 1-4. *JdbcMatchDao, Which Implements the MatchDao Interface and Queries the Database*

```
package com.apress.springbook.chapter01.jdbc;

import javax.sql.DataSource;

import com.apress.springbook.chapter01.MatchDao;

import org.springframework.jdbc.core.JdbcTemplate;

public class JdbcMatchDao implements MatchDao {
  private JdbcTemplate jdbcTemplate;

  public void setDataSource(DataSource dataSource) {
    this.jdbcTemplate = new JdbcTemplate(dataSource);
  }

  public boolean doesMatchExist(long matchId) {
    return 1 == jdbcTemplate.queryForInt(
      "SELECT COUNT(0) FROM T_MATCHES WHERE MATCH_ID = ?",
      new Object[] { new Long(matchId) }
    );
  }
  /* other methods omitted for brevity */
}
```

The code in Listing 1-4 uses JdbcTemplate from the Spring Framework. Chapter 6 covers this class in much more detail. For now, you only need to know that it's a convenient way to query the database. The example shows a SELECT statement that counts how many matches are found in the database with a given identifier. If exactly one match is found, the match exists in the database. In this use case, it's also possible that zero matches are found.

The next sections will discuss how the dependencies of this use case can be satisfied in typical Java applications.

Dealing with the Dependencies in Plain Java

If DefaultTournamentMatchManager was used in a regular Java application—for example, in a Swing application—the objects would probably be created inside the application, as shown in Listing 1-5.

Listing 1-5. *Creating the DefaultTournamentMatchManager and Dependencies in Java*

```java
package com.apress.springbook.chapter01.swing_application;

import org.apache.commons.dbcp.BasicDataSource;

import com.apress.springbook.chapter01.Match;
import com.apress.springbook.chapter01.jdbc.JdbcMatchDao;
import com.apress.springbook.chapter01.TournamentMatchManager;
import com.apress.springbook.chapter01.DefaultTournamentMatchManager;

public class SwingApplication {
  private DefaultTournamentMatchManager tournamentMatchManager;

  public SwingApplication(DefaultTournamentMatchManager tournamentMatchManager) {
    this.tournamentMatchManager = tournamentMatchManager;

    /* other code is omitted for brevity */
  }

  public static void main(String[] args) throws Exception {
    BasicDataSource dataSource = new BasicDataSource();
    /* Setting the properties of the data source. */
    dataSource.setDriverClassName(System.getProperty("jdbc.driverClassName"));
    dataSource.setUrl(System.getProperty("jdbc.url"));
    dataSource.setUsername(System.getProperty("jdbc.username"));
    dataSource.setPassword("pass");

    JdbcMatchDao matchDao = new JdbcMatchDao();
    matchDao.setDataSource(dataSource);

    DefaultTournamentMatchManager tournamentMatchManager =
      new DefaultTournamentMatchManager();
    tournamentMatchManager.setMatchDao(matchDao);

    new SwingApplication(tournamentMatchManager);
  }
}
```

The class shown in Listing 1-5 uses the Swing API to create a GUI. To launch the Swing application, you need to pass the property values for the data source as command-line parameters, as follows:

```
java -classpath %CLASSPATH% ➥
com.apress.springbook.chapter01.swing_application.SwingApplication ➥
-Djdbc.driverClassName=org.hsqldb.jdbcDriver ➥
-Djdbc.url=jdbc:hsqldb:hsql://localhost/ ➥
-Djdbc.username=sa -Djdbc.password=pass
```

The highlighted lines in Listing 1-5 show where collaborating objects are passed to satisfy the dependencies in the application. The objects are created and configured by means of glue code.

This use case is reasonably complex, but small compared with the entire sample application. The glue code that sets up the application can be kept in one place because the client application, the business logic class, and the data-access class are loosely coupled via interfaces. But if we added more glue code here, things would start to get out of hand.

Configuring the application via glue code is not consistent, which is best illustrated by how the properties of the data source are configured. The property values are copied from the system properties. An alternative is to load properties from a file. There's no consistent way to set property values, which means the complexity will grow rapidly without persistent efforts on the part of the developers.

The use of glue code to set up the configuration of an application causes another, subtler problem that becomes apparent when we want to run the Swing application with another implementation of the TournamentMatchManager. When we test the Swing application, we don't want to depend on the state and availability of the database, the data-access code, or the full business logic implementation in DefaultTournamentMatchManager. Instead, we create a dummy or stub implementation that just returns a Match object. This implementation takes five minutes to write and is ideal for testing the user interface components. The stub implementation is shown in Listing 1-6.

Listing 1-6. *A Stub Implementation of the TournamentMatchManager Interface for Testing Purposes*

```
package com.apress.springbook.chapter01.test;

import com.apress.springbook.chapter01.TournamentMatchManager;
import com.apress.springbook.chapter01.Match;
import com.apress.springbook.chapter01.Player;
import com.apress.springbook.chapter01.UnknownMatchException;
import com.apress.springbook.chapter01.MatchIsFinishedException;
import com.apress.springbook.chapter01.PreviousMatchesNotFinishedException;
import com.apress.springbook.chapter01.MatchCannotBePlayedException;

public class StubTournamentMatchManager implements TournamentMachtManager {
  public Match startMatch(long matchId) throws
      UnknownMatchException, MatchIsFinishedException,
      PreviousMatchesNotFinishedException, MatchCannotBePlayedException {
    Player player1 = Player.femalePlayer ();
    player1.setName("Kim Clijsters");

    Player player2 = Player.femalePlayer();
    player2.setName("Justine Henin-Hardenne");

    return new Match(player1, player2);
  }
}
```

When we want to use this stub implementation, we cannot start the client with its own main() method. Instead, we need to create a new class to launch the client in test mode, as shown in Listing 1-7. Because SwingApplication and TournamentMatchManager are loosely coupled, we can start the application with different dependencies, but again the lack of a consistent approach is apparent.

Listing 1-7. *A Separate Class That Launches SwingApplication with StubTournamentMatchManager*

```
package com.apress.springbook.chapter01.test;

import com.apress.springbook.chapter01.swing_application.SwingApplication;

public class LaunchTheSwingApplication {
  public static void main(String[] args) {
    new SwingApplication(new StubTournamentMatchManager());
  }
}
```

Looking Up Dependencies with JNDI

The previous example highlights the lack of consistency in the way the application is configured as the biggest problem. We can try to solve part of this problem by using the Java Naming and Directory Interface (JNDI). JNDI is the standard Java way of looking up objects from an application server. The configuration of the objects happens on the application server and clients can look them up.

When we start our application server, we can look up the data source named env:jdbc/myDataSource, as shown in Listing 1-8.

Listing 1-8. *Looking Up a Data Source Using JNDI*

```
package com.apress.springbook.chapter01.swing_application;

import javax.sql.DataSource;

import javax.naming.Context;
import javax.naming.InitialContext;

import java.util.Hashtable;

import com.apress.springbook.chapter01.Match;
import com.apress.springbook.chapter01.jdbc.JdbcMatchDao;
import com.apress.springbook.chapter01.TournamentMatchManager;
import com.apress.springbook.chapter01.DefaultTournamentMatchManager;

public class SwingApplication {
  private TournamentMatchManager tournamentMatchManager;

  public SwingApplication(TournamentMatchManager tournamentMatchManager) {
    this.tournamentMatchManager = tournamentMatchManager;

    /* other code is omitted for brevity */
  }

  public static void main(String[] args) throws Exception {
    Hashtable properties = new Hashtable();
    properties.put(Context.INITIAL_CONTEXT_FACTORY,
        "weblogic.jndi.WLInitialContextFactory");
    properties.put(Context.PROVIDER_URL,
        "t3://localhost:7001");
    Context ctx = new InitialContext(properties);
    DataSource dataSource = (DataSource)ctx.lookup("env:jdbc/myDataSource");
```

```
        JdbcMatchDao matchDao = new JdbcMatchDao();
        matchDao.setDataSource(dataSource);

        DefaultTournamentMatchManager tournamentMatchManager =
            new DefaultTournamentMatchManager();
        tournamentMatchManager.setMatchDao(matchDao);

        new SwingApplication(tournamentMatchManager);
    }
}
```

The problem of setting the data source property values is solved in Listing 1-8, but it's fair to say some difficulties remain:

- We've coupled our Swing application to an application server to get the data source. This seriously limits the deployment options of the application; it now requires a running application server for the application to start.

- The main consistency problem hasn't been solved yet. There's just as much glue code as in Listing 1-5.

- We still need the TestingTheSwingApplication class in Listing 1-6 to launch the Swing application in test mode.

■**Note** If you're not familiar with JNDI and application servers, you only need to remember that clients can ask a special Java server process for objects by name. Don't worry if you can't follow the discussion on JNDI in this section. You only need to realize that using the standard Java way of locating objects doesn't solve the inconsistency issue.

Overall, JNDI hasn't added much value to the application compared to the previous solution. In fact, it's hard to say which of the two approaches is preferable, as it's a choice between two evils.

Using JNDI adds a dependency to an application server to the application and does nothing to reduce the glue code. JNDI adds a bit of consistency because we can now change the connection settings of the data source in the application server without affecting our application. Compare this to Listing 1-5 and the command line for launching the Swing application, where we need to pass in the database connection setting via command-line parameters.

Using the Spring Framework to Provide Dependencies

The complex setup of the two previous code examples and the lack of consistency are caused by the fact that we, as developers, are responsible for obtaining the collaborating objects for our application. We need to write code to create objects and look up a data source, which bothers us, because it adds no value to our application. The business logic and data-access code are finished, and the Swing application is ready to use, but before we can use both together, we must write glue code to tell our application how to assemble itself.

The solution is to move the configuration code out of our application and use the Spring Framework to create and assemble the application components. This will free us from writing glue code and gives us a consistent way of configuring our application. The key is to use dependency injection.

Introducing Dependency Injection

Dependency injection (DI) is the core feature of the Spring Framework Core Container. It provides a mechanism to pass, or *inject*, dependencies to objects. Dependency injection is a method of *inversion of control* (IoC). Figure 1-1 shows how IoC and dependency injection relate to each other.

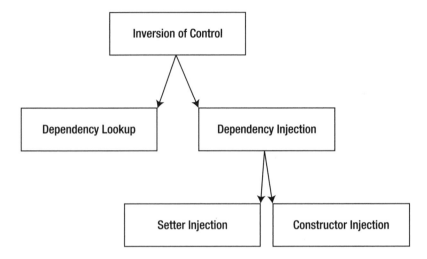

Figure 1-1. *The relationship between IoC and dependency injection*

As shown in Figure 1-1, IoC provides two ways to resolve dependencies: dependency lookup and dependency injection. *Dependency lookup* places the responsibility of resolving dependencies in the hands of the application. The example in Listing 1-8 uses JNDI to obtain a data source, which is a form of dependency lookup. Dependency lookup has been the standard way of resolving dependencies in Java for many years but will always require glue code. The Spring Framework supports dependency lookup, as will be discussed in Chapter 2.

In contrast, dependency injection places the responsibility of resolving dependencies in the hands of an IoC container such as the Spring Framework. A configuration file defines how the dependencies of an application can be resolved. The configuration file is read by the container, which will create the objects that are defined in this file and inject these objects in other application components. The Spring Framework Core Container supports two types of dependency injection to inject collaborating objects: setter injection and container injection.

Setter injection uses set*() methods—also called *setter methods*, or *setters* for short—to inject collaboration objects. set*() and get*() methods together form a JavaBean property, as defined in the JavaBean specifications. To use setter injection, the Spring Framework Core Container must first create an object and then call the setter methods that are defined in the configuration file. Listing 1-9 shows a class with setter methods and a configuration file (you'll see a fuller example of a configuration file in Listing 1-13, later in this chapter). The setter method and the corresponding configuration have been highlighted.

Listing 1-9. *An Example of Setter Injection*

```
package com.apress.springbook.chapter01;

public class DemonstratingBean {
  private String name;
```

```java
  public void setName(String name) {
    this.name = name;
  }

  public String getName() {
    return this.name;
  }
}
```

```xml
<!-- Spring Framework configuration file -->
<beans>

  <!--  Injecting Steven in the name property -->
  <bean id="bean" class="com.apress.springbook.chapter01.DemonstratingBean">
    <property name="name" value="Steven"/>
  </bean>
</beans>
```

Constructor injection calls a constructor to inject collaborating objects. The Spring Framework Core Container creates objects and injects collaborating objects at the same time. Listing 1-10 shows a class with a constructor and a configuration file.

Listing 1-10. *An Example of Constructor Injection*

```java
package com.apress.springbook.chapter01;

public class DemonstratingBean {
  private String name;
  public DemonstratingBean(String name) {
    this.name = name;
  }

  public String getName() {
    return this.name;
  }
}
```

```xml
<!-- Spring Framework configuration file -->
<beans>

  <!--  Injecting Steven in the constructor -->
  <bean id="bean" class="com.apress.springbook.chapter01.DemonstratingBean">
    <constructor-arg value="Steven"/>
  </bean>
</beans>
```

Both of these techniques lead to the same results from the following piece of code, where we load the configuration file and the injected dependencies with an XmlBeanFactory and obtain an instance of the bean:

```java
XmlBeanFactory factory = new XmlBeanFactory(new FileSystemResource("config.xml"));

DemonstratingBean demoBean = (DemonstratingBean)factory.getBean("bean");

System.out.println("Bean property value: " + demoBean.getName());
```

Dependency injection is clearly the preferred way of resolving dependencies, as it enables developers to loosely couple the layers of an application and removes glue code. The result is a cleanly designed application and configuration in one place in a readable and easy-to-change format. In fact, the dependency injection model of the Spring Framework Core Container is a very powerful deployment model. As you create configuration files, you are configuring your application for deployment. Dependency injection is a very important mechanism in the Spring Framework, and the next chapter discusses it in much more detail.

Now, let's continue with the sample use case and see how to handle it with the Spring Framework.

Handling the Use Case with the Spring Framework

The Spring Framework will look at a configuration file (which we need to create) and will automatically create and assemble all objects that are defined in that file. This leaves us with only one task: to bootstrap the Spring Framework and instruct it to read the configuration file and perform the work at hand.

But first, we'll remove all the glue code in our application, as shown in Listing 1-11.

Listing 1-11. *The SwingApplication Class Without Glue Code, Reduced to Its Essence*

```
package com.apress.springbook.chapter01.swing_application;

import com.apress.springbook.chapter01.Match;
import com.apress.springbook.chapter01.TournamentMatchManager;

public class SwingApplication {
  private TournamentMatchManager tournamentMatchManager;

  public SwingApplication(TournamentMatchManager tournamentMatchManager) {
    this.tournamentMatchManager = tournamentMatchManager;

    /* other code is omitted for brevity */
  }
}
```

We've removed the `main()` method as well as the glue code. By looking at the `import` statements of the `SwingApplication` class, we can tell that this class has minimal dependencies on the interfaces of the business logic and the domain classes of the application (`SwingApplication` uses the `Match` class internally). We will come back to this point later in this section, but for now, keep in mind that the `DefaultTournamentMatchManager` and `JdbcMatchDao` classes are not imported anywhere in the application.

Next, we create a skeleton bootstrap class, as shown in Listing 1-12, which will call the API of the Spring Framework. We don't add any implementation to this class for now, but we want to give you a mental hook to where the Spring Framework will fit in the picture.

Listing 1-12. *A Bootstrap Class That Will Launch the Application*

```
package com.apress.springbook.chapter01.spring;

public class SpringBootstrap {
  public static void main(String[] args) throws Exception {

    /* Call the Spring Framework API here! */

  }
}
```

Now we need to create the configuration file that tells Spring which objects to create and how to assemble them. We will use an XML file to hold the configuration instructions. The notation used in this file is defined by the Spring Framework and is consistent for all applications that use it. Listing 1-13 shows the configuration file that will be loaded by the Spring Framework.

Listing 1-13. *The Configuration File That Will Be Loaded by the Spring Framework*

```xml
<?xml version="1.0" encoding="UTF-8"?>
<!DOCTYPE beans PUBLIC "-//SPRING//DTD BEAN//EN"
    "http://www.springframework.org/dtd/spring-beans.dtd">
<beans>
  <bean id="swingApplication"
        class="com.apress.springbook.chapter01.swing_application. ➥
SwingApplication">
    <constructor-arg ref="tournamentMatchManager"/>
  </bean>

  <bean id="tournamentMatchManager"
        class="com.apress.springbook.chapter01.DefaultTournamentMatchManager">
    <property name="matchDao" value="matchDao"/>
  </bean>

  <bean id="matchDao"
        class="com.apress.springbook.chapter01.jdbc.JdbcMatchDao">
    <property name="dataSource" ref="dataSource"/>
  </bean>

  <bean id="dataSource" class="org.apache.commons.dbcp.BasicDataSource">
    <property name="driverClassName" value="org.hsqldb.jdbcDriver"/>
    <property name="url" value="jdbc:hsqldb:hsql://localhost"/>
    <property name="username" value="sa"/>
    <property name="password" value=""/>
  </bean>
</beans>
```

This configuration file instructs the Spring Framework to create four objects and assemble them. We will discuss this file in detail in the next chapter.

The only thing that remains to be done is to implement the main() method of the SpringBootstrap class to call the Spring Framework and instruct it to load the configuration file, as shown in Listing 1-14.

Listing 1-14. *The SpringBootstrap Class Uses the Spring Framework to Load a Configuration File*

```java
package com.apress.springbook.chapter01.spring;

import java.io.FileInputStream;
import java.util.Properties;

import org.springframework.beans.factory.xml.XmlBeanFactory;
import org.springframework.core.io.FileSystemResource;

public class SpringBootstrap {
  public static void main(String[] args) throws Exception {
```

```
    /* Check if the location of the configuration file has been passed
    * as an argument.
    */
    if (args.length == 0) {
      throw new IllegalArgumentException("Please provide the location of a " +
        "Spring configuration file as argument!");
      }

    /* Call the Spring Framework API here! */
    XmlBeanFactory factory =
      new XmlBeanFactory(new FileSystemResource(args[0]));

    /* Pause the application until a key is pressed */
    System.out.println("Press any key to close the application");
    System.in.read();

    /* Key has been pressed; close the application and exit */
  }
}
```

We've modified the `SpringBootstrap` class to first check if the location of the configuration file has been passed as a command-line argument. Next, we create the Spring Framework Core Container and tell it to load the configuration file that has been passed as an argument. These are the lines highlighted in Listing 1-14. The next chapter details how to configure the Spring Framework.

When we launch the application, we need to pass the location of the configuration file as a command-line argument, as follows:

```
java –classpath %CLASSPATH% ➥
com.apress.springbook.chapter01.SpringBootStrap ➥
 ./src/java/com/apress/springbook/chapter01/spring/➥
swingApplicationConfiguration.xml
```

Testing the Application

Because we've configured the application components in a Spring configuration file, we can easily use `StubTournamentMatchManager` by creating a new configuration file, as shown in Listing 1-15.

Listing 1-15. *A Configuration File for Testing the Swing Application*

```
<?xml version="1.0" encoding="UTF-8"?>
<!DOCTYPE beans PUBLIC "-//SPRING//DTD BEAN//EN"
    "http://www.springframework.org/dtd/spring-beans.dtd">

<beans>
  <!-- configuring StubTournamentMatchManager (it doesn't have dependencies) -->
  <bean id="tournamentMatchManager"
        class= "com.apress.springbook.chapter01.test.StubTournamentMatchManager">
  </bean>

  <!-- configuring SwingApplication -->
  <bean id="swingApplication"
        class="com.apress.springbook.chapter01.swing_application.SwingApplication">
    <property name="tournamentMatchManager" ref="tournamentMatchManager"/>
  </bean>
</beans>
```

Next, we can launch the SpringBootstrap class with the test configuration file, as follows:

```
java -classpath %CLASSPATH% ➡
com.apress.springbook.chapter01.spring.SpringBootstrap ➡
./src/java/com/apress/springbook/chapter01/spring/test/➡
swingApplicationTestConfiguration.xml
```

We can change the configuration of the application by modifying the configuration file because we use the Spring Framework. The code of our application is not affected.

Reviewing Loosely Coupled Application Layers

This brings the example full circle. As we've stated before, the DefaultTournamentMatchManager and JdbcMatchDao classes are not imported anywhere in the application. This means the layers of the application are loosely coupled:

- The SwingApplication class is part of the presentation layer (it creates the GUI) and has a dependency on the TournamentMatchManager interface. This dependency is received through the constructor, as shown in Listing 1-11. The configuration file in Listing 1-13 defines which object will be passed in the constructor.

- The DefaultTournamentMatchManager class implements the TournamentMatchManager interface and is part of the business logic layer. It has a dependency on the MatchDao interface, which is received through the setMatchDao() method as shown in Listing 1-2. This type of method is called a setter or setter method, and its purpose is to receive a collaborating object, as demonstrated in Listings 1-5 and 1-8. The configuration file in Listing 1-13 defines which object will be passed to the setMatchDao() method.

- The JdbcMatchDao class implements the MatchDao interface and is part of the data-access layer (it queries the database). It has a dependency on the javax.sql.DataSource interface, which is received through the setDataSource() method. This is again a setter method that receives a collaborating object. The configuration file in Listing 1-13 defines which object will be passed to the setDataSource() method.

One set of classes doesn't fit in any of these layers: the classes of the domain model, such as the Match class. These classes do not implement interfaces and are not controlled by the Spring Framework. Domain model classes encapsulate the business rules of the application. If you look back at Listing 1-2, you will notice DefaultTournamentMatchClass has a supporting role in the overall application by loading players from the database and creating a Match object. Domain model classes are typically used in each layer of the application.

Extending the Application

As other use cases are added to this application, new classes will be added to each layer. However, because we will continue to use clearly defined interfaces comparable to TournamentMatchManager and MatchDao, the layers of the application will remain loosely coupled.

No implementation classes will be imported anywhere in my application, and the Spring Framework will take care of creating objects and managing the dependencies. As the application grows bigger, the size of the configuration file in Listing 1-13 will also increase. The SpringBootstrap class will remain unchanged, no matter how big the application becomes.

However, the clean separation of responsibilities in the application design will remain intact as the configuration grows and the configuration will remain consistent. Compare this with the inconsistent approaches in Listings 1-5 and 1-9. Again, the principle that brings this level of consistency to our application and that's implemented by the Spring Framework is dependency injection.

Integrating the Spring Framework with Java EE

Java EE (formerly J2EE), is an addition to Java Standard Edition that provides APIs that integrate enterprise services in the Java platform. Each enterprise service is a standard defined in specifications that are grouped together under the umbrella of Java EE. Table 1-1 summarizes the enterprise services that are part of Java EE 1.4. Other technologies include accessing mail providers, XML parsing, web services, security, and remote access.

Table 1-1. *Java EE 1.4 Services*

Service	Description
Web application development	The Servlet specifications, under the `javax.servlet.*` package
JavaServer Pages (JSP)	Template technology for rendering X/HTML pages, under the `javax.servlet.jsp.*` and `javax.servlet.jsp.tagext.*` packages
Java Naming and Directory Interface (JNDI)	Directory lookup technology, under the `javax.naming.*` package
Java Transaction API (JTA)	Transaction management abstraction technology supporting distributed transactions, under the `javax.transaction.*` package
Java Messaging Service (JMS)	Message sending and consuming technology, integrating with message queue products, under the `javax.jms.*` package
Enterprise JavaBeans (EJB)	An application model for deploying application components in an environment that transparently configures other parts of the Java EE specifications

The most popular Java EE technologies are servlets, JSP, and EJB. Because Java EE provides a standard way of using enterprise services, developers need to learn only one API.

Spring Framework Integration with Java EE Technologies

The Spring Framework adds one or more extra layers of abstraction on top of the Java EE standards and APIs, either to hide the APIs completely from the developers when it makes sense or to make them easier to use. Some APIs can be completely replaced by alternative solutions, like the EJB specifications, as discussed in the next section.

The following is an overview of how the Spring Framework integrates the most important Java EE APIs to make them less painful to use and more powerful:

JNDI: The Spring Framework has very good JNDI integration in the Core Container. As will be demonstrated in the next chapter, JNDI dependency lookups can be configured in configuration files. The object that's returned by the lookup can then be injected by the Core Container as a collaborating object. Moving dependency lookups out of the application code and into a configuration file helps make existing applications more consistent and easier to maintain.

JTA: Spring's Transaction Management framework fully integrates with the JTA API to support transactions that are orchestrated by an application server. Working with the JTA API is too complicated to allow its usage in application code, so the abstraction offered by the Spring Framework is very useful. Chapter 7 will discuss the JTA API integration in more detail.

JMS: The Spring Framework has excellent integration with the JMS API, which makes it much easier to send and receive messages. Sending messages with JMS requires JNDI lookups that are trivial with the Spring Framework. Sending a message is made very easy by using a helper class that's provided by the Spring Framework. With Spring Framework 2.0, it's now possible to receive messages outside an EJB container with full transactional support. See `http://java.sun.com/products/jms/` for more information about JMS.

Web application development: The Spring Web MVC framework integration with the Servlet API makes it very easy to handle web requests in a consistent way. This framework adds many extensions to the Servlet API that are based on best practices. The Spring Web MVC layer is meant to be very thin and to seamlessly integrate with view technologies. The view abstraction offered by Spring Web MVC and integration with view technologies is unparalleled and uses the Servlet API to hide view rendering details from the developer. Chapter 8 discusses using the Spring Web MVC.

Spring and EJB

EJB integrates with JNDI, JTA, JMS, and other Java EE standards. At the time the Spring Framework was introduced (March 2003), EJB was still the deployment model of choice for many business applications, although its popularity was already declining. At the time of this writing, the EJB specifications are all but dead and buried. The new EJB3 specifications have failed to convince application developers. EJB3 has a very limited dependency injection model and does little to bring consistency to your applications.

EJB and the Spring Framework are often compared because they promise the same thing: *an application deployment model with transparent enterprise service like transaction management, security, messaging, and remote access.*

The Spring Framework matches all the features of EJB3 and goes much further. The Spring Framework is agile and powerful, and reaches out to every kind of application. EJB—including EJB3—caters only to one type of application: centrally deployed business logic running on an application server.

The market has shifted away from intrusive deployment models toward open, flexible, nonintrusive deployment models. That being said, the Spring Framework has excellent integration with EJB3.

The EJB3 specifications consist of two parts: the deployment model and the persistence model. The deployment model manages application components in an *EJB container*. These components are available via JNDI. The Spring Framework has excellent integration with JNDI, so it is easy to acquire references to these objects from within the Spring Framework Core Container and inject these as collaborating objects. Therefore, it is easy to integrate with applications that are deployed in an EJB3 environment. Furthermore, Spring's Transaction Management framework can let objects participate in transactions that are controlled by an application server. This ensures applications deployed with the Spring Framework will work with EJB3 without affecting the business logic code. The Spring Framework also offers integration code for the EJB3 persistence specifications. Chapter 5 discusses this integration in detail.

The Spring Framework also provides excellent integration with older versions of the EJB specifications in the same manner.

Setting Up the Spring Framework in Your Applications

You can download the latest version of the Spring Framework from `http://www.springframework.org`. Make sure you download the distribution archive ending with `with-dependencies`, which contains all the JAR files required by the Spring Framework. This version of the Spring Framework distribution will help you find the JAR files you need to set up your application.

■**Note** Spring 2.0 was first announced at the first edition of The Spring Experience in Miami, Florida, in December 2005. At that time Rod Johnson, founder of the Spring Framework and CEO of Interface21, announced that Spring 2.0 remains fully backward-compatible with Spring 1.2. Furthermore, Spring 2.0 works with Java 1.3 and beyond and with J2EE 1.2 and beyond. This means you are able to drop the Spring 2.0 JAR in your existing projects, and you won't have a single broken dependency.

The Spring distribution contains the following:

- The Spring JARs for the Core Container, the AOP framework, the Data Access framework, the Transaction Management framework, the Remote Access framework, the JMX framework, and the Spring Web MVC framework

- The complete source code of the Spring Framework

- If you've downloaded the distribution with dependencies, all libraries required by the Spring Framework (available in the `lib` folder)

- Reference documentation in HTML and PDF formats

- Sample applications, including JPetStore, PetClinic, and ImageDb

Of the JAR files, two are most important: `spring.jar` and `spring-mock.jar`. `spring.jar` includes the entire Spring Framework and can be found in the `dist` folder of the Spring distribution, and `spring-mock.jar` includes all classes for writing and running tests and can be found in the `dist/modules` folder.

Add the `spring.jar` archive to the classpath of your application to use the Spring Framework in your application. `spring.jar` has a dependency on the `commons-logging.jar` archive, the Jakarta Common Logging API. This file can be found in the `lib/jakarta-commons` folder of the Spring Framework distribution. If you use Spring 2.0, note that the `spring.jar` archive no longer includes the packages with the integration code for the object-relational mapping (ORM) tools Hibernate 2 and 3, JDO, and Oracle TopLink. These packages are moved to their respective JAR archives in the `dist/extmodules` folder of the Spring 2.0 distribution.

■**Tip** When setting up the `spring.jar` archive in your application, we encourage you to attach the Spring source in your integrated development environment (IDE). This allows you to easily look inside the classes of the Spring Framework. Our understanding of the Spring Framework has significantly improved by regularly looking inside the framework's source code. Attaching the source code is simply a matter of pointing your IDE to the `src` folder of the Spring Framework distribution.

If you add the `spring-mock.jar` archive to the classpath of your application, make sure you also add the `junit.jar` archive, the JUnit test framework. This file can be found in the `lib/junit` folder of the Spring Framework distribution.

Furthermore, you need to add the JAR files for the other frameworks you want use in your application. The `lib/readme.txt` file that is included in the Spring Framework distribution lists the JAR files you need to include, depending on how you use the Spring Framework in your application.

SPRING SAMPLE APPLICATIONS

The Spring Framework distribution comes with three sample applications:

- *JPetStore*: Based on the original Java Pet Store application, this sample application uses the Spring Framework to demonstrate how a nontrivial web application can be built. For data access, iBatis is used, and two web layers configurations are available: one with Spring Web MVC and one with Struts. This sample also demonstrates the use of Spring Remoting.

- *PetClinic*: This application demonstrates the use of a data-access layer and has implementations using JDBC, Hibernate, Apache OJB, and Oracle TopLink. It uses Spring Web MVC in the web layer and also demonstrates the use of JMX.

- *ImageDb*: This application demonstrates the use of binary large object (BLOB) handling, file upload with Spring Web MVC, and Velocity as a template technology.

The sample applications are useful examples that demonstrate popular usage patterns of various features of the Spring Framework. Each sample application has a `readme.txt` file with a motivation for the sample application and a list of the features demonstrated in the sample.

Summary

In this chapter, you've learned about dependency injection, a straightforward mechanism to acquired dependent objects. This technique will be further examined in the next chapter where the Spring Framework Core Container is introduced.

You've been introduced to the different modules of the Spring Framework and the concepts behind IoC and dependency injection. The remaining chapters of this book discuss many of the modules in further detail. Now is a good time to download the latest distribution of the Spring Framework.

■■■

The Core Container

The Spring Framework Core Container is essentially a factory that creates objects without revealing the exact classes that are used and how they are created, as we demonstrated in the previous chapter. In software engineering, factories *encapsulate* the process of obtaining objects, which is usually more complex than just creating new objects. The Core Container uses encapsulation to hide from the actual application the details of how an application is created and configured; the application doesn't know how to assemble itself or how to bootstrap. Instead, these tasks are handed off to the Core Container by providing the location of one or more configuration files that contain information about each object in the application that must be created. Next, the Core Container needs to be bootstrapped to launch the application.

This chapter will cover all the details you need to be familiar with to configure application components and load them with the Core Container. We'll cover the following topics:

- How factories work in general, to demonstrate the principle of encapsulation. This principle is important, as it's the foundation of the inversion of control (IoC) principle.

- How the basic container of the Spring Framework is configured. We'll show you how to configure the container to use dependency lookup, dependency injection, setter injection, and constructor injection.

- How the bean life cycle is managed by the Core Container. Each bean can take advantage of optional configuration hooks provided by the Core Container. Each bean also has a predefined scope inside the Core Container.

- How to use factory methods and factory objects in the Core Container. This mechanism can be used to move complex object-creation code from the application code into the Core Container.

- How the XML configuration in version 2.0 of the Core Container has been dramatically simplified for your convenience. We'll show you some new XML tags and how their use compares to the classic XML configuration.

- How the Core Container can be bootstrapped in different environments. This is an interesting discussion, as we'll be configuring the Spring Framework in servlet containers and in integration tests in later chapters.

How Do Factories Work?

Factories solve a common problem in software engineering: hiding the complexity of creating and configuring objects. You can use both factory methods and factory objects.

Factory Methods

To demonstrate the benefits of factory methods, let's look at an example. Let's say we want to read a text file line by line. To do so, we need to use the java.io.BufferedReader class. When creating a BufferedReader object, however, we need to write more code than is convenient:

```
BufferedReader reader =
  new BufferedReader(new InputStreamReader(
    new FileInputStream(new File("myFile.txt"))));
```

Things start to become even more inconvenient if we need to create BufferedReader objects in multiple places in our application. The solution to this problem is to create a factory method that has a java.io.File argument and returns a BufferedReader object:

```
public class ReaderUtils {
  public static BufferedReader createBufferedReader(File file) throws IOException {
    return new BufferedReader(new InputStreamReader(new FileInputStream(file)));
  }
}
```

Now we can call the createBufferedReader() method whenever we need to create a BufferedReader object:

```
BufferedReader reader = ReaderUtils.createBufferedReader(new File("myFile.txt"));
```

By using a factory method, our code becomes more readable, and we've found a convenient way to hide the creation of a complex object. In fact, if at a later time we discover that it makes more sense to use the java.io.FileReader class, we need to change the code only in the factory method, while the calling code remains unaffected:

```
public class ReaderUtils {
  public static BufferedReader createBufferedReader(File file) throws IOException {
    return new BufferedReader(new FileReader(file));
  }
}
```

Using factory methods avoids the following:

- Duplicating complex object-creation code
- Introducing the details of object creation in areas of the application where it doesn't belong

The factory method is a classic example of a *design pattern*—a solution to a common problem in software engineering. It encapsulates object-creation code that is of no concern to other parts of the application. Hiding concerns in software engineering to increase flexibility and robustness of a design is called *separation of concerns*.

It's much more efficient to solve a problem with a factory method once and offer this solution through a consistent API than it is to solve the problem every time it presents itself. The factory method is a very popular encapsulation pattern in applications and frameworks, although it has its limits, primarily because static methods cannot hold state.

Factory Objects

In some cases, a *factory object* is required to encapsulate internal state that is related to its configuration (for example, a list of configuration files to load) or that is created to support its operations. This is often seen as an advantage, and it certainly is in the Spring Framework.

An example of a factory object in the Java SDK is the `javax.net.SocketFactory` class, which provides `java.net.Socket` objects. To use this class, you first need to create and configure it with a `String` hostname and a port number:

```
javax.net.SocketFactory factory = javax.net.SocketFactory.getDefault();
```

This code creates a factory object configured to provide sockets. The factory object can now be used to do the actual factory operations—in this case, providing a socket connected to a host on port 80:

```
java.net.Socket socket = factory.createSocket("localhost", 80);
```

This factory operation—that is, the `createSocket()` method—requires a configured `javax.net.SocketFactory` factory object. Take a look at the Javadoc for the `javax.net.SocketFactory` if you want to learn more about the workings of this class.

The Spring Framework Core Container supports both factory methods and factory objects as an alternative to creating new beans. We'll discuss this in more detail in the "Using Factory Methods and Factory Objects" section later in this chapter.

Introducing the BeanFactory

The Spring Framework Core Container is also a factory object with configuration parameters and factory operations to support IoC. The operations of the Core Container are defined in the `org.springframework.beans.factory.BeanFactory` interface, as shown in Listing 2-1.

Listing 2-1. *The Factory Operations of the org.springframework.beans.factory.BeanFactory Interface*

```
package org.springframework.beans.factory;

import org.springframework.beans.BeansException;

public interface BeanFactory {

  String FACTORY_BEAN_PREFIX = "&";

  Object getBean(String name) throws BeansException;

  Object getBean(String name, Class requiredType) throws BeansException;

  boolean containsBean(String name);

  boolean isSingleton(String name) throws NoSuchBeanDefinitionException;

  Class getType(String name) throws NoSuchBeanDefinitionException;

  String[] getAliases(String name) throws NoSuchBeanDefinitionException;
}
```

The factory operations on the `BeanFactory` interface use the internal state of the factory object that's created based on the specific configuration files that have been loaded.

WHAT IS A BEAN?

The Spring Framework has its own terminology, which includes terms that are borrowed from different areas in software engineering. One term that is a bit challenging is *bean*. This term is used very often in the Spring community, but may leave newcomers confused because they have come across the term when using JavaBeans.

In Spring, a bean is an object—or class instance—that's created and managed by the container. The Spring Framework's beans extend the notion of JavaBeans slightly (hence the confusion).

The Core Container reads its configuration from one or more XML files. Listing 2-2 shows an empty Spring XML configuration file that can be easily edited in your favorite Java IDE.

Listing 2-2. *An Empty Spring XML Configuration File with a DOCTYPE Element*

```
<?xml version="1.0" encoding="UTF-8"?>
<!DOCTYPE beans PUBLIC "-//SPRING//DTD BEAN//EN"
    "http://www.springframework.org/dtd/spring-beans.dtd">

<beans>

</beans>
```

The built-in XML editor takes advantage of the Spring Document Type Definition (DTD) file, which makes adding a bean to the configuration very straightforward, as shown in Listing 2-3.

Listing 2-3. *The <beans> Element with a Single <bean> Element*

```
<?xml version="1.0" encoding="UTF-8"?>
<!DOCTYPE beans PUBLIC "-//SPRING//DTD BEAN//EN"
    "http://www.springframework.org/dtd/spring-beans.dtd">
<beans>
  <bean id="Kim" class="com.apress.springbook.chapter02.Player">
    <property name="fullName" value="Kim Clijsters"/>
    <property name="ranking" value="1"/>
  </bean>
</beans>
```

Creating a BeanFactory Object

It's equally straightforward to create a Spring Core Container or an `org.springframework.beans.factory.BeanFactory` object. Creating a `BeanFactory` requires only one line of code once the configuration file is in the classpath, as shown in Listing 2-4.

Listing 2-4. *Creating an XmlBeanFactory Instance That Loads an XML Configuration File*

```
BeanFactory beanFactory =
  new XmlBeanFactory(
    new ClassPathResource(
      "com/apress/springbook/chapter02/application-context.xml"
    )
  );
```

Using Dependency Lookup

Once the container has been created successfully, you can ask for any bean by name, which is actually an example of dependency lookup. For example, getting the Kim instance is very easy:

```
Player player = (Player)beanFactory.getBean("Kim");
```

The getBean(String) method returns the object registered with the given name in the BeanFactory. If the name cannot be found by the Core Container, an exception will be thrown.

The preceding example can cause a ClassCastException, which is one of the most important disadvantages of dependency lookup. You can avoid a ClassCastException by using the overloaded getBean(String, Class) method on BeanFactory:

```
Player player = (Player)beanFactory.getBean("Kim", Player.class);
```

When you provide the expected type, BeanFactory will throw BeanNotOfRequiredTypeException if the object doesn't match the expected type.

Another disadvantage of using dependency lookup is that you bind your code to the Spring Framework API.

Using Dependency Injection

In Chapter 1, we mentioned that dependency injection is preferred over dependency lookup. Here, we'll examine the XML configuration file from Chapter 1 in detail. Here's a review:

- The SwingApplication class has a dependency on the TournamentMatchManager interface, which is injected via the constructor.

- The DefaultTournamentMatchManager class implements the TournamentMatchManager interface and has a dependency on the MatchDao interface for data-access operations, which is injected via a setter method.

- The JdbcMatchDao class implements the MatchDao interface and has a dependency on the javax.sql.DataSource interface for connecting to the database, which is injected via a setter method.

Listing 2-5 shows how we've configured these classes and dependencies in an XML configuration file.

Listing 2-5. *Configuring Dependency Injection in the Spring XML Configuration File*

```xml
<?xml version="1.0" encoding="UTF-8"?>
<!DOCTYPE beans PUBLIC "-//SPRING//DTD BEAN//EN"
    "http://www.springframework.org/dtd/spring-beans.dtd">
<beans>
  <bean id="swingApplication"
        class="org.apress.springbook.chapter02.SwingApplication">
    <constructor-arg ref="tournamentMatchManager"/>
  </bean>

  <bean id="tournamentMatchManager"
        class="org.apress.springbook.chapter02.DefaultTournamentMatchManager">
    <property name="matchDao" value="matchDao"/>
  </bean>
```

```
  <bean id="matchDao"
        class="org.apress.springbook.chapter02.JdbcMatchDao">
    <property name="dataSource" ref="dataSource"/>
  </bean>

  <bean id="dataSource" class="org.apache.commons.dbcp.BasicDataSource">
    <property name="driverClassName" value="org.hsqldb.jdbcDriver"/>
    <property name="url" value="jdbc:hsqldb:hsql:/localhost/test"/>
    <property name="username" value="sa"/>
    <property name="password" value=""/>
    <property name="initialSize" value="10"/>
    <property name="testOnBorrow" value="true"/>
  </bean>
</beans>
```

The configuration in Listing 2-5 shows four beans: swingApplication, tournamentMatchManager, matchDao, and dataSource. These beans are created in a specific order:

- When the container creates the swingApplication bean, it will detect that in order to call its constructor, the tournamentMatchManager bean is needed (because it is set as a constructor argument in the <constructor-arg> element) and will attempt to create it.

- After the container creates the tournamentMatchManager bean, it will detect that the matchDao bean is needed to inject in the matchDao property and will attempt to create it.

- After the container creates the matchDao bean, it will detect that the dataSource bean is needed to inject in the dataSource property and will attempt to create it.

- After the container creates the dataSource bean, it will find no references to other beans and will set the values to the properties of the bean.

- Next, the container will inject the dataSource bean in the dataSource property of the matchDao bean.

- The container will then inject the matchDao bean in the matchDao property of the tournamentMatchManager bean.

- Finally, the container will create the swingApplication bean and inject the tournamentMatchManager bean via the constructor.

The order in which the bean definitions are defined in the XML configuration file is not relevant, as the container will make sure that beans are created in the correct order.

Now let's take a closer look at how the configuration file in Listing 2-5 works.

Bean Definitions

The <bean> elements in the XML file in Listing 2-5 are called *bean definitions*. The container will convert each <bean> element, its attributes, and child elements to a BeanDefinition object and use this configuration to influence the life cycle of the beans that are created by the container, based on the following information:

How to create the bean: Usually, this is a fully qualified class name. The container will create an object by calling the designated constructor on the class, which is the no-argument constructor if no additional <constructor-arg> elements are provided. Alternatively, the container may also call a factory method or method on a factory object.

How to configure the bean: An optional list of <property> elements tells the container which setter injections to perform. The container can inject values, lists, maps, properties, and references to other beans.

How to initialize the bean: The container can optionally initialize a bean by calling an initialization method. This allows the bean to initialize itself and check if all required dependencies are available.

How to manage the bean life cycle: The container can manage a bean in two ways: as a singleton—always returning the same instance—or as a prototype—creating and returning a new instance on every request.

How to destroy the bean: Singleton beans can optionally be destroyed when the container is closed by calling a destroy method. This step in the bean life cycle is useful to clean up internal resources.

A bean definition instructs the container *how* to create beans and *when*. We'll discuss the details of both in the remainder of this chapter.

Setter Injection

The `<property>` elements in Listing 2-5 specify the setter injections on bean properties. These properties are defined in the JavaBean specifications and are typically used to read and assign class member variables. The method names and types in the getter and setter methods must match. The property names in the XML file refer to this name, although the first letter of the property name must be lowercase. For example, the setFullName() method becomes fullName, the setRanking() method becomes ranking, and so on.

To set a property with the Spring container, you need at least a setter method, as shown in Listing 2-6.

Listing 2-6. *Write-Only JavaBean Properties Have Only Setter Methods*

```
package com.apress.springbook.chapter02;

public class Player {
  private String fullName;
  private int ranking;

  public void setFullName(String fullName) {
    this.fullName = fullName;
  }

  public void setRanking(int ranking) {
    this.ranking = ranking;
  }
}
```

You can optionally add a getter method to make the property readable, as shown in Listing 2-7, but this is not required by the container.

Listing 2-7. *Adding a Getter Method to Make the JavaBean Property Readable*

```
package com.apress.springbook.chapter02;

public class Player {
  private String fullName;
  private int ranking;

  public void setFullName(String fullName) {
    this.fullName = fullName;
  }
```

```
    public void setRanking(int ranking) {
      this.ranking = ranking;
    }

    public String getFullName() {
      return this.fullName;
    }

    public int getRanking() {
      return this.ranking;
    }
  }
}
```

Setter injection can inject values and other beans, as shown in Listing 2-8.

Listing 2-8. *Injecting Values and Other Beans via Setter Methods*

```xml
<?xml version="1.0" encoding="UTF-8"?>
<!DOCTYPE beans PUBLIC "-//SPRING//DTD BEAN//EN"
    "http://www.springframework.org/dtd/spring-beans.dtd">
<beans>
  <bean id="Kim" class="com.apress.springbook.chapter02.Player">
    <property name="fullName" value="Kim Clijsters"/>
    <property name="ranking" value="1"/>
  </bean>

  <bean id="Justine" class="com.apress.springbook.chapter02.Player">
    <property name="fullName" ref="Henin-Hardenne"/>
    <property name="ranking" value="5"/>
  </bean>

  <bean id="Henin-Hardenne" class="java.lang.String">
    <constructor-arg value="Justine Henin-Hardenne"/>
  </bean>
</beans>
```

The value attribute injects a literal value from the XML file, and the ref attribute injects another bean. This example creates a java.lang.String bean, indicating that the container can instantiate any class.

Constructor Injection

We'll rewrite the Player class to use constructor injection, as shown in Listing 2-9.

Listing 2-9. *The Player Class, Which Takes Its Internal State via the Constructor*

```java
package com.apress.springbook.chapter02;

public class Player {
  private String fullName;
  private int ranking;

  public Player(String fullName, int ranking) {
    if (fullName == null || fullName.length() == 0) {
      throw new IllegalArgumentException("Full name is required!");
    }
    this.fullName = fullName;
```

```
    this.ranking = ranking;
  }

  public String getFullName() {
    return this.fullName;
  }

  public int getRanking() {
    return this.ranking;
  }
}
```

By refactoring the Player class, we've introduced one significant change by making the full name required. Checking the state of the object is the most important reason that developers create constructors in their classes. Listing 2-10 shows how the container is instructed to call the constructor.

Listing 2-10. *Instructing the Container to Call the Player Constructor*

```
<?xml version="1.0" encoding="UTF-8"?>
<!DOCTYPE beans PUBLIC "-//SPRING//DTD BEAN//EN"
    "http://www.springframework.org/dtd/spring-beans.dtd">
<beans>
  <bean id="Kim" class="com.apress.springbook.chapter02.Player">
    <constructor-arg value="Kim Clijsters"/>
    <constructor-arg value="1"/>
  </bean>

  <bean id="Justine" class="com.apress.springbook.chapter02.Player">
    <constructor-arg ref="Henin-Hardenne"/>
    <constructor-arg value="5"/>
  </bean>

  <bean id="Henin-Hardenne" class="java.lang.String">
    <constructor-arg value="Justine Henin-Hardenne"/>
  </bean>
</beans>
```

The container must choose which constructor it will invoke based on the information in the bean definition. For the configuration in Listing 2-10, the behavior is predictable since the Player class defines only one constructor. Listing 2-11 shows an example that includes two constructors.

■**Note** In Java, the names of constructor arguments cannot be retrieved from compiled classes by the Reflection API. Other tools, like the open source ASM framework, can retrieve constructor argument names by looking at debug information in the compiled bytecode. However, at the time of this writing, the container does not take the name of arguments into account when invoking constructors.

Listing 2-11. *The ConstructorTestBean Class, Which Has Two Constructors*

```
package com.apress.springbook.chapter02;

public class ConstructorTestBean {
  private boolean constructor1Used = false;
  private boolean constructor2Used = false;
```

```
  public ConstructorTestBean(String name, Integer id) {
    this.constructor1Used = true;
  }

  public ConstructorTestBean(String firstName, String lastName) {
    this.constructor2Used = true;
  }

  public boolean isConstructor1Used() {
    return this.constructor1Used;
  }

  public boolean isConstructor2Used() {
    return this.constructor2Used;
  }
}
```

When you configure the ConstructorTestBean class with two constructor arguments, the container will use the best match, meaning the constructor that is the closest match to the constructor argument types you provide.

The configuration shown in Listing 2-12 has two constructor arguments that are both considered Strings. Why? In XML, all literal values are Strings, and the container does not convert constructor argument values for *finding* a constructor.

Listing 2-12. *Configuring the ConstructorTestBean Class with Two Constructor Arguments*

```
<?xml version="1.0" encoding="UTF-8"?>
<!DOCTYPE beans PUBLIC "-//SPRING//DTD BEAN//EN"
    "http://www.springframework.org/dtd/spring-beans.dtd">
<beans>
  <bean id="testBean"
        class="com.apress.springbook.chapter02.ConstructorTestBean">
    <constructor-arg value="Steven Devijver"/>
    <constructor-arg value="1"/>
  </bean>
</beans>
```

We want to use the first constructor of the ConstructorTestBean class, and we can write a test case to verify it has actually been called, as shown in Listing 2-13.

Listing 2-13. *A Test Case to Verify the First Constructor Is Used*

```
package com.apress.springbook.chapter02;

import junit.framework.TestCase;

import org.springframework.core.io.ClassPathResource;
import org.springframework.beans.factory.BeanFactory;

import org.springframework.beans.factory.xml.XmlBeanFactory;

public class ConstructorTestBeanIntegrationTests extends TestCase {

  private static BeanFactory beanFactory = new XmlBeanFactory(
    new ClassPathResource(
        "com/apress/springbook/chapter02/test-bean-tests.xml"
```

```
    )
  );

private static ConstructorTestBean testBean;

static {
  testBean = (ConstructorTestBean)beanFactory.getBean("testBean");
}

public void testIsConstructor1Used() {
  assertTrue(testBean.isConstructor1Used());
}

public void testIsConstructor2NotUsed() {
  assertFalse(testBean.isConstructor2Used());
}
}
```

■**Note** The "Using an ApplicationContext in Integration Tests" section explains how to load configuration files in test cases more conveniently.

Unfortunately, when we run the test case in Listing 2-13, it appears that the container has used the second constructor of the ConstructorTestBean class. The container has picked the most specific constructor—the one with two String arguments.

We can force the container to use another constructor by providing the type of the constructor arguments. In this case, it is sufficient to change the configuration and specify that the second constructor argument is of type java.lang.Integer, as shown in Listing 2-14.

Listing 2-14. *Forcing the Container to Use the First Constructor*

```
<?xml version="1.0" encoding="UTF-8"?>
<!DOCTYPE beans PUBLIC "-//SPRING//DTD BEAN//EN"
    "http://www.springframework.org/dtd/spring-beans.dtd">
<beans>
  <bean id="testBean"
        class="com.apress.springbook.chapter02.ConstructorTestBean">
    <constructor-arg value="Steven Devijver"/>
    <constructor-arg value="1" type="java.lang.Integer"/>
  </bean>
</beans>
```

Adding the type information to the second constructor argument makes the ConstructorTestBeanIntegrationTests test case run successfully and forces the container to use a specific constructor.

■**Note** You should write your own test cases whenever you want to see how a specific feature of the Spring Framework works. The same goes for any other frameworks, including the classes of the Java Development Kit (JDK).

Setter and Constructor Injection Combination

The container allows the combination of setter injection and constructor injection in the same bean definition, which is especially useful for configuring existing classes in the container. Another use case for combining both forms of dependency injection is to pass required parameters via the constructor and optional parameters via properties.

Let's refactor the Player class to reflect that the full name parameter is required and the ranking parameter is optional, as shown in Listing 2-15.

Listing 2-15. *Refactored Player Class with Required and Optional Parameters*

```
package com.apress.springbook.chapter02;

public class Player {
  private String fullName;
  private int ranking;

  public Player(String fullName) {
    if (fullName == null || fullName.length() == 0) {
      throw new IllegalArgumentException("Full name is required!");
    }
    this.fullName = fullName;
  }

  public String getFullName() {
    return this.fullName;
  }

  public void setRanking(int ranking) {
    this.ranking = ranking;
  }

  public int getRanking() {
    return this.ranking;
  }
}
```

We can now combine setter injection and constructor injection in the configuration file to configure the Player class, as shown in Listing 2-16.

Listing 2-16. *Combining Setter Injection and Constructor Injection in the Same Bean Definition*

```
<?xml version="1.0" encoding="UTF-8"?>
<!DOCTYPE beans PUBLIC "-//SPRING//DTD BEAN//EN"
    "http://www.springframework.org/dtd/spring-beans.dtd">
<beans>
  <bean id="Kim" class="com.apress.springbook.chapter02.Player">
    <constructor-arg value="Kim Clijsters"/>
    <property name="ranking" value="1"/>
  </bean>

  <bean id="Justine" class="com.apress.springbook.chapter02.Player">
    <constructor-arg ref="Henin-Hardenne"/>
    <property name="ranking" value="5"/>
  </bean>
```

```xml
    <bean id="Henin-Hardenne" class="java.lang.String">
      <constructor-arg value="Justine Henin-Hardenne"/>
    </bean>
</beans>
```

Which one is preferred: setter injection or constructor injection? It's largely up to you to choose, although you should pick one and stick to it for the duration of a project for the sake of consistency.

Setter injection is more popular because it's more self-documenting and isn't affected by circular dependency problems, which may occur if you use constructor injection. Setter injection leaves beans in an indeterminate state, something you can avoid with constructor injection, as shown in Listing 2-15. The "Examining the Bean Life Cycle" section later in this chapter offers a solution to the problem of indeterminate state.

Inner Bean Definitions

The container supports inner bean definition, also called anonymous bean definitions since they cannot be referenced by other bean definitions. Inner bean definitions are useful for making the configuration more readable and to avoid exposing beans that are used in only one place.

Listing 2-17 shows a rewritten version of the configuration from Listing 2-5.

Listing 2-17. *Using Inner Bean Definitions to Make the Configuration More Readable*

```xml
<?xml version="1.0" encoding="UTF-8"?>
<!DOCTYPE beans PUBLIC "-//SPRING//DTD BEAN//EN"
    "http://www.springframework.org/dtd/spring-beans.dtd">
<beans>
  <bean id="swingApplication"
        class="org.apress.springbook.chapter02.SwingApplication">
   <constructor-arg ref="tournamentMatchManager"/>
  </bean>

  <bean id="tournamentMatchManager"
        class="org.apress.springbook.chapter02.DefaultTournamentMatchManager">
    <property name="matchDao">
      <bean class="org.apress.springbook.chapter02.JdbcMatchDao">
        <property name="dataSource" ref="dataSource"/>
      </bean>
    </property>
  </bean>

  <bean id="dataSource" class="org.apache.commons.dbcp.BasicDataSource">
    <property name="driverClassName" value="org.hsqldb.jdbcDriver"/>
    <property name="url" value="jdbc:hsqldb:hsql:/localhost/test"/>
    <property name="username" value="sa"/>
    <property name="password" value=""/>
    <property name="initialSize" value="10"/>
    <property name="testOnBorrow" value="true"/>
  </bean>
</beans>
```

The inner bean definition can have a name by adding the id attribute, but it's not available via dependency injection or constructor injection.

PropertyEditors

The bean factory uses PropertyEditors for converting the String values in XML files to the destination type of properties and constructor arguments. The java.beans.PropertyEditor interface, which is part of the Java Software Development Kit (SDK), handles the conversion of Strings to a specific type and back. The container has PropertyEditors for all simple types, their object counterparts, and commonly used objects such as java.math.BigDecimal, java.lang.Class, java.io.File, and java.util.Properties.

Each time a value must be injected, the container uses the PropertyEditor that has been registered for the destination type to do the conversion. The PropertyEditor will throw an exception if the String value cannot be converted to the specific type. For example, the string 'abcdef' cannot be converted to a numeric value. If no PropertyEditor can be found for a destination type, an exception will be thrown.

Let's see how the PropertyEditors work with the PropertyEditorTestBean class. An example is shown in Listing 2-18.

Listing 2-18. *The TestBean Class, Which Has Many Different Property Types*

```
package com.apress.springbook.chapter02;

import java.math.BigDecimal;
import java.io.File;
import java.io.InputStream;
import java.util.Properties;
import java.net.URL;

public class PropertyEditorTestBean {
  private int myNumber;
  private boolean myToggle;
  private byte[] myBytes;
  private String[] myStrings;
  private BigDecimal myAmount;
  private Class myClass;
  private File myFile;
  private InputStream myInputStream;
  private Properties myProperties;
  private URL myUrl;

  public int getMyNumber() {
    return myNumber;
  }

  public void setMyNumber(int myNumber) {
    this.myNumber = myNumber;
  }

  public boolean isMyToggle() {
    return myToggle;
  }

  public void setMyToggle(boolean myToggle) {
    this.myToggle = myToggle;
  }
```

```java
public byte[] getMyBytes() {
  return myBytes;
}

public void setMyBytes(byte[] myBytes) {
  this.myBytes = myBytes;
}

public String[] getMyStrings() {
  return myStrings;
}

public void setMyStrings(String[] myStrings) {
  this.myStrings = myStrings;
}

public BigDecimal getMyAmount() {
  return myAmount;
}

public void setMyAmount(BigDecimal myAmount) {
  this.myAmount = myAmount;
}

public Class getMyClass() {
  return myClass;
}

public void setMyClass(Class myClass) {
  this.myClass = myClass;
}

public File getMyFile() {
  return myFile;
}

public void setMyFile(File myFile) {
  this.myFile = myFile;
}

public InputStream getMyInputStream() {
  return myInputStream;
}

public void setMyInputStream(InputStream myInputStream) {
  this.myInputStream = myInputStream;
}

public Properties getMyProperties() {
  return myProperties;
}

public void setMyProperties(Properties myProperties) {
  this.myProperties = myProperties;
}
```

```
  public URL getMyUrl() {
    return myUrl;
  }

  public void setMyUrl(URL myUrl) {
    this.myUrl = myUrl;
  }
}
```

Next, we can configure the PropertyEditorTestBean class in a configuration file and use String literals, as shown in Listing 2-19. The container will use PropertyEditors to convert these values to the destination type of the properties.

Listing 2-19. *Configuring PropertyEditorTestBean*

```
<?xml version="1.0" encoding="UTF-8"?>
<!DOCTYPE beans PUBLIC "-//SPRING//DTD BEAN//EN"
    "http://www.springframework.org/dtd/spring-beans.dtd">
<beans>
  <bean id="testBean"
        class="com.apress.springbook.chapter02.PropertyEditorTestBean">
    <property name="myNumber" value="500"/>
    <property name="myToggle" value="false"/>
    <property name="myBytes" value="some bytes"/>
    <property name="myStrings" value="Bram,Mark,Seth,Steven"/>
    <property name="myAmount" value="1000000"/>
    <property name="myClass" value="java.util.Collection"/>
    <property name="myFile" value="placeholder.txt"/>
    <property name="myInputStream" value="http://www.google.com"/>
    <property name="myProperties">
      <value>
firstname=Steven
lastname=Devijver
      </value>
    </property>
    <property name="myUrl" value="http://del.icio.us"/>
  </bean>
</beans>
```

The PropertyEditorTestBeanIntegrationTests test case checks if all property values correspond to the expected value, as shown in Listing 2-20.

Listing 2-20. *The PropertyEditorTestBeanIntegrationTest Class*

```
package com.apress.springbook.chapter02;

import junit.framework.TestCase;

import org.apache.commons.io.IOUtils;

import org.springframework.beans.factory.BeanFactory;
import org.springframework.beans.factory.xml.XmlBeanFactory;
import org.springframework.core.io.ClassPathResource;
import org.springframework.util.StringUtils;
```

```java
import java.io.File;
import java.io.IOException;
import java.math.BigDecimal;
import java.net.MalformedURLException;
import java.net.URL;
import java.util.Arrays;
import java.util.Collection;
import java.util.Properties;

public class PropertyEditorTestBeanIntegrationTests
  extends TestCase {

  private static BeanFactory beanFactory = new XmlBeanFactory(
    new ClassPathResource(
        "com/apress/springbook/chapter02/property-editor-test-bean-tests.xml"
    )
  );

  private static PropertyEditorTestBean testBean;

  static {
    testBean = (PropertyEditorTestBean)beanFactory.getBean("testBean");
  }

  public void testMyNumber() {
    assertEquals(500, testBean.getMyNumber());
  }

  public void testMyToggle() {
    assertFalse(testBean.isMyToggle());
  }

  public void testMyBytes() {
    assertTrue(Arrays.equals("some bytes".getBytes(), testBean.getMyBytes()));
  }

  public void testMyStrings() {
    assertTrue(
      Arrays.equals(
        new String[]{
          "Bram",
          "Mark",
          "Seth",
          "Steven"
        },
        testBean.getMyStrings()
      )
    );
  }

  public void testMyAmount() {
    assertEquals(new BigDecimal("1000000"), testBean.getMyAmount());
  }

  public void testMyClass() {
    assertEquals(Collection.class, testBean.getMyClass());
  }
```

```
public void testMyFile() {
  assertEquals(new File("placeholder.txt"), testBean.getMyFile());
}

public void testMyInputStream() throws IOException {
  String content = IOUtils.toString(testBean.getMyInputStream());
  assertTrue(StringUtils.hasText("Google"));
  testBean.getMyInputStream().close();
}

public void testMyProperties() {
  Properties myProps = testBean.getMyProperties();
  assertEquals("Steven", myProps.getProperty("firstname"));
  assertEquals("Devijver", myProps.getProperty("lastname"));
}

public void testMyUrl() throws MalformedURLException {
  assertEquals(new URL("http://del.icio.us"), testBean.getMyUrl());
}
}
```

The use of `PropertyEditors` by the Core Container is an important mechanism, adding a lot of power for configuring applications. Along with the standard `PropertyEditors`, you can also register custom editors and write your own `PropertyEditors`. Chapter 5 of *Pro Spring* (Apress, 2005) covers these more advanced uses of `PropertyEditors`.

Using XML Tags for Bean Configuration

The Core Container's XML notation has tags to make the configuration of bean definitions much easier. All these tags can be used as children of the `<property>` and `<constructor-arg>` tags.

The <value> Element

You can use the `<value>` element to add values:

```
<property name="myToggle">
  <value>false</value>
</property>
```

Before version 1.2, the container did not support the `value` attribute on the `<property>` and `<constructor-arg>` elements, but used the expanded notation. The `<value>` element can still be used to add values to lists and maps, and when unparsable text is used as a literal value, as in this example:

```
<property name="myText">
  <value><![CDATA[Unparsable characters follow: < > & "]]></value>
</property>
```

The <ref> Element

The container also supports an expanded reference notation using the `<ref>` element, which refers to another bean:

```
<property name="tournamentMatchManager">
  <ref bean="tournamentMatchManager"/>
</property>
```

The <list> Element

The next special-purpose element is <list>:

```
<bean id="daysOfWeek" class="java.util.ArrayList">
  <constructor-arg>
    <list>
      <value>Monday</value>
      <value>Tuesday</value>
      <bean class="java.lang.String">
        <constructor-arg type="java.lang.String" value="Wednesday"/>
      </bean>
      <value>Thursday</value>
      <value>Friday</value>
      <value>Saturday</value>
      <value>Sunday</value>
    </list>
  </constructor-arg>
</bean>
```

Child elements of the <list> element can be literal values—they will be converted to strings—inner bean definitions, references to other bean definitions, other lists, maps, properties, and so on. The <list> element creates an object depending on the target type: java.util.List instances, java.util.Set instances, and array objects.

The <map> Element

The <map> element is very similar to the <list> element, except that it creates a java.util.Map instance.

```
<bean id="topPlayers" class="java.util.HashMap">
  <constructor-arg>
    <map>
      <entry key="men.number1">
        <bean class="com.apress.springbook.chapter02.Player">
          <constructor-arg value="Roger Federer"/>
        </bean>
      </entry>
      <entry key="women.number1">
        <bean class="com.apress.springbook.chapter02.Player">
          <constructor-arg value="Kim Clijsters"/>
        </bean>
      </entry>
    </map>
  </constructor-arg>
</bean>
```

The <entry> element takes a key and a value, where the value can be any element that is accepted by the <property> and <constructor-arg> elements. There are special key-ref and value-ref attributes on the <entry> element that take bean definition names as the key and value. The <entry> element also supports a child <key> element that can take any element that is accepted by the <property> and <constructor-arg> elements, as in this example:

```
<?xml version="1.0" encoding="UTF-8"?>
<!DOCTYPE beans PUBLIC "-//SPRING//DTD BEAN//EN"
    "http://www.springframework.org/dtd/spring-beans.dtd">
<beans>
  <bean id="men.number1" class="java.lang.String">
```

```
    <constructor-arg type="java.lang.String" value="men.number1"/>
  </bean>

  <bean id="Federer" class="com.apress.springbook.chapter02.Player">
    <constructor-arg value="Roger Federer"/>
  </bean>

  <bean id="topPlayers" class="java.util.HashMap">
    <map>
      <entry key-ref="men.number1" value-ref="Federer"/>
      <entry>
        <key>
          <value>women.number1</value>
        </key>
        <bean class="com.apress.springbook.chapter02.Player">
          <constructor-arg value="Kim Clijsters"/>
        </bean>
      </entry>
    </map>
  </bean>
</beans>
```

The <props> Element

The <props> element creates a java.util.Properties element that is injected. The Properties class implements java.util.Map and takes Strings for the key and value.

```
<property name="topPlayers">
  <props>
    <prop key="men.number1">Roger Federer</prop>
    <prop key="women.number1">Kim Clijsters</prop>
  </props>
</property>
```

Properties can also be loaded from a properties file. As you saw earlier in the section on PropertyEditors, the <value> element can also be used to inject a java.util.Properties object.

The <set> Element

The <set> element is comparable to the <list> element. This element will create and inject a java.util.Set instance, which is a collection type that enforces uniqueness of its element in the collection.

```
<property name="additivePrimaryColors">
  <set>
    <bean class="java.awt.Color">
      <constructor-arg value="255"/>
      <constructor-arg value="0"/>
      <constructor-arg value="0"/>
    </bean>
    <bean class="java.awt.Color">
      <constructor-arg value="0"/>
      <constructor-arg value="255"/>
      <constructor-arg value="0"/>
    </bean>
```

```
  <bean class="java.awt.Color">
    <constructor-arg value="0"/>
    <constructor-arg value="0"/>
    <constructor-arg value="255"/>
  </bean>
</set>
</property>
```

This overview of the XML tags supported by the Core Container covers the most commonly used elements. The next sections will introduce some attributes of the <bean> element for controlling the life cycle of beans and how beans are created.

Examining the Bean Life Cycle

The container creates and configures a bean based on its bean definition, which provides a single point to configure the life cycle of the bean. Along with dependency injection, the container also provides life-cycle options that address the following:

Scope: The scope of a bean defines the behavior of the container when a bean is requested, either via dependency injection or dependency lookup. By default, beans are *singleton*, which means they are created and configured once and stored in a cache. When a singleton bean is requested, the container returns the instance from the cache. Optionally, beans can be *prototype*, which means they are created and configured by the container on each request. When a prototype bean is requested, the container creates and configures a new bean and doesn't keep track of it.

Initialization: The initialization of beans is available for singleton and prototype beans. The container can invoke a method on a bean if it implements a specific interface that is part of the Spring Framework API or if a custom initialization method has been configured on the bean definition. This is an optional step in the life cycle of a bean.

Destruction: The destruction of beans is available only for singleton beans. The container can invoke a method on a bean if it implements a specific interface that is part of the Spring Framework API or if a custom destroy method has been configured on the bean definition. This is an optional step in the life cycle of a singleton bean.

These options are configured in the bean definition in the XML file, as described in the following sections.

Bean Scope: Singleton or Prototype

Without extra configuration on the bean definition, beans are singleton. This means that the container creates a bean once and puts it in a cache. When the next request for the same bean definition is made, the bean in the cache is returned. All bean definitions we've used so far in this chapter are singleton.

A singleton bean may be used by multiple threads running concurrently, meaning its operations must be implemented in a thread-safe way. The execution of the bean life-cycle process by the container is guaranteed to be thread-safe, so operations that are executed during this process are not subject to thread-safety issues. Once the life-cycle process of the container is over, all operations that are allowed on singleton beans must happen in a thread-safe way.

Updating the state of a shared member variable is a typical operation that is not thread-safe, as shown in Listing 2-21.

Listing 2-21. *Updating the State of a Shared Member Variable*

```
package com.apress.springbook.chapter02;

import java.util.List;
import java.util.ArrayList;

public class ClassWithSharedMemberVariable {
  private List<String> numbers = new ArrayList<String>();

  public void initialize() {
    numbers.add("one");
    numbers.add("two");
    numbers.add("three");
  }
}
```

The initialize() method shown in Listing 2-21 is not thread-safe if executed by multiple threads concurrently on the same bean because it updates a shared member variable. However, as we've already mentioned, the container can call a custom initialization method as part of the bean life cycle. Since this life-cycle process is guaranteed to be thread-safe, the ClassWithSharedMember Variable class can be considered as thread-safe when managed by the container and when the initialize() method is configured as a custom initialization method.

Another type of operation that is potentially not thread-safe involves assigning shared member variables. Dependency injection happens at the start of the bean life-cycle process and typically involves assigning member variables. After the bean life cycle has completed, member variables can safely be read without causing thread-safety issues. Listing 2-5, shown earlier in this chapter, is an example of a configuration that injects a javax.sql.DataSource bean in a JdbcMatchDao bean (shown in Listing 1-4 of the previous chapter). This is a very typical dependency injection scenario that is potentially not thread-safe on a singleton bean, yet occurs in a thread-safe way as guaranteed by the container.

By default, the container creates singleton beans, and you should follow this practice unless you configure classes that are definitely not thread-safe, as discussed next.

Using Prototypes

Prototype beans typically have internal state that is related to a single execution of a business process. Every execution of the business process requires a new bean, and executions that run concurrently cannot share the same bean. For example, Listing 2-22 shows the PrimeIterator class, which returns the next prime number based on an internal prime number. It accepts a start number, in which case the first call to the getNextPrime() method returns the first prime number after the start number. PrimeIterator beans can be used only by one request, since the internal prime number increases on every call to the getNextPrime() method.

Listing 2-22. *The PrimeIterator Class, Which Must Be Configured As a Prototype*

```
package com.apress.springbook.chapter02;

import org.apache.commons.lang.ArrayUtils;

public class PrimeIterator {
  private int start = 2;
  private int current = 0;
  private int[] primesFound = new int[] { 2, 3 };
```

```java
  public void setStart(int start) {
    if (start < 2) {
      throw new IllegalArgumentException("Start should not be less than 2!");
    }
    this.start = start;
  }

  public int getNextPrime() {
    if (current < 2) {
      current = 3;
      if (current > start) {
        return current;
      }
    }
    for (;;) {
      current = current + 2;
      int highestToCheck = (int)(current ^ (1/2));
      boolean isPrime = true;

      for (int i = 0; i < primesFound.length; i++) {
        int prime = primesFound[i];
        if (prime > highestToCheck) {
          break;
        }
        if (current % prime == 0) {
          isPrime = false;
          break;
        }
      }

      if (isPrime && current < start) {
        addToPrimesFound();
      } else if (isPrime) {
        break;
      }
    }

    addToPrimesFound();

    return current;
  }

  private void addToPrimesFound() {
    primesFound = ArrayUtils.add(primesFound, current);
  }
}
```

To configure a bean definition as a prototype, set the `singleton` attribute of the `<bean>` element to `false`, as shown in Listing 2-23.

Listing 2-23. *Configuring the PrimeIterator Class As a Prototype*

```xml
<?xml version="1.0" encoding="UTF-8"?>
<!DOCTYPE beans PUBLIC "-//SPRING//DTD BEAN//EN"
    "http://www.springframework.org/dtd/spring-beans.dtd">
<beans>
  <bean id="primeIterator"
```

```
        class="com.apress.springbook.chapter02.PrimeIterator" singleton="false">
    <property name="start" value="1000"/>
  </bean>
</beans>
```

Now when we request the primeIterator bean definition twice—either via dependency injection or dependency lookup—we get two distinct beans, as demonstrated in the PrototypeIntegrationTests test case in Listing 2-24.

Listing 2-24. *Testing If the Container Returns Two Distinct Beans for the primeIterator Bean Definition*

```
package com.apress.springbook.chapter02;

import junit.framework.TestCase;

import org.springframework.core.io.ClassPathResource;
import org.springframework.beans.factory.BeanFactory;
import org.springframework.beans.factory.xml.XmlBeanFactory;

public class PrototypeIntegrationTests extends TestCase {
  public void testPreInstantiateSingletons() {
    BeanFactory beanFactory =
      new XmlBeanFactory(
        new ClassPathResource(
          "com/apress/springbook/chapter02/prototype.xml"
        )
      );

    PrimeIterator primeNumber1 =
      (PrimeIterator) beanFactory.getBean("primeIterator");
    PrimeIterator primeNumber2 = (PrimeIterator)
    beanFactory.getBean("primeIterator");

    assertNotSame(primeNumber1, primeNumber2);
  }
}
```

Overall, prototype beans are not often configured in the container.

Preinstantiating Singleton Beans

By default, the BeanFactory will not preinstantiate singletons, but will instead create each singleton bean when it's first requested. In contrast, the ApplicationContext, discussed a bit later in this chapter, will preinstantiate singleton beans. In practice, you will almost always use an ApplicationContext, so you will rarely need to deal with this issue.

When you do use the BeanFactory, it makes sense to preinstantiate singletons. For one, you will discover configuration errors that become apparent only when beans are created early on. Let's see how to preinstantiate singletons in the BeanFactory using the InstantiationCounterClass class, which counts the number of instantiations via a static variable, as shown in Listing 2-25.

Listing 2-25. *The InstantiationCounterClass Class, Which Tracks the Number of Instantiations*

```
package com.apress.springbook.chapter02;

import java.util.concurrent.atomic.AtomicInteger;
```

```
public class InstantiationCounterClass {
  private static AtomicInteger instantiationCounter = new AtomicInteger(0);

  public static int getNumberOfInstantiations() {
    /* returns the internal int value */
    return instantiationCounter.get();
  }

  public InstantiationCounterClass() {
    /* increment the internal int value with one */
    instantiationCounter.incrementAndGet();
  }
}
```

We configure the InstantiationCounterClass class in a configuration file, as shown in Listing 2-26.

Listing 2-26. *Configuring the InstantiationCounterClass in a Bean Definition*

```
<?xml version="1.0" encoding="UTF-8"?>
<!DOCTYPE beans PUBLIC "-//SPRING//DTD BEAN//EN"
    "http://www.springframework.org/dtd/spring-beans.dtd">
<beans>
  <bean id="instantiationCounterClass"
        class="com.apress.springbook.chapter02.InstantiationCounterClass"/>
</beans>
```

■**Note** The InstantiationCounterClass uses the java.util.concurrent.atomic.AtomicInteger class introduced in Java 5 to ensure that updates to the static instantiationCounter variable happen atomically, and therefore in a thread-safe fashion. Although this class is used purely for demonstration purposes, we don't want to show you code that updates a shared variable without a second thought. We advise you to take a similar approach when you increment counter variables in your code, even if it's just for testing purposes. We know from experience that you cannot tell who will look at your code after you write it.

Listing 2-27 demonstrates, in the BeanFactoryPreInstantiateSingletonsIntegrationTests test case, how to preinstantiate singletons when using ConfigurableListableBeanFactory. We need to use ConfigurableListableBeanFactory because we are working with the container's configuration. Before we preinstantiate the singletons, we will count the number of instantiations on InstantiationCounterClass.

Listing 2-27. *Testing the Preinstantiation of Singletons on BeanFactory*

```
package com.apress.springbook.chapter02;

import junit.framework.TestCase;

import org.springframework.core.io.ClassPathResource;
import org.springframework.beans.factory.config.ConfigurableListableBeanFactory;
import org.springframework.beans.factory.xml.XmlBeanFactory;

public class BeanFactoryPreInstantiateSingletonsIntegrationTests extends TestCase {
  public void testPreInstantiateSingletons() {
    ConfigurableListableBeanFactory beanFactory =
```

```
    new XmlBeanFactory(
      new ClassPathResource(
        "com/apress/springbook/chapter02/preInstantiate-singletons.xml"
      )
    );

  assertEquals(0, InstantiationCounterClass.getNumberOfInstantiations());

  beanFactory.preInstantiateSingletons();

  assertEquals(1, InstantiationCounterClass.getNumberOfInstantiations());
  }
}
```

Prototype beans are not preinstantiated by the BeanFactory or ApplicationContext container.

Bean Initialization

The container can optionally initialize beans, either via an interface that is implemented by beans or via a custom initialization method. This initialization step can be used to check the internal state of beans. If you use setter injection, it's possible to have forgotten to configure one or more properties. You can use the initialization step to let beans check if all the required collaborating objects are present.

Using the InitializingBean Interface

The container will initialize any bean that implements the org.springframework.beans.factory.InitializingBean interface, as shown in Listing 2-28.

Listing 2-28. *The InitializingBeanNumbersClass Class, Which Implements the InitializingBean Interface*

```
package com.apress.springbook.chapter02;

import org.springframework.beans.factory.InitializingBean;

public class InitializingBeanNameClass implements InitializingBean {
  private String firstName;

  public String getFirstName() {
    return this.firstName;
  }

  public void setFirstName(String firstName) {
    this.firstName = firstName;
  }

  public void afterPropertiesSet() throws Exception {
    if (this.firstName == null) {
      throw new RequiredPropertyNotSetException("firstName property is required.");
    }
  }
}
```

```
  private class RequiredPropertyNotSetException extends Exception {
    private RequiredPropertyNotSetException(String msg) {
      super(msg);
    }
  }
}
```

The afterPropertiesSet() method is invoked by the container and can throw an exception, which will interrupt the life cycle of the bean. In this case, it is a custom RequiredPropertyNotSet Exception that warns about missing properties.

The InitializingBeanNameClass does not require any special configuration, as shown in Listing 2-29.

Listing 2-29. *Configuring InitializingBeanNumberClass in the Container*

```xml
<?xml version="1.0" encoding="UTF-8"?>
<!DOCTYPE beans PUBLIC "-//SPRING//DTD BEAN//EN"
    "http://www.springframework.org/dtd/spring-beans.dtd">
<beans>
  <bean id="numberClass"
        class="com.apress.springbook.chapter02.InitializingBeanNumberClass"/>
</beans>
```

The container calls the afterPropertiesSet() method, as shown in the test case in Listing 2-30.

Listing 2-30. *The InitializingBeanNumberClassIntegrationTests Test Case*

```java
package com.apress.springbook.chapter02;

import junit.framework.TestCase;

import org.springframework.core.io.ClassPathResource;
import org.springframework.beans.factory.BeanFactory;
import org.springframework.beans.factory.xml.XmlBeanFactory;

public class InitializingBeanNameClassIntegrationTests extends TestCase {
  public void testPreInstantiateSingletons() {
    BeanFactory beanFactory =
      new XmlBeanFactory(
        new ClassPathResource(
          "com/apress/springbook/chapter02/initializing-bean.xml"
        )
      );

    InitializingBeanNameClass nameClass =
        (InitializingBeanNameClass)beanFactory.getBean("nameClass");

    assertEquals("Roger", nameClass.getFirstName());
  }
}
```

The test case uses BeanFactory so singleton beans are not preinstantiated. This means that the nameClass bean is created when the getBean() method is called. and any exception thrown by the afterProperties() method is rethrown by the getBean() method. If you try to run this test, you will receive a RequiredPropertyNotSetException before the test executes, because the container won't instantiate the bean without a firstName property.

Using Custom Initialization Methods

The container also supports custom initialization methods, which basically are regular methods. Listing 2-31 shows the CustomInitializationMethodNumberClass class, which has an initialize() method and doesn't implement any interfaces. This is one way to set defaults.

Listing 2-31. *The CustomInitializationMethodNumberClass Class, Which Has an initialize() Method*

```
package com.apress.springbook.chapter02;

import java.util.List;
import java.util.ArrayList;

public class CustomInitializationMethodNumberClass {
  private List<String> numbers = new ArrayList<String>();

  public List<String> getNumbers() {
    return this.numbers;
  }

  public void initialize() throws Exception {
    if (this.numbers.size() < 3) {
      numbers.add("one");
      numbers.add("two");
      numbers.add("three");
    }
  }
}
```

We can now configure the bean definition to set the initialize() method as the custom initialization method, as shown in Listing 2-32.

Listing 2-32. *Configuring the initialize() Method As a Custom Initialization Method*

```
<?xml version="1.0" encoding="UTF-8"?>
<!DOCTYPE beans PUBLIC "-//SPRING//DTD BEAN//EN"
    "http://www.springframework.org/dtd/spring-beans.dtd">
<beans>
  <bean id="numberClass"
        class="com.apress.springbook.chapter02. ➥
CustomInitializationMethodNumberClass"
        init-method="initialize"/>
</beans>
```

The init-method attribute takes the method name of the custom initialization method. The container requires that custom initialization methods have no arguments. They can throw exceptions that are handled in the same way as those thrown by the afterPropertiesSet() method and can return values, but these are ignored by the container.

The test case in Listing 2-33 shows that the custom initialization method is called correctly.

Listing 2-33. *The CustomInitializationMethodNumberClassIntegrationTests Test Case*

```
package com.apress.springbook.chapter02;

import junit.framework.TestCase;
```

```
import org.springframework.core.io.ClassPathResource;
import org.springframework.beans.factory.BeanFactory;
import org.springframework.beans.factory.xml.XmlBeanFactory;

public class InitializingBeanNumberClassIntegrationTests extends TestCase {
  public void testPreInstantiateSingletons() {
    BeanFactory beanFactory =
        new XmlBeanFactory(
          new ClassPathResource(
            "com/apress/springbook/chapter02/custom-initializing-method.xml"
          )
        );

    CustomInitializationMethodNumberClass numberClass =
      (CustomInitializationMethodNumberClass)beanFactory.getBean("numberClass");

    assertEquals(3, numberClass.getNumbers().size());
  }
}
```

We recommend that you use the custom initialization method strategy as much as possible, since it avoids coupling application code to the Spring Framework API. That being said, the `InitializationMethod` interface has one advantage: you can't forget to configure the bean definition correctly. You can, of course, use this interface if your class is otherwise dependent on Spring.

Bean Destruction

Prototype objects are created by the container, returned, and forgotten about. The container does not keep track of prototype beans. The life cycle is restarted for a prototype every time a new object is created.

In contrast, singleton instances are stored in a cache and can be destroyed when the container is closed. The destruction step is useful for cleaning up resources when the application stops. Just like the initialization step, the destruction step can be configured in two ways: through an interface that is implemented by beans or through a custom destruction method.

Java does not support the concept of destructors, so to invoke the destruction part of the life cycle, the container object must be closed by calling the `destroySingletons()` method on `BeanFactory`.

Using the DisposableBean Interface

The container will destroy any bean that implements the `org.springframework.beans.factory.DisposableBean` interface, as shown in Listing 2-34.

Listing 2-34. *The DisposableBeanNumberClass Class, Which Implements the DisposableBean Interface*

```
package com.apress.springbook.chapter02;

import java.util.List;
import java.util.ArrayList;

import org.springframework.beans.factory.DisposableBean;

public class DisposableBeanNumberClass implements DisposableBean {
  private List<String> numbers = new ArrayList<String>();
```

```
  public DisposableBeanNumberClass() {
    this.numbers.add("one");
    this.numbers.add("two");
    this.numbers.add("three");
  }

  public List<String> getNumbers() {
    return this.numbers;
  }

  public void destroy() throws Exception {
    this.numbers = null;
  }
}
```

The DisposableBeanNumberClass class does not require special configuration, as the container will recognize that the class implements the DisposableBean interface, as shown in Listing 2-35.

Listing 2-35. *Configuring the DisposableBeanNumberClass Class*

```
<?xml version="1.0" encoding="UTF-8"?>
<!DOCTYPE beans PUBLIC "-//SPRING//DTD BEAN//EN"
    "http://www.springframework.org/dtd/spring-beans.dtd">
<beans>
  <bean id="numberClass"
        class="com.apress.springbook.chapter02.DisposableBeanNumberClass"/>
</beans>
```

The DisposableBeanNumberClassIntegrationTests test case demonstrates that the destroy() method is called when the container is closed, as shown in Listing 2-36.

Listing 2-36. *The destroy() Method Is Called When the Container Is Closed*

```
package com.apress.springbook.chapter02;

import junit.framework.TestCase;

import org.springframework.core.io.ClassPathResource;
import org.springframework.beans.factory.config.ConfigurableListableBeanFactory;
import org.springframework.beans.factory.xml.XmlBeanFactory;

public InitializingBeanNumberClassIntegrationTests extends TestCase {
  public void testPreInstantiateSingletons() {
    ConfigurableListableBeanFactory beanFactory =
      new XmlBeanFactory(
        new ClassPathResource(
          "com/apress/springbook/chapter02/disposable-bean.xml"
        )
      );

    DisposableBeanNumberClass numberClass =
      (DisposableBeanNumberClass)beanFactory.getBean("numberClass");

    beanFactory.destroySingletons();

    assertNull(numberClass.getNumbers());
  }
}
```

Using a Custom Destroy Method

The container also supports custom destroy methods. Listing 2-37 shows an example of a class that has a custom destroy method.

Listing 2-37. *The CustomDestroyMethodNumberClass, Which Has a Custom Destroy Method*

```
package com.apress.springbook.chapter02;

import java.util.List;
import java.util.ArrayList;

public class CustomDestroyMethodNumberClass {
  private List<String> numbers = new ArrayList<String>();

  public CustomDestroyMethodNumberClass() {
    this.numbers.add("one");
    this.numbers.add("two");
    this.numbers.add("three");
  }

  public List<String> getNumbers() {
    return this.numbers;
  }

  public void close() throws Exception {
    this.numbers = null;
  }
}
```

To configure this class, we need to tell the container to use the close() method as the custom destroy method by setting the destroy-method attribute, as shown in Listing 2-38.

Listing 2-38. *Configuring the close() Method as the Custom Destroy Method*

```
<?xml version="1.0" encoding="UTF-8"?>
<!DOCTYPE beans PUBLIC "-//SPRING//DTD BEAN//EN"
    "http://www.springframework.org/dtd/spring-beans.dtd">
<beans>
  <bean id="numberClass"
      class="com.apress.springbook.chapter02.CustomDestroyMethodNumberClass"
      destroy-method="close"/>
</beans>
```

The CustomDestroyMethodNumberClassIntegrationTests class demonstrates the close() method is actually called when the container is closed, as shown in Listing 2-39.

Listing 2-39. *The close() Method Is Called When the Container Is Closed*

```
package com.apress.springbook.chapter02;

import junit.framework.TestCase;

import org.springframework.core.io.ClassPathResource;
import org.springframework.beans.factory.config.ConfigurableListableBeanFactory;
import org.springframework.beans.factory.xml.XmlBeanFactory;
```

```
public class CustomDestroyMethodNumberClassIntegrationTests extends TestCase {
  public void testPreInstantiateSingletons() {
    ConfigurableListableBeanFactory beanFactory =
        new XmlBeanFactory(
          new ClassPathResource(
            "com/apress/springbook/chapter02/custom-destroy-method.xml"
          )
        );

    CustomDestroyMethodNumberClass numberClass =
      (CustomDestroyMethodNumberClass)beanFactory.getBean("numberClass");

    beanFactory.destroySingletons();

    assertNull(numberClass.getNumbers());
  }
}
```

Custom destroy methods must have no arguments; they can throw any exception and can have a return value, which is ignored by the container.

Exceptions that are thrown by destroy methods are logged by the container, but otherwise swallowed. This makes sense, since exceptions that are thrown by destroy methods should not interrupt the invocations of the entire destruction step.

Using Factory Methods and Factory Objects in the Container

We began this chapter with a discussion on factories that come in two forms: factory methods and factory objects. The container supports both factory types as an alternative to creating new beans. The products of factories are used by the container as beans, which means the container must know how to get objects from the factories.

The beans that are returned by factory methods and factory object methods go through the entire bean life cycle, which means they are subject to the following:

- Singleton/prototype configuration
- Setter injections
- Initialization methods
- Destroy methods, if configured as singleton

When the factory object bean definition is configured as a prototype, each bean definition that calls one of its methods will trigger the creation of a new factory object bean that will be used only for that method invocation.

Factory methods and methods on factory objects may be overloaded, which may require you to use the same selection strategy as discussed in the "Constructor Injection" section earlier in this chapter.

Implementing Factory Methods

As an example, we'll use the compile() method on the java.util.regex.Pattern class as a factory method. To configure this factory method in the container, we need to specify the class and the method to call. The compile() method has one String argument, which we also must specify, as shown in Listing 2-40.

Listing 2-40. *Configuring the compile() Method on java.util.regex.Patterns As a Factory Method in the Container*

```xml
<?xml version="1.0" encoding="UTF-8"?>
<!DOCTYPE beans PUBLIC "-//SPRING//DTD BEAN//EN"
    "http://www.springframework.org/dtd/spring-beans.dtd">
<beans>
  <bean id="pattern" class="java.util.regex.Pattern" factory-method="compile">
    <constructor-arg value="abc"/>
  </bean>
</beans>
```

We use the factory-method attribute on the bean definition in Listing 2-40 to tell the compiler to not create a new Pattern bean, but instead call the static compile() method. Since the compile() method needs a String argument, we've added one <constructor-arg> element.

The way a factory method works is very similar to how a constructor works, so it makes sense to add <constructor-arg> elements to specify the method arguments, which also allows you to inject references. The container uses PropertyEditors to convert the value to the argument types.

The FactoryMethodIntegrationTests test case demonstrates that a Pattern bean is indeed returned by the pattern bean definition in Listing 2-40, as shown in Listing 2-41.

Listing 2-41. *The Container Returns a Pattern Bean by Calling the compile() Factory Method*

```java
package com.apress.springbook.chapter02;

import junit.framework.TestCase;

import org.springframework.core.io.ClassPathResource;
import org.springframework.beans.factory.config.ConfigurableListableBeanFactory;
import org.springframework.beans.factory.xml.XmlBeanFactory;

import java.util.regex.Pattern;
import java.util.regex.Matcher;

public class FactoryMethodIntegrationTests extends TestCase {
  public void testPreInstantiateSingletons() {
    ConfigurableListableBeanFactory beanFactory =
      new XmlBeanFactory(
        new ClassPathResource(
          "com/apress/springbook/chapter02/factory-methods.xml"
        )
      );

    Pattern pattern = (Pattern)beanFactory.getBean("pattern");
    Matcher matcher = pattern.matcher(„abc abc abc");
    int matchCount = 0;

    while (matcher.find()) { matchCount++; }

    assertEquals(3, matchCount);
  }
}
```

Implementing Factory Objects

We've already discussed the advantage of factory objects compared to factory methods: they allow for an extra layer of configuration. Bean definitions that call a method on a factory object use two attributes: the factory-bean attribute, which refers to the factory object, and the factory-method, which indicates the method to call on the factory object.

Listing 2-42 demonstrates configuring the java.text.SimpleDateFormat class as a factory object.

Listing 2-42. *Configuring SimpleDateFormat As a Factory Object in the Container*

```
<?xml version="1.0" encoding="UTF-8"?>

<!DOCTYPE beans PUBLIC "-//SPRING//DTD BEAN//EN"
    "http://www.springframework.org/dtd/spring-beans.dtd">
<beans>
  <!--(1) -->
  <bean id="socketFactory" class="javax.net.SocketFactory"
        factory-method="getDefault">
  </bean>

  <bean id="localhost"
        factory-bean="socketFactory" factory-method="createSocket">
    <constructor-arg value="localhost"/>
    <constructor-arg value="80"/>
  </bean>

  <bean id="apress.com"
        factory-bean="socketFactory" factory-method="createSocket">
    <constructor-arg value="www.apress.com"/>
    <constructor-arg value="80"/>
  </bean>
</beans>
```

In Listing 2-42, we first configure the javax.net.SocketFactory class using the factory-method attribute, which creates beans from a static factory method (in this case, getDefault()). Next, we use the socketFactory bean as a factory object in the two subsequent bean definitions, where we call the createSocket() method and provide it with two arguments.

The configuration in Listing 2-42 is typical for factory objects, where one bean definition configures the factory object and one or more other bean definitions call methods on the factory object. In fact, this method of object construction is not just for factories. It provides a generic mechanism for object construction.

Listing 2-43 shows the integration test for this factory object configuration.

Listing 2-43. *Obtaining the Sockets Created Using the Factory Object*

```
package com.apress.springbook.chapter02;

import junit.framework.TestCase;

import org.springframework.core.io.ClassPathResource;
import org.springframework.beans.factory.BeanFactory;
import org.springframework.beans.factory.config.ConfigurableListableBeanFactory;
import org.springframework.beans.factory.xml.XmlBeanFactory;

public class FactoryObjectIntegrationTests extends TestCase {
  public void testPreInstantiateSingletons() {
```

```
ConfigurableListableBeanFactory beanFactory =
    new XmlBeanFactory(
        new ClassPathResource(
            "com/apress/springbook/chapter02/socket-factory.xml"
        )
    );

java.net.Socket localhost = (java.net.Socket)beanFactory.getBean("localhost");

java.net.Socket apressDotCom =
    (java.net.Socket)beanFactory.getBean("apress.com");

assertTrue(localhost.isConnected());

assertTrue(apressDotCom.isConnected());
    }
}
```

Implementing Factory Objects with the FactoryBean Interface

Spring provides the org.springframework.beans.factory.FactoryBean interface, which is a convenient way to implement factory objects. The FactoryBean interface is chiefly implemented by the classes of the Spring Framework. The biggest advantages gained are a consistent factory model and consistent and straightforward configuration. As a Spring Framework user, you should understand how the container deals with the FactoryBean interface, which is shown in Listing 2-44.

Listing 2-44. *Spring's org.springframework.beans.factory.FactoryBean Interface*

```
public interface FactoryBean {
    Object getObject() throws Exception;

    Class getObjectType();

    boolean isSingleton();
}
```

The FactoryBean interface defines a getObject() method, which returns the product of the factory. The container will create a bean and recognize the FactoryBean interface, after which the getObject() method is called to get the product of the factory, as shown in Listing 2-45.

Listing 2-45. *Configuring org.springframework.beans.factory.config.PropertiesFactoryBean*

```
<?xml version="1.0" encoding="UTF-8"?>
<!DOCTYPE beans PUBLIC "-//SPRING//DTD BEAN//EN"
    "http://www.springframework.org/dtd/spring-beans.dtd">
<beans>
  <bean id="myProperties"
        class="org.springframework.beans.factory.config.PropertiesFactoryBean">
    <property name="location"
              value="classpath:com/apress/springbook/chapter02/PropertyFactory ➥
Bean-context.xml"/>
  </bean>
</beans>
```

The configuration in Listing 2-45 uses the org.springframework.beans.factory.config. PropertiesFactoryBean class, which loads a properties file and returns a java.util.Properties file.

PropertiesFactoryBean is configured—in this case, via setter injection—before the container calls the getObject() method. We'll talk about the classpath: notation in the next section.

When a FactoryBean object is created, it goes through the normal bean life cycle. At the end of the life cycle, the container calls the getObject() method and returns the product of the FactoryBean. The getObject() method is also called on each subsequent request, meaning the product of the FactoryBean is not subject to the normal bean life cycle.

Introducing the ApplicationContext

All of the features we've discussed in this chapter so far are implemented by the BeanFactory, the basic container of the Spring Framework. However, as a user of the Spring Framework, you will chiefly work with another container type called the ApplicationContext.

The ApplicationContext interface inherits all the capabilities of the BeanFactory interface, including dependency lookup, dependency injection, and support for factories and PropertyEditors. The ApplicationContext automates functionalities that are offered by BeanFactory; for example, it automatically preinstantiates singletons and automatically detects beans that implement specific interfaces in the container.

Representing Resources

The most commonly used feature of the ApplicationContext is its generic representation of resources. Resources can reside on the file system, in the classpath, on a web server accessible through a URL, or inside a deployed WAR application.

No matter where resources reside, users can refer to them through a uniform String notation in XML files. Here's an example, which shows the location of a text file:

```
classpath:wordlist.txt
```

The location in this snippet specifies that the wordlist.txt file can be loaded from the root of the classpath.

The next example loads the same file from the current directory, which is the working directory of the Java Virtual Machine (JVM):

```
file:wordlist.txt
```

The next example loads the same file from a URL:

```
http://localhost/wordlist.txt
```

Location strings do not need to specify a prefix, as in the following example:

```
wordlist.txt
```

A resource location without a prefix will be loaded from the default location, which depends on the type of ApplicationContext being used. There are three possible types:

- ClassPathXmlApplicationContext: Reads resources from the classpath by default.

- FileSystemXmlApplicationContext: Reads resources from the file system by default.

- XmlWebApplicationContext: Reads resources from the ServletContext object by default.

You will frequently specify file locations in your XML files. Every time you set a bean property that has the org.springframework.core.io.Resource interface as its type, you can specify a string location that will be converted by the ApplicationContext. This interface is chiefly used by classes of the Spring Framework.

Listing 2-46 shows an example where a Java properties file is loaded using the `org.springframework.beans.factory.config.PropertiesFactoryBean` class that has a `location` property of type `Resource`.

Listing 2-46. *Loading a Properties Files from the Classpath*

```
<bean id="properties"
      class="org.springframework.beans.factory.config.PropertiesFactoryBean">
  <property name="location" value="classpath:environment.properties"/>
</bean>
```

The `PropertiesFactoryBean` also has a `locations` property that has a `Resource[]` type, an array of `Resource` objects. This property takes a wildcard location string and returns all `Resources` that match the location. Listing 2-47 shows an example.

Listing 2-47. *Loading All Properties Files from the Root of the Classpath*

```
<bean id="properties"
      class="org.springframework.beans.factory.config.PropertiesFactoryBean">
  <property name="locations" value="classpath:*.properties"/>
</bean>
```

The example in Listing 2-47 loads all files from the classpath with the extension `.properties` into one `java.util.Properties` object.

Creating ApplicationContext Objects

The three most common ways of creating `ApplicationContext` objects are as follows:

- Creating an `ApplicationContext` in Java code
- Creating an `ApplicationContext` in an integration test
- Creating an `ApplicationContext` in a web application

Creating an ApplicationContext in Java Code

Creating an `ApplicationContext` in Java code is straightforward. You can choose between two types, depending on the default resource location, as discussed in the previous section.

The following `applicationContext.xml` file will be loaded from the classpath:

```
ApplicationContext applicationContext =
  new ClassPathXmlApplicationContext("applicationContext.xml");
```

And this `applicationContext.xml` file will be loaded from the file system:

```
ApplicationContext applicationContext =
  new FileSystemXmlApplicationContext("applicationContext.xml");
```

You should, however, use the classpath as much as possible.

The `ApplicationContext` allows you to load multiple XML files that will be merged into a set of bean definitions, as shown in Listing 2-48.

Listing 2-48. *Creating an Application Context from Multiple XML Files*

```
ApplicationContext applicationContext =
  new ClassPathXmlApplicationContext(
    new String[] {
```

```
        "service-context.xml",
        "data-access-context.xml"
    }
);
```

You should configure the modules of your applications in separate configuration files and load them together in one ApplicationContext. This will keep your configuration files small enough to manage conveniently.

Using an ApplicationContext in Integration Tests

The Spring Framework ships classes that you can use to write integration tests, which test the overall functionalities of an application. Integration tests are important to ensure all components of an application work together correctly when the application is loaded by the ApplicationContext.

Chapter 10 covers integration testing with the Spring Framework in much more detail. Here, we will load the configuration file shown earlier in Listing 2-5 in an integration test. To do so, we need to extend the org.springframework.test.AbstractDependencyInjectionSpringContextTests class, which is a subclass of junit.framework.TestCase. We'll need to override the getConfigLocations() method to return a String array of XML file locations that are to be loaded by the ApplicationContext that is created by AbstractDependencyInjectionsSpringContextTests, as shown in Listing 2-49.

Listing 2-49. *Implementing an Integration Test Using AbstractDependencyInjectionSpringContextTests*

```
package com.apress.springbook.chapter02;

import org.springframework.test.AbstractDependencyInjectionSpringContextTests;

public class TournamentMatchManagerIntegrationTests
  extends AbstractDependencyInjectionSpringContextTests {

  protected String[] getConfigLocations() {
    return new String[] {
        "classpath:com/apress/springbook/chapter02/application-context.xml"
    };
  }

  private TournamentMatchManager tournamentMatchManager;

  public void setTournamentMatchManager(TournamentMatchManager tmm) {
    this.tournamentMatchManager = tmm;
  }

  public void testCreateMatch() throws Exception {
    Match match = this.tournamentMatchManager.startMatch(2000);
  }
}
```

The test case in Listing 2-49 looks at its own setter methods and will try to inject beans from the container that match the types. For the setTournamentMatchManager() method, the container will look for a bean that is assignable to the TournamentMatchManager interface—the tournamentMatchManager bean in Listing 2-5—and inject that bean. If no matching bean is found, the container will not throw an exception; if more than one bean is assignable to the type, an exception will be thrown.

Loading an ApplicationContext in a Web Application

In web applications, the ApplicationContext is configured in the web.xml file. If your servlet container supports the Servlet 2.3 specification, you can use org.springframework.web.context.ContextLoaderListener, as shown in Listing 2-50.

Listing 2-50. *Configuring ContextLoaderListener in web.xml*

```
<listener>
  <listener-class>
    org.springframework.web.context.ContextLoaderListener
  </listener-class>
</listener>
```

ContextLoaderListener is not compatible with some Servlet 2.3 containers. If you are using such a servlet container, you need to configure the org.springframework.web.context.ContextLoaderServlet servlet in the web.xml file instead of ContextLoaderListener. ContextLoaderListener is known not to work properly with these Servlet 2.3 containers:

- BEA WebLogic 8.1 SP2 and older

- IBM WebSphere versions prior to version 6.0

- Oracle OC4J versions prior to version 10g

If you use a Servlet 2.2 container, you also must use ContextLoaderServlet, as shown in Listing 2-51.

Listing 2-51. *Configuring ContextLoaderServlet in web.xml*

```
<servlet>
  <servlet-name>contextLoaderServlet</servlet-name>
  <servlet-class>
    org.springframework.web.context.ContextLoaderServlet
  </servlet-class>
  <load-on-startup>1</load-on-startup>
</servlet>
```

The <load-on-startup> element in Listing 2-51 must have a lower numeric value than other servlet classes that use the ApplicationContext loaded by ContextLoaderServlet, such as Spring Web MVC's DispatcherServlet (discussed in Chapter 8).

The ApplicationContext object that is created by ContextLoaderListener and ContextLoaderServlet is placed in the ServletContext object of the web application. The org.springframework.web.context.support.WebApplicationContextUtil class returns the ApplicationContext object if you provide the ServletContext object, as follows:

```
ApplicationContext applicationContext =
  WebApplicationContextUtils.getWebApplicationContext(servletContext);
```

By default, ContextLoaderListener and ContextLoaderServlet load the /WEB-INF/applicationContext.xml file. This location can be overwritten by defining the contextConfigLocation context parameter in web.xml, as shown in Listing 2-52.

Listing 2-52. *Specifying XML File Locations with the contextConfigLocation Parameter*

```
<context-param>
  <param-name>contextConfigLocation</param-name>
  <param-value>
    classpath:service-context.xml
```

```
    classpath:data-access-context.xml
  </param-value>
</context-param>
```

If multiple locations are specified by the `contextConfigLocation` parameter, they can be separated by comma, semicolon, space, tab, or newline characters.

The default resource location for the application context loaded by `ContextLoaderListener` and `ContextLoaderServlet` is the `ServletContext` object of the web application. This corresponds to the root of the WAR archive or exploded WAR folder.

Chapter 8 demonstrates how to load the `ApplicationContext` works in conjunction with the Spring Web MVC framework.

■**Note** You can learn about auto-wiring dependencies and extending the bean life cycle of the `Application Context` in Chapter 5 of *Pro Spring* (Apress, 2005). The Spring Framework reference documentation also covers these topics, as well as advanced features of the `ApplicationContext`, including event processing, internalization, and application context hierarchies.

Configuring the Container with Spring 2.0 XML Tags

The Spring Framework version 2.0 adds a new feature to the container that simplifies the Spring XML notation, including new tags to do common tasks. One of these tasks is loading a properties file into a `java.util.Properties` object. Other new tags configure transaction management and aspect-oriented programming (AOP), which is discussed in Chapters 3 and 4. Vendors can also create their own XML simplifications for your convenience.

To support custom XML tags and attributes for the XML simplifications, the container supports XML Schema for validation along with the classic DTD validation, so you can combine files that use both types of XML validation. Listing 2-53 shows an XML file using XML Schema.

Listing 2-53. *A Spring XML File Set Up to Use XML Schema*

```
<?xml version="1.0" encoding="UTF-8"?>
<beans
        xmlns="http://www.springframework.org/schema/beans"
        xmlns:xsi="http://www.w3.org/2001/XMLSchema-instance"
        xmlns:util="http://www.springframework.org/schema/util"
        xsi:schemaLocation="http://www.springframework.org/schema/beans
          http://www.springframework.org/schema/beans/spring-beans.xsd
          http://www.springframework.org/schema/util
          http://www.springframework.org/schema/util/spring-util.xsd">

</beans>
```

All Java IDEs have good support for XML Schema and support completion when you edit Spring XML files. To demonstrate the ease of use of the XML simplification, the following shows the `<util:properties>` XML tag as it is completed by the IDE:

```
<util:properties id="" location=""
```

The IDE automatically adds the required attributes for the XML element, so you no longer need to think about which class to use and which properties to configure.

The following line shows the complete notation of the `<util:properties>` tag, which loads a properties file:

```
<util:properties id="properties" location="classpath:environment.properties"/>
```

Compare this single XML tag to the configuration in the "Representing Resources" section, which shows how properties files are loaded in the classic way.

Using the Container As a Deployment Model

When you decide to use the Spring Framework in your projects, you will soon find out the Spring container is actually a deployment model. Once all components of your application are configured in Spring XML files, your application can be loaded in a stand-alone application, a web application, or any other type of application.

The Spring Framework offers support to deploy applications in these deployment environments:

- *Servlet containers*: Tomcat, Jetty, and Resin
- *Application servers*: BEA WebLogic, IBM WebSphere, and JBoss
- *Portlet servers*: JetSpeed 2 and Pluto
- *Thin clients*: Java desktop applications that call remote services over a network
- *Thick clients*: Java desktop applications that directly connect to a database
- *Messaging*: Applications that connect to message queues and handle incoming messages

People use the Spring Framework in a wide range of settings. Although this book is primarily focused on web applications, the chapters that don't cover web-related topics apply to all other environments as well.

Part of the reason the Spring Framework is gradually becoming the de facto deployment model for Java EE applications is its integration with almost all popular Java frameworks, which is an extra stimulus to get started with the Spring Framework today.

Summary

In this chapter, we introduced the Spring container. You learned about Spring's XML format and the basic features of the container. You also learned about the life cycle of beans that are managed by the container and how to configure factories.

We then talked about the `ApplicationContext`, which has all of the features of the `BeanFactory` and adds generic resource locations, among other features, to the mix. You've learned how to create `ApplicationContext` objects in Java code, in integration tests, and in web applications.

The next two chapters cover AOP in the Spring Framework.

CHAPTER 3

■ ■ ■

Aspect-Oriented Programming

The biggest part of an application's life starts when it's first deployed in a production environment. Developing the first version may take a while, but once deployed, the application must be maintained and improved, typically for many years. Applications that are deployed and used by businesses and organizations need some form of maintenance over time, which means they need to be maintainable in the first place; that is, applications should be easy to develop and test during development, and afterward they should be easy to maintain. Organizations that can improve their business processes in small incremental steps when they see fit have an important advantage over their competitors.

In this chapter, we'll cover some traditional object-oriented solutions and expose some of the problems in their approach. In so doing, we'll cover a couple of design patterns that can apply to our sample application. However, we'll also see why we can't always rely on them in all situations where maximum flexibility is required. This will lead us to aspect-oriented programming (AOP), which helps us write functionality that is difficult to implement efficiently with pure object-oriented techniques.

The Spring Framework provides its own AOP framework called Spring AOP. This chapter discusses the classic Spring AOP framework, which is still available in Spring 2.0 and is the AOP framework for versions of the Spring Framework prior to 2.0. This framework has been completely revamped for Spring 2.0, which is discussed in the next chapter. The revamped 2.0 AOP framework borrows a lot of features from the classic AOP framework, so understanding these features is important when using Spring 2.0.

Extending Applications the Traditional Way

Applications should be developed with the flexibility for later changes and additions. A sure way to hamper maintenance tasks is to overload applications with complexity and make them hard to configure. Another sure way to hinder maintenance is to overload classes with complexity by giving them more than one responsibility. This makes the code hard to write, test, and understand, and it frustrates the efforts of maintenance developers. Classes that perform more tasks than they should suffer from a lack of abstraction, which makes them generally harder for developers to use. Finally, code that is not properly tested is riskier, since unintended effects caused by changes are less likely to be spotted.

Making applications more functional without having to change core business logic is an important part of their maintainability. Changing core application code is really warranted only when the rules of the core business logic change. In all other cases, testing the entire application again for less important changes is often considered too expensive. Getting approval for small changes that would make an application more useful is often postponed until big changes need to be made, reducing the flexibility of the organization that depends on the application to improve its efficiency.

When maintenance developers need to touch the core of the application to change secondary features, the application becomes less straightforward to test and thus is probably not fully tested. This may result in subtle bugs being introduced and remaining unnoticed until after data corruption has occurred.

Let's look at an example and some typical solutions.

Extending a Base Class

Listing 3-1 shows the NotifyingTournamentMatchManager class, which sends text messages to selected mobile phones to notify tournament officials when a match has finished.

Listing 3-1. *Sending Text Messages When a Match Ends*

```
package com.apress.springbook.chapter03;

public class TextMessageSendingTournamentMatchManager
    extends DefaultTournamentMatchManager
{
  private MessageSender messageSender;

  public void setMessageSender(MessageSender messageSender) {
    this.messageSender = messageSender;
  }

  public void endMatch(Match match) throws
      UnknownMatchException, MatchIsFinishedException,
      MatchCannotBePlayedException, PreviousMatchesNotFinishedException {
    super.endMatch(match);
    this.messageSender.notifyEndOfMatch(match);
  }
}
```

This is an example of a class that performs too many tasks. Although creating the specialized class TextMessageSendingTournamentMatchManager by extending DefaultTournamentMatchManager may seem sensible, this technique fails if you need to add more functionality. The root problem lies in the location of the TextMessageSendingTournamentMatchManager class in the class hierarchy, as shown in Figure 3-1.

Because it extends DefaultTournamentMatchManager, it is too deep in the class hierarchy, which makes it hard to create other specialized classes. Also, when writing tests for the endMatch() method on TextMessageSendingTournamentMatchManager, you need to test the functionality inside DefaultTournamentMatchManager since the super method is called. This means TextMessageSending TournamentMatchManager is part of the core application code.

Implementing, changing, and removing actions always require changing core application code. For this particular case, you can use at least two other object-oriented solutions to add the text-message-sending functionality to the sample application without affecting the core application code, which we'll look at next.

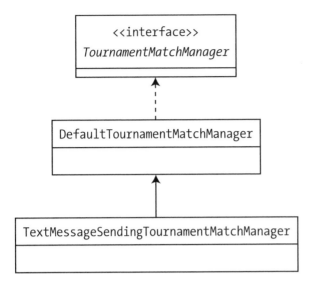

Figure 3-1. *TextMessageSendingTournamentMatchManager in the class hierarchy*

Using the Observer Design Pattern

One solution is to implement the observer design pattern in the application. This approach uses observer objects that are registered to listen to specific events that occur in the application code and act on them. Developers can implement functionality in observer objects and register them with specific events through configuration. The application code launches the events but is not responsible for registering observer objects.

　　Listing 3-2 shows the MatchObserver interface.

Listing 3-2. *The MatchObserver Interface Acts on Match-Related Events*

```
package com.apress.springbook.chapter03;

public interface MatchObserver {
    void onMatchEvent(Match match);
}
```

　　The MatchObserver interface is only part of the solution. Its onMatchEvent() method is called by the application code to notify it of the occurrence of predefined events. The ObservingTournament MatchManager extends DefaultTournamentMatchManager and announces the end of a match event to all MatchObservers that are registered, as shown in Listing 3-3.

Listing 3-3. *Announcing the End of a Match Event to Registered Observer Objects*

```
package com.apress.springbook.chapter03;

public class ObservingTournamentMatchManager extends DefaultTournamentMatchManager {
    private MatchObserver[] matchEndsObservers;

    public void setMatchEndsObservers(MatchObserver[] matchEndsObservers) {
        this.matchEndsObservers = matchEndsObservers;
    }
```

```
public void endMatch(Match match) throws
        UnknownMatchException, MatchIsFinishedException,
        MatchCannotBePlayedException, PreviousMatchesNotFinishedException {
    super.endMatch(match);
    for (MatchObserver observer : matchEndsObservers) {
      observer.onMatchEvent(match);
    }
  }
}
```

ObservingTournamentMatchManager notifies registered MatchObserver objects when a match ends, which allows you to implement the MatchObserver interface to send the text messages, as shown in Listing 3-4.

Listing 3-4. *Implementing the MatchObserver Interface to Send Text Messages*

```
package com.apress.springbook.chapter03;

public class TextMessageSendingOnEndOfMatchObserver implements MatchObserver {
  private MessageSender messageSender;

  public void setMessageSender(MessageSender messageSender) {
    this.messageSender = messageSender;
  }

  public void onMatchEvent(Match match) {
    this.messageSender.notifyEndOfMatch(match);
  }
}
```

Code that calls registered observer objects when specific events occur, as shown in Listing 3-3, provides a hook in the application logic to extend its functionality. The Unified Modeling Language (UML) diagram shown in Figure 3-2 provides an overview of the classes that implement the observer design pattern in the application.

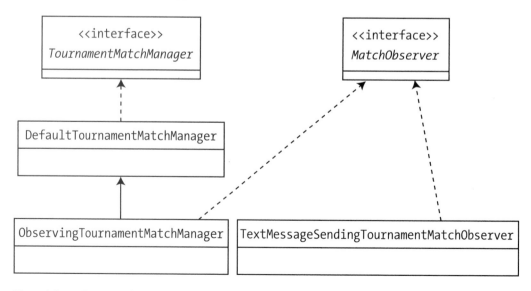

Figure 3-2. *We have implemented the observer design pattern in our application.*

TextMessageSendingOnEndOfMatchObserver has access to the Match object, yet the code is factored out of the core application logic and can be easily registered, as shown in Listing 3-5.

Listing 3-5. *Registering the MatchObserver Object with ObservingTournamentMatchManager*

```
<beans>
  <bean id="tournamentMatchManager"
        com="com.apress.springbook.chapter03.ObservingTournamentMatchManager">
    <property name="matchEndsObservers">
      <list>
        <bean com="com.apress.springbook.chapter03. ➥
TextMessageSendingOnEndOfMatchObserver">
          <property name="messageSender" ref="messageSender"/>
        </bean>
      </list>
    </property>
  </bean>
</beans>
```

As shown in Listing 3-5, registering MatchObserver objects is straightforward and flexible with the Spring container, so you can easily configure additional actions. Also, you can extend the implementation of ObservingTournamentMatchManager to observe other events, leaving this class responsible only for raising events. In the end, it's probably better to add the observer logic to DefaultTournamentMatchManager instead of creating a separate class, since this will facilitate testing.

However, some inconvenient side effects curtail the usability of observer objects for the purpose of adding functionality. The addition of observer code to the application is the most important side effect, since it reduces flexibility—you can register observer objects only if a hook is in place. You can't extend existing (or third-party) code with extra functionality if no observer code is in place. In addition, observer code must be tested; hence, the less code you write, the better. Also, developers need to understand up front where to add observer hooks or modify the code afterward.

Overall, the observer design pattern is an interesting approach and certainly has its uses in application code, but it doesn't offer the kind of flexibility you want.

Using the Decorator Design Pattern

As an alternative to observer objects, you can use the decorator design pattern to add functionality to existing application classes by wrapping the original classes with decorator classes that implement that functionality. Listing 3-6 shows the TournamentMatchManagerDecorator class, which implements the TournamentMatchManager interface and delegates each method call to a TournamentMatchManager target object.

Listing 3-6. *The TournamentMatchManagerDecorator Class*

```
package com.apress.springbook.chapter03;

public class TournamentMatchManagerDecorator implements TournamentMatchManager {
  private TournamentMatchManager target;

  public void setTournamentMatchManager(TournamentMatchManager target) {
    this.target = target;
  }

  public void endMatch(Match match) throws
      UnknownMatchException, MatchIsFinishedException,
      MatchCannotBePlayedException, PreviousMatchesNotFinishedException {
```

```
      this.target.endMatch(match);
   }

   /* other methods omitted */
}
```

The `TournamentMatchManagerDecorator` class in Listing 3-6 is type-compatible with the `TournamentMatchManager` interface, meaning you can use it anywhere you use the `Tournament MatchManager` interface. It can serve as a base class for other decorator implementations for the `TournamentMatchManager` interface, yet it's possible to configure this class with a target object to demonstrate its purpose more clearly, as shown in Listing 3-7.

Listing 3-7. *Configuring TournamentMatchManagerDecorator with a Target Object*

```
<beans>
  <bean id="tournamentMatchManager"
        class="com.apress.springbook.chapter03.TournamentMatchManagerDecorator">
    <property name="target">
      <bean class="com.apress.springbook.chapter03.DefaultTournamentMatchManager">
        <!-- other properties omitted -->
      </bean>
    </property>
  </bean>
</beans>
```

As the configuration in Listing 3-7 shows, the decorator class sits in front of a target and delegates all method calls to that target. It's now trivial to implement another decorator class that sends text messages after the `endMatch()` method has been called, as shown in Listing 3-8.

Listing 3-8. *Sending Text Messages from a Decorator Class*

```
package com.apress.springbook.chapter03;

public class TextMessageSendingTournamentMatchManagerDecorator
   extends TournamentMatchManagerDecorator {
  private MessageSender messageSender;

  public void setMessageSender(MessageSender messageSender) {
    this.messageSender = messageSender;
  }

  public void endMatch(Match match) throws
      UnknownMatchException, MatchIsFinishedException,
      MatchCannotBePlayedException, PreviousMatchesNotFinishedException {
    super.endMatch(match);
    this.messageSender.notifyEndOfMatch(match);
  }
}
```

Now let's look at the subtle yet important difference between the `TextMessageSending TournamentMatchManagerDecorator` class in Listing 3-8 and the `TextMessageSendingTournament MatchManager` class in Listing 3-1.

In Listing 3-8, a decorator class is extended, meaning any class that implements the `TournamentMatchManager` interface can serve as its target, including sibling decorator objects. In Listing 3-1, a concrete implementation class is extended, restricting the text-message-sending functionality strictly to the base class and restricting the options to add other actions or functionalities.

Listing 3-1 uses class inheritance to hook into the class hierarchy and add new functionality, as shown in Figure 3-1. Listing 3-8 uses composition, which is generally more flexible since it's not rooted in the class hierarchy at such a deep level, as shown in Figure 3-3.

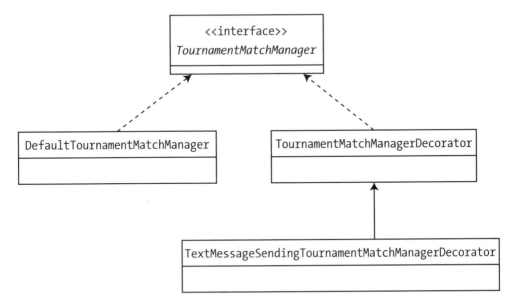

Figure 3-3. *TextMessageSendingTournamentMatchManagerDecorator is not rooted deep in the class hierarchy.*

Listing 3-9 shows the configuration of the decorator and its target bean.

Listing 3-9. *Configuring TextMessageSendingTournamentMatchManagerDecorator with Its Target Object*

```
<beans>
  <bean id="tournamentMatchManager"
      class="com.apress.springbook.chapter03. ➥
TextMessageSendingTournamentMatchManagerDecorator">
    <property name="target">
      <bean class="com.apress.springbook.chapter03.DefaultTournamentMatchManager">
        <!-- other properties omitted -->
      </bean>
    </property>
    <property name="messageSender" ref="messageSender"/>
  </bean>
</beans>
```

Decorator objects are an interesting alternative to observer objects since they take a different approach to solving the same problem. As with observers, you can combine multiple decorator objects—one decorating the other and the target object—to add multiple actions to one method. But again, this approach has some unfortunate side effects: you need to implement a decorator object per functionality and per target interface. This may leave you with many decorator classes to write, test, and maintain, which takes you further away from a flexible solution.

So again, we've discussed an interesting approach that doesn't quite cut it—it doesn't offer the full flexibility you would like to see.

Benefits of Separating Concerns

What have we gained by using the decorator and observer design patterns? Because we've separated the text-message-sending code from the business logic code, we've achieved a clean *separation of concerns*. In other words, the business logic code is isolated from other concerns, which allows you to better focus on the requirements of your application.

You can add functionality to the business logic code more effectively by adding separate classes to your code base. This makes for a more effective design process, implementation, testing methodology, and modularity.

More Effective Design Process

While initially designing an application, it's unlikely developers or designers fully understand the problem domain; thus, it's unlikely they will be able to incorporate every feature of the application into their design.

Ironically, it's often more effective to start developing core features with the understanding that you will add other features later whose exact details aren't clear yet. The decorator and observer design patterns can reasonably efficiently accommodate this way of working. This trade-off allows developers to design the core functionalities—which as a bare minimum give them a better understanding of the problem—and it buys them and the users more time to think about other features.

Adding new features throughout an application's life span stretches the design process over a longer period of time, which most likely will result in a better application. Alternatively, spending time on functionality for sending mail messages, for instance, when core application logic remains unimplemented, is not very efficient.

More Effective Implementation

Having to think about only one problem at a time is a blessing and an efficient way of working. Solving a Sudoku puzzle and reading the newspaper at the same time is hard and probably inefficient, and so is implementing two features at the same time, for the same reason.

Developers become much more efficient when the number of concerns they need to implement at any given time is reduced to one. It gives them a better chance to solve a problem efficiently. Also, the code they produce will be cleaner, easier to maintain, and better documented. Working on one problem at a time has another interesting advantage: developers who work on a single problem also work on one class, meaning any class in the application will likely be dedicated to only one concern.

How can you implement a complex problem as many different subproblems, each implemented as one class? Well, you think about the different logical steps and how you will implement them in the application. For example, if you need to create a tournament in the database and create tennis matches for all the players who are registered, the logical steps are as follows:

1. Load all registered players from the database.

2. Create pools of players based on their ranking, age, gender, or other properties.

3. Create matches for each pool based on the number of players while assigning players to matches by drawing.

4. Plan matches in the timetables so players who play in multiple pools have as much time as possible between matches.

You can further simplify each of these logical steps into technical steps. As such, it's possible to assemble small classes into a bigger whole, which, as we've seen already, is separation of concerns.

More Effective Testing

Testing the business logic of an application is an incremental process; it's about testing each class and method. If all the parts of the business logic are tested, the entire business logic is tested. Writing unit tests for classes that implement only one concern is much easier and takes much less time than creating tests for classes that implement many concerns.

Since typically a lot of tests must be written for any given application, it's important to note that if writing a single test becomes easier, writing all the tests becomes much easier. Chapter 10 talks in more detail about testing applications and provides some guidelines on how to test business logic.

Enhanced Modularity

Lastly, by using decorator or observer objects, you can plug in concerns as required. It's now possible to effectively decide which concerns should be part of the application and which implementations of these concerns should be part of the application.

This leaves a lot of room for optimization outside the scope of the core application logic. If you're not happy with the way text messages are being sent, for example, you can change the implementation and use a different one; all it takes is changing one XML file.

Limitations of Object-Oriented Solutions

So far, we've discussed three ways of adding functionality to existing code without affecting the code directly:

- Extending a base class and adding code in method bodies
- Using observer objects that can be registered with application components
- Using decorator objects that can sit in front of target objects

However, none of these options offers the kind of flexibility you want: being able to add new functionality to existing classes or third-party code anywhere in the application. What's wrong?

You're experiencing the limits of object-oriented development technology as implemented by the Java programming language. Neither composition nor class inheritance provides sufficient flexibility for these purposes, so you can either give up or look further.

Let's review your goals again:

- Add nice-to-have features to existing applications
- Not affect core application code
- Extend functionality yet keep code integrity intact

The goals you're trying to achieve are important for any application, and you should consider them carefully. Without finding a flexible, easy-to-use solution, you will probably be left behind with a suboptimal application that is not capable of fully satisfying your business needs, which will undoubtedly result in suboptimal business processes.

Enter AOP

Any functionality that exists in an application, but cannot be added in a desirable way is called a *cross-cutting concern*. If you look back at the text-message-sending requirement, we couldn't find a sufficiently flexible means to add this functionality to the application without some undesirable side effect, which is a sure sign we were dealing with a cross-cutting concern.

What you need is a means of working with cross-cutting concerns that offers the flexibility to add any functionality to any part of the application. This allows you to focus on the core of the application separately from the cross-cutting concerns, which offers you a win-win situation, since both areas will get your full attention.

The field in computer science that deals with cross-cutting concerns is called aspect-oriented programming (AOP). It deals with the functionality in applications that cannot be efficiently implemented with pure object-oriented techniques.

AOP started as an experiment and has become stable and mature over the course of ten years. It was originally intended to extend the field of object-oriented programming with its own feature set. Each popular language has its own AOP framework, sometimes as part of the language. AOP has gained the most popularity within the Java community because of the availability of powerful AOP frameworks for many years.

Because the Java programming language supports only a subset of object-oriented programming features, and because AOP has many powerful features to extend the functionality of Java, developers can perform complicated operations with simple AOP instructions. This power, however, comes at a price: AOP can be complex to use and developers need to become familiar with many concepts.

The Spring Framework provides its own AOP framework, called Spring AOP.

The Classic Spring AOP Framework

The Spring AOP framework has specifically been designed to provide a limited set of AOP features yet is simple to use and configure. Most applications need the features offered by Spring AOP only if more advanced features are required. The Spring Framework integrates with more powerful AOP frameworks, such as AspectJ (discussed in the next chapter).

To use Spring AOP, you need to implement cross-cutting concerns and configure those concerns in your applications.

Implementing Cross-Cutting Concerns

One of the core features of AOP frameworks is implementing cross-cutting concerns once and reusing them in different places and in different applications. In AOP jargon, the implementation of a cross-cutting concern is called an *advice*.

Listing 3-10 shows the text-message-sending cross-cutting concern implemented for the Spring AOP framework.

Listing 3-10. *Cross-Cutting Concern Implemented with Spring AOP for Sending Text Messages*

```
package com.apress.springbook.chapter03;

import java.lang.reflect.Method;

import org.springframework.aop.AfterReturningAdvice;

public class TextMessageSendingAdvice implements AfterReturningAdvice {
  private MessageSender messageSender;

  public void setMessageSender(MessageSender messageSender) {
    this.messageSender = messageSender;
  }
```

```
  public void afterReturning(
    Object returnValue, Method method, Object[] args, Object target)
      throws Throwable {
    Match match = (Match)args[0];
    this.messageSender.notifyEndOfMatch(match);
  }
}
```

The TextMessageSendingAdvice class shown in Listing 3-10 implements the AfterReturning Advice Spring AOP interface, meaning it will be executed after a target method is executed. Other types of advice are available in Spring AOP, which we will discuss in the "Selecting Advice Types" section later in this chapter. All of them operate solely on the execution of public methods on target objects.

The afterReturning() method has arguments for the value that was returned by the execution of the target method, the Method object that was invoked, the arguments passed to the target method, and the target object itself. We'll discuss this method and how to use AfterReturningAdvice in the "After Advice" section later in this chapter.

The next step is to use this advice in the application by configuring it in the Spring container. The advice class is written and compiled once—it's a regular Java class—and can be reused many times, meaning it needs to be tested only once.

Configuring AOP in the Spring Container

Any advice written for Spring AOP is configurable in the Spring container through a simple, consistent configuration. This configuration is an important aspect of using AOP in Spring because it is the only one you need to remember for creating extension points to existing classes.

Listing 3-11 shows the configuration of the TextMessageSendingAdvice class with the DefaultTournamentMatchManager class, the target. The default is to call the advice for each public method invoked, which is what we are configuring here. You'll see how to specify which methods to target shortly, in the "Filtering Methods" section.

Listing 3-11. *Configuring the TextMessageSendingAdvice Class with the Spring AOP Framework*

```
<beans>
  <bean id="tournamentMatchManager"
      class="org.springframework.aop.framework.ProxyFactoryBean">
    <property name="target">
      <bean class="com.apress.springbook.chapter03.DefaultTournamentMatchManager">
        <!-- other properties omitted -->
      </bean>
    </property>
    <property name="interceptorNames">
      <list>
        <idref bean="textMessageSendingAdvice"/>
      </list>
    </property>
  </bean>

  <bean id="textMessageSendingAdvice"
      class="com.apress.springbook.chapter03.TextMessageSendingAdvice">
    <property name="messageSender" ref="messageSender"/>
  </bean>
</beans>
```

The configuration in Listing 3-11 creates an object that brings the advice (TextMessageSending Advice) and the target (DefaultTournamentMatchManager) together. The advice is configured as a bean definition and is referred to in the interceptorNames property on ProxyFactoryBean by name.

This object, called a *proxy* object, is type-compatible with the target object and acts as a stand-in for the target. Any method that is called on the proxy object is delegated to the target object, and any advice that is configured for the specific method is executed. The proxy, instead of the target object, must be passed to callers.

Figure 3-4 illustrates the execution path of the endMatch() method on the proxy object created by the configuration in Listing 3-11.

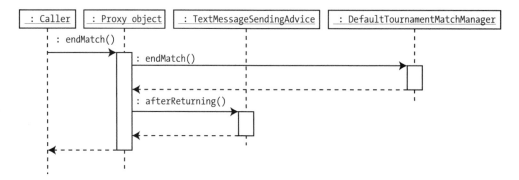

Figure 3-4. *The execution path of endMatch() on the proxy object*

Using Proxy Objects

Proxy objects are created at runtime by ProxyFactoryBean; you don't need to write any code to create them. All public methods on the target object are available on the proxy object, and you can decorate any of these methods with advice.

Spring AOP supports two proxy types: Java Development Kit (JDK) proxies and bytecode proxies. If you specify interface names in the ProxyFactoryBean configuration, as shown in Listing 3-12, you'll create a JDK proxy; otherwise, you'll create a bytecode proxy.

Listing 3-12. *Creating a JDK Proxy Object*

```
<bean id="schedulingService"
      class="org.springframework.aop.config.ProxyFactoryBean">
  <property name="target">
    <bean class="com.apress.springbook.chapter03.DefaultTournamentManager">
      <!-- other properties omitted -->
    </bean>
  </property>
  <property name="proxyInterfaces">
    <list>
      <value>com.apress.springbook.chapter03.TournamentMatchManager</value>
    </list>
  </property>
  <property name="interceptorNames">
    <list>
      <idref bean="textMessageSendingAdvice"/>
    </list>
  </property>
</bean>
```

JDK proxies are created using the `java.lang.reflect.Proxy` class and can implement only interfaces. This means the proxy object that is created by `ProxyFactoryBean` is type-compatible with the interfaces you list and not with the implementation classes of those interfaces. Since interfaces can define only public methods, all their methods can be called from the proxy object.

If you want to create proxy objects with `ProxyFactoryBean` that are type-compatible with the class of the target object, you can leave out the definition of interfaces, as shown in Listing 3-13, or set the `proxyTargetClass` property on `ProxyFactoryBean` to true.

Listing 3-13. *Creating a Bytecode Proxy Object*

```
<bean id="tournamentMatchManager"
      class="org.springframework.aop.config.ProxyFactoryBean">
  <property name="target">
    <bean class="com.apress.springbook.chapter03.DefaultTournamentMatchManager">
      <!-- other properties omitted -->
    </bean>
  </property>
  <property name="interceptorNames">
    <list>
      <idref bean="textMessageSendingAdvice"/>
    </list>
  </property>
</bean>
```

`protected` methods on target objects can be called on proxy objects in Spring AOP 2.0, and these methods can be decorated with advice. `final` classes and methods cannot be proxied, which is the sole limitation of bytecode-generated proxy objects.

■Note In some cases, proxy objects are created without a target object. The most common case for this is for creating remote access and Java Management eXtension (JMX) client-side stub objects using the Spring AOP framework. This is the most likely scenario when the target object that is passed to advice objects is null.

Now that we can attach an advice to our bean, we can choose to which methods the advice applies.

Filtering Methods

AOP frameworks allow you to define which advice is applied to which methods. The proxy object created by `ProxyFactoryBean` in the previous examples calls `TextMessageSendingAdvice` for each method invoked, which is the default behavior. However, only when a match ends should a text message be sent. To achieve this, we can specify that the advice we're configuring should be invoked only for the `endMatch()` method.

Specifying the advice and method involves using what AOP terms *join points* and *pointcuts*. Although the term *join point* has a broader meaning, Spring AOP supports only method invocations as join points. A *pointcut* selects zero or more join points on the target object. Spring AOP has a number of pointcut classes you can use to select join points:

`org.springframework.aop.support.NameMatchMethodPointcut`: Selects join points based on method names. This class matches method names using an Ant-style wildcard notation (for example, both *Match or end* select the `endMatch()` method name). It's used like this:

```
<bean id="endMatchMethodPointcut"
      class="org.springframework.aop.support.NameMatchMethodPointcut">
  <property name="mappedName" value="endMatch"/>
</bean>
```

org.springframwork.aop.support.JdkRegexpMethodPointcut: Selects join points based on method names. This class matches method names using regular expressions and works only with Java 1.4 and newer because it uses the java.util.regexp package.

org.springframwork.aop.support.Perl5RegexpMethodPointcut: Selects join points based on method names. This class matches method names using regular expressions and uses the Jakarta ORO open source regular expression library; thus, it supports Java 1.3.

When using the regular expression–based pointcut classes to match method names, the package name, class name, or method name can be matched, offering a more powerful selection mechanism. Here's an example of the string to match:

com.apress.springbook.chapter03.TournamentMatchManager.endMatch

To match the endMatch() method, use the regular expression \.endMatch$, which will select the last part of the full method name. Here's this regular expression in use:

```
<bean id="endMatchMethodPointcut"
      class="org.springframework.aop.support.JdkRegExpMethodPointcut">
  <property name="pattern" value="\.endMatch$"/>
</bean>
```

You should use the simplest pointcut class that works for your use case. NameMatchMethodPointcut suffices in almost all situations.

Adding Advisors

Pointcuts select zero or more join points (their selection may select no methods). You need to use them in combination with an advice to define to which methods the advice applies. An *advisor* takes a pointcut and an advice object and is passed to ProxyFactoryBean. Listing 3-14 shows an example.

Listing 3-14. *Using DefaultPointcutAdvisor to Configure a Pointcut and an Interceptor*

```
<bean id="sendTextMessageWhenMatchEnds"
      class="org.springframework.aop.support.DefaultPointcutAdvisor">
  <property name="pointcut" ref="endMatchMethodPointcut"/>
  <property name="advice" ref="textMessageSendingAdvice"/>
</bean>

<bean id="tournamentMatchManager"
      class="org.springframework.aop.config.ProxyFactoryBean">
  <property name="target">
    <bean class="com.apress.springbook.chapter03.DefaultTournamentMatchManager">
      <!-- other properties omitted -->
    </bean>
  </property>
  <property name="interceptorNames">
    <list>
      <value>sendTextMessageWhenMatchEnds</value>
    </list>
  </property>
</bean>
```

This example passes the name of the sendTextMessageWhenMatchEnds advisor to ProxyFactoryBean. This advisor applies textMessageSendingAdvice to all methods selected by the sendTextMessageWhenMatchStarts pointcut (both of which we've configured in earlier sections). Other methods that are called on the proxy objects do not cause the advice to be invoked.

Methods on proxy objects can have more than one advisor assigned to them. In this case, the order of execution is defined by the order in the XML configuration file. To control the proper ordering of multiple advisors, Spring AOP uses an *advisor chain* to execute all configured advisors sequentially.

Using PointcutAdvisors

Spring AOP provides convenience classes for the pointcut classes discussed earlier. These classes turn pointcut classes into advisors. Three classes are available:

- org.springframework.aop.support.NameMatchMethodPointcutAdvisor

- org.springframework.aop.support.JdkRegExpMethodPointcutAdvisor

- org.springframework.aop.support.Perl5RegExpMethodPointcutAdvisor

These convenience classes inherit the properties defined in the pointcut class they extend and add the advice property. You should use these classes instead of a separate pointcut and an advisor class to reduce the number of lines in the XML configuration files, as shown in Listing 3-15.

Listing 3-15. *Using NameMatchMethodPoincutAdvisor to Simplify the XML Configuration*

```
<bean id="sendTextMessageWhenMatchStarts"
      class="org.springframework.aop.support.NameMatchMethodPointcutAdvisor">
  <property name="mappedName" value="endMatch"/>
  <property name="advice" ref="textMessageSendingAdvice"/>
</bean>

<bean id="tournamentMatchManager"
      class="org.springframework.aop.config.ProxyFactoryBean">
  <property name="target">
    <bean class="com.apress.springbook.chapter03.DefaultTournamentMatchManager">
      <!-- other properties omitted -->
    </bean>
  </property>
  <property name="interceptorNames">
    <list>
      <value>sendTextMessageWhenMatchStarts</value>
    </list>
  </property>
</bean>
```

So, what happens when an advice is passed to ProxyFactoryBean without an advisor? Spring AOP uses an advisor for the advice that matches all methods on the target object. As a result, an advice that is configured without an advisor will be applied to all methods of the target object.

Specifying the Bean Definition Name

As you've seen in earlier examples, ProxyFactoryBean takes a list of advice names. These are the names of bean definitions that are looked up by ProxyFactoryBean in the container. But what happens if one of the advice names is not correct? The container will throw an exception because it cannot find the bean definition.

The cause of this exception—the incorrect name passed to `ProxyFactoryBean`—may not be clear. By using the `<idref>` element to specify the bean definition name, if the container cannot find the bean definition, a more appropriate exception will be thrown. Listing 3-16 shows an example.

Listing 3-16. *Causing a Nice Exception in Case the Bean Definition Name Is Incorrect*

```
<bean id="tournamentMatchManager"
      class="org.springframework.aop.config.ProxyFactoryBean">
  <property name="target">
    <bean class="com.apress.springbook.chapter03.DefaultTournamentManager">
      <!-- other properties omitted -->
    </bean>
  </property>
  <property name="interceptorNames">
    <list>
      <idref bean="textMessageSendingAdvice"/>
    </list>
  </property>
</bean>
```

When the container parses the XML fragment in Listing 3-16, a clear exception will be thrown if the bean definition name in the `<idref>` element cannot be found.

Selecting Advice Types

Spring AOP supports four advice types that each represents a specific scenario for advice implementations:

Around advice: Controls the execution of a join point. This type is ideal for advice that needs to control the execution of the method on the target object.

Before advice: Is executed before the execution of a join point. This type is ideal for advice that needs to perform an action before the execution of the method on the target object.

After advice: Is executed after the execution of a join point. This type is ideal for advice that needs to perform an action after the execution of the method on the target object.

Throws advice: Is executed after the execution of a join point if an exception is thrown. This type is ideal for advice that needs to perform an action when the execution of the method on the target object has thrown an exception.

■**Note** Actually, the Spring AOP framework supports one more advice type: the introduction advice. We won't discuss this fifth advice type in this book since it's not often used. You can just remember it is available and that it can be used to add methods and properties to the advised class.

The advice type is determined by the interface that is implemented by advice classes. Spring AOP advice type interfaces are based on the interfaces defined by the AOP Alliance project. These interfaces are supported by other AOP frameworks as well and ensure optimal reuse of advice.

ADVICE VS. INTERCEPTOR

When reading about the Spring AOP framework, you will probably find that the term *interceptor* is often used instead of *advice*. Technically speaking, Spring AOP is an interception-based framework, and the terms *interceptor* and *advice* are interchangeable in this context. However, these terms are not interchangeable for AOP in general.

Technically, the only advice type supported by Spring AOP that is an interceptor is around advice. You may encounter the terms *around interceptor* and *method interceptor*, which are synonymous with *around advice*.

Before advice, after advice, and throws advice are semantically different from around advice, since they do not control method invocations on a target object; hence, they are not interceptors. However, you may encounter the terms *before interceptor, after interceptor,* and *throws interceptor.* Since Spring AOP is interception-based, these terms are valid, but we prefer to stick to the term *advice* in this book.

Additionally, you may encounter the term *interceptor chain* in literature in Spring AOP, which is synonymous with *advisor chain.*

Some people are confused about the Spring AOP architecture and use the terms *advisor* and *interceptor* interchangeably. This is incorrect since an *interceptor* is a specific type of advice (and synonymous to advice in the context of the Spring AOP framework), while an *advisor* brings a pointcut and an advice together.

Around Advice

The around advice type (also called a *method interceptor*) controls the flow of method invocations on target objects. This advice type is ideal for cross-cutting concerns that need to control the method invocation. It is called before the method on the target object is executed and exits after this method returns.

Around advice sits around a method invocation and can prevent the advice chain execution from continuing. The org.aopalliance.intercept.MethodInterceptor interface must be implemented to create around advice, as shown in Listing 3-17.

Listing 3-17. *The AOP Alliance MethodInterceptor Interface*

```
package org.aopalliance.intercept;

public interface MethodInterceptor extends org.aopalliance.intercept.Interceptor {
  Object invoke(MethodInvocation methodInvocation) throws Throwable;
}
```

The advice implementation is responsible for continuing the interceptor chain by calling the proceed() method on MethodInvocation and returning a value. The interceptor implementation may also choose not to continue the invocation by not calling the proceed() method.

Listing 3-18 shows around advice that records the duration of the method invocation on the target object.

Listing 3-18. *A Simple Profiling Around Advice Class*

```
package com.apress.springbook.chapter03;

import org.aopalliance.intercept.MethodInterceptor;
import org.aopalliance.intercept.MethodInvocation;

import org.springframework.util.StopWatch;
```

```java
public class SimpleProfilingAroundAdvice implements MethodInterceptor {

  public Object invoke(MethodInvocation invocation) throws Throwable {
    StopWatch stopWatch = new StopWatch();
    stopWatch.start();

    try {
      return invocation.proceed();
    } finally {
      stopWatch.stop();
      System.out.println(stopWatch.prettyPrint());
    }
  }
}
```

The around advice in Listing 3-18 shows how this advice class sits around the execution of the method on the target object. When the proceed() method is called, any additional advice is executed, before the method on the target object is executed. When the target method exits and any additional advice returns control, the proceed() method exits and returns the original return value (or null in the case of the return type void).

Figure 3-5 shows the execution flow when the endMatch() method is executed on the proxy object created by the configuration in Listing 3-19.

Listing 3-19. *Creating a Proxy Object with SimpleProfilingAroundAdvice*

```xml
<bean id="sendTextMessageWhenMatchStarts"
      class="org.springframework.aop.support.NameMatchMethodPointcutAdvisor">
  <property name="mappedName" value="endMatch"/>
  <property name="advice" ref="textMessageSendingAdvice"/>
</bean>

<bean id="profilingAdvice"
      class="com.apress.springbook.chapter03.SimpleProfilingAroundAdvice"/>

<bean id="tournamentMatchManager"
      class="org.springframework.aop.config.ProxyFactoryBean">
  <property name="target">
    <bean class="com.apress.springbook.chapter03.DefaultTournamentMatchManager">
      <!-- other properties omitted -->
    </bean>
  </property>
  <property name="interceptorNames">
    <list>
      <idref bean="profilingAdvice"/>
      <idref bean="sendTextMessageWhenMatchStarts"/>
    </list>
  </property>
</bean>
```

As shown in Figure 3-5, around advice uses a cascading mechanism, where the advice decides when to pass control to the AOP framework by calling the proceed() method.

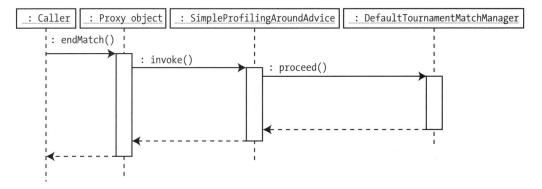

Figure 3-5. *The sequence of events when around advice is used*

Around advice classes can access the arguments passed to the method on the proxy object by calling the MethodInvocation.getArguments() method. This method returns an object array that contains the arguments that were passed to the method on the proxy object. You are free to change the content of this array as you see fit, as long as the values remain type-compatible with the corresponding argument types of the target method. Primitive types are translated to their class wrapper counterparts, meaning you will be using the Java class wrapper types when reading and writing primitive variables.

Before Advice

Before advice is ideal for actions that must occur before a method on a target object is called. It is called before the target method is invoked and can interrupt the invocation only by throwing an exception. You need to implement the org.springframework.aop.MethodBeforeAdvice interface to create before advice, as shown in Listing 3-20.

Listing 3-20. *Spring's MethodBeforeAdvice Interface*

```
package org.springframework.aop;

import java.lang.reflect.Method;

public interface MethodBeforeAdvice extends org.aopalliance.aop.BeforeAdvice {
  void before(Method method, Object[] arguments, Object target) throws Throwable;
}
```

The before() method provides access to the arguments of the method invocation and the target object. Since the target method has not been executed when the before advice is called, you are free to change the method arguments, as long as they are type-compatible with the argument types of the target method. The before() method also provides access to the target object, which is almost always present.

As an example of before advice, Listing 3-21 shows a class that checks all the arguments that are passed and checks whether they are not null. This advice can solve the occurrence of NullPointerExceptions with some methods.

Listing 3-21. *NullArgumentsNotAllowedBeforeAdvice Checks Method Arguments Are Not Null and Throws IllegalArgumentException If One of Them Is*

```
package com.apress.springbook.chapter03;

import org.springframework.aop.MethodBeforeAdvice;
import java.lang.reflect.Method;

public class NullArgumentsNotAllowedBeforeAdvice implements MethodBeforeAdvice {
  public void before(Method method, Object[] arguments, Object target)
      throws Throwable {
    if (arguments == null || arguments.length == 0) {
      return;
    }

    for (int i = 0; i < arguments.length; i++) {
      Object argument = arguments[i];
      if (argument == null) {
        throw new IllegalArgumentException(
          "Value for argument [" + i + "] is required but not present " +
          "for method [" + method + "]!"
        );
      }
    }
  }
}
```

As you can see from the example in Listing 3-21, writing before advice that checks the arguments of method invocations is straightforward. The only requirement is to implement the MethodBeforeAdvice interface.

You can now configure this advice using ProxyFactoryBean on any target object, as shown in Listing 3-22.

Listing 3-22. *Configuring NullArgumentsNotAllowedBeforeAdvice Using ProxyFactoryBean*

```
<bean id="myBean" class="org.springframework.aop.framework.ProxyFactoryBean">
  <property name="target" ref="myTarget"/>
  <property name="interceptorNames" value="nullArgumentsNotAllowedBeforeAdvice"/>
</bean>

<bean id="nullArgumentsNotAllowedBeforeAdvice"
      class="com.apress.springbook.chapter03.NullArgumentsNotAllowedBeforeAdvice"/>
```

Figure 3-6 shows the sequence of events when a method is called on the myBean proxy object.

After Advice

We've discussed after advice already. It is called if the method invocation on the target object exits normally, so it's not called if the target method throws an exception. This advice type is ideal for actions that need access to the value returned by the target method and otherwise do not need to control the execution of the target method.

After advice cannot interrupt the execution of the method on the target object, since it's called after that. However, this advice type can interrupt the further invocation of the advisor chain by throwing an unchecked exception (java.lang.RuntimeException or java.lang.Error) or a checked exception that is declared in the signature of the method on the proxy object.

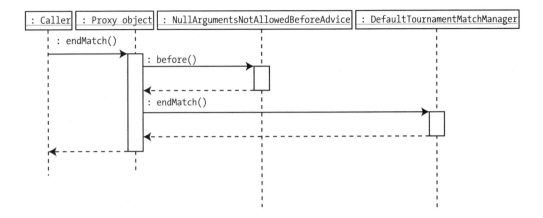

Figure 3-6. *The sequence of events when before advice is used*

You need to implement the `org.springframework.aop.AfterReturningAdvice` interface to create after advice, as shown in Listing 3-23.

Listing 3-23. *Spring's AfterReturningAdvice Interface*

```
package org.springframework.aop;

public interface AfterReturningAdvice extends org.aopalliance.aop.Advice {
  void afterReturning(
    Object returnValue,
    Method method,
    Object[] arguments,
    Object target) throws Throwable;
}
```

The `afterReturning()` method has the same arguments as the `before()` method on the `MethodBeforeAdvice` interface and adds the return value of the method invocation on the target object. The return value will be null if the target method returns null or has the return type void. See Listing 3-10, shown earlier in this chapter, for an example of after advice.

Throws Advice

Throws advice is called when the method execution on the target object throws a specific exception type. This advice type is ideal for actions that need access to exceptions or otherwise need control when specific exception types are thrown. Throws advice does not control the method execution because it's called after exceptions are thrown.

You need to implement the `org.springframework.aop.ThrowsAdvice` interface to create throws advice, as shown in Listing 3-24.

Listing 3-24. *Spring's ThrowsAdvice Interface*

```
package org.springframework.aop;

public interface ThrowsAdvice extends org.aopalliance.aop.Advice {
}
```

ThrowsAdvice is probably the strangest interface that is part of the Spring Framework, since it doesn't define any methods and yet must be implemented by advice classes. Instead of defining methods in the interface, Spring AOP recognizes and supports magic methods in classes that implement this interface. (A *magic method* is any method in a Java class that is not defined in an interface or a base class, yet is expected to be implemented by a framework or container.) The magic methods for throws advice supported by Spring AOP need to be named afterThrowing(). These methods must have either of the two method signatures shown in Listings 3-25 and 3-26.

Listing 3-25. *ThrowsAdvice That Catches RuntimeExceptions with Short Method*

```
public class RuntimeExceptionThrowsAdvice implements ThrowsAdvice {
  public void afterThrowing(RuntimeException ex) {
    // do something with exception
  }
}
```

Listing 3-26. *ThrowsAdvice That Catches RuntimeExceptions with Extended Method*

```
public class RuntimeExceptionThrowsAdvice implements ThrowsAdvice {
  public void afterThrowing(
    Method method,
    Object[] arguments,
    Object target,
    RuntimeException ex) {
    // access to runtime information
    // do something with exception
  }
}
```

The exception type defined as the method argument may vary. The only limitation is that the argument type must be type-compatible with java.lang.Throwable.

Spring AOP will call the most specific afterThrowing() method defined in throws advice, which is the method with an exception argument type that's type-compatible with the actual type that is thrown and closest to it in the class hierarchy. The advice classes in Listings 3-25 and 3-26 implement the two supported method signatures to catch RuntimeException. Any exception type that is type-compatible with RuntimeException will thus be caught; other exception types will be ignored by these throws advice implementations.

When throws advice is called by an exception that's thrown, that exception will be thrown to the caller. The only way to prevent this exception from being thrown is by throwing another exception.

Throwing Exceptions with Spring AOP Advice

Each of the Spring AOP advice interfaces discussed allows you to throw exceptions. When an exception is thrown from an advice, one of three things happens:

- Unchecked exceptions are passed to any other advice in the advisor chain and eventually to the caller.

- Checked exceptions that are declared in the method signature of the target method are also passed to any other advice in the advisor chain and eventually to the caller.

- Checked exceptions that are *not* declared in the method signature of the target method will be wrapped in java.lang.reflect.UndeclaredThrowableException, which is unchecked.

So if you get the mysterious UndeclaredThrowableException, you know an advice has thrown a checked exception that's not declared in the method signature of the target method.

AOP Usage in the Spring Framework

Many of the services offered by the Spring Framework use the Spring AOP framework internally. Each service typically has one or more *ProxyFactoryBean classes to simplify the AOP configuration. These include the following:

Transaction management: Around advice starts and ends transactions using a transaction manager (org.springframework.transaction.interceptor.TransactionProxyFactoryBean). We'll discuss this in more detail in Chapter 7.

Remote access: For client-side remote access, around advice makes a connection to the server and returns the method execution result received from the server (for example, org.springframework.remoting.httpinvoker.HttpInvokerProxyFactoryBean). For server-side remote access, a proxy object without advice makes sure only the methods of selected interfaces are exported (for example, org.springframework.remoting.httpinvoker.HttpInvokerServiceExporter).

JMX: Around advice acts as a client to access remote objects exported via JMX (for example, org.springframework.jmx.access.MBeanProxyFactoryBean).

By using the specific *ProxyFactoryBean classes, you no longer need to set up a Spring AOP configuration. Each *ProxyFactoryBean class uses an advice class internally that can also be configured with org.springframework.aop.framework.ProxyFactoryBean.

Other Advice Classes

Some additional advice classes ship with the Spring Framework distribution that need to be configured using org.springframework.aop.framework.ProxyFactoryBean. These classes are not used by the Spring Framework internally but are provided for your convenience.

Logging Messages with Around Advice

The CustomizableTraceInterceptor around advice logs customizable messages using the Jakarta Commons Logging framework. Messages are logged on the trace level when methods are invoked. Listing 3-27 shows how to configure this advice.

Listing 3-27. *Configuring CustomizableTraceInterceptor with Spring AOP*

```
<bean id="traceInterceptor"
      class="org.springframework.aop.interceptor.CustomizableTraceInterceptor">
  <property name="enterMessage"
            value="Entered $[methodName] on $[targetClassShortName]"/>
</bean>

<bean id="tournamentMatchManager"
      class="org.springframework.aop.config.ProxyFactoryBean">
  <property name="target">
    <bean class="com.apress.springbook.chapter03.DefaultTournamentMatchManager">
    <!-- other properties omitted -->
    </bean>
```

```
    </property>
    <property name="interceptorNames">
      <list>
        <idref bean="traceInterceptor"/>
      </list>
    </property>
  </bean>
```

CustomizableTraceInterceptor has three message properties: enterMessage, exitMessage, and exceptionMessage. The message strings can have placeholder strings to customize the content. Refer to the Javadoc for this class for more details.

Notice in Listing 3-27 that no pointcut is configured, meaning the advice will be called for all methods of the proxy object.

Debugging with Around Advice

The org.springframework.aop.interceptor.DebugInterceptor around advice logs a full method invocation message plus a method invocation count on the trace level. This advice also uses the Jakarta Commons Logging framework and should be used only for debugging purposes.

This advice class is stateful since it keeps track of the method invocation count, so it must be configured as a prototype in the Spring container.

Limiting Concurrent Method Execution with Around Advice

The org.springframework.aop.interceptor.ConcurrencyThrottleInterceptor around advice limits the maximum number of concurrent executions of one or more methods. This advice is stateful, meaning it should be configured as a prototype, as shown in Listing 3-28. It actually limits the maximum number of concurrent executions of all methods selected by one pointcut.

Listing 3-28. *Limiting the Maximum Number of Executions of One Method*

```
<bean id="concurrencyThrottleInterceptor"
      class="org.springframework.aop.interceptor.ConcurrencyThrottleInterceptor"
      singleton="false">
  <property name="concurrencyLimit" value="5"/>
</bean>

<bean id="endMatchPointcutAdvisor"
      class="org.springframework.aop.support.NameMatchMethodPointcutAdvisor"
      singleton="false">
  <property name="advice" ref="concurrencyThrottleInterceptor"/>
  <property name="mappedName" value="endMatch"/>
</bean>

<bean id="tournamentMatchManager"
      class="org.springframework.aop.config.ProxyFactoryBean">
  <property name="target">
    <bean class="com.apress.springbook.chapter03.DefaultTournamentMatchManager">
      <!-- other properties omitted -->
    </bean>
  </property>
  <property name="interceptorNames">
    <list>
```

```
        <idref bean="endMatchPointcutAdvisor"/>
      </list>
    </property>
  </bean>
```

The configuration in Listing 3-28 limits the maximum number of concurrent executions of the endMatch() method. Notice both the advice and advisor bean definitions are configured as the prototype.

Since the advisor holds a reference to the advice and the advice must be configured as a prototype, the advisor must also be configured as a prototype.

Summary

So, what do we gain by using Spring AOP instead of decorator or observer classes? You need to implement a cross-cutting concern only once and can reuse it anywhere. Besides being able to apply cross-cutting concerns anywhere, you don't even need to write your own implementations for the most common concerns. The cross-cutting concern implementations offered by Spring are high-quality implementations that are widely used and well tested.

Also, it doesn't matter what the target object is; Spring AOP can apply any advice to any target object. This means a cross-cutting concern must be written only once and can be applied anywhere.

The next chapter covers Spring AOP 2.0, which is built on top of the Spring AOP features discussed in this chapter.

CHAPTER 4

■■■

Spring AOP 2.0

Welcome to the chapter on the future of Spring AOP. In Chapter 3, we described how Spring AOP has been used up to the Spring 1.2.*x* releases. This chapter covers features added to Spring AOP in the 2.0 release.

That's right, new features have been *added*, so everything you learned about AOP so far is still applicable and available. This really is proof that the Spring 2.0 release remains fully backward-compatible with Spring 1.2.*x*. We strongly recommend upgrading your Spring version to the latest 2.0 release. Full backward-compatibility is assured.

If you haven't done so already, now is a good time to review the concepts covered in Chapter 3, as they continue to be the foundations of Spring AOP.

The following are the new features that will be covered in detail in this chapter:

- The @AspectJ-style of writing aspects with Java 5 annotations, including the supported advice types

- The AspectJ pointcut language

- The Spring AOP XML tags to declare aspects in XML for those cases where Java 5 is not available or existing classes must be used as advice

- The Spring AOP XML advisor tag to combine classic Spring AOP advice classes and the AspectJ pointcut language

Introducing AspectJ and Aspects

While classic Spring AOP (covered in Chapter 3) works with advice, pointcuts, and advisors, the new Spring AOP works with advice, pointcuts, advisors, and *aspects*. Not much of a difference you may think, but as you'll find out soon, things have changed significantly. Literally all the new Spring AOP features are built on top of the integration with the AspectJ AOP framework. (The proxy-based interception mechanism remains in place, so the skills you've gained from the previous chapter will remain useful.)

So what is AspectJ? The AspectJ FAQ (`http://www.eclipse.org/aspectj/doc/released/faq.html`) answers this question as follows:

> *AspectJ is a simple and practical extension to the Java programming language that adds to Java aspect-oriented programming (AOP) capabilities. AOP allows developers to reap the benefits of modularity for concerns that cut across the natural units of modularity. In object-oriented programs like Java, the natural unit of modularity is the class. In AspectJ, aspects modularize concerns that affect more than one class.*

And what is an aspect? That is also answered by the same FAQ as follows:

Aspects are how developers encapsulate concerns that cut across classes, the natural unit of modularity in Java.

From the previous chapter, you know that cross-cutting concerns are modularized as advice. These are *encapsulated* by an advisor, which combines one advice and one pointcut. This encapsulation tells at which join points in the software the advice is executed.

Aspects and advisors seem to have much in common: they both encapsulate concerns that cut across classes. Advice is executed at join points that are matched by a pointcut; however, a given pointcut may not match any join points in an application.

Now let's look at what you can do with an aspect:

- You can declare pointcuts.

- You can declare errors and warnings for each join point that is selected by the associated pointcut.

- You can declare new fields, constructors, and methods in classes. These are called inter-type declarations in AspectJ.

- You can declare one or more advices, each one executed for all joint points matched by a pointcut.

When comparing the two, it quickly becomes clear an aspect is a much more sophisticated construct than an advisor. For now, it's sufficient to understand aspects and advisors both encapsulate cross-cutting concerns yet take a different approach.

Join Points and Pointcuts in AspectJ

AspectJ supports many more join point types than Spring AOP, which supports only method executions. The following is a selection of join points supported by AspectJ:

- Calls to methods and execution of instance and static methods

- Calls to get and set values on instance fields and static fields

- Calls to constructors and execution of constructors

- Classes and packages

None of these additional join points are featured in Spring AOP. However, it's useful to have an idea about which join points are supported by AspectJ when discussing pointcuts.

To select the rich set of supported join points, AspectJ has its own pointcut language. The following pointcut selects all static and instance methods named `relax`, regardless of their arguments, return type, or classes:

```
execution(* relax(..))
```

When you consider all the join point types supported by AspectJ, a proper language is the only flexible way to define pointcuts. Any other means, including XML configuration or an API, would be a nightmare to write, read, and maintain.

Spring AOP integrates with this AspectJ pointcut language, which is covered later in this chapter, in the "Working with Pointcuts" section. For now, all you need to know is that the asterisk (*) matches any method or class name or any argument type, and the double dot (..) matches zero or more arguments.

AspectJ Aspect Creation

AspectJ has its own language that extends the Java language specifications for creating aspects. Originally, this was the only way to declare aspects with AspectJ. Because aspects and pointcuts are treated as first-class citizens, it's a very practical AOP language. Spring AOP does not integrate with this language, but to give you a better understanding of AspectJ aspects, here's a very simple example:

```
package com.apress.springbook.chapter04.aspects;

public aspect MySimpleAspectJAspect {
  before(): execution(* relax(..)) {
    System.out.println("relax() method is about to be executed!");
  }
}
```

As you can see, the aspect is somewhat comparable to a Java class, but you wouldn't be able to compile it with a regular Java compiler.

AspectJ 1.5 has introduced Java 5 annotations to allow programmers to write AspectJ aspects as an alternative to the AspectJ language. (If you're not familiar with Java 5 annotations, you can find an introduction at http://www.developer.com/java/other/article.php/3556176.) Spring AOP integrates with this way of writing aspects, as detailed in this chapter.

Listing 4-1 shows how the previous aspect looks when it's rewritten with annotations. This style is called the @AspectJ-style, although the @Aspect annotation is used. As you can see, aspects become regular Java classes.

Listing 4-1. *A Simple AspectJ Aspect Written in the @AspectJ-Style*

```
package com.apress.springbook.chapter04.aspects;

import org.aspectj.lang.annotation.Aspect;
import org.aspectj.lang.annotation.Before;

@Aspect
public class MySimpleAtAspectJAspect {
  @Before("execution(* relax(..))")
  public void beforeRelaxingMethod() {
    System.out.println("relax() method is about to be executed!");
  }
}
```

The aspect in Listing 4-1 declares a regular Java class that is annotated with the @AspectJ-style Java 5 annotations. The class declares one pointcut/advice pair. The @Aspect annotation on the class declaration indicates that this class is an @AspectJ-style aspect. A class needs to have this annotation to qualify as an aspect.

The @Before annotation is used to turn the regular beforeRelaxingMethod() method into an advice declaration and holds the pointcut declaration for the advice. In AspectJ, an advice cannot exist without a pointcut.

The annotation type also defines the advice type; in this case, it's before advice. The @AspectJ-style supports the advice types defined in Chapter 3 plus one more. Only instance methods with an @AspectJ advice type annotation are advice declarations, so an aspect class can also have regular methods.

The @AspectJ annotations *can* be used on abstract classes and even interfaces, although this is not very useful, as the annotations are not inherited.

Listing 4-2 shows a class with one method that will be one of the join points matched by the pointcut in Listing 4-1.

Listing 4-2. *The relax() Method in the SunnyDay Class Is Selected As a Join Point*

```
package com.apress.springbook.chapter04;

public class SunnyDay {
  public void relax() {
    // go to the beach
  }
}
```

Before the `relax()` method is executed, a message will be printed on the console. The print statement is the actual advice that is executed.

The @AspectJ-style requires Java 5. Also, existing classes that don't declare the @AspectJ annotations cannot be used as advice.

In the typical Spring style, you can declare aspects in Spring AOP without using Java 5 and annotations. By making clever use of the Spring 2.0 XML Schema support (introduced in Chapter 2), the Spring developers have been able to define AOP tags for declaring aspects, advice, and pointcuts. There is also a new tag to declare advisors. This chapter covers these new XML tags after introducing the @AspectJ-style of declaring aspects and the pointcut language in more detail.

Now, without further ado, here comes Spring 2.0 AOP.

■**Note** You can find much more information about AspectJ at `http://www.eclipse.org/aspectj/`. Another excellent resource is *AspectJ in Action* by Ramnivas Laddad (Manning, 2003).

Configuring @AspectJ-Style Aspects in Spring

By now, you know what an aspect looks like and how you can write one yourself. In this section, we'll start with an example of an @AspectJ-style aspect that's configured in the Spring container. This will demonstrate how the Spring AOP framework uses aspects and creates proxy objects. After the example, we'll look at the details of advice types, pointcuts, and proxy objects.

A Simple @AspectJ-Style Aspect

@AspectJ-style aspects must be configured in the Spring container to be usable by Spring AOP. From the previous chapter, you'll remember proxy objects were created by using `ProxyFactoryBean` in the Spring container. In that case, we took our first AOP steps with a configuration per target object to create proxy objects. With @AspectJ-style aspects, Spring AOP takes a different approach to creating proxy objects based on the pointcuts in aspects, as this example will demonstrate. In this example, we'll use one simple pointcut so we can focus on the aspects. As the chapter progresses, we'll use more elaborate pointcut examples.

Aspect Definition

The aspect for this example is shown in Listing 4-3. It has one pointcut that selects all `startMatch()` methods it can find and an advice that prints a message to the console when this occurs. In the next sections, we'll look in more detail at how join points are searched for and what happens if they are found.

Listing 4-3. *Aspect with Pointcut That Selects All startMatch() Methods and Advice That Prints a Message Before the Join Point Is Executed*

```
package com.apress.springbook.chapter04.aspects;

import org.aspectj.lang.annotation.Aspect;
import org.aspectj.lang.annotation.Before;

@Aspect
public class MessagePrintingAspect {
  @Before("execution(* startMatch(..))")
  public void printMessageToInformMatchStarts() {
    System.out.println("Attempting to start tennis match!");
  }
}
```

■**Note** You need to include the aspectjweaver.jar and aspectjrt.jar in your classpath. Both files can be found in the Spring Framework distribution under the lib/aspectj directory.

The MessagePrintingAspect in Listing 4-3 is a regular Java class with Java 5 annotations. It's also an aspect declaration because of the @AspectJ-style annotations.

The @Aspect annotation on the class declaration turns this class into an aspect declaration. It can now hold pointcut declarations and advice/pointcut combinations. The aspect is called MessagePrintingAspect, indicating its responsibility is to print messages to the console. When we want to print messages for other join points, we can add more advice/pointcut combinations to this aspect. By organizing (or modularizing) advice that logically belongs together in aspects, it will be trivial to get an overview of which messages are printed to the console for which join points.

The @Before annotation on the printMessageToInformMatchStarts() method declaration has two roles: it defines the advice type (before advice), and it holds the pointcut declaration. Again, we've chosen a name, printMessageToInformMatchStarts, that explains the responsibilities of the advice.

■**Tip** Giving descriptive names to advice helps to organize your thoughts and organize advices. If you're having trouble coming up with names for your advices that exactly describe what they do, maybe they're overloaded with responsibilities and should be split into smaller parts.

The pointcut declaration selects all instance methods named startMatch(), regardless of the number of arguments, argument types, throws declarations, return type, visibility, or classes that declare them.

Now that you understand the aspect declaration, it's time to look at the target class of this example.

Target Class

The target class in this example is our friend DefaultTournamentMatchManager, as shown in Listing 4-4.

Listing 4-4. *DefaultTournamentMatchManager Class*

```
package com.apress.springbook.chapter04;

public class DefaultTournamentMatchManager implements TournamentMatchManager {
  public Match startMatch(long matchId) throws
      UnknownMatchException, MatchIsFinishedException,
      MatchCannotBePlayedException, PreviousMatchesNotFinishedException {
    // implementation omitted
  }

  /* other methods omitted */
}
```

The startMatch() method matches the criteria of the pointcut in Listing 4-3. This doesn't mean, however, that Spring AOP will start creating proxy objects just like that. First, we must configure a target object and the @AspectJ-style aspect in the Spring container, as discussed in the next section.

Aspect Configuration

Listing 4-5 shows the required configuration in a Spring XML configuration file to have the printMessageToInformMatchStarts advice print a message to the console before the startMatch() method is executed (there is another way to do this, which we'll explore in the "Using AOP XML Tags" section later in this chapter).

Listing 4-5. *aspect-config.xml: Required Configuration in a Spring XML File*

```
<?xml version="1.0" encoding="UTF-8"?>
<!DOCTYPE beans PUBLIC "-//SPRING//DTD BEAN//EN"
    "http://www.springframework.org/dtd/spring-beans.dtd">
<beans>
  <bean class="org.springframework.aop.aspectj.annotation. ➥
AnnotationAwareAspectJAutoProxyCreator"/>

  <bean class="com.apress.springbook.chapter04.aspects.MessagePrintingAspect"/>

  <bean id="tournamentMatchManager"
        class="com.apress.springbook.chapter04.DefaultTournamentMatchManager">
    <!-- properties omitted -->
  </bean>
</beans>
```

Spring AOP provides a powerful integration with the Spring container called *auto-proxy* creation. Spring AOP will extend the bean life cycle of the Spring container to create proxy objects for those beans in the container that have join points that are matched by one or more pointcuts.

We'll look into the details of how the proxy is created in the next sections. For now, it's sufficient to understand that an object for the AnnotationAwareAspectJAutoProxyCreator bean definition in Listing 4-5 will be created first when the Spring container (ApplicationContext) loads. Once this is done, the Spring container detects any classes that have @Aspect annotation and uses them to configure Spring AOP.

The AnnotationAwareAspectJAutoProxyCreator bean has the potential to affect all other beans that are created by the container. During the bean life cycle of the tournamentMatchManager bean, AnnotationAwareAspectJAutoProxyCreator will create a proxy object for this bean and replace the original bean with the proxy object because one of its join points (the startMatch() method) is matched by the advice/pointcut combination in the MessagePrintingAspect.

The printMessageToInformMatchStarts advice will be called when the startMatch() method is executed on the tournamentMatchManager bean. Now, let's find out if the printMessageToInform MatchStarts advice actually gets called and prints a message before the startMatch() method is executed.

An Integration Test for the Configuration and Aspect

We can now use a simple integration test to verify if the message is printed to the console when the startMatch() method is called on the tournamentMatchManager bean. We'll also add a test that creates a new DefaultTournamentMatchManager object and calls its startMatch() method to verify that *no* message is printed when this method is called. Listing 4-6 shows the integration test case.

Listing 4-6. *Integration Test Case for the Spring AOP Configuration and the Aspect*

```
package com.apress.springbook.chapter04;

import org.springframework.test.AbstractDependencyInjectionSpringContextTests;

public class MessagePrintingAspectIntegrationTests extends
        AbstractDependencyInjectionSpringContextTests {

  protected String[] getConfigLocations() {
    return new String[] {
      "classpath:com/apress/springbook/chapter04/" +
        "aspect-config.xml"
    };
  }

  private TournamentMatchManager tournamentMatchManager;

  public void setTournamentMatchManager(
          TournamentMatchManager tournamentMatchManager) {
    this.tournamentMatchManager = tournamentMatchManager;
  }

  public void testCallStartMatchMethodOnBeanFromContainer()
      throws Exception {
    System.out.println("=== GOING TO CALL METHOD " +
          "ON BEAN FROM CONTAINER ===");

    this.tournamentMatchManager.startMatch(1);

    System.out.println("=== FINISHED CALLING METHOD " +
          "ON BEAN FROM CONTAINER ===");
  }

  public void testCallStartMatchMethodOnNewlyCreatedObject()
      throws Exception {
    TournamentMatchManager newTournamentMatchManager =
      new DefaultTournamentMatchManager();

    System.out.println("=== GOING TO CALL METHOD " +
          "ON NEWLY CREATED OBJECT ===");

    newTournamentMatchManager.startMatch(1);
```

```
        System.out.println("=== FINISHED CALLING METHOD " +
                "ON NEWLY CREATED OBJECT ===");
    }
}
```

The test case in Listing 4-6 loads the Spring XML configuration file (Listing 4-5). It declares two tests:

testCallStartMatchMethodOnBeanFromContainer(): This test uses a tournamentMatchManager object that is injected from the container. This is the tournamentMatchManager bean defined in the Spring XML configuration file. The test calls the startMatch() method on this object. The tournamentMatchManager bean is a proxy object that has been created by the AnnotationAware AspectJAutoProxyCreator bean. A proxy object was created because the sole pointcut in the MessagePrintingAspect matches the startMatch() join point. When the startMatch() method is executed on the proxy object, the printMessageToInformMatchStarts advice, which prints its message to the console, will be executed, and then the actual method on the target object will be executed.

testCallStartMatchMethodOnNewlyCreatedObject(): This test creates a new DefaultTournament MatchManager object. This object is not a proxy and is in no way touched or affected by Spring AOP. When its startMatch() method is called, no advice will be executed. Because this object is not created by the Spring container, it is not affected by the MessagePrintingAspect.

When the test case in Listing 4-6 is executed, messages will be printed on the console as follows:

```
=== GOING TO CALL METHOD ON BEAN FROM CONTAINER ===
Attempting to start tennis match!
=== FINISHED CALLING METHOD ON BEAN FROM CONTAINER ===
=== GOING TO CALL METHOD ON NEWLY CREATED OBJECT ===
=== FINISHED CALLING METHOD ON NEWLY CREATED OBJECT ===
```

The printMessageToInformMatchStarts() advice method declared in MessagePrintingAspect is executed when the startMatch() join point is executed on the tournamentMatchManager bean.

Our example touches many facets of how Spring AOP deals with aspects. You've been exposed to all the requirements that must be met in order to use @AspectJ-style aspects with Spring AOP:

- Join points need to be public or protected instance methods on objects.
- Objects must be created by the Spring container.
- Callers need to call methods on the proxy objects, not on the original objects.
- Aspect instances must also be created by the Spring container.
- A special bean must be created by the Spring container to take care of auto-proxy creation.

Now, let's look at the advice types supported by aspects in Spring AOP.

@AspectJ-Style Advice Types

Aspects in Spring AOP are not declared by interfaces as is the case for classic Spring AOP. Instead, an advice is declared as a regular Java method, which can have arguments, return objects, and throw exceptions. As you saw in the previous example, the advice type is defined by the @Aspect annotation declaration on methods. The following advice types are supported:

Before advice (@Before): Executed before a join point is executed. It has the same semantics as before advice described in the previous chapter. It can prevent method execution on the target object from happening only by throwing an exception.

After returning advice (@AfterReturning): Executed after a join point has been executed without throwing an exception. It has the same semantics as after returning advice described in the previous chapter. It can have access to the return value of the method execution if it wants to, but can't replace the return value.

After throwing advice (@AfterThrowing): Executed after executing a join point that threw an exception. It has the same semantics as throws advice described in the previous chapter. It can have access to the exception that was thrown if it wants to, but can't prevent this exception from being thrown to the caller unless it throws another exception.

After (finally) advice (@After): Always called after a join point has been executed, regardless of whether the join point execution threw an exception or not. This is a new advice type that is not available in classic Spring AOP. It can't get access to the return value or an exception that was thrown.

Around advice (@Around): Executed as an interceptor around the execution of a join point. As with around advice described in the previous chapter, it's the most powerful advice type, but also the one that requires the most work.

■**Note** Actually, the Spring 2.0 AOP framework supports a sixth advice type: the introduction advice. We won't discuss this advice type in this book since it's not often used. You can just remember it is available and that it can be used to add methods and properties to the advised class.

You saw an example of before advice in the previous examples; MessagePrintingAspect contained before advice. Let's take a quick look at the other advice types and how to declare them in an @AspectJ-style aspect.

After Returning Advice

After returning advice is called when a join point has been executed and has exited with a return value or without a return value if the return type is void. Listing 4-7 shows MessagePrintingAspect with after returning advice.

Listing 4-7. *Printing a Message After a Join Point Has Been Executed Normally*

```
package com.apress.springbook.chapter04.aspects;

import org.aspectj.lang.annotation.Aspect;
import org.aspectj.lang.annotation.AfterReturning;

@Aspect
public class MessagePrintingAspect {
  @AfterReturning("execution(* startMatch(..))")
  public void printMessageWhenTennisMatchHasBeenStartedSuccessfully() {
    System.out.println("Tennis match was started successfully!");
  }
}
```

After Throwing Advice

If you want to do some work when a join point throws an exception, you can use after throwing advice. Listing 4-8 shows MessagePrintingAspect with after throwing advice that prints out a warning when an exception is thrown.

Listing 4-8. *Printing a Warning Message After a Join Point Has Thrown an Exception*

```
package com.apress.springbook.chapter04.aspects;

import org.aspectj.lang.annotation.Aspect;
import org.aspectj.lang.annotation.AfterThrowing;

@Aspect
public class MessagePrintingAspect {
  @AfterThrowing("execution(* startMatch(..))")
  public void printMessageWhenSomethingGoesWrong() {
    System.out.println("Oops, couldn't start the tennis match. " +
        "Something went wrong!");
  }
}
```

After (Finally) Advice

After (finally) advice is always executed after a join point has been executed, but it can't get hold of the return value or any exception that is thrown. In other words, this advice type can't determine the outcome of the execution of the join point. It's typically used to clean up resources, such as to clean up objects that may still be attached to the current thread.

Listing 4-9 shows MessagePrintingAspect with after (finally) advice that prints a message to bring closure to the tennis match-starting event.

Listing 4-9. *Printing a Message When a Tennis Match Start Has Been Attempted*

```
package com.apress.springbook.chapter04.aspects;

import org.aspectj.lang.annotation.Aspect;
import org.aspectj.lang.annotation.After;

@Aspect
public class MessagePrintingAspect {
  @After("execution(* startMatch(..))")
  public void printMessageToConcludeTheTennisMatchStartAttempt() {
    System.out.println("A tennis match start attempt has taken place. " +
        "We haven't been informed about the outcome but we sincerely " +
        "hope everything worked out OK and wish you very nice day!");
  }
}
```

Around Advice

Around advice is the most complicated type to use because it hasn't been specifically designed for any particular tasks. Instead, it's based on an interception model that allows you to take full control over the join point execution.

Its semantics are the same as those of MethodInterceptor, which was discussed in the previous chapter. As is the case with MethodInterceptor, this advice needs to able to proceed with the ongoing method execution. For this purpose, every around advice method *must* have a ProceedingJoinPoint declared as its first argument, as shown in Listing 4-10.

Listing 4-10. *Passing on Our Regards and Then Getting on with Things*

```
package com.apress.springbook.chapter04.aspects;

import org.aspectj.lang.annotation.Aspect;
import org.aspectj.lang.annotation.Around;

import org.aspectj.lang.ProceedingJoinPoint;

@Aspect
public class MessagePrintingAspect {
  @Around("execution(* startMatch(..))")
  public Object printMessageToTellHowNiceTheLifeOfAnAdviceIs(
          ProceedingJoinPoint pjp) throws Throwable {

    System.out.println("Greetings, Master, how are you today? I'm " 
          "very glad you're passing by today and hope you'll enjoy " +
          "your visit!");

    try {
      return pjp.proceed();
    } finally {
      System.out.println("Au revoir, Master, I'm sorry you can't stay " +
          "longer, but I'm sure you'll pay me a visit again. Have a very " +
          "nice day yourself, sir!");
    }
  }
}
```

The example of around advice in Listing 4-10 looks different from the previous examples. The first thing to notice is the advice method signature. Three things are special about this signature:

- The return type is java.lang.Object; the other advice types have return type void.

- The first argument is of type org.aspectj.lang.ProceedingJoinPoint.

- The method declares java.lang.Throwable in its throws clause.

Another interesting thing to notice in Listing 4-10 is the call to the proceed() method on the ProceedingJoinPoint object. The entire advice method is actually very comparable to the invoke() method on MethodInterceptor used by classic Spring AOP:

```
package org.aopalliance.intercept;

public interface MethodInterceptor extends Interceptor {
  Object invoke(MethodInvocation invocation) throws Throwable;
}
```

If you're familiar with how the MethodInceptor and its MethodInvocation object work, you'll find around advice and ProceedingJoinPoint very easy to use.

Pointcut Declaration and Reuse

You can also declare named pointcuts in @AspectJ-style aspects. These pointcuts are a great way to reuse pointcut declarations throughout your aspects.

Listing 4-11 shows an example of an aspect with a named pointcut declaration.

Listing 4-11. *An Aspect That Declares Systemwide Pointcuts*

```
package com.apress.springbook.chapter04.aspects;

import org.aspectj.lang.annotation.Aspect;
import org.aspectj.lang.annotation.Pointcut;

@Aspect
public class SystemPointcutsAspect {
  @Pointcut("within(com.apress.springbook.chapter04.service..*)")
  public void inServiceLayer() {}
}
```

The inServiceLayer pointcut selects all join points in the com.apress.springbook.chapter04. service package, meaning all public and protected methods of all classes in this package and its subpackages. within() is a *pointcut designator*, which we'll discuss in the "Working with Pointcuts" section later in this chapter.

The inServiceLayer() method is a pointcut declaration, but also a regular Java method. However, Spring AOP will never execute this method; instead, it will read its @Pointcut annotation. So it's not useful to add any implementation to the method body, and it's not even useful to call this method yourself, *because* it's a pointcut declaration. We recommend that methods with the @Pointcut annotation always have an empty method body. It's the name of the method that's important here.

We can now reuse the inServiceLayer pointcut in other aspects, as shown in Listing 4-12 (if you do this, remember to configure both aspects).

Listing 4-12. *Reusing the inServiceLayer Pointcut in Another Aspect*

```
package com.apress.springbook.chapter04.aspects;

import org.aspectj.lang.annotation.Aspect;
import org.aspectj.lang.annotation.Before;

@Aspect
public class SecurityAspect {
  @Before("com.apress.springbook.chapter04.aspects." +
          "SystemPointcutsAspect.inServiceLayer()")
  public void denyAccessToAll() {
    throw new IllegalStateException("This system has been compromised. " +
          "Access is denied to all!");
  }
}
```

Pointcut reuse provides you with a powerful tool to select join points in one place and reuse these declarations anywhere. In Listing 4-11, we've defined the pointcut that selects the service layer of our application. In Listing 4-12, we decide to deny access to the system for all, since there's an unresolved security issue.

We can add more behaviors to the service layer by reusing the same pointcut in other aspects. Reusing pointcut declarations will make your applications easier to maintain.

Auto-Proxy Creation in the Spring Container

We've already covered how to use `AnnotationAwareAspectJAutoProxyCreator` in the Spring container to enable auto-proxy creation, which is a requirement to use @AspectJ-style aspects with Spring AOP. In this section, we'll discuss another way of enabling auto-proxy creation. We'll also explain how Spring AOP 2.0 decides which proxy types to use, and we'll shed some more light on how Spring AOP decides to create proxy objects for beans.

Auto-Proxy Creation with the AOP XML Schema

The other way of enabling auto-proxy creation is to use the Spring AOP XML Schema and its `<aop:aspectj-autoproxy>` tag. Listing 4-13 shows a Spring XML configuration file that uses the AOP XML Schema and the `aop` namespace.

Listing 4-13. *Using Spring's AOP XML Schema to Enable @AspectJ-Style Aspects in the Spring Container*

```
<?xml version="1.0" encoding="UTF-8"?>
<beans xmlns="http://www.springframework.org/schema/beans"
       xmlns:xsi="http://www.w3.org/2001/XMLSchema-instance"
       xmlns:aop="http://www.springframework.org/schema/aop"
       xsi:schemaLocation="http://www.springframework.org/schema/beans
                    http://www.springframework.org/schema/beans/spring-beans.xsd
                    http://www.springframework.org/schema/aop
                    http://www.springframework.org/schema/aop/spring-aop.xsd">

    <aop:aspectj-autoproxy/>

</beans>
```

Using the `<aop:aspectj-autoproxy>` XML tag has an advantage: if you accidentally define this tag more than once in your Spring configuration, no harm is done. If you configure the `AnnotationAwareAspectJAutoProxyCreator` more than once in your configuration, auto-proxy creation will occur twice for each bean—something you want to avoid. Otherwise, both approaches have exactly the same effect: auto-proxy creation is enabled for the entire Spring container.

Proxy Type Selection

The proxy type selection strategy in Spring AOP 2.0 has changed slightly from the previous version of Spring AOP. Since version 2.0, JDK proxy objects will be created for target objects that implement at least one interface. For target objects that implement no interfaces, CGLIB proxy objects will be created.

You can force the creation of CGLIB proxies for all target classes by setting the `proxy-target-class` option to `true`:

```
<aop:aspectj-autoproxy proxy-target-class="true"/>
```

Forcing the use of CGLIB proxy objects is required when at least one object for which a proxy object is created in the Spring container implements one or more interfaces, but is used as the class type by its callers. In this case, a JDK proxy object that implements only the interfaces would not be type-compatible for certain callers. Proxy objects created by CGLIB remain type-compatible with the target object.

In all other cases, you can safely leave the `proxy-target-class` option disabled.

The Proxying Process

In the example in Listing 4-5, we configured three beans to be loaded by the Spring container. A proxy object was created for only one of them. Let's review the role of each bean definition in Listing 4-5:

`AnnotationAwareAspectJAutoProxyCreator`: This class is responsible for auto-proxy creation. There's no need to create a proxy object for this bean, since it's not called by the application itself. Instead, it will enhance the bean life cycle for all other beans in the container.

`MessagePrintingAspect`: This is a regular Java class *and* an @AspectJ-style aspect. No proxy object is created for this bean, since it's also not called by the application. Instead, it embeds advices and pointcuts that will determine for which other beans in the container proxy objects will be created.

`DefaultTournamentMatchManager`: This class is part of the application logic. What's more, it has a join point that is matched by the pointcut in the `MessagePrintingAspect`: its `startMatch()` method. Because at least one join point is matched, a proxy object will be created and will replace the original bean in the container during the bean life cycle. So once the bean life cycle has been completed successfully for the `tournamentMatchManager` bean, the container will return a proxy object with advice and its target object.

So let's wrap up the rules for auto-proxy creation in the Spring container based on the example:

- Beans that implement the `org.springframework.beans.factory.BeanPostProcessor` or `org.springframework.beans.factory.BeanFactoryPostProcessor` interfaces will never be proxied. `AnnotationAwareAspectJAutoProxyCreator` implements the `BeanPostProcessor` interface, which allows it to enhance the bean life cycle for beans created by the Spring container.

- @AspectJ-style aspects, beans that implement the `org.springframework.aop.Advisor` or `org.springframework.aop.Pointcut` interfaces, and beans that implement any of the classic Spring AOP advice-type interfaces discussed in the previous chapter are excluded from auto-proxy creation because they have infrastructural roles.

- All other beans that are created by the Spring container are eligible for auto-proxy creation. During the life cycle of each bean created by the Spring container—both singleton and prototype beans—the container will ask all aspects and advisors found in the container if one or more of the bean join points are matched by one of their pointcuts. If there is at least one match, a proxy object will be created for the bean and will replace that bean. The proxy object will have all the advice embedded for all join points that were matched.

To fully understand the last rule, you need to know how join points will be matched by any given pointcut. If you look back at the example and its pointcut in Listing 4-3, it's obvious that only methods named `startMatch()` will be matched. Later in this chapter, in the "Working with Pointcuts" section, we'll discuss other pointcuts that select join points in specific ways.

Advice and Aspect Ordering

Advice declared in aspects is automatically selected and added to a proxy object during auto-proxy creation. It is entirely possible that two advices apply to the same join point. Consider the `MessagePrintingAspect` @AspectJ-style aspect shown in Listing 4-14.

Listing 4-14. *Two Advices Will Be Executed for the Same Join Points*

```
package com.apress.springbook.chapter04.aspects;

import org.aspectj.lang.annotation.Aspect;
import org.aspectj.lang.annotation.Pointcut;
import org.aspectj.lang.annotation.Before;

@Aspect
public class MessagePrintingAspect {
  @Pointcut("execution(* startMatch(..))")
  public void atMatchStart() {}

  @Before("atMatchStart()")
  public void printHowAnnoyedWeAre() {
    System.out.println("Leave it out! Another tennis match!?");
  }

  @Before("atMatchStart()")
  public void printHowExcitedWeAre() {
    System.out.println("Hurray for another tennis match!");
  }
}
```

The aspect in Listing 4-14 declares two advices that will be executed for the same join points. This may leave you wondering in what order they will be executed,

In this example, the actual order is not very important, but in other scenarios, it may be important to understand the exact order. And what would the order be if these two advices were defined in different aspects?

Ordering Advice

In those cases where advices are declared in the same aspect and they are both executed for the same join point, Spring AOP uses the same order as AspectJ: the order of declaration. So, advices in the same aspect that are executed for the same join point will maintain their order of declaration. For the aspect in Listing 4-14, consider the Spring configuration in Listing 4-15.

Listing 4-15. *Configuring DefaultTournamentMatchManager with Two Advices Declared in the Same Aspect*

```
<beans>
  <bean class="org.springframework.aop.aspectj.annotation. ➡
AnnotationAwareAspectJAutoProxyCreator"/>

  <bean class="com.apress.springbook.chapter04.aspects.MessagePrintingAspect"/>

  <bean id="tournamentMatchManager"
        class="com.apress.springbook.chapter04.DefaultTournamentMatchManager">
    <!-- properties omitted -->
  </bean>
</beans>
```

When the startMatch() method on the tournamentMatchManager bean is executed, the following messages are printed on the console:

```
Leave it out! Another tennis match!?
Hurray for another tennis match!
```

So, the two aspects are executed in the order in which they are declared.

Ordering Aspects

When two advices that are declared in *different* aspects are executed for the same join point, the order is determined by the `org.springframework.core.Ordered` interface, as shown in Listing 4-16.

Listing 4-16. *Spring's Ordered Interface*

```
package org.springframework.core;

public interface Ordered {
  int getOrder();
}
```

The Spring Framework uses the `Ordered` interface whenever a list of object needs to be processed in a particular order. By implementing the `Ordered` interface aspects, you can place your advices in a specific spot in the order of advice execution for join points. The ordering rules for aspects are as follows:

- Aspects that don't implement the `Ordered` interface are in an undetermined order and come after the aspects that do implement the interface.

- Aspects that implement the `Ordered` interface are ordered according to the return value of the `getOrder()` method. The lowest values get the first position.

- Two or more aspects that have the same return value for the `getOrder()` method are in an undetermined order.

To demonstrate how the ordering of aspects works, we first create a common pointcut, as shown in Listing 4-17.

Listing 4-17. *A Common Pointcut*

```
package com.apress.springbook.chapter04.aspects;

import org.aspectj.lang.annotation.Aspect;
import org.aspectj.lang.annotation.Pointcut;

@Aspect
public class TennisMatchEventsAspect {
  @Pointcut("execution(* startMatch(..))")
  public void atMatchStart() {}
}
```

Next, we'll declare two advices in separate aspects, as shown in Listings 4-18 and 4-19.

Listing 4-18. *Aspect That Implements Spring's Ordered Interface*

```
package com.apress.springbook.chapter04.aspects;

import org.aspectj.lang.annotation.Aspect;
import org.aspectj.lang.annotation.Before;
```

```
import org.springframework.core.Ordered;

@Aspect
public class HappyMessagePrintingAspect implements Ordered {
  private int order = Integer.MAX_VALUE;

  public int getOrder() { return this.order; }

  public void setOrder(int order) { this.order = order; }

  @Before("com.apress.springbook.chapter04.aspects." +
          "TennisMatchEventsAspect.atMatchStart()")
  public void printHowExcitedWeAre() {
    System.out.println("Hurray for another tennis match!");
  }
}
```

Listing 4-19. *Aspect That Doesn't Implement the Ordered Interface*

```
package com.apress.springbook.chapter04.aspects;

import org.aspectj.lang.annotation.Aspect;
import org.aspectj.lang.annotation.Before;

@Aspect
public class AnnoyedMessagePrintingAspect {
  @Before("com.apress.springbook.chapter04.aspects." +
          "TennisMatchEventsAspect.atMatchStart()")
  public void printHowAnnoyedWeAre() {
    System.out.println("Leave it out! Another tennis match!?");
  }
}
```

Next, we load these two aspects in the Spring container, as shown in Listing 4-20.

Listing 4-20. *Configuring the Two Aspects for Loading by the Spring Container*

```
<beans>
  <bean class="org.springframework.aop.aspectj.annotation. ➥
AnnotationAwareAspectJAutoProxyCreator"/>

  <bean class="com.apress.springbook.chapter04.aspects.HappyMessagePrintingAspect"/>

  <bean class="com.apress.springbook.chapter04.aspects. ➥
AnnoyedMessagePrintingAspect"/>

  <bean id="tournamentMatchManager"
        class="com.apress.springbook.chapter04.DefaultTournamentMatchManager">
    <!-- properties omitted -->
  </bean>
</beans>
```

When we call the startMatch() method on the tournamentMatchManager bean, the following messages will be printed to the console:

```
Hurray for another tennis match!
Leave it out! Another tennis match!?
```

We get this order of messages because the `HappyMessagePrintingAspect` implements the `Ordered` interface and the `AnnoyedMessagePrintingAspect` doesn't.

Because we have implemented the `setOrder()` method in `HappyMessagePrintingAspect`, we can change the order value via the bean definition, as follows:

```
<bean class="com.apress.springbook.chapter04.aspects.HappyMessagePrintingAspect"/>
  <property name="order" value="20"/>
</bean>
```

Although we can control the order of aspects and thus their advices, the order of declaration for advices within individual aspects remains.

So far, we've discussed only @AspectJ-style aspects in this chapter, but there is an alternative, which we'll cover next.

Using AOP XML Tags

The Spring developers have come up with a way to define aspects in XML by creating an AOP XML Schema for the Spring 2.0 custom XML Schema support. It allows you to turn any public instance methods on beans created by the Spring container into advice methods. These methods are comparable to the methods annotated with @Aspect in @AspectJ-style aspects.

@AspectJ-style aspects use Java 5 annotations, so they are not an option when Java 5 is not used in the production environment (many organizations still use Java 1.4). Also, you may want to use methods on existing classes as advice methods.

This section explains how to create aspects in XML, which solves these problems. We will also show how you can replace the pointcut classes covered in the previous chapter with the AspectJ pointcuts discussed in this chapter.

As you will notice, XML aspects and advice declarations are straightforward to understand and work with when you're familiar with @AspectJ-style aspects. You may also notice that with XML declarations, the advice type and pointcut are separated from the advice method (which some see as a disadvantage because it splits a unit of functionality). For this reason, we recommend that you to write aspects with the @AspectJ-style when possible.

AOP Configuration Tags

The first step to using the AOP XML tags for declaring aspects, pointcuts, and advisors is to create a Spring XML file, as shown in Listing 4-21.

Listing 4-21. *A Spring XML Configuration File Based on Spring 2.0 XML Schemas*

```
<?xml version="1.0" encoding="UTF-8"?>
<beans xmlns="http://www.springframework.org/schema/beans"
       xmlns:xsi="http://www.w3.org/2001/XMLSchema-instance"
       xmlns:aop="http://www.springframework.org/schema/aop"
       xsi:schemaLocation="http://www.springframework.org/schema/beans
               http://www.springframework.org/schema/beans/spring-beans.xsd
               http://www.springframework.org/schema/aop
               http://www.springframework.org/schema/aop/spring-aop.xsd">

</beans>
```

You can load this file, together with other, classic, Spring XML configuration files, into the Spring container. To declare aspects and advisors in XML, add the `<aop:config>` tag to the XML file, as shown in Listing 4-22.

Listing 4-22. *Creating an AOP Configuration Unit in XML with the aop:config Tag*

```
<?xml version="1.0" encoding="UTF-8"?>
<beans xmlns="http://www.springframework.org/schema/beans"
       xmlns:xsi="http://www.w3.org/2001/XMLSchema-instance"
       xmlns:aop="http://www.springframework.org/schema/aop"
       xsi:schemaLocation="http://www.springframework.org/schema/beans
               http://www.springframework.org/schema/beans/spring-beans.xsd
               http://www.springframework.org/schema/aop
               http://www.springframework.org/schema/aop/spring-aop.xsd">

    <aop:config>

    </aop:config>

</beans>
```

You can declare multiple `<aop:config>` tags in one or multiple XML files. The `<aop:config>` tag can contain zero or more of the following tags:

- `<aop:aspect>`: Allows you to create aspects in XML that are comparable to @AspectJ-style aspects.

- `<aop:advisor>`: Allows you to create an advisor object with an AspectJ pointcut and a classic Spring AOP advice object.

- `<aop:pointcut>`: Allows you to declare and reuse pointcuts in XML aspects.

We'll cover these tags in more detail as we work through our next example. Now we'll re-create the @AspectJ-style aspect from Listing 4-3 in XML.

XML Aspect Configuration

The @AspectJ-style concepts we've discussed in the chapter also apply to aspects declared in XML. The only difference is the use of XML instead of annotations.

The first step for creating an aspect with XML is to add the `<aop:aspect>` tag to `<aop:config>`, as shown in Listing 4-23.

Listing 4-23. *xml-aspect-context.xml: Creating an Empty XML Aspect*

```
<?xml version="1.0" encoding="UTF-8"?>
<beans xmlns="http://www.springframework.org/schema/beans"
       xmlns:xsi="http://www.w3.org/2001/XMLSchema-instance"
       xmlns:aop="http://www.springframework.org/schema/aop"
       xsi:schemaLocation="http://www.springframework.org/schema/beans
               http://www.springframework.org/schema/beans/spring-beans.xsd
               http://www.springframework.org/schema/aop
               http://www.springframework.org/schema/aop/spring-aop.xsd">

    <aop:config>
      <aop:aspect ref="messagePrinter">

      </aop:aspect>
    </aop:config>

    <bean id="messagePrinter"
          class="com.apress.springbook.chapter04.MessagePrinter"/>
```

```
<bean id="tournamentMatchManager"
      class="com.apress.springbook.chapter04.DefaultTournamentMatchManager">
   <!-- properties omitted -->
</bean>
</beans>
```

The `<aop:aspect>` tag takes a `ref` attribute that holds the name of a bean definition (`messagePrinter`). Listing 4-24 shows the `MessagePrinter` class.

Listing 4-24. *The MessagePrinter Class*

```java
package com.apress.springbook.chapter04;

public class MessagePrinter {
  public void printMessageToInformMatchStarts() {
    System.out.println("Attempting to start tennis match!");
  }
}
```

The `MessagePrinter` class is comparable to the `MessagePrintingAspect` in Listing 4-3, but without the @AspectJ-style annotations. So `MessagePrinter` is a regular Java class and not an aspect declaration.

But we've configured `MessagePrinter` in a bean definition in Listing 4-23, *and* we've let the `<aop:aspect>` tag refer to the `messagePrinter` bean definition. This configuration declares the `messagePrinter` *bean* as an aspect, not the `MessagePrinter` class. We've also added the `tournamentMatchManager` bean to the configuration in Listing 4-23.

So far, this aspect configuration won't do anything out of the ordinary. However, we can add more configuration to the `<aop:aspect>` tag to turn the `printMessageToInformMatchStarts()` method on the `messagePrinter` *bean* into an advice method, as shown in Listing 4-25.

Listing 4-25. *xml-aspect-context.xml: Turning the printMessageToInformMatchStarts() Method on the messagePrinter Bean into an Advice Method*

```xml
<?xml version="1.0" encoding="UTF-8"?>
<beans xmlns="http://www.springframework.org/schema/beans"
       xmlns:xsi="http://www.w3.org/2001/XMLSchema-instance"
       xmlns:aop="http://www.springframework.org/schema/aop"
       xsi:schemaLocation="http://www.springframework.org/schema/beans
              http://www.springframework.org/schema/beans/spring-beans.xsd
              http://www.springframework.org/schema/aop
              http://www.springframework.org/schema/aop/spring-aop.xsd">

  <aop:config>
    <aop:aspect ref="messagePrinter">
      <aop:before method="printMessageToInformMatchStarts"
                  pointcut="execution(* startMatch(..))"/>
    </aop:aspect>
  </aop:config>

  <bean id="messagePrinter"
        class="com.apress.springbook.chapter04.MessagePrinter"/>

  <bean id="tournamentMatchManager"
        class="com.apress.springbook.chapter04.DefaultTournamentMatchManager">
    <!-- properties omitted -->
  </bean>
</beans>
```

That's it—we've created the XML aspect. The `<aop:before>` tag declares that the `printMessageToInformMatchStarts()` method on the `messagePrinter` bean becomes before advice and also declares the pointcut.

Let's run through the configuration in Listing 4-25 to look at all elements and their roles.

- The `<aop:config>` tag activates auto-proxy creation in the Spring container. It also holds the configuration for one or more XML aspect, pointcut, or advisor declarations.

- The `<aop:aspect>` tag refers to the `messagePrinter` *bean* and declares that *bean* as an aspect. This bean itself is not touched or affected in any way. In fact, the `messagePrinter` bean is not aware that it's being declared as an aspect. This tag by itself won't trigger the creation of proxy objects during auto-proxy creation. The tag only declares an aspect that can hold zero or more pointcut and advice/pointcut declarations in XML.

- The `<aop:before>` tag is an advice/pointcut declaration that will execute the `printMessageToInformMatchStarts()` method on the `messagePrinter` bean for the execution of all join points that are matched by the pointcut.

- The `messagePrinter` bean is an ordinary bean created and configured based on an ordinary bean definition by the Spring container. It is not aware of Spring AOP, advice, auto-proxy creation, or pointcuts. In fact, you can get this bean and execute its methods, and you'll find they will respond as expected.

- The `tournamentMatchManager` bean is affected by auto-proxy creation during its bean life cycle since it has one join point—the `startMatch()` method—that is matched by the pointcut in the XML aspect declaration. When its `startMatch()` method is executed, the `printMessageToInformMatchStarts()` method on the `messagePrinter` bean will be executed first.

Next, we'll load `xml-aspect-context.xml` into a test case to verify the `tournamentMatchManager` bean is proxied correctly. The test case in Listing 4-26 shows `MessagePrintingXmlAspectIntegration Tests`, which extends `MessagePrintingAspectIntegrationTests` from Listing 4-6.

Listing 4-26. *Test Case to Verify the XML Aspect Works As Expected*

```
package com.apress.springbook.chapter04;

public class MessagePrintingXmlAspectIntegrationTests extends
    MessagePrintingAspectIntegrationTests {

  protected String[] getConfigLocations() {
    return new String[] {
      "classpath:com/apress/springbook/chapter04/" +
        "xml-aspect-context.xml"
    };
  }
}
```

The test case in Listing 4-26 runs the test methods declared in Listing 4-6 and overwrites the `getConfigLocations()` method to load the Spring XML file in Listing 4-25. The following messages shown are printed to the console when the test runs:

```
=== GOING TO CALL METHOD ON BEAN FROM CONTAINER ===
Attempting to start tennis match!
=== FINISHED CALLING METHOD ON BEAN FROM CONTAINER ===
=== GOING TO CALL METHOD ON NEWLY CREATED OBJECT ===
=== FINISHED CALLING METHOD ON NEWLY CREATED OBJECT ===
```

Pointcut Declaration and Reuse with XML

You can declare and reuse pointcuts in the AOP XML configuration, and you can reuse pointcuts declared in @AspectJ-style aspects. Listing 4-27 reuses the pointcut declared in the SystemPointcutsAspect (Listing 4-11). The SecurityEnforcer class is the same as the SecurityAspect class, but has been stripped of its aspect status.

Listing 4-27. *Reusing a Pointcut Declared in an @AspectJ-Style Aspect*

```
<?xml version="1.0" encoding="UTF-8"?>
<beans xmlns="http://www.springframework.org/schema/beans"
       xmlns:xsi="http://www.w3.org/2001/XMLSchema-instance"
       xmlns:aop="http://www.springframework.org/schema/aop"
       xsi:schemaLocation="http://www.springframework.org/schema/beans
                http://www.springframework.org/schema/beans/spring-beans.xsd
                http://www.springframework.org/schema/aop
                http://www.springframework.org/schema/aop/spring-aop.xsd">

   <aop:config>
     <aop:aspect ref="securityEnforcer">
       <aop:before method="denyAccessToAll"
                 pointcut="com.apress.springbook.chapter04.aspects. ➥
SystemPointcutsAspect.inServiceLayer()"/>
     </aop:aspect>
   </aop:config>

   <bean id="securityEnforcer"
         class="com.apress.springbook.chapter04.SecurityEnforcer"/>
</beans>
```

You can also declare pointcuts in XML, and you can declare them in two places. The first option is shown in Listing 4-28, which declares a pointcut inside the <aop:aspect> tag. This pointcut can be reused only inside this aspect.

Listing 4-28. *Declaring and Reusing a Pointcut in an XML Aspect*

```
<?xml version="1.0" encoding="UTF-8"?>
<beans xmlns="http://www.springframework.org/schema/beans"
       xmlns:xsi="http://www.w3.org/2001/XMLSchema-instance"
       xmlns:aop="http://www.springframework.org/schema/aop"
       xsi:schemaLocation="http://www.springframework.org/schema/beans
                http://www.springframework.org/schema/beans/spring-beans.xsd
                http://www.springframework.org/schema/aop
                http://www.springframework.org/schema/aop/spring-aop.xsd">

   <aop:config>
     <aop:aspect ref="securityEnforcer">
       <aop:pointcut id="inServiceLayer"
                   expression="within(com.apress.springbook.chapter04..*)"/>
       <aop:before method="denyAccessToAll"
                 pointcut-ref="inServiceLayer"/>
     </aop:aspect>
   </aop:config>

   <bean id="securityEnforcer"
         class="com.apress.springbook.chapter04.SecurityEnforcer"/>
</beans>
```

The `<aop:pointcut>` tag declares a pointcut and takes a name (id) and pointcut expression (expression). This pointcut is then reused by the `<aop:before>` tag (pointcut-ref).

Listing 4-29 shows a pointcut that is declared inside the `<aop:config>` tag. This pointcut can be reused inside `<aop:aspect>` tags in this and other Spring XML files.

Listing 4-29. *Declaring a Pointcut Outside an Aspect and Reusing It Inside an XML Aspect*

```
<?xml version="1.0" encoding="UTF-8"?>
<beans xmlns="http://www.springframework.org/schema/beans"
       xmlns:xsi="http://www.w3.org/2001/XMLSchema-instance"
       xmlns:aop="http://www.springframework.org/schema/aop"
       xsi:schemaLocation="http://www.springframework.org/schema/beans
                http://www.springframework.org/schema/beans/spring-beans.xsd
                http://www.springframework.org/schema/aop
                http://www.springframework.org/schema/aop/spring-aop.xsd">

  <aop:config>
    <aop:pointcut id="inServiceLayer"
                  expression="within(com.apress.springbook.chapter04..*)"/>
    <aop:aspect ref="securityEnforcer">
      <aop:before method="denyAccessToAll"
                  pointcut-ref="inServiceLayer"/>
    </aop:aspect>
  </aop:config>

  <bean id="securityEnforcer"
        class="com.apress.springbook.chapter04.SecurityEnforcer"/>
</beans>
```

Pointcuts declared in XML have certain limitations, in that they cannot be reused in @AspectJ-style aspects. Also, they cannot take dynamic pointcut designators such as args() and @annotation() (pointcut designators are discussed in the "Working with Pointcuts" section later in this chapter). The reason has to do with the fact that pointcut declarations are not coupled to a method, as they are in @AspectJ-style aspects.

Advice Declaration in XML

The aspects that are declared in XML support the same advice types as @AspectJ-style aspects with exactly the same semantics. As explained in the previous section, advice declarations in XML use regular Java methods on an object as advice methods.

Now we'll look at how to declare each of the different advice types in XML. Later, in the "Binding Advice Arguments" section, we'll rewrite the aspects we've used to explain how to bind advice arguments on @AspectJ-style advice methods and show the equivalent XML, so that you can easily compare the two.

Listing 4-30 shows an example for a before advice XML declaration.

Listing 4-30. *Before Advice Declaration in XML*

```
<?xml version="1.0" encoding="UTF-8"?>
<beans xmlns="http://www.springframework.org/schema/beans"
       xmlns:xsi="http://www.w3.org/2001/XMLSchema-instance"
       xmlns:aop="http://www.springframework.org/schema/aop"
       xsi:schemaLocation="http://www.springframework.org/schema/beans
                http://www.springframework.org/schema/beans/spring-beans.xsd
                http://www.springframework.org/schema/aop
                http://www.springframework.org/schema/aop/spring-aop.xsd">
```

```
<aop:config>
  <aop:aspect ref="messagePrinter">
    <aop:before method="printMessageToInformMatchStarts"
               pointcut="execution(* startMatch(..))"/>
  </aop:aspect>
</aop:config>

<bean id="messagePrinter"
      class="com.apress.springbook.chapter04.MessagePrinter"/>

<bean id="tournamentMatchManager"
      class="com.apress.springbook.chapter04.DefaultTournamentMatchManager">
  <!-- properties omitted -->
</bean>
</beans>
```

Listing 4-31 shows an example of using after returning advice.

Listing 4-31. *After Returning Advice Declared in XML*

```
<?xml version="1.0" encoding="UTF-8"?>
<beans xmlns="http://www.springframework.org/schema/beans"
       xmlns:xsi="http://www.w3.org/2001/XMLSchema-instance"
       xmlns:aop="http://www.springframework.org/schema/aop"
       xsi:schemaLocation="http://www.springframework.org/schema/beans
               http://www.springframework.org/schema/beans/spring-beans.xsd
               http://www.springframework.org/schema/aop
               http://www.springframework.org/schema/aop/spring-aop.xsd">

<aop:config>
  <aop:aspect ref="messagePrinter">
    <aop:after-returning method="printMessageToInformMatchHasStarted"
                         pointcut="execution(* startMatch(..))"/>
  </aop:aspect>
</aop:config>

<bean id="messagePrinter"
      class="com.apress.springbook.chapter04.MessagePrinter"/>

<bean id="tournamentMatchManager"
      class="com.apress.springbook.chapter04.DefaultTournamentMatchManager">
  <!-- properties omsitted -->
</bean>
</beans>
```

Declaring after throwing advice in XML is equally straightforward, as shown in Listing 4-32.

Listing 4-32. *After Throwing Advice Declared in XML*

```
<?xml version="1.0" encoding="UTF-8"?>
<beans xmlns="http://www.springframework.org/schema/beans"
       xmlns:xsi="http://www.w3.org/2001/XMLSchema-instance"
       xmlns:aop="http://www.springframework.org/schema/aop"
       xsi:schemaLocation="http://www.springframework.org/schema/beans
               http://www.springframework.org/schema/beans/spring-beans.xsd
               http://www.springframework.org/schema/aop
               http://www.springframework.org/schema/aop/spring-aop.xsd">
```

```
  <aop:config>
    <aop:aspect ref="messagePrinter">
      <aop:after-throwing method="printMessageWhenMatchIdentifierIsNotFound"
                          pointcut="execution(* startMatch(..) throws ➡
com.apress.springbook.chapter04.UnknownMatchException)"/>
    </aop:aspect>
  </aop:config>

  <bean id="messagePrinter"
        class="com.apress.springbook.chapter04.MessagePrinter"/>

  <bean id="tournamentMatchManager"
        class="com.apress.springbook.chapter04.DefaultTournamentMatchManager">
    <!-- properties omitted -->
  </bean>
</beans>
```

In the after (finally) advice example shown in Listing 4-33, we again use a pointcut to match the startMatch() method.

Listing 4-33. *After (Finally) Advice Declared in XML*

```
<?xml version="1.0" encoding="UTF-8"?>
<beans xmlns="http://www.springframework.org/schema/beans"
       xmlns:xsi="http://www.w3.org/2001/XMLSchema-instance"
       xmlns:aop="http://www.springframework.org/schema/aop"
       xsi:schemaLocation="http://www.springframework.org/schema/beans
                http://www.springframework.org/schema/beans/spring-beans.xsd
                http://www.springframework.org/schema/aop
                http://www.springframework.org/schema/aop/spring-aop.xsd">

  <aop:config>
    <aop:aspect ref="messagePrinter">
      <aop:after method="printMessageWhenStartMatchAttemptIsOver"
                 pointcut="execution(* startMatch(..))"/>
    </aop:aspect>
  </aop:config>

  <bean id="messagePrinter"
        class="com.apress.springbook.chapter04.MessagePrinter"/>

  <bean id="tournamentMatchManager"
        class="com.apress.springbook.chapter04.DefaultTournamentMatchManager">
    <!-- properties omitted -->
  </bean>
</beans>
```

The code in Listing 4-34 shows the printMessageWhenStartMatchAttemptIsOver() method on MessagePrinter.

Listing 4-34. *The printMessageWhenStartMatchAttemptIsOver() Method on MessagePrinter*

```
package com.apress.springbook.chapter04;

public class MessagePrinter {
  public void printMessageWhenStartMatchAttemptIsOver() {
    System.out.println("Tried to start a match and this attempt is now over!");  }
}
```

Again, there are no surprises since the after (finally) advice XML declaration is very similar to the @AspectJ-style declaration we've discussed previously.

And last, but not least, is the around advice as an XML declaration. As you may suspect, this advice type requires the declaration of a `ProceedingJoinPoint` argument in the advice method. This binds the `MessagePrinter` class to the AspectJ API. Listing 4-35 shows an around advice declaration in XML.

Listing 4-35. *Around Advice Declared in XML*

```xml
<?xml version="1.0" encoding="UTF-8"?>
<beans xmlns="http://www.springframework.org/schema/beans"
       xmlns:xsi="http://www.w3.org/2001/XMLSchema-instance"
       xmlns:aop="http://www.springframework.org/schema/aop"
       xsi:schemaLocation="http://www.springframework.org/schema/beans
                  http://www.springframework.org/schema/beans/spring-beans.xsd
                  http://www.springframework.org/schema/aop
                  http://www.springframework.org/schema/aop/spring-aop.xsd">

  <aop:config>
    <aop:aspect ref="messagePrinter">
      <aop:around method="controlStartMatchMethodExecution"
                  pointcut="execution(* startMatch(..))"/>
    </aop:aspect>
  </aop:config>

  <bean id="messagePrinter"
        class="com.apress.springbook.chapter04.MessagePrinter"/>

  <bean id="tournamentMatchManager"
        class="com.apress.springbook.chapter04.DefaultTournamentMatchManager">
    <!-- properties omitted -->
  </bean>
</beans>
```

Listing 4-36 shows the `controlStartMatchMethodExecution()` method on `MessagePrinter`.

Listing 4-36. *The controlStartMatchMethodExecution() Method on MessagePrinter*

```java
package com.apress.springbook.chapter04;

import org.aspectj.lang.ProceedingJoinPoint;

public class MessagePrinter {
  public Object controlStartMatchMethodExecution(ProceedingJoinPoint pjp)
        throws Throwable {
    System.out.println("A match is about to be started!");

    try {
      Object result = pjp.proceed();
      System.out.println("The match has been started successfully!");
      return result;
    } catch (Throwable t) {
      System.out.println("Oops, something went wrong while starting the match.");
      throw t;
    }
  }
}
```

The `controlStartMatchMethodExecution()` method on `MessagePrinter` is a classic example of interception advice.

Advice Ordering in XML

Proxy objects for aspects declared in XML are also created via auto-proxy creation. Declaring the `<aop:config>` tag once will automatically configure the Spring container. As we've discussed previously in this chapter, auto-proxy creation means the order of advice is undetermined, and you may need control over the advice order. Ordering aspects declared in XML is very similar to ordering aspects declared in @AspectJ-style aspects:

- Advices declared in the same XML aspect that is executed on one join point are ordered according to their order of declaration in the XML file.

- If you want to control the order of advice declared in different XML aspects, you must implement the `org.springframework.core.Ordered` interface on the classes where advice methods are declared (like the `MessagePrinter` class in Listing 4-24).

By implementing the `Ordered` interface, you can also control the order between XML advice and @AspectJ-style advice on the same join point.

Advisors with AspectJ Pointcuts

In the previous chapter, you learned that an advisor holds an advice object and a pointcut object. When you add an advisor to the Spring container and configure auto-proxy creation, its pointcut can match join points on beans in the container; when it does, proxy objects will be created.

Consider the example in Listing 4-37. Note that you must define advisors before aspects.

Listing 4-37. *Configuring a PointcutAdvisor with the <aop:advisor> Tag*

```xml
<?xml version="1.0" encoding="UTF-8"?>
<beans xmlns="http://www.springframework.org/schema/beans"
       xmlns:xsi="http://www.w3.org/2001/XMLSchema-instance"
       xmlns:aop="http://www.springframework.org/schema/aop"
       xsi:schemaLocation="http://www.springframework.org/schema/beans
                http://www.springframework.org/schema/beans/spring-beans.xsd
                http://www.springframework.org/schema/aop
                http://www.springframework.org/schema/aop/spring-aop.xsd">

  <aop:config>
    <aop:advisor advice-ref="loggingAdvice" pointcut="execution(* startMatch(..))"/>
  </aop:config>

  <bean id="loggingAdvice"
        class="org.springframework.aop.interceptor.CustomizableTraceInterceptor">
    <property name="enterMessage"
              value="Entering $[methodName] on $[targetClassShortName]"/>
  </bean>

  <bean id="tournamentMatchManager"
        class="com.apress.springbook.chapter04.DefaultTournamentMatchManager">
    <!-- properties omitted -->
  </bean>
</beans>
```

Auto-proxy creation will create a proxy for the `tournamentMatchManager` bean, since its `startMatch()` method is matched by the advisor's pointcut.

The advisors take part in auto-proxy creation, which means their advice objects can be executed together with other advices on the same join point. To set the order of an advisor, you can configure the `order` attribute, as shown in Listing 4-38.

Listing 4-38. *Setting the Order of the Advice for This Advisor*

```xml
<?xml version="1.0" encoding="UTF-8"?>
<beans xmlns="http://www.springframework.org/schema/beans"
      xmlns:xsi="http://www.w3.org/2001/XMLSchema-instance"
      xmlns:aop="http://www.springframework.org/schema/aop"
      xsi:schemaLocation="http://www.springframework.org/schema/beans
              http://www.springframework.org/schema/beans/spring-beans.xsd
              http://www.springframework.org/schema/aop
              http://www.springframework.org/schema/aop/spring-aop.xsd">

  <aop:config>
    <aop:advisor advice-ref="loggingAdvice"
                 order="20"
                 pointcut="execution(* startMatch(..))"/>
  </aop:config>

  <bean id="loggingAdvice"
        class="org.springframework.aop.interceptor.CustomizableTraceInterceptor">
    <property name="enterMessage"
              value="Entering $[methodName] on $[targetClassNameShort]"/>
  </bean>

  <bean id="tournamentMatchManager"
        class="com.apress.springbook.chapter04.DefaultTournamentMatchManager">
    <!-- properties omitted -->
  </bean>
</beans>
```

Proxy Type Selection in XML

When working with aspect declarations in XML, you can choose between automatic proxy type detection—JDK or CGLIB proxy objects—or forced use of CGLIB proxy objects. You can toggle between these two modes by setting the `proxy-target-class` property to `true` on the `<aop:config>` XML tag, as shown in Listing 4-39.

Listing 4-39. *Forcing the Use of CGLIB Proxy Objects*

```xml
<?xml version="1.0" encoding="UTF-8"?>
<beans xmlns="http://www.springframework.org/schema/beans"
      xmlns:xsi="http://www.w3.org/2001/XMLSchema-instance"
      xmlns:aop="http://www.springframework.org/schema/aop"
      xsi:schemaLocation="http://www.springframework.org/schema/beans
              http://www.springframework.org/schema/beans/spring-beans.xsd
              http://www.springframework.org/schema/aop
              http://www.springframework.org/schema/aop/spring-aop.xsd">
```

```
<aop:config proxy-target-class="true">

</aop:config>
```

```
</beans>
```

Since you can add multiple `<aop:config>` tags to your configuration and toggle the `proxy-target-class` attribute value in each one, it may not be clear which proxy object creation mode is active. The rule for setting this mode is simple: when at least one `<aop:config>` tag sets the `proxy-target-class` value to true or `<aop:aspectj-autoproxy>` sets the value to `true`, Spring AOP will always create CGLIB proxy objects.

So, now that you've seen the two different ways to configure Spring AOP, let's look at pointcuts in more detail.

Working with Pointcuts

In this chapter, we've used the same simple pointcut in aspects over and over. The AspectJ pointcut language is extremely powerful and versatile in how it can select join points. Remember that Spring AOP supports only method executions as join points. While this is far less than what is supported by AspectJ, you can still do some pretty neat things with method executions alone. Specifically, point-cuts allow you to select methods based on a wide variety of criteria, and you can combine criteria with logical operators to narrow down the selection.

In Spring AOP, the goal of pointcuts is to select public or protected methods. Methods are declared in Java classes, but when selecting them, you often want to escape the narrow boundary of classes and generalize. Here are just some examples of what you may want to select:

- All methods of a specific class
- All methods of all classes in a specific package
- All methods of all classes in a specific package and its subpackages
- All methods with a specific annotation
- All methods of a class with a specific annotation
- All methods with a specific name
- All methods where the name contains a specific string
- All methods with specific argument types

To select methods, you can use these constructs in pointcut expressions:

- *Pointcut designators*: We've already used `execution()` and `within()`. Spring AOP supports more designators, as you'll see in the following examples. They narrow down the selection of the join points based on some property. Other constructs in this list are used in combination with these designators.

- *Boolean operators*: You can combine pointcut designators to narrow down the selection. The AND (&&) and OR (||) operators, as well as the NOT operator (!), are supported.

- *Class names*: Often, you need to specify class names, such as to narrow down the selection to a target type or a method argument type. These class names must always be fully qualified (including the full package name), even for classes in the `java.lang` package.

- *Visibility operators*: You can narrow the search to only `public` or `protected` methods.

- *Wildcards*: Frequently, you will want to use a wildcard operator. Supported wildcard operators are the asterisk (*) for any method or class name or any argument type and double dot (..) for zero or more arguments.

- *Method names*: These can be the full name, a partial match of the name, or a wildcard (any name).

- *Annotations*: You can select methods based on annotations, as discussed in the next sections.

Let's start with how to select methods directly.

Selecting Methods Directly

Most of the time, you want to select methods based on some of their parts, such as the name, return type, throws declaration, or arguments. When selecting based on method parts, you will use the execution() or args() pointcut designators or a combination of these designators.

Selecting on Method Names

The simplest way to select methods is by narrowing down the selection based on their names. Listing 4-40 shows a pointcut that selects all relax(), enjoy(), and chillOut() methods.

Listing 4-40. *Selecting Some Enjoyable Methods*

```
package com.apress.springbook.chapter04.aspects;

import org.aspectj.lang.annotation.Aspect;
import org.aspectj.lang.annotation.Pointcut;

@Aspect
public class SystemPointcutsAspect {
  @Pointcut("execution(* relax(..)) || execution(* enjoy(..)) || " +
         "execution(* chillOut(..))")
  public void goodTimes() {}
}
```

Each execution() pointcut designator in Listing 4-40 selects methods based on their names, regardless of all other properties.

You can also use wildcards in method names. Listing 4-41 shows a pointcut that selects all methods whose names start with do.

Listing 4-41. *Selecting All Methods Whose Names Start with do*

```
package com.apress.springbook.chapter04.aspects;

import org.aspectj.lang.annotation.Aspect;
import org.aspectj.lang.annotation.Pointcut;

@Aspect
public class SystemPointcutsAspect {
  @Pointcut("execution(* do*(..))")
  public void performAction() {}
}
```

Selecting methods on their names is one of the most basic pointcut criteria. They can be combined with other criteria to narrow the selection to make sure only the intended methods are selected.

One powerful way to narrow down the method selection is to also select on method arguments.

Selecting on Argument Types

You can also select on the argument declarations of methods. Listing 4-42 shows pointcuts that narrow down the selection to the following:

- All methods without arguments
- All methods with one argument, regardless of its type
- All methods with one java.lang.String argument
- All methods with java.lang.String as the first argument and zero or more other arguments
- All methods with java.lang.String as the second argument and zero or more other arguments

Listing 4-42. *Selecting Methods Based on Their Arguments*

```
package com.apress.springbook.chapter04.aspects;

import org.aspectj.lang.annotation.Aspect;
import org.aspectj.lang.annotation.Pointcut;

@Aspect
public class SystemPointcutsAspect {
  @Pointcut("execution(* *())")
  public void allMethodsWithoutArguments() {}

  @Pointcut("execution(* *(*))")
  public void allMethodsWithOneArgumentRegarlessOfType() {}

  @Pointcut("execution(* *(java.lang.String))")
  public void allMethodsWithOneArgumentOfTypeString() {}

  @Pointcut("execution(* *(java.lang.String,..))")
  public void
    allMethodsWithFirstArgumentOfTypeStringAndZeroOrMoreOtherArguments() {}

  @Pointcut("execution(* *(*,java.lang.String,..))")
  public void
    allMethodsWithSecondArgumentOfTypeStringAndZeroOrMoreOtherArguments () {}
}
```

When narrowing down the selection based on arguments with the execution() pointcut designator, Spring AOP will look at the static method declarations. This is a safe option in combination with auto-proxy creation, since Spring AOP can look at method metadata to determine if there is a match. Remember that this matching is important to decide if a proxy object must be created for any given bean in the Spring container.

Another way to select arguments is based on the actual types that are passed to method executions of the proxy object. Listing 4-43 shows an aspect with a pointcut that selects methods with one argument.

Listing 4-43. *Selecting Methods Based on Actual Argument Values Instead of Argument Declaration*

```
package com.apress.springbook.chapter04.aspects;

import org.aspectj.lang.annotation.Aspect;
import org.aspectj.lang.annotation.Pointcut;
import org.aspectj.lang.annotation.Before;

@Aspect
public class MessagePrintingAspect {
  @Before("args(java.util.Hashtable)")
  public void printWarningForUsageOfHashtable() {
    System.out.println("Warning: java.util.Hashtable is passed as argument!");
  }
}
```

java.util.Hashtable is a synchronized class meant to be used in scenarios where one map object is shared in a multithreaded environment. Hashtable performs poorly compared to nonsynchronized maps, and we want to print a warning when it's being used in a single-threaded setting. Three method signatures will all be selected by this pointcut:

```
public java.util.List getUniqueValuesFromMap(java.util.Map map) { … }
```

```
public Object getLowestKeyValueFromMap(java.util.Map map) { … }
```

```
public String transformObjectToString(Object o) { … }
```

These three method signatures will be matched by the pointcut in Listing 4-43 during auto-proxy creation since Spring AOP has no way of determining which argument value will be passed to these methods. Spring AOP knows any of these single-argument methods can be potentially matched by this pointcut. But even though Spring AOP will decide to create a proxy object for beans that implement any of these methods, that does not mean that the advice will always be executed for these methods. Spring AOP will need to do a match each time these methods are executed to decide whether or not to execute the advice, based on the argument value that is passed. This process may have the undesired side effect of creating many more proxy objects than intended.

In Spring AOP, proxy creation is relatively inexpensive and of no concern for singleton beans. It's a different story for prototype beans, since a proxy object needs to be created each time it's requested via dependency lookup or dependency injection. You should be aware of the performance impact dynamic pointcuts *may* have on prototype bean creation in the Spring container if you're going to create many prototype objects.

Selecting on a Return Type Declaration

Another way to select methods is based on their return type declaration, which can be any type or void. Let's consider the pointcut we used at the start of this chapter to select all methods named startMatch():

```
execution(* startMatch(..))
```

The asterisk (*) in this pointcut matches any return type; the return type and the method signature are both required fields for the execution() pointcut designator. We can change this pointcut to match only startMatch() methods that return the type we expect, like this:

```
execution(com.apress.springbook.chapter04.Match startMatch(..))
```

Why do we want to specify the return type when we have only one startMatch() method in the entire application and * is much less typing?

When writing pointcuts, you need to be careful about which join points you will select. Any join point that is selected as an unintended side effect is overhead. When applications grow, many small overheads often become significant.

You can also use the void keyword as the return type to select only methods that don't return anything.

■**Note** Selecting methods on their return type declaration does not require a dynamic pointcut since Spring AOP can look at static method signatures at auto-proxy creation time.

Selecting on a throws Declaration

Sometimes you want to select methods based on their throws declaration. These pointcuts are not strictly related to after throwing advice; they can be used with any advice type.

To match an exception type, it must be declared in method signatures. As you are probably aware, Java has two exception types:

Unchecked exceptions: These are unrecoverable exceptions, meaning there is usually little or nothing an application can do in response to these exceptions when they occur. Because of their unrecoverable nature, Java does not require these exceptions to be declared in method signatures or caught by application code. Exceptions that are type-compatible with java.lang.Error and java.lang.RuntimeException are unchecked.

Checked exceptions: These are usually recoverable exceptions, meaning the application logic can do something significant in response to their occurrence. These exceptions must be either caught in a try/catch block or declared in the method signature to pass them on to the caller. Exceptions that are *not* type-compatible with java.lang.Error and java.lang.Runtime Exception are checked.

Checked exceptions must be declared in method signatures if not caught in the method body; unchecked exceptions *may* be declared, but this is not required. Unchecked exceptions are sometimes declared in method signatures to inform callers they may be thrown. However, even when unchecked exceptions are declared in method signatures, they don't need to be caught by the caller. This leads us to conclude the following:

- Checked exceptions are typically declared in method signatures.

- Unchecked exceptions are often *not* declared in method signatures.

Since pointcuts can match only methods that declare exceptions in their signatures, you will typically be able to match only against checked exceptions, as shown in Listing 4-44.

Listing 4-44. *Matching Against java.io.IOException*

```
package com.apress.springbook.chapter04.aspects;

import org.aspectj.lang.annotation.Aspect;
import org.aspectj.lang.annotation.Pointcut;
import org.aspectj.lang.annotation.Before;

@Aspect
public class MessagePrintingAspect {
  @Before("execution(* *(..) throws java.lang.IOException)")
  public void printWarningIOExceptionMayBeThrown() {
```

```
    System.out.println("Warning: IOException may be thrown. Brace yourselves!");
  }
}
```

You need to specify only the exception types you want to match against. Method signatures may declare additional types yet will still be matched. The following method signatures will be matched by the pointcut in Listing 4-44:

```
public String readFileToString(java.io.File file) throws
    java.io.IOException, java.lang.IllegalArgumentException { … }

public void copy(java.io.InputStream in, java.io.OutputStream out)
    java.io.IOException, java.lang.IllegalStateException { … }
```

When we talk about binding advice method arguments later in this chapter, we'll look at how to respond to exceptions that are actually thrown by methods.

■Note Selecting methods on their `throws` declaration does not require a dynamic pointcut since Spring AOP can look at static method signatures at auto-proxy creation time.

Selecting Methods via Classes, Packages, and Inheritance

Selecting methods directly is very useful when writing advice for specific methods or methods with specific properties. The most interesting use of aspects, however, is enforcement of systemwide policies, as in the following examples:

- *Logging*: You want to learn exactly how your application components interact, or you want to measure the performance of method executions.

- *Auditing*: You have a requirement to log who executes operations on a series of components.

- *Security*: You want to enforce user roles when invoking methods, or you want to filter return values based on security policies.

- *Optimization*: You want to learn how your users use your domain logic to learn where you can add more features or how you can improve performance, reduce memory usage, or reduce database access for common operations.

Each of these requirements typically has an impact on large sets of methods based on generic properties, such as containing classes, containing packages, or inheritance hierarchies. Some of these requirements can be implemented only by binding advice methods arguments, which we'll discuss later in this chapter. Here, we'll focus on how to select methods based on classes, packages, and inheritance.

Selecting on a Class

There are two important distinctions when selecting all methods within one class:

- Pointcuts that can determine matches based on static (as in nondynamic) class and method information. The `execution()` and `within()` pointcut designators will look only at static information and are great to narrow down the selection on a pointcut.

- Pointcuts that require a method execution context to determine a match. Pointcuts that require method execution can't always be avoided, but it's important that you know how to limit the number of objects that will be proxied to only the intended ones.

You're already familiar with execution(), but we haven't discussed yet how you can select methods in one class. The within() pointcut designator can also narrow the selection to all methods on a specific type. Here are two pointcuts that select exactly the same join points:

```
execution(* com.apress.springbook.chapter04.DefaultTournamentMatchManager.*(..))
```

```
within(com.apress.springbook.chapter04.DefaultTournamentMatchManager)
```

These pointcuts select all methods on the DefaultTournamentMatchManager class. They use static information so don't require the context of the method execution. However, sometimes you need this, specifically when using advice method argument binding, as we'll discuss shortly.

We've already discussed the args() pointcut designator, which enforces dynamic pointcuts. Two other dynamic pointcut designators are target() and this(). The target() designator narrows down the selection on the target object of a proxy object. The this() designator narrows down the selection on the proxy object itself. (See Chapter 6 of the Spring 2.0 reference manual for more details on target() and this().)

Selecting Methods via Inheritance

You can very easily apply what you've learned in the previous section to class hierarchies that are created through inheritance. The DefaultTournamentMatchManager class implements the TournamentMatchManager interface so is part of this interface's hierarchy. We can rewrite the pointcuts shown in the previous section to match all members of a class hierarchy instead of one specific class, like this:

```
execution(* com.apress.springbook.chapter04.TournamentMatchManager+.*(..))
```

```
within(com.apress.springbook.chapter04.TournamentMatchManager+)
```

These pointcuts will select all objects that are type-compatible with the TournamentMatch Manager interface. Notice the use of the + operator to tell Spring AOP to take the class hierarchy into account.

Selecting Methods on all Classes in a Package

It's very easy to narrow the selection of join points to all classes in a package, and you can optionally include all subpackages. To select all methods on all classes in the com.apress.springbook. chapter04 package, simply use the asterisk (*) operator:

```
execution(* com.apress.springbook.chapter04.*.*(..))
```

```
within(com.apress.springbook.chapter04.*)
```

If you want to include all subpackages, you need to provide on extra dot (..). Compare the preceding pointcuts to these:

```
execution(*com.apress.springbook.chapter04..*.*(..))
```

```
within(com.apress.springbook.chapter04..*)
```

Narrowing down on the package level helps you to select specific methods.

Selecting Methods via Annotations

Selecting all methods of all classes in a package may be too coarse-grained for certain aspects. For example, with auditing, you know in advance which methods on which classes require the retention of audit information.

Here, we'll use the example of auditing to demonstrate how to select methods with annotations and methods in classes with annotations. Throughout this example, we'll use the @Audit annotation shown in Listing 4-45.

Listing 4-45. *The @Audit Annotation*

```
package com.apress.springbook.chapter04;

import java.lang.annotation.Retention;
import java.lang.annotation.RetentionPolicy;

@Retention(RetentionPolicy.RUNTIME)
public @interface Audit {
}
```

We can now use this annotation on the BusinessOperations class, in shown Listing 4-46.

Listing 4-46. *Using the @Audit Annotation to Mark a Method That Requires Retention of Audit Information*

```
package com.apress.springbook.chapter04;

public class BusinessOperations {
    @Audit
    public void sensitiveOperation(long recordId) { … }
}
```

By declaring the @Audit annotation on the sensitiveOperation() method, we've indicated we need to retain audit information for this method. We haven't determined, however, which information to retain, where to store this information, and for how long.

The information that is to be stored and how it is to be stored is very likely defined in a policy document and is equal for all methods. We've only marked a method and can now implement the retention policy with an aspect.

Selecting on Method Annotation Declarations

We need to write an aspect that implements the audit retention policy. Selecting which methods are subject to audit information retention is a separate effort and of no concern to the aspect or the developers who implement it. Because we can base the pointcut on a Java 5 annotation, we get fine-grained semantics.

We will select only the methods that declare the @Audit annotation and leave other methods unaffected. This is a great way of working, since we can be sure there will be no side effects. We'll delegate the actual saving of audit information to the AuditInformationRetentionPolicy interface, as shown in Listing 4-47.

Listing 4-47. *The AuditInformationRetentionPolicy Interface*

```
package com.apress.springbook.chapter04;

public interface AuditInformationRetentionPolicy {
  public void retainMethodInvocationInformation(
      String currentUser, String methodDescription, Object[] arguments);
}
```

As you'll notice, the retainMethodInvocationInformation() method on the AuditInformation RetentionPolicy interface requires the name of the current user. We need to get this name, but we don't want to tie the implementation of our aspect to a specific authentication mechanism. We create the CurrentUserInformation interface, as shown in Listing 4-48.

Listing 4-48. *The CurrentUserInformation Interface*

```
package com.apress.springbook.chapter04;

public interface CurrentUserInformation {
  public String getUsername();
}
```

We now know how to retain audit information and how to get the current username. Since we delegate these two responsibilities to collaboration objects, we will need to configure our aspect in the Spring container.

The first step is to add a pointcut to the SystemPointcutsAspect, since we want to centralize systemwide pointcuts, as shown in Listing 4-49.

Listing 4-49. *Adding a Systemwide Pointcut*

```
package com.apress.springbook.chapter04.aspects;

import org.aspectj.lang.annotation.Aspect;
import org.aspectj.lang.annotation.Pointcut;

@Aspect
public class SystemPointcutsAspect {
  @Pointcut("@annotation(com.apress.springbook.chapter04.Audit)")
  public void auditableMethods() {}
}
```

The pointcut in Listing 4-49 uses the @annotation() pointcut designator to select join points that have declared the @Audit annotation (we'll discuss the @annotation() pointcut designator more in the "Binding Annotations" section later in this chapter). Spring AOP can now select only those beans in the Spring container during auto-proxy creation.

Notice that we're not selecting specific methods, classes, or packages anymore. We can obviously further narrow down the selection of the pointcut if desired.

Listing 4-50 shows the AuditInformationRetentionAspect that is responsible for trapping all executions of methods that are marked with the @Audit annotation and call the retainMethod InvocationInformation() on the AuditInformationRetentionPolicy interface.

Listing 4-50. *The AuditInformationRetentionAspect Is Responsible for Saving Audit Information for Sensitive Operations*

```
package com.apress.springbook.chapter04.aspects;

import com.apress.springbook.chapter04.CurrentUserInformation;
import com.apress.springbook.chapter04.AuditInformationRetentionPolicy;

import org.aspectj.lang.annotation.Aspect;
import org.aspectj.lang.annotation.Before;

import org.aspectj.lang.JoinPoint;

@Aspect
public class AuditInformationRetentionAspect {
```

```
  private AuditInformationRetentionPolicy auditInformationRetentionPolicy;
  private CurrentUserInformation currentUserInformation;

  public void setAuditInformationRetentionPolicy(
    AuditInformationRetentionPolicy auditInformationRetentionPolicy
  ) {
    this.auditInformationRetentionPolicy = auditInformationRetentionPolicy;
  }

  public void setCurrentUserInformation
  (
    CurrentUserInformation currentUserInformation
  ) {
    this.currentUserInformation = currentUserInformation;
  }

  public void init() {
    if (this.auditInformationRetentionPolicy == null) {
      throw new IllegalStateException("AuditInformationRetentionPolicy " +
          "object is not set!");
    }
    if (this.currentUserInformation == null) {
      throw new IllegalStateException("CurrentUserInformation " +
          "object is not set!");
    }
  }

  @Before("com.apress.springbook.chapter04.aspects." +
          "SystemPointcutsAspect.auditableMethods()")
  public void retainMethodInvocationInformation(JoinPoint joinPoint) {
    String currentUser = this.currentUserInformation.getUsername();
    String methodDescription = joinPoint.getSignature().toLongString();
    Object[] arguments = joinPoint.getArgs();

    this.auditInformationRetentionPolicy.retainMethodInvocationInformation(
        currentUser, methodDescription, arguments);
  }
}
```

In Listing 4-50, the retainMethodInvocationInformation() advice method has a JoinPoint argument. Any advice method, except around advice, can have a first argument of this type. If this argument is declared, Spring AOP will pass a JoinPoint object that contains information about the current join point.

The aspect in Listing 4-50 uses the org.aspectj.lang.JoinPoint object to obtain a description of the method that is executed and the arguments that have been passed.

Listing 4-51 shows the Spring XML configuration file for the BusinessOperations class and the AuditInformationRetentionAspect aspect.

Listing 4-51. *Configuring the Auditable Class and Audit Aspect*

```
<beans>
  <bean class="org.springframework.aop.aspectj.annotation. ➥
AnnotationAwareAspectJAutoProxyCreator"/>

  <bean class="com.apress.springbook.chapter04.aspects. ➥
AuditInformationRetentionAspect"
        init-method="init">
```

```
        <property name="auditInformationRetentionPolicy"
                  ref="auditInformationRetentionPolicy"/>
        <property name="currentUserInformation" ref="currentUserInformation"/>
    </bean>

    <bean id="businessOperations"
          class="com.apress.springbook.chapter04.BusinessOperations">
      <!-- properties omitted -->
    </bean>
</beans>
```

The Spring configuration in Listing 4-51 configures the AuditInformationRetentionAspect with AuditInformationRetentionPolicy and CurrentUserInformation objects. It's not important for this example and the aspect how these interfaces are implemented. The aspect delegates these two responsibilities, so that its advice implementation is small, easy to maintain, and easy to implement.

Selecting on Class Annotation Declarations

The example in the previous section elaborates on how to match methods with @Audit declaration. Sometimes you also want to mark an entire class with an annotation to enforce a policy for all methods in this class. This is a viable approach in those cases where all the responsibilities of a class require the enforcement of a policy such as auditing. Methods that don't require these policies consequently don't belong in this class.

While this is an interesting approach, you need to take into account one consequence. If you recall, one of the requirements of working with aspects in Spring AOP is that callers use the proxy object, not the target object.

Consider the MoreBusinessOperations class in Listing 4-52.

Listing 4-52. *The MoreBusinessOperations Class*

```
package com.apress.springbook.chapter04;

@Audit
public class MoreBusinessOperations {
  public void someSensitiveOperation(long recordId) {
    // do some work
    someOtherSensitiveOperation(recordId);
  }

  public void someOtherSensitiveOperation(long recordId) {
   // work with sensitive data
  }
}
```

In Listing 4-52, the someSensitiveOperation() method calls the someOtherSensitiveOperation() method on the same object. This object, however, is the target object—the original object for which a proxy object *may have been* created.

Whether or not the someSensitiveOperation() method has been called via a proxy object is not relevant. This method calls another method on the same object, so that the method call will not pass through a proxy object. This means the auditing policy will not be enforced for the someOtherSensitiveOperation(). Although this sounds dramatic, we need to consider if saving audit information when the someSensitiveOperation() is executed is sufficient to cover both method executions. If this is not sufficient, then do two methods that both require audit information retention, one called by the other, belong in the same class? It's entirely possible that placing these two methods in the same class overloads the class with responsibilities.

If the someOtherSensitiveOperation() method always requires audit information to be saved, it should probably be moved to a separate class. An object of that class can then be injected in a MoreBusinessOperations object, which can then call the someOtherSensitiveOperation() method on the injected object.

There are no hard-and-fast rules for solving this kind of conflict between application design and limitations imposed by technical frameworks such as Spring AOP. We recommend that you use some common sense and consider the class, the methods, and the policy to be enforced to come to a solution.

To match methods in classes that declare the @Audit annotation, we need to change the auditableMethods() pointcut in SystemPointcutsAspect, as shown in Listing 4-53.

Listing 4-53. *Also Match Methods in Classes That Declare the @Audit Annotation*

```
package com.apress.springbook.chapter04.aspects;

import org.aspectj.lang.annotation.Aspect;
import org.aspectj.lang.annotation.Pointcut;

@Aspect
public class SystemPointcutsAspect {
  @Pointcut("@within(com.apress.springbook.chapter04.Audit)")
  public void auditableMethods() {}
}
```

The @within() pointcut designator used in the auditableMethods() pointcut in Listing 4-53 also matches methods declared *within* classes that declare the @Audit annotation. In other words, the @within() pointcut designator matches only @Audit annotations at the class level.

Now that we've covered how to match Java 5 annotations with pointcuts, let's look at how to bind advice.

Binding Advice Arguments

We're going to take what you've learned about pointcuts so far a couple of steps further. Now, we'll add arguments to advice methods. This is called *argument binding*, and it allows you to create much more powerful advice methods. You can add arguments to advice methods and bind any method argument value, exception, return value, or annotation object.

Let's start with the aspect from the first examples in this chapter, shown in Listing 4-54.

Listing 4-54. *Printing a Message When a Tennis Match Starts*

```
package com.apress.springbook.chapter04.aspects;

import org.aspectj.lang.annotation.Aspect;
import org.aspectj.lang.annotation.Before;

@Aspect
public class MessagePrintingAspect {
  @Before("execution(* startMatch(..))")
  public void printMessageToInformMatchStarts() {
    System.out.println("Attempting to start tennis match!");
  }
}
```

The `printMessageToInformMatchStarts()` advice method in Listing 4-54 has no arguments. Let's look again at the `TournamentMatchManager` interface and its `startMatch()` method, shown in Listing 4-55.

Listing 4-55. *The TournamentMatchManager Interface*

```
package com.apress.springbook.chapter04;

public interface TournamentMatchManager {
  public Match startMatch(long matchId) throws
        UnknownMatchException, MatchIsFinishedException,
        MatchCannotBePlayedException, PreviousMatchesNotFinishedException;
}
```

Say we want to print the match identifier that is passed to `startMatch()` in the `printMessage ToInformMatchStarts()` advice method. We need to get the argument somehow. We've already used the `JoinPoint` argument before, and we can use it again here to obtain the match identifier argument value of the `startMatch()` method, as shown in Listing 4-56.

Listing 4-56. *Getting an Argument Value via the JoinPoint Object*

```
package com.apress.springbook.chapter04.aspects;

import org.aspectj.lang.annotation.Aspect;
import org.aspectj.lang.annotation.Before;

import org.aspectj.lang.JoinPoint;

@Aspect
public class MessagePrintingAspect {
  @Before("execution(* startMatch(..))")
  public void printMessageToInformMatchStarts(JoinPoint jp) {
    Long matchId = (Long)jp.getArgs()[0];
    System.out.println("Attempting to start tennis match with identifier " +
          matchId + "!");
  }
}
```

Spring AOP will detect that the `printMessageToInformMatchStarts()` advice method has `JoinPoint` as its first argument type and will pass a `JoinPoint` object, which has an `Object` array with the argument values of the method invocation.

So we now have the match identifier, but there is a problem: the pointcut expression must be changed to avoid errors. The current pointcut expression will select *any* `startMatch()` method, regardless of its argument types. We need to change the pointcut to select only methods that have a first argument of type `long`, as shown in Listing 4-57, because the advice method assumes it's present.

Listing 4-57. *Changing the Pointcut Expression to Further Narrow the Method Selection*

```
package com.apress.springbook.chapter04.aspects;

import org.aspectj.lang.annotation.Aspect;
import org.aspectj.lang.annotation.Before;

import org.aspectj.lang.JoinPoint;
```

```
@Aspect
public class MessagePrintingAspect {
  @Before("execution(* startMatch(long,..))")
  public void printMessageToInformMatchStarts(JoinPoint jp) {
    Long matchId = (Long)jp.getArgs()[0];
    System.out.println("Attempting to start tennis match with identifier " +
            matchId + "!");
  }
}
```

This is better, but Listing 4-57 can still be improved. Spring AOP allows us to declare a long
argument in the printMessageToInformMatchStarts() advice method, instead of having to use the
JoinPoint object, as the next sections demonstrate.

Spring AOP supports advice argument binding as follows:

- Binding values, possible for all advice types

- Binding return values, possible only for after returning advice

- Binding exception objects, possible only for after throwing advice

- Binding annotation objects, possible for all advice types

▮**Note** You need to configure your Java compiler to include debug information in Java classes to make argument
binding work correctly. Typically, the compilers in IDEs are configured this way by default. See Chapter 6 of the
Spring 2.0 reference manual for more details.

Binding Method Argument Values

You can bind argument values that were passed to the method execution on the proxy object to
arguments of advice methods. Binding method argument values is possible for all advice types.

For the example, we want to bind the match identifier value to an argument of the print
MessageToInformMatchStarts() advice method, so first we need to add an argument to this method.
However, we also need to use the args() pointcut designator to specify that we want to bind
method arguments. We've changed the MessagePrintingAspect as shown in Listing 4-58.

Listing 4-58. *Binding the Match Identifier Value to the Advice Method*

```
package com.apress.springbook.chapter04.aspects;

import org.aspectj.lang.annotation.Aspect;
import org.aspectj.lang.annotation.Before;

import org.aspectj.lang.JoinPoint;

@Aspect
public class MessagePrintingAspect {
  @Before("execution(* startMatch(..)) && args(matchId, ..)")
  public void printMessageToInformMatchStarts(long matchId) {
    System.out.println("Attempting to start tennis match with identifier " +
            matchId + "!");
  }
}
```

The pointcut in Listing 4-58 tells Spring AOP to bind the first argument value of the join point to the sole argument of the printMessageToInformMatchStarts() advice method. When this advice method is executed, its argument will contain the value that was passed to the startMatch() method execution on the proxy object.

Note the following about the pointcut and advice method in Listing 4-58:

- We've kept the static argument selection in the execution() point designator. Remember that execution() uses static method signature information, while args() needs a dynamic pointcut. To avoid selecting too many startMatch() methods as join points that *can* match the pointcut at auto-proxy creation time, we add as much static criteria as we can.

- The printMessageToInformMatchStarts() advice method cannot change the value of the match identifier. To change argument values, the JoinPoint object must be used.

- When adding the argument to the printMessageToInformMatchStarts() advice methods, this argument must be bound by the pointcut, so we *must* add the args() pointcut designator. When we add more arguments, we will need to change the pointcut so that these extra arguments will also be bound. The names used in the args() pointcut designator must match the argument names in the advice method arguments.

To do this in XML, add the following to your configuration file:

```
<aop:aspect ref="messagePrinter">
  <aop:before method="printMessageToInformMatchStarts"
              arg-names="matchId"
              pointcut="execution(* startMatch(..)) && args(matchId, ..)"/>
</aop:aspect>
```

Binding Return Values

You can also bind the return value to arguments of advice methods, but this is only possible for after returning advice. Listing 4-59 shows the MessagePrintingAspect that gets access to the return value of the startMatch() method.

Listing 4-59. *Getting the Return Value*

```
package com.apress.springbook.chapter04.aspects;

import com.apress.springbook.chapter04.Match;

import org.aspectj.lang.annotation.Aspect;
import org.aspectj.lang.annotation.AfterReturning;

import org.aspectj.lang.JoinPoint;

@Aspect
public class MessagePrintingAspect {
  @AfterReturning(
      value = "execution(com.apress.springbook.chapter04.Match" +
          " startMatch(..))",
      returning = "match"
  )
  public void printMessageToInformMatchHasStarted(Match match) {
    System.out.println("This match has been started: " + match);
  }
}
```

Binding the return value is a special kind of static pointcut. Spring AOP doesn't need to do any matching at runtime, but it does need to pass the return value as an argument to the `printMessage ToInformMatchHasStarted()` advice method. Notice that we provide the return type in the `execution()` pointcut designator as a safety measure, so that the advice method will be executed for only the `startMatch()` methods with the correct return type.

We've specified the `returning` property on the `@AfterReturning` annotation in Listing 4-59 to indicate we want to bind the return value to the advice method. The value we pass to the `returning` property is the argument name to which we want to bind. To do this in XML, add the `returning` attribute:

```
<aop:aspect ref="messagePrinter">
  <aop:after-returning method="printMessageToInformMatchHasStarted"
                       returning="match"
                       pointcut="execution(* startMatch(..))"/>
</aop:aspect>
```

Binding Exceptions

When an exception occurs, you can also bind this object as an argument to your advice methods, but only if you're using after throwing advice. Listing 4-60 shows the `MessagePrintingAspect` that gets access to one exception type thrown by the `startMatch()` method on `DefaultTournamentMatch Manager`.

Listing 4-60. *Getting Exceptions That Are Thrown by the startMatch() Method*

```
package com.apress.springbook.chapter04.aspects;

import com.apress.springbook.chapter04.UnknownMatchException;

import org.aspectj.lang.annotation.Aspect;
import org.aspectj.lang.annotation.AfterThrowing;

import org.aspectj.lang.JoinPoint;

@Aspect
public class MessagePrintingAspect {
  @AfterThrowing(
     value = "execution(* startMatch(..) throws " +
        "com.apress.springbook.chapter04." +
        "UnknownMatchException)",
     throwing = "exception"
  )
  public void printMessageWhenMatchIdentifierIsNotFound(
     UnknownMatchException exception) {
    System.out.println("No match found for match identifier " +
        exception.getInvalidMatchIdentifier() + "!");
  }
}
```

The pointcut in Listing 4-60 uses only the `execution()` pointcut designator, meaning it will use only static method signature information to match join points at auto-proxy creation time. When the `UnknownMatchException` type is thrown by the `startMatch()` method, the `printMessageWhen MatchIdentifierIsNotFound()` advice method will be executed.

However, what will happen if another exception type is thrown by the startMatch() method? The startMatch() declares three other exception types in addition to UnknownMatchException and can also throw any unchecked exception.

The printMessageWhenMatchIdentifierIsNotFound() advice method will be executed only if the exception type declared in its sole argument is thrown; otherwise, the advice will not be executed at all. This allows us to add more @AfterThrowing advice to handle specific exception types. We don't necessarily need to use the exception object, but by binding it to advice methods, Spring AOP can choose the correct advice.

Note, however, the pointcut in Listing 4-60 is not a dynamic pointcut. Spring AOP will match join points based on the static execution() pointcut designator. When an exception is thrown, Spring AOP will decide per advice if it needs to be executed, based on the binding information. This means the static pointcut must be sufficiently strict to select only the methods that can actually throw the exception. A pointcut that is not strict enough will trigger the creation of proxy objects for too many beans during auto-proxy creation.

The throwing property on the @AfterThrowing annotation must be present when binding exceptions and should have the name of the exception argument that is declared in the advice method as its value.

To bind on the exception using XML notation, you would do the following:

```
<aop:aspect ref="messagePrinter">
  <aop:after-throwing method="printMessageWhenMatchIdentifierIsNotFound"
                      throwing="exception"
                      pointcut="execution(* startMatch(..) throws ➡
com.apress.springbook.chapter04.UnknownMatchException)"/>
  </aop:aspect>
```

Binding Annotations

Since annotations are added to the bytecode of classes and are part of class and method declarations, they are static and immutable. This means Spring AOP can get annotations with static (nondynamic) pointcuts.

We will continue to look at binding annotation objects to advice method arguments that come from two locations:

- Annotations declared on methods
- Annotations declared on classes

In this section, we will extend the @Audit example we used when we introduced annotations earlier in this chapter. First, we will add a property to the @Audit annotation, as shown in Listing 4-61.

Listing 4-61. *Adding a Property to the @Audit Annotation*

```
package com.apress.springbook.chapter04;

import java.lang.annotation.Retention;
import java.lang.annotation.RetentionPolicy;

@Retention(RetentionPolicy.RUNTIME)
public @interface Audit {
  String value() default "";
}
```

By adding a value to the @Audit annotation, we can pass specific information that we can use while retaining audit information.

Next, we'll change the auditableMethods() pointcut declaration on the SystemPointcutsAdvice to work with argument binding, as shown in Listing 4-62.

Listing 4-62. *Changing the auditableMethods() Pointcut Declaration to Work with Argument Binding*

```
package com.apress.springbook.chapter04.aspects;

import com.apress.springbook.chapter04.Audit;

import org.aspectj.lang.annotation.Aspect;
import org.aspectj.lang.annotation.Pointcut;

@Aspect
public class SystemPointcutsAspect {
  @Pointcut("@annotation(audit)")
  public void auditableMethods(Audit audit) {}
}
```

We've changed the pointcut declaration to support binding @Audit annotation objects that are declared on method execution join points. The @annotation() pointcut designator takes the name of the audit argument in the auditableMethods() method. @annotation() takes a variable name, instead of a type, to specify that we want to bind an annotation object. auditableMethods() declares an argument of type Audit to tell Spring AOP that only @Audit annotations are to be selected by this pointcut.

Listing 4-63 shows the BusinessOperations class with the @Audit annotation.

Listing 4-63. *Declaring the @Audit Annotation with Additional Information*

```
package com.apress.springbook.chapter04;

public class BusinessOperations {
  @Audit("top secret")
  public void sensitiveOperation(long recordId) { … }
}
```

We need to change the AuditInformationRetentionAspect aspect slightly from Listing 4-50 to enable the argument binding of the annotation object that is declared on a join point, as shown in Listing 4-64.

Listing 4-64. *Binding Annotation Objects Declared on Objects*

```
package com.apress.springbook.chapter04.aspects;

import com.apress.springbook.chapter04.Audit;
import com.apress.springbook.chapter04.CurrentUserInformation;
import com.apress.springbook.chapter04.AuditInformationRetentionPolicy;

import org.aspectj.lang.annotation.Aspect;
import org.aspectj.lang.annotation.Before;

import org.aspectj.lang.JoinPoint;
```

```
@Aspect
public class AuditInformationRetentionAspect {
  private AuditInformationRetentionPolicy auditInformationRetentionPolicy;
  private CurrentUserInformation currentUserInformation;

  public void setAuditInformationRetentionPolicy(
      AuditInformationRetentionPolicy auditInformationRetentionPolicy) {
    this.auditInformationRetentionPolicy = auditInformationRetentionPolicy;
  }

  public void setCurrentUserInformation(
      CurrentUserInformation currentUserInformation) {
    this.currentUserInformation = currentUserInformation;
  }

  public void init() {
    if (this.auditInformationRetentionPolicy == null) {
      throw new IllegalStateException("AuditInformationRetentionPolicy " +
          "object is not set!");
    }

    if (this.currentUserInformation == null) {
      throw new IllegalStateException("CurrentUserInformation " +
          "object is not set!");
    }
  }

  @Before("com.apress.springbook.chapter04.aspects." +
          "SystemPointcutsAspect.auditableMethods(audit)")
  public void retainMethodInvocationInformation(JoinPoint joinPoint, Audit audit) {
    String currentUser = this.currentUserInformation.getUsername();
    String methodDescription = audit.value() + ":" +
            joinPoint.getSignature().toLongString();
    Object[] arguments = joinPoint.getArgs();

    this.auditInformationRetentionPolicy.retainMethodInvocationInformation(
        currentUser, methodDescription, arguments);
  }
}
```

The `auditableMethods()` pointcut on `SystemPointcutsAspect` takes the name of the argument in the `retainMethodInvocationInformation()` advice method. Notice this advice method still has the `JoinPoint` argument as its first argument and the audit annotation type as the second argument. The `JoinPoint` argument is bound automatically by Spring AOP, and `auditableMethods()` calls `@annotation()` to bind the `Audit` annotation argument.

Because the pointcut doesn't specify the annotation type, Spring AOP decides that the argument in `@annotation()` is referred to by name. In this way, the `retainMethodInvocationInformation()` advice method is executed only for join points that declare the `@Audit` annotation.

Notice the pointcut in Listing 4-64 doesn't reuse another pointcut. The reuse of pointcuts doesn't support binding arguments to advice methods.

We can also bind annotations that are declared on classes to advice methods using the `@within()` pointcut designator. Consider again the `MoreBusinessOperations` class, as shown in Listing 4-65.

Listing 4-65. *The MoreBusinessOperations Class Is Now Classified Top Secret*

```
package com.apress.springbook.chapter04;

@Audit("top secret")
public class MoreBusinessOperations {
  public void someSensitiveOperation(long recordId) {
    // do some work
    someOtherSensitiveOperation(recordId);
  }

  public void someOtherSensitiveOperation(long recordId) {
    // work with sensitive data
  }
}
```

Getting the @Audit annotation object on the MoreBusinessOperations class and binding it to the retainMethodInvocationInformation() advice method requires a change to the SystemPointcuts Aspect, as shown in Listing 4-66.

Listing 4-66. *SystemPointcutsAspect Selects @Audit Annotations on Classes*

```
package com.apress.springbook.chapter04.aspects;

import org.aspectj.lang.annotation.Aspect;
import org.aspectj.lang.annotation.Pointcut;

@Aspect
public class SystemPointcutsAspect {
  @Pointcut("@within(audit)")
  public void auditableMethods(Audit audit) {}
}
```

Again, the @within() point designators matches @Audit annotation declarations on the class level. Also notice that no dynamic pointcut is used, since @within() can match join points based on static method signature information during auto-proxy creation.

Being able to create your own annotations, annotate your methods and classes, and bind the annotation objects to your advice method arguments is an extremely interesting feature of Spring AOP. See Chapter 6 of the Spring reference manual for more details about binding advice arguments, as well as other Spring AOP topics.

Summary

The popularity of the Spring Framework is in part thanks to Spring AOP and how other parts of the framework use it. In Spring 2.0, the already excellent integration between Spring AOP and the Spring container has been improved by introducing aspects and the AspectJ pointcut language. AspectJ aspects are rich, fine-grained, and powerful constructs that allow you to change and augment the behavior of Java classes.

This chapter covered all you need to know to get started with the new Spring AOP features and aspects in your application. Aspects are supported for Java 5 by leveraging the @AspectJ-style annotations and for older Java versions by leveraging the AOP XML Schema.

The next chapter introduces data access with the Spring Framework.

CHAPTER 5

■ ■ ■

Introduction to Data Access

Welcome to Chapter 5, where we will lay out the cornerstones of working with databases. This chapter is an introduction to the integration with popular Java data-access frameworks provided by the Spring Framework. From the perspective of applications and their developers, we can say that *data access* is all the Java code and other details that come with it to create, read, update, and delete data (CRUD operations) in relational databases.

But before we can explain the Spring solutions, we need to look at the challenges of data access. Then we will show you how Spring helps you overcome those challenges.

In this chapter, we will cover the following topics:

- Spring integration with popular data-access frameworks

- The challenges of working with data access in your applications

- The solutions to these challenges offered by Spring

- An abstraction mechanism for data-access code that you can use in your applications

- The DataSource interface and connection pools

We assume you have a basic understanding of working with databases, SQL, and JDBC. We will be working with relational databases, and we assume that you will too. It's also useful to have read Chapters 1 through 4 before reading this chapter. We expect you to know about the Spring container and its XML configuration files, dependency injection, advice, aspects, pointcuts, and join points.

Spring Integration with Data-Access Frameworks

In Java, the oldest way of carrying out data-access operations is JDBC. It's part of the Java Standard Edition and requires a specific driver that is supplied by your database vendor. JDBC is the standard way of working with SQL for Java. Although JDBC is popular and has been around for many years, it's notoriously difficult. This is because JDBC is a low-level API that provides the basics for working with SQL and relational databases, and nothing more. The Spring Framework makes it much easier to work with JDBC *and* keeps all of its powers.

The Spring Framework integrates with all popular Java data-access frameworks. Apart from JDBC, all the other supported frameworks are object-relational mapping (ORM) tools:

- Hibernate 2 and 3 (LGPL)

- iBATIS (Apache license, partial ORM implementation)

- Java Data Objects (JDO) 1 and 2 (specifications with commercial and open source implementations)

- Oracle TopLink (commercial)

- Apache ObjectRelationalBridge (OJB) (Apache license)

- EJB3 persistence (specification with commercial and open-source implementations, also called Java Persistence API, or JPA)

The Spring Framework offers integration code that covers all the infrastructural aspects of working with these frameworks and APIs. The integration also makes it easier to set up and configure these tools in your applications and adds features that make them easier to work with for developers.

The Spring Framework makes it as easy as possible to use these tools and never harder than it should be for the way you want to use them. Their full power and entire feature set remains available *if you choose to use them*. This is an important distinction to make, since all of these tools are powerful and offer great features, but can also be difficult to use and integrate into your applications. This is because their APIs are designed to offer all available features, but not necessarily to make these features easy to use. This can put developers off when they intend to use these tools in straightforward ways.

For example, Hibernate is a popular open source framework released under the Lesser General Public License (LGPL). Hibernate is an ORM framework that uses relational databases to automatically read, save, and delete Java objects. It offers powerful features and uses JDBC behind the scenes to execute automatically generated SQL statements. But using Hibernate directly is often a painful experience because its resources must be managed by developers. Using Hibernate in an application server such as JBoss solves many of these problems, but ties applications to a restrictive programming model. Only the Spring Framework offers a consistent, noninvasive integration with Hibernate and other ORM frameworks.

Spring provides this integration in exactly the same way for each tool. Spring gives developers the full power of their favorite frameworks and APIs for data access, and adds ease of use and consistency.

The Challenges of Data Access

One of the hardest tasks in software development is to integrate one system with another. This is especially difficult if the system to integrate with is a black box with elaborate requirements on how to interact with it and use its resources.

One of the best examples is integrating an application with a relational database system. Any application that wants to work with such a database needs to respect and accept its interaction rules. The application also must use specific communication protocols and languages to get access to database resources and functionality. Successful integration can yield great results, but getting there can be quite difficult.

Here are some examples that illustrate why developers find it hard to integrate databases and applications:

- There are as many SQL dialects as there are database vendors. Almost all relational databases require the use of SQL to add data to tables and read, modify, and delete data.

- You can't just modify sets of data and expect the database to elegantly save the changes under any condition. Instead, you need to take control over the entire modification process by executing SQL statements inside transactions. By using these transactions, you can make sure the modifications happen as you expect. It's up to you, as a developer, to decide how you expect them to occur and to use transactions to meet your goals.

- Network connections to database systems are typically hard to control for Java developers. Typically, these connections are not thread-safe, so they can be used by only a single thread. They must be created and released in such a way that applications can do any arbitrary set of work with one database connection. Also, the life span of a connection is important when working with transactions. A connection should only be closed after every transaction has ended.

- Databases use system resources such as CPU cycles, memory, network connections, processes, and threads. These resources can be easily exhausted and must therefore be carefully managed. This comes on top of the connectivity problems.

The main reason why Java developers find it hard to work with the JDBC API is because it's a thin layer on top of the peculiar database systems. It implements only the communication protocols; all other aspects of interacting with databases must be handled by the developers.

Effects of Data-Access Leakage

The inner workings of databases and their restrictions are plainly present when writing data-access code with JDBC. Application code that is somehow restricted or negatively affected by its data-access requirements is said to suffer from *leakage of data-access details*.

The following are some typical examples of how application code can be affected by this leakage:

Data-access exceptions: Application code must deal with checked exceptions related to data access yet is unable to respond in a meaningful way. Alternatively, data-access code throws unchecked exceptions that don't provide sufficient contextual information about the root cause for the errors.

Database resource management: Data-access code either completely shields the creation and release of database connections or leaves it up to the calling code to manage the connections. Applications can't take control of how connections are managed in either case without being affected by leakage of data-access *responsibilities*.

Database transaction management: Data-access code doesn't properly delegate responsibilities and prevents applications from controlling when and how transactions are created and ended.

Application design: Data-access details such as relationships between tables or table constraints can ripple through applications. Alternatively, changes to data-access details can cause applications to become inflexible.

Certain data-access details that leak into your applications can result in undesired side effects when applications are adapted to change. This likely results in applications that are inflexible and hard (read *costly*) to change.

Developers don't want to have to deal with any of this. Their goal is to properly contain the responsibilities of data-access code and operations. However, when you look at the list of potential leakage examples, it becomes obvious that developers are being faced with too many responsibilities.

Listing 5-1 shows an example of raw JDBC code to demonstrate the real-life consequences of leakage.

Listing 5-1. *Using Raw JDBC to Access a Database*

```
package com.apress.springbook.chapter05;

public class JDBCTournament {

  private javax.sql.DataSource dataSource;

  public int countTournamentRegistrations(int tournamentId)
      throws MyDataAccessException {
    java.sql.Connection conn = null;
    java.sql.Statement statement = null;
    java.sql.ResultSet rs = null;
    try {
      conn = dataSource.getConnection();
      statement = conn.createStatement();
      rs = statement.executeQuery(
        "SELECT COUNT(0) FROM t_registrations WHERE " +
        "tournament_id = " + tournamentId
        );
      rs.next();
      return rs.getInt(1);
    } catch (java.sql.SQLException e) {
      throw new MyDataAccessException(e);
    } finally {
      if (rs != null) {
        try {
          rs.close();
        } catch (java.sql.SQLException e) {
          // exception must be caught, can't do anything with it.
          e.printStackTrace();
        }
      }
      if (statement != null) {
        try {
          statement.close();
        } catch (java.sql.SQLException e) {
          // exception must be caught, can't do anything with it.
          e.printStackTrace();
        }
      }
      if (conn != null) {
        try {
          conn.close();
        } catch (java.sql.SQLException e) {
          // exception must be caught, can't do anything with it.
          e.printStackTrace();
        }
      }
    }
  }
}
```

The lines highlighted in bold in Listing 5-1 are the actual meaningful lines of the countTournamentRegistrations() method, because they are the SQL statement that is executed. All the other code is required to create and release database resources and deal with the checked JDBC java.sql.SQLException.

Let's look at how this code deals with the technical details of data access:

- We've used a method, `countTournamentRegistrations()`, to encapsulate data-access code from other parts of the application.

- The call to `getConnection()` on the `javax.sql.DataSource` object is problematic since this method obtains its own database connection. What will happen when this call is made depends entirely on the underlying `DataSource` object. In general, however, data-access code should never obtain database connections in this way. A single `java.sql.Connection` object must be shared by all data-access methods that want to participate in one database transaction, like `countTournamentRegistrations()`. The `Connection` object should be obtained by other means than from a `DataSource`. It's fair to say that this way of obtaining database connections is a leakage, since it restricts the application on how it can organize database transactions.

- The call to `createStatement()` on the `java.sql.Connection` is also problematic. SQL statements that contain variable parts should always be executed with `java.sql.PreparedStatement`, not `java.sql.Statement`. Objects of this type can be cached to improve performance. It's fair to say this is a leakage because it affects the application by performing poorly. While no one would ever consider this approach, you can see how JDBC has the potential to make things worse.

- The calls to `next()` and `getInt()` on the `java.sql.ResultSet` object are required to obtain the result of the `COUNT` statement. It's not leakage but the archaic JDBC API.

- Catching the checked `java.sql.SQLException` is unfortunate but required by the JDBC API. It's JDBC's only exception type and typically reveals very little about the root cause of an error.

- Throwing the unchecked `MyDataAccessException` instead of `SQLException` is useless, since it doesn't supply any additional contextual information about the cause of the exception. The only benefit of throwing an unchecked exception is that calling code doesn't have to catch it. However, this particular exception type does nothing to make debugging easier in case of database errors. In this respect, it's leakage, since application code is restricted in how it can deal with specific database errors.

- The `finally` block contains the biggest chunk of code in the method. Inside this block, the `java.sql.ResultSet`, `java.sql.Statement`, and `java.sql.Connection` objects are closed as required. Closing these resource objects properly prevents resource exhaustion in the database caused by cursors and connections that remain open longer than they should. Each call to the `close()` method again must be wrapped in a `try/catch` block, since a `SQLException` can be thrown. By catching this exception and not throwing another exception, the other `try/catch` blocks will always be executed. Swallowing these exceptions is not ideal, but an unfortunate necessity when developers are responsible for cleaning up database resources. Notice how the `Connection` object is being closed, making it impossible for other methods to reuse it, which definitely qualifies as a leakage.

The code in Listing 5-1 suffers from four leakages, which is a big concern. Developers will need to clean them up, if they ever become aware of them. And this is the biggest problem for developers who need to write raw data-access code: *they need to have a profound understanding of the underlying framework in order to avoid leakages.*

■**Note** The `try/catch` blocks in Listing 5-1 could be moved to reusable utility methods. We've chosen to show the full JDBC code in the examples in this chapter to highlight all the responsibilities developers must shoulder.

Concerns of leakage also exist when working with ORM tools. However, they are often much less visible and more complicated, and as such less understood.

Next, we'll look at the most important categories of leakages and discuss why they are important to fix. These categories apply whenever you write data-access code. To our knowledge, all data-access tools available today can be affected by any of these categories.

Database Resources

Data-access code can show three forms of leakage when dealing with database resources:

Resource exhaustion: Occurs when database cursors, result sets, and connections are not closed properly. Resources on both sides of the database connection remain locked indefinitely, until a timeout occurs or until cleaned up by the garbage collector. This can lead to slow performance, unrecoverable errors, and memory leaks. These are bad forms of leakage because memory and other valuable resources, both on the server and the client, remain open for too long. They can be fixed by developers, but detecting them can be hard. One form of resource exhaustion is *connection leakage*.

Poor performance: Occurs when database Connection and Statement objects are created in inefficient ways that affect performance negatively. Typically, Connection and Statement objects are cached and reused by the JDBC driver or *connection pools*. Reusing these objects improves performance compared to creating them from scratch every time such an object is needed. To enable caching and reuse, you typically need to set some configuration and write specific JDBC code.

Inappropriate connection life cycles: Occurs when data-access code can't automatically adapt to one of two connection life cycle scenarios. The first one is obtaining and releasing a Connection object for each execution of data-access code. The second one is reusing a Connection object that was created by another party without closing it. Data-access code that doesn't support both is never going to be flexible.

Let's look at JDBC examples of each of these three types of leakage.

Resource Exhaustion

Database connections or other resources are represented in JDBC as shown in Table 5-1. These JDBC types typically cause resource exhaustion, as demonstrated by the examples in this section.

Table 5-1. *JDBC Resource Representation*

Resource	JDBC Interface Type
Connection to the database	java.sql.Connection
Execution and potentially results of SQL statement	java.sql.Statement
Execution and potentially results of parameterized and precompiled SQL statement	java.sql.PreparedStatement
Cursor (client or server side)	java.sql.ResultSet

Listing 5-2 shows JDBC code that doesn't properly close the Connection object when an exception occurs.

Listing 5-2. *JDBC Connection Is Not Properly Closed When Exception Occurs*

```
private javax.sql.DataSource dataSource;

public int countTournamentRegistrations(int tournamentId)
  throws MyDataAccessException {
  try {
    java.sql.Connection conn = dataSource.getConnection();
    java.sql.Statement statement = conn.createStatement();
    java.sql.ResultSet rs = statement.executeQuery(
      "SELECT COUNT(0) FROM t_registrations WHERE " +
      "tournament_id = " + tournamentId
      );
    rs.next();
    int result = rs.getInt(1);
    rs.close();
    statement.close();
    conn.close();
    return result;
  } catch (java.sql.SQLException e) {
    throw new MyDataAccessException(e);
  }
}
```

When a SQLException is thrown, the code will not close the Connection object. Each line between the call to getConnection() and the return statement can potentially throw a SQLException, and with each exception, a database connection hangs indefinitely or until database administrators clean up connections. This typically leads to situations where the database server needs to be restarted every few days to clean up unclosed connections.

Listing 5-3 shows JDBC code that doesn't close the Statement and ResultSet objects properly.

Listing 5-3. *JDBC Code That Doesn't Close the Statement and ResultSet Objects Properly*

```
private javax.sql.DataSource dataSource;

public List findRegisteredPlayers(int tournamentId) throws MyDataAccessException {
  java.sql.Connection conn = null;
  try {
    conn = dataSource.getConnection();
    java.sql.Statement statement = conn.createStatement();
    java.util.List results = new java.util.ArrayList();
    java.sql.ResultSet rs = statement.executeQuery(
      "SELECT p.player_id, p.first_name, p.last_name " +
      "FROM t_registrations r, t_players p WHERE " +
      "r.player_id = p.player_id AND" +
      "r.tournament_id = " + tournamentId
      );
    while (rs.next()) {
      int playerId = rs.getInt(1);
      String firstName = rs.getString(2);
      String lastName = rs.getString(3);
      Player player = new Player(playerId, firstName, lastName);
      results.add(player);
    }
    return results;
  } catch (java.sql.SQLException e) {
    throw new MyDataAccessException(e);
```

```
  } finally {
    if (conn != null) {
      try {
        conn.close();
      } catch (java.sql.SQLException e) {
        // exception must be caught, can't do anything with it.
        e.printStackTrace();
      }
    }
  }
}
```

As you can see in Listing 5-3, the Statement and Result objects are not explicitly closed. The effects of this depend on the cursor type used by the Statement object. The following resources can be locked longer than they should:

- Memory used on the client side of the connection by the Statement object is freed only on garbage collection. A call to close() would free this memory as soon as possible.

- Any server-side cursor may not be released in a timely fashion. A call to close() would free these resources as early as possible.

- Temporary table space in the database that has been allocated to store the results returned by the query is not cleaned up in a timely fashion. A call to close() would free these resources as early as possible.

So by not calling the close() methods on the Statement and ResultSet objects, this code doesn't handle its responsibilities to clean up resources when it knows they can be freed. Remember that we said database resources are scarce and should be managed carefully.

Listing 5-4 doesn't close the PreparedStatement object it creates.

Listing 5-4. *JDBC Code That Doesn't Close the PreparedStatement Object*

```
private javax.sql.DataSource dataSource;

public List findRegisteredPlayers(int tournamentId) throws MyDataAccessException {
  java.sql.Connection conn = null;
  try {
    conn = dataSource.getConnection();
    java.sql.PreparedStatement statement = conn.prepareStatement(
        "SELECT p.player_id, p.first_name, p.last_name " +
        "FROM t_registrations r, t_players p WHERE " +
        "r.player_id = p.player_id AND" +
        "r.tournament_id = ?"
        );
    statement.setInt(1, tournamentId);
    java.sql.ResultSet rs = statement.executeQuery();
    java.util.List results = new java.util.ArrayList();
    while (rs.next()) {
      int playerId = rs.getInt(1);
      String firstName = rs.getString(2);
      String lastName = rs.getString(3);
      Player player = new Player(playerId, firstName, lastName);
      results.add(player);
    }
    return results;
  } catch (java.sql.SQLException e) {
    throw new MyDataAccessException(e);
```

```
    } finally {
      if (conn != null) {
        try {
          conn.close();
        } catch (java.sql.SQLException e) {
          // exception must be caught, can't do anything with it.
          e.printStackTrace();
        }
      }
    }
  }
}
```

PreparedStatement objects are often cached by JDBC drivers or connection pools to avoid having to recompile identical SQL statements over and over. You would need to consult the vendor documentation to find out whether this caching is enabled or disabled for your configuration.

These caching mechanisms will reuse a PreparedStatement object after its close() method has been called. But since the code in Listing 5-4 never calls this method, the cache hands out objects that are never returned. This may lead to the creation of large amounts of objects that are not garbage-collected (possibly leading to memory leaks) or exceptions that are thrown, depending on the type and configuration of your caching mechanism.

Resource exhaustion by itself is a complicated topic. It can be avoided depending on how you write your JDBC code. And it's just one of three categories where database resource management can fail.

Poor Performance

Three expensive operations typically occur when working with JDBC:

- Resource creation, such as database connections
- SQL statement compilation
- SQL statement execution

The execution of SQL statements is always going to be the most expensive operation, since it will occur most often. Some SQL statements make inefficient use of database resources and can be rewritten to become less expensive.

It's relatively easy to avoid the recompilation of the same SQL statements by using PreparedStatements and a caching mechanism. Not doing so means the database must recompile the same statements over and over again. This consumes resources, is expensive, and can be easily avoided.

Note Some databases, such as Oracle, will cache compiled SQL statements (not prepared statements). If you don't use PreparedStatement and your SQL statements have no variable parts so that they are identical for all executions, this cache *may* be used. However, configuring this cache inside the database so that it will always be used as expected under load requires strong database performance tuning skills. On top of that, it usually takes time and testing to get the configuration right. Also, not all database vendors have such a cache and not all caches perform equally well. That's why PreparedStatement objects are a far more developer-friendly way to improve data-access performance.

However, the most expensive operation is setting up a database connection. Not only does it require a TCP/IP connection between client and server, which is notoriously expensive, but the database server also needs to do a lot of work before it's ready to accept requests from the client.

Connection creation becomes especially troublesome under load. The resources of the underlying operating system and hardware must be shared among executing SQL statements *and* setting up the environments for new client connections. What's more, when connections are closed by the client, the database again must do a lot of work to clean up resources.

So JDBC code should never create database connections. Instead, connection creation should be delegated to a DataSource object. We'll discuss the javax.sql.DataSource interface later in this chapter, in the "The DataSource Interface and Connection Pooling" section.

Inappropriate Connection Life Cycles

When you've studied hard and long, and understand how to avoid resource exhaustion and performance bottlenecks, you're still not out of the woods. You need to design your data-access infrastructure in such a way that your applications remain fully flexible.

As an example, consider the addNewsletterSubscription() method on the Newsletter SubscriptionDataAccess class in Listing 5-5. This method saves an e-mail address to the database to subscribe a tennis club member to the monthly newsletter.

Listing 5-5. *The NewsletterSubscriptionDataAccess Class*

```
package com.apress.springbook.chapter05;

import javax.sql.DataSource;

import java.sql.Connection;
import java.sql.PreparedStatement;
import java.sql.SQLException;

public class NewsletterSubscriptionDataAccess {

  private DataSource dataSource;

  public void setDataSource(DataSource dataSource) {
    this.dataSource = dataSource;
  }

  public void addNewsletterSubscription(int memberId, String emailAddress)
    throws MyDataAccessException {

    Connection conn = null;
    PreparedStatement statement = null;
    try {
      conn = dataSource.getConnection();
      statement = conn.prepareStatement(
          "INSERT INTO t_newsletter_subscriptions (" +
          "(subscription_id, member_id, email_address) " +
          " VALUES (" +
          "newsletter_subscription_seq.nextVal(), ?, ?)"
          );
      statement.setInt(1, memberId);
      statement.setString(2, emailAddress);
      statement.executeUpdate();
    } catch (SQLException e) {
      throw new MyDataAccessException(e);
```

```
        } finally {
          if (statement != null) {
            try {
              statement.close();
            } catch (java.sql.SQLException e) {
              // exception must be caught, can't do anything with it.
              e.printStackTrace();
            }
          }
          if (conn != null) {
            try {
              conn.close();
            } catch (java.sql.SQLException e) {
              // exception must be caught, can't do anything with it.
              e.printStackTrace();
            }
          }
        }
      }
    }
}
```

While the addNewsletterSubscription() method avoids resource leakage and poor performance, it suffers from another kind of leakage: it obtains its own database connection and closes that
connection again.

This method is inflexible because the application doesn't get the chance to let this method
participate in a database transaction. We'll cover the caveats of database transaction managment
shortly. Here, we'll show you the consequence of the way addNewsletterSubscription() implements
its connection life cycle.

First, let's call this method to add a newsletter subscription for one registered member. The
execution of the addNewsletterSubscription() method is the only data-access operation we perform. We just want to add the subscription details to the database when a member enters an e-mail
address in a form on our website.

Listing 5-6 shows how the addNewsletterSubscription() method is called for this use case.

Listing 5-6. *Calling the addNewsletterSubscription() Method*

```
private NewsletterSubscriptionDataAccess subscriptionDataAccess;

public void subscribeMemberToNewsletter(Member member, String email)
    throws MyDataAccessException {
  subscriptionDataAccess.addNewsletterSubscription(member.getId(), email);
}
```

The addNewsletterSubscription() method performs the use case in Listing 5-6 excellently. It
creates its own Connection object and closes it again. As such, the application code that calls it
doesn't have to worry about the details of the data-access code.

However, things become more complicated when a tennis player registers for membership on
our website. We need to add a newsletter subscription to the database, and the obvious way forward
is to reuse the addNewsletterSubscription() method. The difficulty of this use case is that adding
the membership registration details and the subscription details to the database requires calling
two data-access methods: saveMembershipRegistration() and addNewsletterSubscription(). We
call both methods as shown in Listing 5-7.

Listing 5-7. *Saving the Registration of a New Player*

```
private NewsletterSubscriptionDataAccess subscriptionDataAccess;
private MembershipDataAccess membershipDataAccess;

public void saveMembershipRegistrationDetails(
    MembershipRegistration details,
    String emailForNewsletter) throws MyDataAccessException {

  int membershipId =
    membershipDataAccess.saveMembershipRegistration(details);

  if (emailForNewsletter != null && emailForNewsletter.length() > 0) {
    subscriptionDataAccess
      .addNewsletterSubscription(membershipId, emailForNewsletter);
  }
}
```

When this code is executed, addNewsletterSubscription() will create its own Connection object and close it again. This is troublesome for two reasons:

- We execute two data-access methods, but they don't share the same Connection object. This means we must obtain and close two Connection objects. If the DataSource object we're using is a connection pool, we'll potentially avoid the creation of an actual database connection. Yet it makes sense to reuse a Connection object for all data-access operations that are executed for one use case. We need to be careful with resources and shouldn't spend CPU cycles and memory on obtaining and releasing a Connection object twice if it can be avoided, even if we're using a connection pool.

- What is worse, the data-access operations that are called by the saveMembership RegistrationDetails() method can't work in the same database transaction. For data-access methods to operate in the same database transaction, they must use one and the same Connection object. So because of the way the addNewsletterSubscription() method implements its connection life cycle, it's impossible for the application to use database transactions for this use case.

The connection life cycle as is implemented by the addNewsletterSubscription() method is inappropriate. It assumes that the application does not want to use this method as part of a database transaction. This is a misguided decision to make at the data-access level, and it leads to inflexibility for the overall application.

Database transactions should be extremely easy to control and configure for developers. It must be possible for applications to let data-access operations participate in transactions without needing to change data-access code.

■**Note** It's possible to obtain Connection objects from a javax.sql.DataSource object that automatically participates in database transactions. This requires the use of an application server and the Java Transaction API (JTA). Even when depending on JTA, it's still inflexible to obtain Connection objects directly from a DataSource object in data-access code. We'll cover transaction management and the JTA in detail in Chapter 7.

For example, suppose that we also want to bill newly registered members for an annual membership fee. This requires that additional information is saved to the database, say, to the t_invoice table. This would mean calling yet another data-access method as part of saving the membership details.

We would use a database transaction to make sure a set of modifications in the database (adding data, modifying data, or deleting data) is either saved together or not saved at all. (We'll discuss transactions in detail in Chapter 7.) It's perfectly valid to expect data-access operations to work transparantly with *and* without database transactions. In fact, it would be very convenient to be able to write data-access operations that transparently work in this way. However, if developers who work with JDBC are responsible for setting up this behavior, we would expect them to write an enormous amount of infrastructure code, which is unfeasible. This code would be so elaborate and complex that we won't even attempt to solve this problem with code examples.

What's important for you to remember about the connection life cycle of data-access operations is any data-access code *must* be able to transparently work with *and* without database transactions. Otherwise, you're confronted with a leakage of data-access responsibilities. This can seriously harm the flexibilty of your entire application.

Exceptions Related to Data Access

As if managing database resources correctly and in a flexible way weren't difficult enough, the problems with JDBC coding don't stop there. As mentioned earlier, SQLException causes leakage in applications for two important reasons:

- Passing SQLException to calling code is unacceptable and is clearly an example of a data-access detail that leaks into other parts of the application. It's a checked exception, and calling code has no way of responding in a meaningful way. The only sensible thing to do would be to declare SQLException in the throws clause of method signatures. This would have disastrous consequences, since your entire application would become dependent on the JDBC API.

- Wrapping SQLException in a generic unchecked exception such as GenericDataAccess Exception is equally fruitless. It solves the problem of the checked exception, but this approach is equally uninformative. You will still need to consider the error codes inside SQLException to understand the root cause of the exception.

The problems are relevant to applications that use JDBC, as well as to applications that use tools and frameworks that depend on JDBC behind the scenes.

The single most important question is, "What has caused this error?" And to learn the cause, you need to look at the information inside SQLException.

SQLException does contain two error codes that you can sometimes use to get information: the vendor code and the SQLState code. However, the exact same error condition will return different error codes for different database vendors. Therefore, application code that relies on these error codes is not portable. This constitutes a serious leakage related to data access.

Another problem comes when debugging SQLException occurrences. Consider the SQLException retrieved from the following log trace:

```
java.sql.SQLException: ORA-00942: table or view does not exist
```

The underlying database is Oracle. We're being informed that *a* table or view does not exist, but we don't know the table name or the SQL statement that caused the exception. We can look at the stack trace to identify where the exception originated. But database administrators or other maintenance personnel who see this exception won't have much use for a stack trace if they either don't have access to the source code or don't have the Java skills to look at the source code and find the erroneous SQL statement. So, even if we understand the codes, we don't always get sufficient information to understand the cause of the problem, and an application that runs in a production environment and throws data-access exceptions that can't immediately be solved is a serious problem.

> **■Tip** An article on the Oracle website titled "Add Some Spring to Your Oracle JDBC Access" (`http://www.oracle.com/technology/pub/articles/marx_spring.html`) shows some interesting uses of the Spring data-access exception hierarchy.

Database Transactions

We've already covered the problem of inappropriate connection life cycles and how this can prevent applications from working with database transactions. We concluded that we can't expect developers to come up with a solution that fixes this problem because it's too much work and very challenging to get it exactly right. But even if developers do manage to fix this problem, they will have solved only one piece of the database transaction puzzle.

Data-access details can be leaked in three areas related to transactions, which apply to all data-access frameworks in Java, not just JDBC:

Connection life cycles: As discussed earlier, data-access code *must* be able to transparently work with *and* without database transactions to avoid leakage. This leads us to the next point.

Transaction demarcation: We need to decide where database transactions must be declared in the flow of the application. In other words, the boundaries need to be marked. However, application code should preferably not decide on this in order to keep maximum flexibility.

Transaction management: Transactions need to be started and ended. In the case of JDBC, we need to call specific methods on the `java.sql.Connection` class. However, application code should not be aware of how this works; otherwise, we're faced with leakage of data-access details.

Let's take a closer look at the areas of transaction demarcation and transaction management.

Transaction Demarcation

Developers need a mechanism to declare where transactions start and end in applications. This mechanism shouldn't leak data-access details. Its declaration can ideally be changed without having to change application code. Such a mechanism is called *transaction demarcation* and is a transaction-control mechanism that's placed around a point in the flow of a program. Transaction attributes define what will happen to transactions when the execution of a program reaches such a point. These transaction attributes declare properties such as isolation level and transaction time-out. They are also used to decide how a transaction ends (commit or rollback).

Transactions start when the flow of control enters a transaction demarcation point and end when the flow of control exits again. The specific behavior depends on the settings of the transaction attributes for the transaction demarcation point.

A transaction demarcation point is sometimes called a *transactional boundary*. Transaction *demarcation* refers to the act of defining transaction *demarcations* in an application.

Only AOP can offer the kind of flexibility that transaction demarcation requires (see Chapters 3 and 4). Transaction demarcation is ideal to be externalized from the application code in an advice, since it's a very common requirement.

Superficially, it doesn't sound that hard to write a basic around advice that starts and ends transactions. However, matters are more complex. We also need to look at transaction management, which implements the actual starting and ending of transactions.

Transaction management is a complicated field with many corner cases to be covered. There's a risk that a custom transaction demarcation advice will not properly support some corner cases; hence, it may limit the application in its abilities to work with database transactions.

Transaction Management

To see how transaction-management code could create leakage, we need to take a closer look at the relationship between transaction demarcation and transaction management. Transaction demarcation advice depends on transaction management code. Also, transactions can potentially be started and ended through other means than transaction demarcation.

This suggests that transaction-management functionalities are best defined in an API to keep the contract as clear and simple as possible. This alone will avoid the most obvious cases of leakage. However, there's another point to consider.

We mentioned at the start of this section that working with database transactions is a problem shared by all Java data-access frameworks. This means the transaction-management API should be sufficiently flexible to support transaction management for JDBC and the various ORM tools. All these tools define their own APIs for doing transaction management. And it doesn't stop there. The Java EE specifications define the JTA for transaction management. The JTA must be used when you want a transaction manager to manage transactions for you.

You will typically find these transaction managers that implement the JTA in application servers such as JBoss, GlassFish, IBM WebSphere, and BEA WebLogic. Unfortunately, the JTA is not interesting as a generic transaction-management API.

While the JTA may not be suitable for our needs—we want to avoid leakage of data-access and transaction-management details—an abstract transaction management API should also support the use of the JTA behind the scenes. We need a transaction management API that is flexible and reveals only the most basic details about transaction management.

At this point, you won't be surprised when we tell you that writing a transaction-management API that effectively avoids leakage of data-access details is totally out of scope for developers who work on applications. Only an adequately defined API can guarantee that applications remain flexible and can adapt to change without serious overhead.

We'll cover database transactions in more detail in Chapter 7 where we discuss Spring's transaction management framework.

Abstractions

We present you one final challenge, yet another example of how data-access details can ripple through the entire application. Imagine for a moment that we have solved all the issues involving resource management, data-access exceptions, and database transactions. Say you can download one JAR file through a magical Internet portal from a place where applications are flexible and powerful because of the way the data-access challenges have been solved for them. Say the classes in this JAR file allow you to write the most flexible data-access code you've ever seen. This code automatically cleans up resources, transparently works with *and* without transactions, and demonstrates optimal performance characteristics. And above all, the way you write your data-access code is incredibly easy. It's so easy that your data-access code actually becomes readable.

Even when you have all of this, it's still possible to cripple your applications if you don't properly abstract your data-access code for the rest of the application. To understand how insufficient abstraction of data-access code can cause leakage, we need to look beyond databases and technical data-access issues.

One of the most influential thought leaders on object-oriented design is Robert C. Martin (a.k.a. Uncle Bob). He outlined many key principles of object-oriented design in his book *Agile Software Development, Principles, Patterns, and Practices* (Prentice Hall, 2002). The quote from this book that's probably most applicable to the design of data-access code is, "Every dependency in the design should target an interface, or an abstract class." It should be noted this author doesn't discuss dependency injection in his book. As such, his discussion on managing dependencies is somewhat outdated. His ideas on *defining* dependencies, however, are timeless.

In his book, Martin says that the most important reason to use abstractions is to "prevent you from depending upon volatile [code]." This requires a bit more explanation in the context of data-access code. If you look back to the `NewsletterSubscriptionDataAccess` class in Listing 5-5, you'll find a concrete class with a concrete `addNewsletterSubscription()` method. Why is *concrete* associated with *volatile* when this concrete method is very specific in what it does?

So, we could rephrase the reason to this: abstractions prevent you from depending on code characterized by or subject to rapid or unexpected change. This starts to make a little more sense in the light of data-access code. After all, the `addNewsletterSubscription()` method serves as a hinge point between the application logic and the structure of the database. Hence, for a change on either side of the hinge, there's a good chance that data-access code must be changed as well.

Remember we started this chapter by saying nothing is more difficult in software development than integrating two systems? No matter how effective we are in tackling leakage of data-access details, we must remain aware that the structure of the database can change for a multitude of reasons. In many cases, these changes have no affect on the *application logic*. For example, changes to table or field names won't affect the behavior of our core application code at all. However, those changes will affect our data-access code. Without responding to the changes in the database, the SQL statements that are embedded in the data-access code will fail.

We've used only one very innocent scenario for change, but already we can see the effects of leakage rippling throughout the application. After all, the code in Listing 5-7 *depends* on the concrete `addNewsletterSubscription()` method and `NewsletterSubscriptionDataAccess` class.

In fact, what we've just discovered is that the structure of a database leaks in the form of SQL statements. It doesn't stop there, however. Any specific behavior, constraint, or requirement that is defined in or specific for the database has the potential to leak through the entire application.

So we can safely say after this little thought experiment that *concrete* is indeed equal to *volatile*, which the Merriam-Webster Online Dictionary defines as "characterized by or subject to rapid or unexpected change." So in order to avoid leakage of data-access details into the application, we must place an *abstraction* between the data-access code and its callers. This abstraction, however, will be able to abstract only certain details. Others will still leak into the application. We'll look at this further in the "Abstraction and the Repository Adapter" section later in this chapter.

If you look back at all the challenges we've discussed, you should realize that we haven't even covered a fairly large set of other issues. However, we believe you've heard enough to conclude that working with databases and writing data-access code is indeed very, very hard.

In fact, if this were not a Spring book, the only possible conclusion would be that writing adequate data-access code in Java is impossible. But since this is a Spring book, we can say that the Spring Framework has solved almost all of these issues we've discussed, and the solutions are readily available. In the remainder of this chapter, we'll look at how Spring achieves this small miracle.

■**Note**   Chapter 10 of *Expert One-on-One J2EE Development without EJB* (Wrox, 2004) gives a good high-level overview of data access and its challenges for J2EE applications.

The Spring Solutions to Data Access

After many pages recounting problems with data-access code, it's time to look at some solutions. The central theme of the first half of this chapter has been the enormous difficulties developers face when writing data-access code. The recurring problem is leakage of data-access details into other parts of the application. You now have a solid understanding of the many issues that come with writing data-access code.

Without further ado, we'll look at how Spring solves these issues. In this section we'll focus on JDBC. Where relevant, we will mention that similar solutions are also available for the ORM tools supported by the Spring Framework.

Managing Database Resources

To show how Spring manages database resources for you, we've rewritten the JDBC example in Listing 5-1 as shown in Listing 5-8.

Listing 5-8. *Simple Things Should Be Easy to Do*

```
private org.springframework.jdbc.core.JdbcTemplate jdbcTemplate;

public void setDataSource(javax.sql.DataSource dataSource) {
  this.jdbcTemplate =
    new org.springframework.jdbc.core.JdbcTemplate(dataSource);
}

public int countTournamentRegistrations(int tournamentId) {
  return this.jdbcTemplate.queryForInt(
      "SELECT COUNT(0) FROM t_registrations WHERE " +
      "tournament_id = ?", new Object[] { new Integer(tournamentId) }
    );
}
```

The code in Listing 5-8 is much shorter than the original JDBC code. A JdbcTemplate object is created by passing a DataSource object into its constructor. JdbcTemplate is a thread-safe data-access broker class for working with JDBC. It solves the following concerns for developers:

Resource exhaustion: All JDBC resources will be properly closed to avoid resource exhaustion.

Poor performance: JdbcTemplate uses PreparedStatement for variable SQL statements.

Inappropriate connection life cycles: JdbcTemplate will effectively check if an existing Connection object is available for reuse and will reuse it in a thread-safe way. If no such object can be found, it will obtain a Connection object from the DataSource object and close it again.

Uninformative exceptions: JdbcTemplate will always translate SQLException to a more specific exception in an exception hierarchy. This exception will contain the SQL statement that caused the error and the full stack trace of the SQLException.

Looking at Listing 5-8, notice what you cannot see in the data-access code:

- Obtaining a reusable Connection object
- Creating a new Connection object if no reusable Connection was found
- Creating a PreparedStatement object
- Binding the tournamentId parameter
- Executing the SQL on the statement object
- Working with the ResultSet object and returning the result of the COUNT operation
- Catching any SQLException that might be thrown, translating it to another exception type, and closing all resources that are not reused
- Closing all resources that are not reused

This sequence of operations happens inside JdbcTemplate and is specific for the code in Listing 5-8, yet is comparable to many other operations. The next chapter will cover JdbcTemplate in more detail. For now, remember that JdbcTemplate is extremely powerful and flexible, and can handle many corner cases of working with JDBC.

Spring has a Template class for all other data-access frameworks with which it integrates. (Chapters 8, 9, and 10 of *Pro Spring* cover the usage of JdbcTemplate, Hibernate, and iBATIS with Spring.)

Handling Data-Access Exceptions

As mentioned earlier, the issues that come with SQLException also affect ORM tools. So the solution that the Spring Framework provides for SQLException applies beyond JDBC. How does Spring enrich SQLException to help debugging and problem-solving efforts? It's a combination of two approaches:

- Spring will always include the SQL statement that is being executed when the exception occurs. On top of that, the SQLException object is always preserved.

- Spring will translate SQLException to a more specific exception type from its own hierarchy of unchecked data-access exceptions. Spring looks at the error codes inside SQLException and will determine the type of error for your database (based on a list of error codes per database product). This exception-translation mechanism is configurable and can be easily extended.

■**Note** Supported databases for SQLException error code lookup are IBM DB2, Hypersonic SQL (HSQLDB), Microsoft SQL Server, MySQL, Oracle, Informix, PostgreSQL, and Sybase. Others can be configured through custom configuration.

These two approaches are simple yet effectively solve the SQLException leakage problems. See Chapter 6 for more details on the Spring data-access exception hierarchy.

Working with Database Transactions

Earlier, we identified three requirements for letting applications work with database transactions in a truly flexible way:

Appropriate connection life cycles: As you've learned, JdbcTemplate implements this mechanism so that Connection objects can be reused in a thread-safe way. Other template classes for other data-access frameworks and APIs have similar behavior.

Abstract transaction management API: We need an API that can support any form of transaction management, such as that provided by the JDBC Connection or the JTA.

Transaction demarcation: We need flexible ways to determine where or when transactions start and end in applications, preferably through configuration.

The Spring Framework actually has an API that abstracts various forms of transaction management: org.springframework.transaction.PlatformTransactionManager. If you took a look at it, you would find that it's surprisingly simple for the kind of power if abstracts. This interface has many implementation classes, one of which is org.springframework.jdbc.datasource.DataSource TransactionManager. This class knows how to obtain JDBC Connection objects from a DataSource object and close them again. It also knows how to start and end JDBC transactions, and how to make Connection objects available in a thread-safe manner so that JdbcTemplate can reuse them.

As for transaction demarcation, Spring offers a number of alternatives (many of which we'll cover in more detail in Chapter 7):

- A programmatic way to transparently start and end transactions. This approach will use the implementation class of `PlatformTransactionManager` you've selected to start and end transactions.

- A Java 5 annotation type (`@Transactional`) to demarcate methods and entire classes. Spring 2.0 needs only one line of XML configuration to create proxy objects in the Spring container during auto-proxy creation. Spring 2.0 also has convenient XML tags for configuring transaction attributes.

- A transaction advice that can be used in combination with AspectJ pointcuts to demarcate methods and objects in the Spring container.

- A transaction aspect for AspectJ (located in the `aspectj` directory of the Spring 2.0 distribution).

- A special-purpose `org.springframework.transaction.interceptor.TransactionProxy FactoryBean` class, which is the Spring 1.x way of configuring transaction on objects in the Spring container.

The Spring Framework is extremely flexible when it comes to transaction management. You simply cannot find a framework or container that comes close to what Spring offers. Working with database transactions in Spring is flexible and convenient. All the problems are solved for you, every popular transaction-management API in Java is supported, and you can choose how you will integrate Spring's transaction demarcation features into your applications.

SOLVING PROBLEMS IN YOUR APPLICATION

We've gone to a lot of trouble in this chapter to expose you to many issues that you are likely to encounter when writing data-access code. Even though the Spring Framework solves almost all of these issues, it's important for any developer to be aware of them. For one, your understanding may help to communicate the main concerns to people who are uninitiated in the challenges of data access. Also, when considering the data-access requirements of a project, it will be easier for you to spot code smells and areas or ways of working that are likely to lead to problems.

When you start designing an application, you shouldn't use Spring's data-access infrastructure simply because it's convenient. Instead, we advise you to look at how your application interacts with the database without regard to data-access code, JDBC, ORM tools, or Spring. You'll find it easy to notice the pervasive effects of data-access requirements on the application based on what you've learned so far in this chapter.

We find this a far more interesting approach to discover exactly how databases affect applications. You can continue this exercise as long as necessary, until you've eliminated as many pervasive effects by accommodating for them by changing your application. At a later stage, you can pick your data-access API of choice and look at the picture again, and so on. As you may start to realize, by doing this kind of iterative search for pervasive effects of databases and data-access APIs on your applications, it becomes far easier to spot the areas of concern.

By solving problems in your application instead of through Spring, you'll find it becomes easier to adapt to changes. This means, however, that every change in the database or the application requires a new investigation for pervasiveness. When you're happy with the structure of your application and the way the effects of the integration with the database have been countered, you can count on Spring's data-access frameworks to solve the remaining problems.

Try to hold on to these ideas when we talk about abstracting data-access code for other parts of an application.

Data-Access Leakage

In this chapter, we've discussed how database-specific details can easily ripple through an entire application. It doesn't stop there. Details of data-access code can also leak into the application. Each data-access framework or API leaks its own specific characteristics. This makes sense, since each framework or API is unique in how it works with the underlying database.

These remaining data-access details can be stopped from leaking into the application in two ways:

- You can study the application to learn how it is affected by details of the database and change the application or database to resolve some of these issues.

- You can abstract certain remaining issues that are related to data-access code behind interfaces to prevent other parts of the application from being affected. Other issues are impossible or impractical to abstract.

Changing the Application

Let's look at an example of when the database schema is not appropriate as a model for the application logic. In our sample application, we store information about tennis club members in the t_players database table. This makes sense, since by definition all members are also tennis players.

The t_players table is central in the database schema and has relationships with tables that store information about tournament registrations, future and past tennis matches, player statistics, and membership information. All the information in these tables relates to individual *members and players*. In fact, we have a least three roles for the records that are stored in the t_players table:

- We can perform tasks that are related to their membership (members can, for example, subscribe to a newsletter); we can send our members bills for their membership fees and tournament participation fees; and we can query and update membership information.

- Our members are tennis players in the first place. They can register for and participate in tennis tournaments.

- Members can get access to historic player and match statistics.

This schema can't simply be mapped to one Player class in our application. It would simply place too much responsibility on this class. Instead we should create three immutable classes:

- A Member class to contain all the data and functionality related to managing members and memberships

- A Player class used only to identify a player in a tournament

- A PlayerStatistics class to aggregate information about the performance of a player for one tennis season

Each class performs a specific role in the application and their responsibilities don't collide. Each class is used in an area of the application where specific information about individual members or players is managed. We have three classes that represent the three roles we've assigned to our members (registered club member, participant in tennis tournaments, and tennis player with historic match statistics).

So how does this work when we bring the application and the database together? We need to be able to create three different types of objects from the t_players table. Only via the membership part of the application can records be added or modified. We never delete records from this table.

Are there any details about the database schema that can ripple through the application and make this approach impractical? Not at first sight, not for this application anyway. Does this three-class approach prevent details from leaking into the application? Yes, it does. As mentioned earlier, a single `Member` or `Player` class would be overloaded with responsibilities and roles and would not fit naturally in any part of the application.

Abstractions for Data-Access Code

When abstracting data-access code, we want to set realistic expectations for developers. We want to abstract the sensible details, yet we don't want to be ignorant about details that cannot be abstracted. Also, we want to adapt between the database and the database schema on one hand and the application code on the other. We recognize that the database schema and application code are interconnected on a logical level. We also recognize that the features of the data-access framework or API will always ripple through the application.

We think the commonly used approach of the Data Access Object (DAO) pattern is not suitable. We suggest a new approach: the *repository adapter*.

The repository adapter is an integration pattern between application code and relational databases. It abstracts some data-access details from application code by declaring data-access operations as methods on an interface. Application code depends on this interface and can remain unaware of details like the actual data-access code, checked exceptions, and SQL or query statements as defined by the single responsibility principle (see http://en.wikipedia.org/wiki/Single_responsibility_principle).

Many other details—such as required fields, indices, table structures, relationships between tables, triggers, features offered by data-access frameworks, and so on—can be much harder to abstract. The repository adapter abstracts only the sensible details and offers control but no transparency over data access.

Before answering the question of how data-access code should be abstracted, let's review the goals such an abstraction mechanism should make possible:

- Its aim is abstraction and control, not transparency.

- It should work as an adapter between a *specific* application and a *specific* relational database schema using a *specific* type of data-access framework or API.

Developers must have realistic expectations from the abstractions they use and the data-access code they write. Because some issues with data access can be attributed only to aiming for unrealistic outcomes.

We believe transparency is a misguided principle for data-access code. The following is a partial list of implementation details of databases that are impossible or impractical to hide from applications; in order words, they will always ripple into your applications.

- Indices and constraints, required fields, field types, relationships, access rights, and triggers

- The resource usage and performance characteristics of SQL statements, given they have been properly tuned for performance

- The impact of the database schema on the performance of SQL statements, the amount and type of data stored by the database, and the configuration of the database and its impact on performance

- The amount of available memory and number of available CPUs for the database or any other runtime factors

It's more useful to abstract issues. For example, the SQL statements for performing operations on the database are best abstracted from the application code. We know which operations we want to perform, but we don't want to know how they are performed. We may expect these operations to be performed within certain ranges. The actual data-access code is best abstracted simply because it's a separate responsibility and can be quite complex to implement. Application code does not have to be aware of those details that are practical to hide. As you've seen in this chapter, that's quite a lot.

Realistic aims are very important when working with databases. If you know which issues can be abstracted and which cannot, you'll be better informed and more sensitive about the health of your database, data-access code, and application.

When Java developers want to abstract data-access code behind an interface, they almost naturally reach for the DAO pattern. This pattern is part of the Core J2EE Patterns and is motivated as follows: "Access to data varies depending on the source of the data. Access to persistent storage, such as to a database, varies greatly depending on the type of storage [...] and the vendor imple- mentation" (http://java.sun.com/blueprints/corej2eepatterns/Patterns/ DataAccessObject.html).

We believe this motivation is too vague for an abstraction mechanism that is used at the hinge point between application code and the database. The website discusses at length the problems that are solved by the DAO. However, searching for terms like "goal" or "aim" on the lengthy page that describes DAO returns no results. The DAO does not define the semantics we're seeking. We believe this pattern is impractical and plain wrong for abstracting data-access code, and its use should be deprecated. It doesn't focus on any of the real issues of data-access code and has created wildly unrealistic expectations.

The DAO inhibits the idea of replacing one data-access framework or API with another without affecting application code. Such a swap is only possible between data-access frameworks or APIs that are very much alike. However, no two frameworks in Java behave the same. Each one has its strengths and weaknesses. So application code that is written for either JDBC or ORM is likely to have a hard dependency—one that can't be undone by a data-access abstraction. In fact, it's so common for application code to be tied to either JDBC or ORM that it makes no sense to hide this dependency from the application code. This means it should be expected that application code is tied to the features of a specific framework or API.

The best example of this is the COUNT aggregate function in SQL statements. We can count the number of records that are selected by a SQL SELECT statement using JDBC without actually retrieving records from the database. If we want to replace JDBC in an application with another data-access framework or API, we should still be able to perform these COUNT operations. If the replacement tool doesn't support COUNT, all records of a query may need to be processed and counted instead. This approach would perform terribly slowly when compared to COUNT. This is a leakage of data-access details, but not one we can possibly prevent.

■**Note** The EJB 2.0 Query Language doesn't support COUNT although some vendors did add it. It is included in EJB 2.1.

The DAO also promotes the idea that an application can work with any database schema. This is a confusing and slightly ridiculous proposition. First of all, it's very uncommon for an application to move away from it original database schema to one that is structurally different *without affecting this application beyond its data-access abstraction*. Such a need simply does not have to be accom- modated. Secondly, the application code will always exhibit logical connections to the database schema. This is normal and no attempts should be made to avoid this via data-access abstraction or any other forms of abstraction.

A good example of this logical connection is relationships between tables in the database. There is a logical connection in the domain of the sample application between a member and their invoices. Each member has a set of these invoices, which forms a unit for a specific part of the application. Therefore, this part of the application needs a member and the member's invoices to do its work. The database stores all members and all invoices. It must be possible to get a list of all invoices per member, which means the database needs to maintain this relationship. Since it's a one-to-many relationship (one member has many invoices; one invoice belongs to one member) and we're using a relational database, we can design the t_invoice table to hold a foreign key of the member (member_id) that links to the t_player table.

When the application wants to load all the invoices for a member from the database, it must know the identifier of the member, as it does when it wants to insert a new invoice. So it's fair to say that the outlines of the schema in the database ripple through the application. This example will work a bit differently for ORM tools, but the logical connection between the database and application will remain. Application code and database schemas will always be connected at some level.

The adapter nature has an interesting consequence: applications should be built with the database and data access in mind. This means that unless your data-access needs are trivial, you will need a fairly accurate database schema in place to find out how fit your application code actually is.

Some applications are built believing that no concessions should be made for the data-access requirements. This is a misguided approach to data access that can be linked to the transparency claim of the DAO. When you look closely, you will find data-access details rippling through all applications that work with databases. It's impractical and often impossible to hide this.

Using the Repository Adapter

To demonstrate how the repository adapter works in practice. we're going to rewrite the code in Listings 5-5 and 5-7. We'll start with the NewsletterSubscriptionRepositoryAdapter interface, as shown in Listing 5-9.

Listing 5-9. *The NewsletterSubscriptionRepositoryAdapter Interface*

```
package com.apress.springbook.chapter05;

public interface NewsletterSubscriptionRepositoryAdapter {
  void addNewsletterSubscription(int memberId, String emailAddress);
}
```

Notice that the addNewsletterSubscription() method has been written with JDBC in mind. Next, we'll implement this interface in the JdbcNewsletterSubscriptionRepositoryAdapter class, as shown in Listing 5-10.

Listing 5-10. *The JdbcNewsletterSubscriptionRepositoryAdapter Class*

```
package com.apress.springbook.chapter05;

import org.springframework.jdbc.core.support.JdbcDaoSupport;

public class JdbcNewsletterSubscriptionRepositoryAdapter
  extends JdbcDaoSupport
  implements NewsletterSubscriptionRepositoryAdapter {

  public void addNewsletterSubscription(int memberId, String emailAddress) {
    getJdbcTemplate().update(
        "INSERT INTO t_newsletter_subscriptions (" +
        "(subscription_id, member_id, email_address) " +
        " VALUES (" +
        "newsletter_subscription_seq.nextVal(), ?, ?",
        new Object[] { new Integer(memberId), emailAddress }
    );
  }
}
```

JdbcNewsletterSubscriptionRepositoryAdapter extends the Spring org.springframework. jdbc.core.support.JdbcDaoSupport class. This class has a setDataSource() method and creates a JdbcTemplate instance that is accessible via the getJdbcTemplate() method. It's a convenience base class that eases the implementation of classes that work with Spring's data-access integration.

Why do we use a class called JdbcDaoSupport when we just denounced the DAO? From the Spring perspective, a data-access object is any class that implements data-access logic, regardless of its intentions, goals, or definitions. Spring uses the DAO abbreviation in multiple places across the framework code. This is a historic coincidence more than anything else. While this may be a little confusing, it makes sense to reuse convenient base classes when they are available. (Chapters 11 and 12 of the Spring 2.0 reference manual provide more rationale and technical details on Spring's JDBC framework and the integration with the various ORM frameworks.)

Why do we need an interface and a class when the interface itself is only meant to work with JDBC? Couldn't we just use a class? To explain this, we refer again to the single responsibility principle: "There should never be more than one reason for a class to change" (Robert C. Martin). This principle should be considered in the light of dependency management. We need to place data-access code behind an interface to keep our application code flexible. To understand how this works for data-acces code, we need to consider two things:

- Data-access code is an axis of change, meaning that it's a separate responsibility for actual application code that is subject to change over time.

- A class that depends on repository adapter interfaces will not have to *change and be recompiled* when the data-access code it depends on is subject to change.

In practice, we have the NewsletterSubscriptionRepositoryAdapter interface, which is geared towards JDBC. This interface binds us to SQL and JDBC, but not to a specific framework. We can choose between at least JdbcTemplate, iBATIS (another data-access framework on top of JDBC), and raw JDBC code.

Because we define the data-access operations as methods on a repository adapter interface, classes that depend on this interface will not need to change and recompile when the data-access code they depend on changes. We can inject, using dependency injection, any implementation we want, which is what the single responsibility principle says.

Let's put this in practice by rewriting the code in Listing 5-7 to use the repository adapter interface, as shown in Listing 5-11.

Listing 5-11. *Using the Repository Adapter Interface in Application Code*

```
package com.apress.springbook.chapter05;

public class MembershipRegistrationService {
  private NewsletterSubscriptionRepositoryAdapter subscriptionRepositoryAdapter;
  private MembershipRepositoryAdapter membershipRepositoryAdapter;

  public MembershipRegistrationService(
    NewsletterSubscriptionRepositoryAdapter subscriptionRepositoryAdapter,
    MembershipRepositoryAdapter membershipRepositoryAdapter) {

    this.subscriptionRepositoryAdapter = subscriptionRepositoryAdapter;
    this.membershipRepositoryAdapter = membershipRepositoryAdapter;
  }

  public void saveMembershipRegistrationDetails(
        MembershipRegistration details,
        String emailForNewsletter) {
```

```
    int membershipId =
        membershipRepositoryAdapter.saveMembershipRegistration(details);

    if (emailForNewsletter != null && emailForNewsletter.length() > 0) {
        subscriptionRepositoryAdapter
            .addNewsletterSubscription(membershipId, emailForNewsletter);
    }
  }
}
```

We've almost come full circle with the repository adapter example. In the next section, we'll discuss the `javax.sql.DataSource` interface and connection pools. There, we'll configure the `JdbcNewsletterSubscriptionRepositoryAdapter` and `MembershipRegistrationService` classes in a Spring XML configuration file.

The DataSource Interface and Connection Pools

We've already used the `javax.sql.DataSource` interface in this chapter, and if you've ever written JDBC code, chances are you've used this interface yourself. The `DataSource` interface is part of the Java Standard Edition and is a factory for `java.sql.Connection` objects. Listing 5-12 shows its most important method, which is the actual factory method.

Listing 5-12. *Partial javax.sql.DataSource Interface with getConnection() Factory Method*

```
package javax.sql;

import java.sql.Connection;
import java.sql.SQLException;

public interface DataSource {
  Connection getConnection() throws SQLException;

  // other methods omitted
}
```

As you can see, the `DataSource` interface is very simple. However, it has some powerful implementations. Here are the three typical types of `DataSource` implementations:

Simple implementations: These create a new `Connection` object using the `java.sql.DriverManager` class. The `org.springframework.jdbc.datasource.DriverManagerDataSource` is such an implementation. It will create a `Connection` object when `getConnection()` is called, return it, and forget about it. This kind of `DataSource` should never be used in production environments, since it doesn't support the reuse of database connections and would cause performance issues.

Connection pooling implementations: These return a `Connection` object from an internal pool when the `getConnection()` method is called. Each `Connection` object that comes from a connection pool is placed back into the pool when its `close()` method is called. Connection pools are favorable for production environments since they avoid excessive database connection creation and closure. They create a number of `Connection` objects at startup (this number is configurable) and can create more objects if demand increases. Because `Connection` objects are constantly returned to the pool and reused, an application can handle a large number of requests with a small number of open database connections. Application servers such as JBoss, GlassFish, and Geronimo and servlet engines such as Tomcat can provide this kind of DataSource connection pool implementations through JNDI. Jakarta Commons Database Connection Pool (DBCP) and C3P0 are stand-alone open source DataSource implementations.

DataSources that support distributed transactions: These are provided by application servers such as BEA WebLogic and IBM WebSphere. The DataSource objects must be acquired via JNDI. Their Connection objects automatically participate with JTA transactions. This type of DataSource typically also provides connection pooling.

If you do not require distributed transactions (if you're not sure about this, then you don't), you should use the second type of DataSource implementation for obtaining database connections.

Setting Up Connection Pools

The easiest way to set up a connection pool DataSource implementation for your applications that is safe to use in production environments is to get the commons-dbcp.jar, commons-pool.jar, and common-collections.jar files from the lib/jakarta-commons directory of the Spring distribution and add them to your classpath. Next, you can add a DataSource bean definition to a Spring XML file, as shown in Listing 5-13.

Listing 5-13. *Setting Up a Local Connection Pool Using Jakarta Commons DBCP*

```
<bean id="dataSource"  class="org.apache.commons.dbcp.BasicDataSource"
      destroy-method="close">
  <property name="driverClassName" value="org.hsqldb.jdbcDriver"/>
  <property name="url" value="jdbc:hsqldb:mem:."/>
  <property name="username" value="sa"/>
  <property name="password" value=""/>
</bean>
```

You should replace the values of the properties with the correct values to connect to your database. The dataSource bean created by this configuration is a local connection pool object. This is the most portable type of connection pool and can also be used inside an application server.

Notice that the destroy-method attribute is configured. The close() method on the BasicDataSource object must be called when the Spring container is closed to properly release all database connections held by the connection pool.

If you're using an application server and want to obtain one of its DataSource objects, you can add the bean definition in Listing 5-14.

Listing 5-14. *Looking Up a JNDI Data Source from an Application Server*

```
<bean id="dataSource" class="org.springframework.jndi.JndiObjectFactoryBean">
  <property name="jndiName" value="java:env/myDataSource"/>
</bean>
```

Alternatively, you can use the Spring 2.0 <jndi:lookup> XML convenience tag, as shown in Listing 5-15.

Listing 5-15. *Spring 2.0 <jndi:lookup> XML Convenience Tag*

```
<?xml version="1.0" encoding="UTF-8"?>
<beans xmlns="http://www.springframework.org/schema/beans"
       xmlns:xsi="http://www.w3.org/2001/XMLSchema-instance"
       xmlns:jndi="http://www.springframework.org/schema/jndi"
       xsi:schemaLocation="http://www.springframework.org/schema/beans
```

```
                    http://www.springframework.org/schema/beans/spring-beans.xsd
                    http://www.springframework.org/schema/jndi
                    http://www.springframework.org/schema/jndi/spring-jndi.xsd">

  <jndi:lookup id="dataSource" jndi-name="java:env/myDataSource"/>

</beans>
```

■**Note** To obtain a `DataSource` object via JNDI from an application server, you first need to configure a data source in its management console or configuration files. Check your vendor documentation for details.

Using Value Placeholders and Property Files

When you've configured a local connection pool in a Spring XML file, like the one in Listing 5-13, you can externalize the database connection settings to a property file. By replacing the actual values with placeholder symbols, you prevent having to change your Spring XML files when the database connection settings must be modified.

Listing 5-16 shows the `BasicDataSource` bean definition with property value placeholders.

Listing 5-16. *Using Placeholders in the Spring XML File*

```
<bean id="dataSource" class="org.apache.commons.dbcp.BasicDataSource"
      destroy-method="close">
  <property name="driverClassName" value="${jdbc.driverClassName}"/>
  <property name="url" value="${jdbc.url}"/>
  <property name="username" value="${jdbc.username}"/>
  <property name="password" value="${jdbc.password}"/>
</bean>
```

The values for these placeholders go into a property file, as shown in Listing 5-17. This property file can be placed in the classpath of your application or in any other location where it's accessible when your application is deployed.

Listing 5-17. *jdbc.properties: Property File That Holds the Values for the Database Connection Settings*

```
jdbc.driverClassName=org.hsqldb.jdbcDriver
jdbc.url=jdbc:hsqldb:mem:.
jdbc.username=sa
jdbc.password=
```

The only item you need to add to your configuration is the `org.springframework.beans.factory.config.PropertyPlaceholderConfigurer` class, as shown in Listing 5-18. This bean definition will make sure that the property value placeholders are replaced when the Spring container is loaded.

Listing 5-18. *Configuring PropertyPlaceholderConfigurer with one Property File*

```
<bean class="org.springframework.beans.factory.config. ➥
PropertyPlaceholderConfigurer">
  <property name="location" value="classpath:jdbc.properties"/>
</bean>
```

Summary

This chapter introduced you to some of the challenges of data access. Data access is the single most influential factor for applications that build on top of databases. The Spring Framework offers an amazing library of solutions for both JDBC and ORM. However, without an understanding of the problems, you wouldn't be able to benefit very much from the solution.

In this chapter, you've learned that the Spring Framework offers solutions to problems with database resources, data-access exceptions, and transaction management. Combined, they provide solutions to problems that are caused when the Java world meets the database world. These solutions are versatile and flexible, so they can accommodate a lot of situations and corner cases.

The problems that remain are mostly influenced by the integration of databases and data-access frameworks and APIs into applications. These problems are not unique to Java, and there are no straightforward ways to solve them. Each database schema and application that uses it is unique, and developers need to find compromises and work-arounds for the most urgent problems.

After reading this chapter, we hope you now understand that you can't just connect your application to a database and expect it will have no consequences—or think that you can code your way around all consequences. We've offered an approach that's practical in what it promises to solve and more realistic in what it does not attempt to solve.

The repository adapter is a practical way to solve certain data-access issues elegantly, while at the same time acknowledging that many other issues cannot be solved by abstraction alone. An abstraction doesn't work for those issues that leak through it and have an influence on your application. Instead of ignoring them, you can try to work on these influences by changing your application.

The next two chapters cover `JdbcTemplate` and Spring's transaction management framework. You'll find practical information on how to use Spring's data-access infrastructure in your applications.

■ ■ ■

CHAPTER 6

Persistence with JDBC

The previous chapter introduced the Spring Framework's integration with Java data-access frameworks. This chapter provides more detailed insight into Spring's support for persistence using JDBC, covering the following topics:

- How the `JdbcTemplate` class takes care of the boilerplate code you usually encounter and simplifies working with the JDBC API.

- How to use the `JdbcTemplate` class to perform common database tasks, such as selecting, inserting, updating, and deleting data.

- How to use a convenient base class for your data access objects (DAOs) that builds on the `JdbcTemplate` class.

- How to use callbacks, which make performing more complex tasks easier.

- How to use executable query objects, which allow you to work with database operations in a more object-oriented manner.

- How to perform batch operations, working with large chunks of data in the form of large objects (LOBs), and obtaining native JDBC objects, while still leveraging the power of Spring's data abstraction framework.

- The features that are new in Spring 2.0, including the `SimpleJdbcTemplate` class, an even more lightweight template class for performing JDBC operations.

Defining the Data Layer

It is of great importance to separate your applications into three tiers. One of those tiers is the data tier. Because this chapter deals with persistence, we'll start by showing you how to define (part of) the data tier. Specifically, you'll define a domain object that you will use for the duration of this chapter.

A *domain object* is a Java representation of part of your domain model. It is typically a data holder that is shared across the different layers of your application. We'll define a `Member` domain object as shown in Listing 6-1. Notice the other domain objects: `Name`, `Address`, and `PhoneNumber`.

Listing 6-1. *The Member Domain Object*

```
package com.apress.springbook.chapter06;

import java.util.List;
import java.util.ArrayList;
import java.util.Collections;
```

```java
public class Member {
  private Integer id;
  private Name name = new Name();
  private Integer age;
  private Sex sex;
  private Address address = new Address();
  private List<PhoneNumber> phoneNumbers = new ArrayList<PhoneNumber>();

  public Member() { }

  public Member(String firstName, String lastName) {
    this.getName().setFirst(firstName);
    this.getName().setLast(lastName);
  }

  void setId(Integer id) {
    this.id = id;
  }

  public Integer getId() {
    return id;
  }

  public Address getAddress() {
    return address;
  }

  public Integer getAge() {
    return age;
  }

  public void setAge(Integer age) {
    this.age = age;
  }

  public Name getName() {
    return name;
  }

  public List<PhoneNumber> getPhoneNumbers() {
    return Collections.unmodifiableList(phoneNumbers);
  }

  public void addPhoneNumber(PhoneNumber phoneNumber) {
    this.phoneNumbers.add(phoneNumber);
  }

  public void removePhoneNumber(PhoneNumber phoneNumber) {
    this.phoneNumbers.remove(phoneNumber);
  }

  public void removePhoneNumber(int index) {
    this.phoneNumbers.remove(index);
  }
```

```
  public Sex getSex() {
    return sex;
  }

  public void setSex(Sex sex) {
    this.sex = sex;
  }
}
```

Next, we need to define an interface that provides access to instances of the Member class, as shown in Listing 6-2. You'll gradually implement this DAO interface throughout this chapter (though, as we explained in Chapter 5, DAO in the Spring sense is different from traditional DAO). Defining a DAO interface is considered a best practice because it allows your business logic code to depend on the DAO interface instead of the actual implementation. This enables you to change the implementation of the DAO interface without needing to refactor the rest of your application code.

Listing 6-2. *The MemberDao Interface*

```
package com.apress.springbook.chapter06;

import java.io.InputStream;
import java.io.OutputStream;

import java.util.List;

public interface MemberDao {
  int getTotalNumberOfMembers();

  Member load(Integer id);
  void add(Member member);
  void delete(Member member);

  void updateAge(Integer memberId, Integer age);

  long getTotalAge();
  long getAverageAge();
  long getOldestAge();
  long getYoungestAge();

  List getMembersForLastNameAndAge(String lastName, Integer age);
  void addImageForMember(Integer memberId, InputStream in);
  void getImage(Integer id, OutputStream out);
  void importMembers(List<Member> members);
  List loadAll();
}
```

Using the JdbcTemplate Class

As mentioned in the previous chapter, Spring greatly simplifies using the JDBC API. Take another look at the first two code examples in the previous chapter. The first introduces a count query using JDBC the traditional way. The second uses Spring's template class to eliminate most of the boiler-plate code.

Spring provides the org.springframework.jdbc.core.JdbcTemplate class, which simplifies working with JDBC. As with all Spring template classes, it provides resource management, exception handling, and transparent participation in ongoing transactions. So, you don't need to open and close database connections, handle unrecoverable exceptions, or write code to participate in a transaction.

■**Tip** The JdbcTemplate class is a stateless and thread-safe class, so you can use a single instance that many classes can use. However, you should use only one JdbcTemplate instance per data source.

The Spring template classes offer more than the advantages of working directly with JDBC. They provide convenience methods for obtaining integers, objects, and so on directly. So instead of needing to obtain a ResultSet, read the first row, and then get the first value in the row, you can use the convenience method queryForInt() on the template class to return an integer directly. Table 6-1 lists some of those methods.

Table 6-1. *Some Convenience Methods Provided by JdbcTemplate*

Method	Description
execute()	Executes a SQL statement that returns either null or the object that was the result of the statement
query()	Executes a SQL query and returns the result as a list of objects
queryForInt()	Executes a SQL query and returns the result as an integer
queryForLong()	Executes a SQL query and returns the result as a long
queryForMap()	Executes a SQL query and returns the single row result as a Map (each column being an entry in the map)
queryForList()	Executes a SQL query and returns the result as a List (containing the result of the queryForMap() method for each row in the result)
queryForObject()	Executes a SQL query and returns the result as an object (either by specifying a class or by providing a callback)
queryForRowSet()	Executes a SQL query and returns an instance of SqlRowSet (a wrapper for a javax.sql.RowSet), which eliminates the need to catch SqlException

We'll start by implementing the first method of the MemberDao interface using the JdbcTemplate class, as shown in Listing 6-3. This is in a class called MemberDaoImpl.

Listing 6-3. *Using the Convenience Methods Provided by the JdbcTemplate Class*

```
public int getTotalNumberOfMembers() {
  return new JdbcTemplate(dataSource).queryForInt(
    "SELECT COUNT(0) FROM members"
  );
}
```

Again, compare this code with the two first examples of the previous chapter, and notice the absence of a lot of code that you would normally need to write in order to perform this operation:

- You do not need to manage resources. A connection to the database is automatically opened and closed, even when an error occurs. In addition to eliminating all the boilerplate code, this automatic resource management also prevents resource leaks due to incorrectly managed connections.

- The code will automatically participate in any ongoing Spring-managed transactions without you needing to write code to manage transactions (that is, commit and roll back). We'll discuss transaction management in the next chapter.

- It eliminates the need for exception handling.

The JDBC API is notorious for its exception handling. This is mainly because it requires you to handle numerous unrecoverable exceptions, such as when a connection to the database could not be established. In most cases, a SQLException indicates an unrecoverable error, and it is therefore not desirable to need to handle them.

Spring will translate any data-access-related exception into a fine-grained, hierarchical tree of unchecked exceptions (an instance of java.lang.RuntimeException). These exceptions do not need to be declared in your method signature and therefore do not need to be handled. Obviously, you may want to catch some exceptions, especially those you anticipate and know how to handle. All other exceptions will be treated as unrecoverable and will be handled in the front-end tier. We discussed Spring's data-access exception translation in detail in the previous chapter. Figure 6-1 shows the part of the Spring data-access exception hierarchy that is related to using the JDBC API.

Figure 6-1. *JDBC-related part of the DataAccessException hierarchy*

The most important exceptions related to working with the JDBC API in this hierarchy are as follows:

DataAccessResourceFailureException: This exception (or one of its subtypes) is thrown when a problem occurs while connecting to the database, such as not being able to connect to the database.

DataIntegrityViolationException: This exception indicates a data-integrity problem, such as specifying no data for a column that requires data to be set or inserting a duplicate unique value.

DataRetrievalFailureException: This exception is thrown when a problem occurs while retrieving data from the database, such as querying for a single result and getting more than one result.

Using the JdbcDaoSupport Class

In addition to offering the JdbcTemplate class to provide powerful JDBC support to your application, Spring also provides convenient base classes to implement DAOs for all supported persistence APIs; therefore, it offers one for working with the JDBC API. This important org.springframework.jdbc. core.support.JdbcDaoSupport class provides convenient access to a JdbcTemplate instance through the getJdbcTemplate() method. You can either inject a JdbcTemplate into your DAO in the configuration directly or inject just a preconfigured DataSource instance. In this example, we will use an injected data source to generate a JdbcTemplate instance.

First, the initial implementation of the MemberDao that will be used by the middle-tier logic is shown in Listing 6-4. This implementation will extend the DAO support class provided by Spring for working with the JDBC API.

Listing 6-4. *Using the JdbcDaoSupport Class As the Base Class for the DAO Implementation*

```
package com.apress.springbook.chapter06;

import org.springframework.jdbc.core.JdbcTemplate;
import org.springframework.jdbc.core.support.JdbcDaoSupport;

public class MemberDaoImpl extends JdbcDaoSupport implements MemberDao {

  public int getTotalNumberOfMembers() {
    return getJdbcTemplate().queryForInt("SELECT COUNT(0) FROM members");
  }

}
```

The difference between the previous implementation of getTotalNumberOfMembers() and this one is that we do not instantiate a new JdbcTemplate instance, but rather ask the superclass for an instance.

To be able to get an instantiated JdbcTemplate, you need to configure the DAO implementation in a Spring application context. You need to provide it with a valid data source that it will use to create a template, as shown in Listing 6-5.

Listing 6-5. *Part of the data-layer.xml Application Context Defining the DAO*

```
<bean id="dataSource" class="org.apache.commons.dbcp.BasicDataSource"
      destroy-method="close">
  <property name="driverClassName" value="org.hsqldb.jdbcDriver"/>
  <property name="url" value="jdbc:hsqldb:mem:."/>
  <property name="username" value="sa"/>
  <property name="password" value=""/>
</bean>

<bean id="memberDao" class="com.apress.springbook.chapter06.MemberDaoImpl">
  <property name="dataSource" ref="dataSource"/>
</bean>
```

Depending on the database you are using, you need to modify the properties of the data source. You can find more information about using data sources in the previous chapter.

■**Caution** Make sure to set the destroy-method parameter on the data source. This will guarantee that the connection pool and all underlying connections are closed properly.

Now we can look at working with the data in the database.

Working with Database Data

The following sections demonstrate the most common data-access and manipulation tasks using the JdbcTemplate class. First, we revisit how to select data from the database. Next, we discuss how to insert new data and update and delete existing data. Finally, we discuss aggregate functions to perform on data in the database.

Selecting Data

When working with databases, probably the most common task is accessing data that is already in the database. To do this, you need to write a SQL query that retrieves only the data of interest.

Listing 6-6 demonstrates using a SELECT statement to obtain all Member instances from the database.

Listing 6-6. *Selecting Data Using a SELECT Statement*

```
public List<Member> loadAll() {
    return (List<Member>)
        getJdbcTemplate().query("SELECT * FROM member", new MemberRowMapper());
}
```

The last argument to the query() method is an implementation of the org.springframework. jdbc.core.RowMapper interface that is part of Spring. We discuss the RowMapper interface in more detail in the "Using Callbacks" section later in this chapter. For now, just note that the implementation maps the SQL ResultSet to a Member instance.

Inserting Data

Most applications want to add data to the database as well. To do this, use an INSERT statement. Listing 6-7 inserts a new Member instance into the database.

Listing 6-7. *Inserting Data Using an INSERT Statement*

```
public void add(Member member) {
  getJdbcTemplate().update(
    "INSERT INTO member (name_first, name_middle, name_last, address_line1, " +
    "address_line2, address_city, address_state, address_zip, age) " +
    "VALUES (?, ?, ?, ?, ?, ?, ?, ?, ?)",
    new Object[] {
      member.getName().getFirst(),
      member.getName().getMiddle(),
      member.getName().getLast(),
      member.getAddress().getLine1(),
      member.getAddress().getLine2(),
      member.getAddress().getCity(),
      member.getAddress().getState(),
      member.getAddress().getZip(),
      member.getAge()
    }
  );
}
```

To insert data into the database, you use the update() method on the JdbcTemplate class and provide it with a SQL INSERT statement and the arguments to put in the INSERT statement. This statement is executed, and no result is returned. Note that we are using an object array to supply the template method with the arguments to insert into the placeholders inside the SQL query. Specifying question marks in your SQL queries and providing the arguments to replace them with is common when working with the JDBC API. In later sections, you will see some more advanced examples of inserting data. We will also discuss how to externalize the actual SQL statements from your methods.

Tip It is considered a best practice to use the update() method of the JdbcTemplate class for both INSERT and UPDATE statements.

Updating Data

Another common task for applications is updating existing entries in the database. You do this using the UPDATE SQL statement. In the following example, we want to update an existing Member instance. When the member has a birthday, we want to update the age field. Therefore, we add a method to the DAO interface that updates the age of the member to the age that was passed in as a parameter, as shown in Listing 6-8.

Listing 6-8. *Updating Data Using an UPDATE Statement*

```
public void updateAge(Integer memberId, Integer age) {
  getJdbcTemplate().update(
    "UPDATE member SET age = ? WHERE id = ?",
    new Object[] { age, memberId }
  );
}
```

The only difference from the previous example is the SQL statement, which updates only the column that needs to be changed. Note that you can update multiple columns by separating the column/value pairs with a comma.

Deleting Data

Another common task related to persistence is removing existing data from the database. Suppose that we want to provide the user with the means to clean up the database by removing specific member instances. Listing 6-9 demonstrates how to do this.

Listing 6-9. *Deleting Data Using a DELETE Statement*

```
public void delete(Member member) {
  getJdbcTemplate().update(
    "DELETE FROM member WHERE id = ?",
    new Object[] { member.getId() }
  );
}
```

Again, this example is similar to the previous examples. However, it uses a SQL DELETE statement to remove the data from the database.

Using Aggregate Functions

Table 6-2 provides an overview of the SQL aggregate functions. Most databases offer a number of additional aggregate functions, but they are mostly vendor-specific and therefore tie your code to a particular database vendor.

Table 6-2. *Common SQL Aggregate Functions*

Function	Description
AVG(column)	Returns the average value of a certain column
COUNT(0)	Returns the number of selected rows
COUNT(column)	Returns the number of rows of a certain column (excluding rows with a null value for this column)
MAX(column)	Returns the highest value of a certain column
MIN(column)	Returns the lowest value of a certain column
SUM(column)	Returns the sum of all values of a certain column

Revisit the first JDBC example of this chapter (Listing 6-3). It uses the COUNT(0) aggregate function to determine the total number of members. Listing 6-10 shows a few more examples of using aggregate functions to get some statistics on existing members.

Listing 6-10. *Examples of Using Aggregate Functions*

```
public long getTotalAge() {
  return getJdbcTemplate().queryForLong("SELECT SUM(age) FROM member");
}

public long getAverageAge() {
  return getJdbcTemplate().queryForLong("SELECT AVG(age) FROM member");
}

public long getOldestAge() {
  return getJdbcTemplate().queryForLong("SELECT MAX(age) FROM member");
}

public long getYoungestAge() {
  return getJdbcTemplate().queryForLong("SELECT MIN(age) FROM member");
}
```

You could also implement the examples in Listing 6-10 by retrieving all the data from the database and determining the average and sum programmatically. However, because these aggregate functions are implemented natively by the database, using them greatly improves performance. Furthermore, using aggregate functions greatly reduces network traffic by transferring only the result of the function instead of the entire data set on which the function is performed.

Note that we are using the queryForLong() method provided by the JdbcTemplate class to avoid having to inspect the result set and cast the content of the result set to a long. We can do this because we know the result of the aggregate function is of the long type.

■**Tip** Because aggregate functions generally outperform doing the same operation programmatically in terms of CPU cycles as well as network traffic, use aggregate functions wherever applicable.

So far, we have created an incomplete implementation of the MemberDao interface. We will continue to implement the entire interface during the remainder of this chapter, but to do this, we need to discuss some more advanced features of the Spring JdbcTemplate class.

Using Callbacks

As mentioned earlier, Spring's template classes hide most of the complexity of working with the underlying persistence technology. However, in some cases, you do want access to the underlying API to perform operations on it. Fortunately, Spring provides support for doing that. Spring does this by means of callbacks. A *callback* is really nothing more than an implementation of an interface that is passed into a method call as an argument. The internals of the method call—in this case, method calls on the JdbcTemplate—will use these callbacks to either get data or set data depending on the callback.

Note that the methods on these callbacks are allowed to throw a SQLException, which is often needed when working with the JDBC API directly, such as when obtaining values from a ResultSet. The JdbcTemplate class will handle these exceptions and translate them to Spring's data-access exception hierarchy.

In a previous example (Listing 6-6), you were introduced to the RowMapper interface, which was used to map the result of the SELECT statement to an actual Member instance. This is an example of a callback that you can use to obtain access to the JDBC API. Table 6-3 provides an overview of the different callbacks Spring's JDBC support classes provide.

Table 6-3. *Callbacks Provided by Spring's JDBC Support Classes*

Callback	Description
CallableStatementCreator	Allows for the creation of a CallableStatement, a JDBC interface that can be used to execute stored procedures, using the provided Connection instance
CallableStatementCallback	Allows for performing additional calls on the CallableStatement
ConnectionCallback	Allows for direct interaction on an active JDBC Connection instance
PreparedStatementCreator	Allows for the creation of a PreparedStatement (a precompiled SQL statement) using the provided Connection instance
PreparedStatementCallback	Allows for performing additional calls on the PreparedStatement
PreparedStatementSetter	Allows for setting the values on a prepared statement (also comes in a batch version: BatchPreparedStatementSetter)
ResultSetExtractor	Allows for stateless extracting of all results from the ResultSet
RowCallbackHandler	Allows for stateful extracting of all results from the ResultSet
RowMapper	Allows for mapping individual rows in the ResultSet to an object instance
StatementCallback	Allows for setting the values on a Statement (a static SQL statement)
PreparedStatementCallback	Allows for execution of a number of methods on an active PreparedStatement

The most commonly used callback interfaces are PreparedStatementSetter and RowMapper. We will discuss these two callbacks in more detail in the next sections. Note that most of the principles for working with those two callback interfaces apply to all of the callback interfaces.

Using the RowMapper Interface

In Listing 6-6, we used the RowMapper interface to map each row in the result set to a Member instance. Listing 6-11 shows the load() method implementation, which is similar to loadAll(). In this case, for illustrative purposes, we are implementing the RowMapper interface as an anonymous inner class.

Listing 6-11. *Using the RowMapper Callback Interface*

```
public Member load(Integer id) {
  return (Member)getJdbcTemplate().queryForObject(
    "SELECT * FROM member WHERE id = ?",
    new Object[] { id },
    new RowMapper() {
      public Object mapRow(ResultSet resultSet, int row) throws SQLException {
        Member member = new Member();
        member.setId(resultSet.getInt("id"));
        member.getName().setFirst(resultSet.getString("name_first"));
        member.getName().setMiddle(resultSet.getString("name_middle"));
        member.getName().setLast(resultSet.getString("name_last"));
        member.getAddress().setLine1(resultSet.getString("address_line1"));
        member.getAddress().setLine2(resultSet.getString("address_line2"));
        member.getAddress().setCity(resultSet.getString("address_city"));
        member.getAddress().setState(resultSet.getString("address_state"));
        member.getAddress().setZip(resultSet.getString("address_zip"));
        member.setAge(resultSet.getInt("age"));
        return member;
      }
    }
  );
}
```

The RowMapper callback interface defines one method that you need to implement: mapRow(). In this code example, we implemented it as an anonymous inner class that provides a convenient way to have all related code in one place. Of course, you could also use a named inner class or even a separate class as an implementation of the RowMapper interface. As the implementation gets longer and more complex, your code may become more difficult to read. In that case, using an anonymous class is discouraged, and using inner classes or package protected classes is more useful. It allows other parts of your application to reuse the same mappings.

Using a RowMapper implementation for the query method on the JdbcTemplate class ensures that the framework will iterate over all rows in the ResultSet and call the mapRow() method on the RowMapper callback. The mapRow() method is called by the framework for each row in the result set, passing in the ResultSet and the row number as arguments. The implementation of the method gets the needed values from the ResultSet and sets them on a newly created Member instance. After setting all the values on the Member instance, it is returned by the method implementation.

The framework will handle maintaining a list of results or just returning the single instance, depending on the query method you called. In this case, only a single instance is returned because the queryForObject() method was called, which returns a single object instance. In the case of Listing 6-6, a List of Member objects is returned.

Working with the ResultSet directly usually requires you to handle the SQLException that is thrown by all the getters, but because the mapRow() method on the callback interface declares a thrown SQLException, there is no need to handle it. The framework will handle it for you and transparently translate it to an exception in Spring's data-access exception hierarchy.

Using the PreparedStatementSetter Interface

Another frequently used callback interface is org.springframework.jdbc.core.
PreparedStatementSetter. Suppose we want to query the database for all Member instances that
were created on a certain date. Listing 6-12 uses the PreparedStatementSetter to ease the creation
and initialization of the query.

Listing 6-12. *Using the PreparedStatementSetter Callback Interface*

```
public List getMembersForLastNameAndAge(final String lastName, final Integer age) {
  return getJdbcTemplate().query(
    "SELECT * FROM member WHERE name_last = ? AND age = ?",
    new PreparedStatementSetter() {
      public void setValues(PreparedStatement ps) throws SQLException {
        ps.setString(0, lastName);
        ps.setInt(1, age);
      }
    },
    new RowMapper() {
      public Object mapRow(ResultSet resultSet, int i) throws SQLException {
        Member member = new Member();
        member.setId(resultSet.getInt("id"));
        member.getName().setFirst(resultSet.getString("name_first"));
        member.getName().setMiddle(resultSet.getString("name_middle"));
        member.getName().setLast(resultSet.getString("name_last"));
        member.getAddress().setLine1(resultSet.getString("address_line1"));
        member.getAddress().setLine2(resultSet.getString("address_line2"));
        member.getAddress().setCity(resultSet.getString("address_city"));
        member.getAddress().setState(resultSet.getString("address_state"));
        member.getAddress().setZip(resultSet.getString("address_zip"));
        member.setAge(resultSet.getInt("age"));
        return member;
      }
    }
  );
}
```

Listing 6-12 uses PreparedStatementSetter to create the query to execute and set the values on
the prepared statement. The framework will create the actual prepared statement from the specified
SQL statement. PreparedStatementSetter will obtain the created prepared statement and allows the
developer to just set the required values on the statement. Again, when using the JdbcTemplate
class, the framework handles the possible SQLException, which needs to be handled when accessing
values in the result set.

Note that you could rewrite the code in Listing 6-11 to use a prepared statement, but that
would be a fairly trivial use of the PreparedStatementSetter callback interface (not a bad thing,
because it is precompiled by the database and therefore will outperform a regular SQL statement).
In more complex cases, you also want to use PreparedStatement for creating the query and setting
the arguments on it. For instance, when working with a date or time stamp as one of the arguments
to the query, you should use PreparedStatement and set the argument values using the corresponding setter methods to ensure the correct conversion from Java type to SQL type.

Using Executable Query Objects

So far, we have written our SQL statements as `String` arguments or prepared statements, which are passed into the `JdbcTemplate` methods. Spring provides a more elegant way to write SQL statements, which offers the means to access the database in a more object-oriented manner. Spring supports this by providing several executable query objects for performing database operations.

■**Tip** These query objects are thread-safe once they are compiled. Therefore, declare and initialize them in the constructor to avoid thread-safety issues. Once compiled, you can use a single instance for several classes.

Each of these executable query objects is used to map a database operation to a Java object. This object can be created, initialized, and used to query the database in an object-oriented manner.

Using the MappingSqlQuery Class

The most common task when working with databases is to query for data in the database. The `org.springframework.jdbc.object.MappingSqlQuery` class makes it easier to execute the same query multiple times.

Suppose we want to reuse the query from Listing 6-12 and refactor it out of the DAO class, as shown in Listing 6-13. First, we need to implement the query in a separate query class, which extends the abstract `MappingSqlQuery` class. Second, we need to implement the `mapRow()` method in the same manner as discussed in the "Using the RowMapper Interface" section.

Listing 6-13. *Implementing the MappingSqlQuery Class*

```
package com.apress.springbook.chapter06;

import java.sql.ResultSet;
import java.sql.Types;
import java.sql.SQLException;

import javax.sql.DataSource;

import org.springframework.jdbc.object.MappingSqlQuery;
import org.springframework.jdbc.core.SqlParameter;

public class LastNameAndAgeQuery extends MappingSqlQuery {
  private static final String SQL_QUERY =
    "SELECT * FROM member WHERE name_last = ? AND age = ?";

  public LastNameAndAgeQuery (DataSource ds) {
    super(ds, SQL_QUERY);
    declareParameter(new SqlParameter("name_last", Types.VARCHAR));
    declareParameter(new SqlParameter("age", Types.INTEGER));
    compile();
  }

  protected Object mapRow(ResultSet resultSet, int row) throws SQLException {
    Member member = new Member();
    member.setId(resultSet.getInt("id"));
    member.getName().setFirst(resultSet.getString("name_first"));
    member.getName().setMiddle(resultSet.getString("name_middle"));
```

```
        member.getName().setLast(resultSet.getString("name_last"));
        member.getAddress().setLine1(resultSet.getString("address_line1"));
        member.getAddress().setLine2(resultSet.getString("address_line2"));
        member.getAddress().setCity(resultSet.getString("address_city"));
        member.getAddress().setState(resultSet.getString("address_state"));
        member.getAddress().setZip(resultSet.getString("address_zip"));
        member.setAge(resultSet.getInt("age"));
        return member;
    }
}
```

Note that the string containing the actual SQL query to execute is declared as a static and final field for readability. Then one of the available constructors is overridden in order to pass in the query to use.

Next, we need to declare the parameters to the query. The MappingSqlQuery superclass provides the declareParameter() convenience method to do this. We need to declare the two parameters, depicted by question marks in the SQL query, in the correct order. JDBC relies on the ordering of the parameters rather than the name of the parameters. Naming the parameters while declaring them is not necessary, but it improves the readability and maintainability of our code.

■Tip Always name the declared parameters in your query objects. This greatly improves the readability and maintainability of your code.

The parameters are declared by creating an instance of the SqlParameter class, a convenience class offered by Spring's JDBC support that eases the creation of a SQL parameter. The constructor you should always use takes the name and a SQL type as arguments. The types are defined by the java.sql.Types class, which is part of the JDBC API.

Now that we have implemented our query object, we can rewrite our DAO to reuse the query object for all queries, as shown in Listing 6-14.

Listing 6-14. *The Rewritten DAO That Uses the Externalized Query Object*

```
private LastNameAndAgeQuery lastNameAndAgeQuery;

protected void initDao() throws Exception {
  super.initDao();

  lastNameAndAgeQuery = new LastNameAndAgeQuery (getDataSource());
}

public List getMembersForLastNameAndAge (String lastName, Integer age) {
  return lastNameAndAgeQuery.execute(new Object[] { lastName, age });
}
```

Note that the lastName and age arguments no longer need to be declared final. The MappingSqlQuery class also provides some convenience execute() methods when, for instance, you have only a few int parameters or a single long parameter. In this case, for clarity, you use the execute() method with an object array as argument.

As mentioned earlier, query objects are thread-safe only after they have been initialized and compiled. Therefore, you create the query inside the initDao() method, which is overridden. This method is called on the JdbcDaoSupport class after all the properties have been set but before any other method call is allowed on the DAO. This ensures the query object is in a thread-safe state once it is first used.

Using the SqlUpdate Class

Next, to provide support for externalizing queries, Spring's JDBC support offers a way to externalize your UPDATE and INSERT statements. You can externalize both kinds of statements by extending the org.springframework.jdbc.object.SqlUpdate query object. Listing 6-15 shows how to use the SqlUpdate class to execute an UPDATE statement.

Listing 6-15. *Implementing the SqlUpdate Class to Do an Update*

```
package com.apress.springbook.chapter06;

import java.sql.Types;

import javax.sql.DataSource;

import org.springframework.jdbc.object.SqlUpdate;
import org.springframework.jdbc.core.SqlParameter;

public class UpdateAgeQuery extends SqlUpdate {
   private static final String SQL_QUERY =
         "UPDATE member SET age = ? WHERE id = ?";

   public UpdateAgeQuery (DataSource dataSource) {
      super(dataSource, SQL_QUERY);
      declareParameter(new SqlParameter("age", Types.INTEGER));
      declareParameter(new SqlParameter("id", Types.INTEGER));
      compile();
   }
}
```

This example is similar to the MappingSqlQuery example. The main difference is that the SqlUpdate implementation does not need to implement a method to map the row to an object, because the update() methods on SqlUpdate always return an int indicating the number of rows that were affected by the update.

To be able to use this externalized UPDATE statement, we need to rewrite the DAO to use the query, as shown in Listing 6-16. Just as with the MappingSqlQuery example, we need to initialize the query object in the initDao() method. This ensures that the query is correctly initialized (and compiled) before it is being called. That way, we are sure no thread-safety issues occur.

Listing 6-16. *The Rewritten DAO That Uses the Externalized Update Object*

```
private UpdateAgeQuery updateAgeQuery;

protected void initDao() throws Exception {
  super.initDao();

  lastNameAndAgeQuery = new LastNameAndAgeQuery (getDataSource());
  updateAgeQuery = new UpdateAgeQuery (getDataSource());
}

public void updateAge(Integer memberId, Integer age) {
  updateAgeQuery.update(new Object[] { age, memberId });
}
```

The SqlUpdate class is not only for performing updates as the name suggests. It also allows you to externalize your INSERT statements in the same manner. Listing 6-17 demonstrates externalizing an INSERT statement.

Listing 6-17. *Implementing SqlUpdate to Do an Insert*

```
package com.apress.springbook.chapter06;

import java.sql.Types;

import javax.sql.DataSource;

import org.springframework.jdbc.object.SqlUpdate;
import org.springframework.jdbc.core.SqlParameter;

public class AddMemberQuery extends SqlUpdate {
  private static final String SQL_QUERY =
    "INSERT INTO member (name_first, name_middle, name_last, address_line1, " +
    "address_line2, address_city, address_state, address_zip, age) " +
    "VALUES (?, ?, ?, ?, ?, ?, ?, ?, ?)";

  public AddMemberQuery (DataSource dataSource) {
    super(dataSource, SQL_QUERY);
    declareParameter(new SqlParameter("name_first", Types.VARCHAR));
    declareParameter(new SqlParameter("name_middle", Types.VARCHAR));
    declareParameter(new SqlParameter("name_last", Types.VARCHAR));
    declareParameter(new SqlParameter("address_line1", Types.VARCHAR));
    declareParameter(new SqlParameter("address_line2", Types.VARCHAR));
    declareParameter(new SqlParameter("address_city", Types.VARCHAR));
    declareParameter(new SqlParameter("address_state", Types.VARCHAR));
    declareParameter(new SqlParameter("address_zip", Types.VARCHAR));
    declareParameter(new SqlParameter("age", Types.INTEGER));
    compile();
  }
}
```

We need to change the rewritten version of the DAO in the same way as the previous examples. We create the query in the initDao() method and rewrite the actual insert method to use the created query, as shown in Listing 6-18.

Listing 6-18. *The Rewritten DAO That Uses the Externalized Insert Object*

```
private AddMemberQuery addMemberQuery;

protected void initDao() throws Exception {
  super.initDao();

  lastNameAndAgeQuery = new LastNameAndAgeQuery (getDataSource());
  updateAgeQuery = new UpdateAgeQuery (getDataSource());
  addMemberQuery = new AddMemberQuery (getDataSource());
}

public void add(Member member) {
  addMemberQuery.update(new Object[] {
    member.getName().getFirst(),
    member.getName().getMiddle(),
    member.getName().getLast(),
```

```
    member.getAddress().getLine1(),
    member.getAddress().getLine2(),
    member.getAddress().getCity(),
    member.getAddress().getState(),
    member.getAddress().getZip(),
    member.getAge(),
  });
}
```

Using the StoredProcedure Class

All previous examples of executable query objects so far just provided a more elegant way to implement your data-access code. However, the main reason to use executable query objects is that they allow you to work with stored procedures in the same manner. A *stored procedure* is a routine (or program) that is physically stored in the database. Stored procedures are not part of the core SQL standard and are therefore not supported by all databases. However, Spring's data-access features also provide support for working with stored procedures by means of the org.springframework. jdbc.object.StoredProcedure class.

This class works in a similar manner as the previous executable query objects. First, you need to create an extension of the StoredProcedure class, which will call the stored procedure. We'll assume a stored procedure exists in the database with the name aggregate_members and that it takes two arguments—the starting age and the ending age—that define the range of members to aggregate, as shown in Listing 6-19.

Listing 6-19. *Implementing StoredProcedure*

```
package com.apress.springbook.chapter06;

import java.util.Map;
import java.util.HashMap;

import java.sql.Types;

import javax.sql.DataSource;

import org.springframework.jdbc.object.StoredProcedure;
import org.springframework.jdbc.core.SqlParameter;
import org.springframework.jdbc.core.SqlOutParameter;

public class CallAggregateMembers extends StoredProcedure {
  private static final String STORED_PROCEDURE_NAME = "aggregate_members";

  public CallAggregateMembers(DataSource dataSource) {
    super(dataSource, STORED_PROCEDURE_NAME);
    declareParameter(new SqlParameter("start_age", Types.INTEGER));
    declareParameter(new SqlParameter("end_age", Types.INTEGER));
    declareParameter(new SqlOutParameter("number_aggregated", Types.INTEGER));
    compile();
  }

  public int aggregate(Integer start, Integer end) {
    Map<String, Integer> inParameters = new HashMap<String,Integer>(2);
    inParameters.put("start_age", start);
    inParameters.put("end_age", end);
```

```
  Map outParameters = execute(inParameters);
  if (outParameters.size() > 0) {
    return (Integer) outParameters.get("number_aggregated");
  } else {
    return 0;
  }
  }
}
```

You will notice that Listing 6-19 looks similar to all the previous examples. However, it has two important differences:

- For stored procedures, we also need to declare one or more out parameters. This is necessary only when the stored procedure actually returns one or more values. In this case, the stored procedure named aggregate_members returns the number of rows that were aggregated. Therefore, we need to declare one out parameter.

- In the aggregate() method, we need to first declare a map containing all the input parameters, and that map is then used to execute the actual stored procedure. The execution returns a Map containing all the out parameters that were returned by the stored procedure. We just need to get the parameters by the name we specified when declaring the out parameters.

Tip It is considered a best practice to have the method on the implementation resemble the signature of the actual stored procedure. So, in this case, the stored procedure accepts two integers, and the aggregate method also accepts two integer arguments.

Because most of the actual code for executing the query is already inside the stored procedure implementation, calling the stored procedure from our DAO is straightforward:

```
CallAggregateMembers procedure = new CallAggregateMembers(getDataSource());
int numberOfAffectedRecords = procedure.aggregate(1, 2);
```

Creating Batches

One of the major advantages of using JDBC over most ORM solutions is its support for batch operations. Suppose that we want to create an import tool that allows us to import a number of old members. Say we have a comma-separated file containing the data that we read and transform to a list of Member instances.

To insert such instances into a database, most ORM solutions force you to call a save method on all of them separately. When working with the JDBC API, you can create a batch containing all the INSERT statements and send them to the database together for execution, which improves performance greatly.

Creating a batch is fairly straightforward using Spring's JDBC support. We just need to call a different method on the JdbcTemplate class and use a specific callback implementation, as shown in Listing 6-20.

Listing 6-20. *Performing a Batch Update Using the JdbcTemplate Class*

```
public void importMembers(final List<Member> members) {
  getJdbcTemplate().batchUpdate(
    "INSERT INTO member (name_first, name_middle, name_last, address_line1, " +
```

```
    "address_line2, address_city, address_state, address_zip, age) " +
    "VALUES (?, ?, ?, ?, ?, ?, ?, ?, ?)",
    new BatchPreparedStatementSetter() {
      public void setValues(PreparedStatement ps, int i) throws SQLException {
        Member member = members.get(i);
        ps.setString(1, member.getName().getFirst());
        ps.setString(2, member.getName().getMiddle());
        ps.setString(2, member.getName().getLast());
        ps.setInt(9, member.getAge());
      }

      public int getBatchSize() {
        return members.size();
      }
    }
  );
}
```

Here, we've used the batchUpdate() method with the same SQL statement as we used previously to insert member instances into the database and a specific callback. The org.springframework. jdbc.core.BatchPreparedStatementSetter callback defines two methods we need to implement:

- setValues(), which is the same as previous examples, but in this case, it is called for each item in the batch

- getBatchSize(), which is used by JdbcTemplate to determine the batch size and therefore the number of times the setValues() method must to be called

Working with LOBs

Some applications require you to work with large chunks of data, such as images, documents, and so on. These items need to be persisted in the same way as any other piece of data. Most databases support storing these larger amounts of data by means of a large object (LOB). Two kinds of LOBs exist: binary large objects (BLOBs) for large chunks of binary data and character large objects (CLOBs) for large chunks of character data. These kinds of objects are not supported by all databases and require special handling when storing and retrieving them.

Spring provides support for handling LOBs through the JdbcTemplate class. Listing 6-21 demonstrates how to store a BLOB in the database.

Listing 6-21. *Storing a BLOB Using the LobHandler Class*

```
private LobHandler lobHandler = new DefaultLobHandler();

public void addImageForMember(final Integer memberId, final InputStream in)
throws IOException {
  final int imageSize = in.available();

  getJdbcTemplate().execute(
    "INSERT INTO member_image (member_id, image) VALUES (?, ?)",
    new AbstractLobCreatingPreparedStatementCallback(lobHandler) {
      protected void setValues(PreparedStatement ps, LobCreator lobCreator)
      throws SQLException, DataAccessException {
        ps.setInt(1, memberId);
        lobCreator.setBlobAsBinaryStream(ps, 2, in, imageSize);
```

```
      }
    }
  );
}
```

First, notice that we need to declare an org.springframework.jdbc.support.lob.LobHandler instance. In this case, the org.springframework.jdbc.support.lob.DefaultLobHandler is used, which just delegates to the underlying JDBC API. When working with Oracle (more specifically, the Oracle 9*i* driver), you need to use the more specific OracleLobHandler implementation that handles some of the peculiarities of Oracle for handling LOBs.

Next is just a normal INSERT statement, as you saw earlier on in this chapter. However, the execute() method is called with a PreparedStatementCallback callback, which is specific for working with LOBs (org.springframework.jdbc.core.support.AbstractLobCreating PreparedStatementCallback). The abstract callback provides us with an additional org.springframework.jdbc.support.lob.LobCreator instance, which we need in order to handle the BLOB.

In the setValues() implementation, we set the ID of the member with which we want to associate the image. Furthermore, we need to set the input stream on the prepared statement. This is where the LobCreator class comes in; it provides a few convenience methods for setting the LOB data on the prepared statement. For BLOBs, you can set the content either as a binary stream or as bytes. For CLOBs, you can set the content as an ASCII stream, a character stream, or a string. The LobCreator class handles the content and the encoding.

Now that we are able to store LOBs in the database, Listing 6-22 shows how to retrieve them using the LobHandler class.

Listing 6-22. *Retrieving a BLOB Using LobHandler*

```
public void getImage(Integer id, final OutputStream out) {
  getJdbcTemplate().query("SELECT image FROM member_image WHERE id = ?",
    new AbstractLobStreamingResultSetExtractor() {
      protected void streamData(ResultSet rs) throws SQLException, IOException {
        FileCopyUtils.copy(lobHandler.getBlobAsBinaryStream(rs, 1), out);
      }
    }
  );
}
```

As you can see in Listing 6-22, retrieving a LOB is similar to executing a normal query. You just need to specify a specific callback and use the LobHandler class to obtain the stream to the LOB content.

Working with LOBs using the JDBC API without a framework such as Spring can be cumbersome. As you saw in the previous two examples, Spring makes working with LOBs easy.

Using the NativeJdbcExtractor Interface

As mentioned in the previous chapter, you can obtain a connection to a database in multiple ways: through a direct connection, connection pooling, or the connection provided by an application server. All of these are transparently wrapped in a DataSource, which is inserted into the JdbcTemplate class. So you don't need to know about the underlying native objects as provided by the database.

Sometimes, however, you might want to gain access to the underlying objects in order to perform database-specific operations on them, such as for changing the connection timeout. Spring's JDBC support provides access to the underlying objects by using one of the implementations of the NativeJdbcExtractor interface. Spring provides a SimpleNativeJdbcExtractor implementation, which works for many connection pools and application servers, but it also offers more specific implementations for a number of well-known connection pools and application servers, as shown in Table 6-4.

Table 6-4. *Specific Native JDBC Extractor Implementations*

Pooling/Platform	Implementation
C3PO	`org.springframework.jdbc.support.nativejdbc.` `C3PONativeJdbcExtractor`
Jakarta Commons DBCP	`org.springframework.jdbc.support.nativejdbc.` `CommonsDbcpNativeJdbcExtractor`
JBoss (3.2+)	`org.springframework.jdbc.support.nativejdbc.` `JBossNativeJdbcExtractor`
WebLogic (6.1+)	`org.springframework.jdbc.support.nativejdbc.` `WebLogicNativeJdbcExtractor`
WebSphere (4+)	`org.springframework.jdbc.support.nativejdbc.` `WebSphereNativeJdbcExtractor`
ObjectWeb XA Pool	`org.springframework.jdbc.support.nativejdbc.` `XAPoolNativeJdbcExtractor`
Other	`org.springframework.jdbc.support.nativejdbc.` `SimpleNativeJdbcExtractor`

To use any of these native JDBC extractors, you need to set them on the `JdbcTemplate` class you are using. You can do this in one of two ways: programmatically or in your application context. Here is an example of how to set the extractor programmatically, assuming the same Commons DBCP data source configuration shown in Listing 6-5:

```
getJdbcTemplate().setNativeJdbcExtractor(new SimpleNativeJdbcExtractor());
```

The other way is to specify the extractor in your application context and set it in `JdbcTemplate`, as shown in Listing 6-23. Note that in this case, you need to configure the `JdbcTemplate` class in the application context in order to be able to set the extractor on it. This requires you to set the `JdbcTemplate` class on the DAO instead of the data source directly.

Listing 6-23. *Setting the Extractor on the JdbcTemplate Class in the Application Context*

```
<bean id="dataSource" class="org.apache.commons.dbcp.BasicDataSource"
      destroy-method="close">
  <property name="driverClassName" value="org.hsqldb.jdbcDriver"/>
  <property name="url" value="jdbc:hsqldb:mem:."/>
  <property name="username" value="sa"/>
  <property name="password" value=""/>
</bean>

<bean id="nativeJdbcExtractor"
      class="org.springframework.jdbc.support.nativejdbc. ➡
CommonsDbcpNativeJdbcExtractor"/>

<bean id="jdbcTemplate" class="org.springframework.jdbc.core.JdbcTemplate">
  <property name="dataSource" ref="dataSource"/>
  <property name="nativeJdbcExtractor" ref="nativeJdbcExtractor"/>
</bean>
```

Introducing New Spring 2.0 Features

The release of Spring 2.0 introduced several improvements to Spring in general and two improvements specific to persistence. Both features are extras provided by Spring for convenience. Of course, you are not required to use them.

Using the SimpleJdbcTemplate Class

Version 2.0 of the Spring Framework introduced a new version of the `JdbcTemplate`: `org.springframework.jdbc.core.simple.SimpleJdbcTemplate`. This wrapper class for the original template uses Java 5 (and newer) facilities such as varargs and autoboxing. This simplifies the use of the template for performing database operations through the JDBC API. It also exposes only the most commonly used methods of the normal `JdbcTemplate` class, as shown in Table 6-5, and offers a more convenient method signature.

Table 6-5. *Methods Provided by SimpleJdbcTemplate*

Method	Description
`query()`	Allows you to query by specifying a SQL statement, a parameterized row mapper, and optionally any parameters
`queryForInt()`	Allows you to query for an `int` by specifying a SQL statement and optionally any parameters
`queryForLong()`	Allows you to query for a `long` by specifying a SQL statement and optionally any parameters
`queryForMap()`	Allows you to query for a `Map` by specifying a SQL statement and optionally any parameters
`queryForList()`	Allows you to query for a `List` by specifying a SQL statement and optionally any parameters
`queryForObject()`	Allows you to query for a specific object by specifying a SQL statement, either the class of the object to convert to or a parameterized row mapper, and optionally any parameters
`update()`	Allows you to execute an update statement by specifying the update statement and optionally any parameters

All methods of `SimpleJdbcTemplate` allow you to specify the optional parameters as comma-separated arguments, instead of needing to create an object array to pass in the arguments. Furthermore, the `SimpleJdbcTemplate` class uses a strongly typed `org.springframework.jdbc.core.simple.ParameterizedRowMapper` interface instead of the normal `RowMapper` interface, which is created for a specific type of object, so you do not need to cast the result of the query.

Using `SimpleJdbcTemplate`, we can rewrite the implementation of the `load()` method (Listing 6-11) as shown in Listing 6-24.

Listing 6-24. *Rewritten load() Method Implementation Using the SimpleJdbcTemplate Class*

```
public Member load(Integer id) {
  return new SimpleJdbcTemplate(getDataSource()).queryForObject(
    "SELECT * FROM member WHERE id = ?",
    new ParameterizedRowMapper<Member>() {
      public Member mapRow(ResultSet resultSet, int row)
          throws SQLException {
        Member member = new Member();
```

```
            member.setId(resultSet.getInteger("id"));
            member.getName().setFirst(resultSet.getString("name_first"));
            member.getName().setLast(resultSet.getString("name_last"));

            member.setAge(resultSet.getInteger("age"));
            return member;
        }
    }, id);
}
```

Note that we do not need to cast the object resulting from the query to the specific implementation class, and we do not need to create an object array to pass in the ID. Even when multiple arguments must be provided, we can just add them as extra arguments.

Let's assume we have a more complex query to obtain the total number of members that exist for a certain age range and have a certain first name. We can implement this as shown in Listing 6-25.

Listing 6-25. *Using the Convenient Syntax Provided by the SimpleJdbcTemplate Class*

```
public int getTotalNumberOfMembers(Integer startAge,
                                   Integer endAge,
                                   String firstName) {
  return new SimpleJdbcTemplate(getDataSource()).queryForInt(
    "SELECT COUNT(0) FROM member " +
    "WHERE age > ? AND age < ? AND first_name = ?",
    startAge, endAge, firstName);
}
```

From this example, it is more obvious why using the new syntax is a more convenient way to perform database operations.

■Caution The SimpleJdbcTemplate class uses Java 5 (and newer) syntax, so you can use it only when you are actually running in a Java 5 (or newer) environment.

Performing JNDI Data Source Lookups

As explained in the previous chapter, you can look up a data source through JNDI. The namespace support offered by Spring 2.0 discussed earlier allows for an easier configuration, as shown in Listing 6-26.

Listing 6-26. *Spring 2.0 Syntax for Looking Up a Data Source Through JNDI*

```
<?xml version="1.0" encoding="UTF-8"?>
<beans xmlns="http://www.springframework.org/schema/beans"
    xmlns:xsi="http://www.w3.org/2001/XMLSchema-instance"
    xmlns:jndi="http://www.springframework.org/schema/jndi"
    xsi:schemaLocation="http://www.springframework.org/schema/beans
          http://www.springframework.org/schema/beans/spring-beans.xsd
          http://www.springframework.org/schema/jndi
          http://www.springframework.org/schema/jndi/spring-jndi.xsd">

  <jndi:lookup id="dataSource" jndiName="jdbc/MyDataSource"/>

</beans>
```

This is an example of the simplest kind of JNDI lookup. Of course, Spring 2.0 also supports more complex lookups. Refer to the Spring reference documentation for more information about JNDI lookups.

Summary

In this chapter, you learned how to perform the most common database operations, as well as more complex tasks, using Spring's data-access support. Spring provides a powerful abstraction framework that simplifies working with the JDBC API. This chapter also showed you how the new features provided by Spring 2.0 make working with the JDBC API easier. The concepts and examples provided in this chapter should give you enough information to start building your own application that uses database persistence.

Now that you've seen how Spring handles data access, the next chapter looks at bundling database operations into transactions.

CHAPTER 7

■■■

Transaction Management

Welcome to Chapter 7, where you'll learn how to organize transaction management in your applications with the Spring Framework. This chapter builds on top of all that has been discussed in the previous chapters.

Before we start with the Spring details, we need to take a closer look at database transactions and exactly what they help us to achieve. Then we'll discuss Spring transaction managers. As you'll recall from Chapter 5, there are at least eight APIs in Java to manage transactions, plus the JTA. We'll look at how Spring adds flexibility to applications by taking away these differences.

The last part of this chapter talks about transaction demarcation. We'll first describe how this works in earlier Spring versions, and then discuss the new options in Spring 2.0. This will stand you in good stead if you need to upgrade an old installation (which you should). All options use Spring AOP, which we covered in Chapters 3 and 4, either directly or behind the scenes.

Database Transactions

Transactions are used to guarantee data integrity. They organize changes made to data in a database in *units*, which must be either completed entirely or aborted. They must also be treated in a coherent and reliable way, which is where the ACID properties (or features) come into play. The ACID properties form the minimal contract that databases must respect to ensure data integrity, as follows:

Atomicity: All changes that are made between the start and the end of a transaction must either succeed or abort all together. To ensure this, a database will roll back (that is, undo) all changes that have occurred since the start of the transaction when internal errors occur or when asked to do so.

Consistency: After a transaction ends—is either committed or rolled back—the data should be left in a consistent state, meaning no constraints or indices can be violated and field constraints like not-nullable, field length, and field type must be respected.

Isolation: Transactions can run concurrently, meaning multiple transactions can insert, read, update, and delete data at the same time. Transactions should not be affected by the actions of other transactions. Because full isolation between transactions that work on the same data often involves locks, it may cause slow performance. For this reason, databases support different isolation levels that offer a trade-off between performance and the risk of being affected by the actions of other transactions.

Durability: After a transaction has been committed, the changes must be stored in a durable way; for example, by saving them on the file system.

The idea of a database transaction is straightforward. While connected to the database, you notify the database that you want to start a new transaction, execute a number of SQL statements, and then notify the database that you want to commit any changes.

A database connection can have only one active (or current) transaction. (Other transactions may be suspended; these are called *nested transactions*, and they are commonly used on databases that support them.) The database will automatically roll back the transaction (and all changes that were made after its start) when errors—such as invalid field values, other forms of integrity violations, deadlocks, and so on—occur. As a database user, you can also ask the database to roll back the active transaction by issuing a rollback command.

Two main issues make database transactions complicated for developers to work with and difficult for database vendors to implement:

Concurrency control: Databases need to protect against data loss or ghost data, yet allow concurrent access to the same data. Generally, developers can choose an isolation level to control the level of protection. Another form of concurrency control is protecting against lost updates. (For more information, see http://en.wikipedia.org/wiki/Concurrency_control, http://en.wikipedia.org/wiki/Multiversion_concurrency_control, and http://en.wikipedia.org/wiki/Optimistic_concurrency_control.)

Synchronization between transactions: Complex applications often need a way to synchronize two or more databases or other resources so that their local transactions are guaranteed to commit or roll back in a group. The technique used for this is called *two-phase commit* (or 2PC), *distributed transactions*, or *global transactions*.

We will take a "sunny day" approach to database transactions in this chapter and assume that you connect to only one database. We won't go into the details of concurrency control and isolation levels. And although many types of databases and resource types support transactions, we'll focus on transactions in relational databases, where they are most commonly used. Your database vendor documentation is a good place to start if you want to learn more about how transactions work for your database.

Transaction Management in Spring

The first step in setting up transaction management with Spring is choosing a transaction management strategy. This basically means selecting which of the transaction-management APIs in Java you want to use. Your choice will be dictated by the data-access framework or API you use in your applications.

As discussed in Chapter 5, Spring has a transaction-management API that is used to abstract the details of and differences between more than eight transaction-management APIs in Java. The main interface of this API is org.springframework.transaction.PlatformTransactionManager. Spring provides a number of implementations of this interface that support the most popular transaction-management APIs in Java, as shown in Table 7-1.

Table 7-1. *Transaction Manager Implementations in Spring*

Class	Target API
org.springframework.jdbc.datasource. DataSourceTransactionManager	java.sql.Connection (JDBC)
org.springframework.orm.hibernate. HibernateTransactionManager	net.sf.hibernate.Session (Hibernate 2)
org.springframework.orm.hibernate3. HibernateTransactionManager	org.hibernate.Session (Hibernate 3)

Class	Target API
`org.springframework.orm.jdo.` `JdoTransactionManager`	`javax.jdo.PersistenceManager` (JDO)
`org.springframework.orm.jpa.` `JpaTransactionManager`	`javax.persistence.EntityManager` (JPA)
`org.springframework.jta.` `JtaTransactionManager`	`javax.transaction.UserTransaction` (JTA)

Each transaction manager listed in Table 7-1 needs a factory object to obtain an object of the target API, except for `JtaTransactionManager`. The type of factory object that is required depends on the underlying data-access framework or API.

In the case of `DataSourceTransactionManager`, which manages transactions via the JDBC `Connection` interface, the factory object is `javax.sql.DataSource`. As we discussed in Chapter 5, `DataSource` is indeed a factory interface for JDBC `Connection` objects.

All the other APIs in Table 7-1, except JTA, are the unit of work types for the various ORM tools. These types have methods for managing transactions, and they use one JDBC `Connection` object behind the scenes. Each of these types has a factory class, which must be passed to their respective transaction manager implementation. Table 7-2 lists the factory type per Spring transaction manager implementation. The factory instance that is passed to the transaction manager must also be passed to the respective Spring template objects in data-access code. For example, the `DataSource` object that is passed to the `DataSourceTransactionManager` must also be passed to instances of `JdbcTemplate`.

Table 7-2. *Required Factory Types for Spring Transaction Managers*

Class	Target API
`org.springframework.jdbc.datasource.` `DataSourceTransactionManager`	`javax.sql.DataSource` (JDBC)
`org.springframework.orm.hibernate.` `HibernateTransactionManager`	`net.sf.hibernate.SessionFactory` (Hibernate 2)
`org.springframework.orm.hibernate3.` `HibernateTransactionManager`	`org.hibernate.SessionFactory` (Hibernate 3)
`org.springframework.orm.jdo.` `JdoTransactionManager`	`javax.jdo.PersistenceManagerFactory` (JDO)
`org.springframework.orm.jpa.` `JpaTransactionManager`	`javax.persistence.EntityManagerFactory` (JPA)

■**Tip** `JdbcTemplate` will work with any of the transaction manager implementations listed in Table 7-1. This allows you to seamlessly combine the use of ORM tools and JDBC in the same transactions and even on the same tables. The only requirement is to use `JdbcTemplate` with the same `DataSource` that is used by the ORM framework.

Next, we'll discuss how to configure Spring transaction managers for JDBC and the JTA.

Configuring Spring's Transaction Manager for JDBC

To set up transaction management for your applications, you need to configure the transaction manager of your choice. The simplest way to start is to use the DataSourceTransactionManager. It's suitable when working with JDBC or iBATIS.

Listing 7-1 shows the configuration for a connection pool and DataSourceTransactionManager.

Listing 7-1. *Configuring DataSourceTransactionManagement*

```
<beans>
  <bean id="dataSource" class="org.apache.commons.dbcp.BasicDataSource"
      destroy-method="close">
    <property name="driverClassName" value="${jdbc.driverClassName}"/>
    <property name="url" value="${jdbc.url}"/>
    <property name="username" value="${jdbc.username}"/>
    <property name="password" value="${jdbc.password}"/>
  </bean>

  <bean class="org.springframework.beans.factory.config. ➥
PropertyPlaceholderConfigurer">
    <property name="location" value="classpath:jdbc.properties"/>
  </bean>

  <bean id="transactionManager"
      class="org.springframework.jdbc.datasource. ➥
DataSourceTransactionManager">
    <property name="dataSource" ref="dataSource"/>
  </bean>
</beans>
```

We will use the transactionManager bean in Listing 7-1 when we configure transaction demarcation later in the chapter. In the most straightforward scenario, DataSourceTransactionManager will obtain a new Connection object from the DataSource object and bind it to the current thread when a transaction starts. It will remove the Connection object from the current thread when the transaction ends and commit or roll back the active transaction, as necessary, and close the Connection object.

Configuring Spring's Transaction Manager for JTA

An alternative transaction-management strategy is to use a JTA transaction manager. All application servers come with such a transaction manager, although some stand-alone implementations exist. You don't automatically need to use JTA when deploying applications in an application server. Nothing stops you from using DataSourceTransactionManager, which gives you the advantage of more independence from the deployment environment.

However, in a minority of cases, you want to delegate transaction management to the JTA transaction manager of your application server. The most common reason for this is to work with *distributed transactions*.

■Note Distributed transactions are required when you want to synchronize the transactions of multiple resources—for example, across multiple database connections. This is a requirement in only a small number of cases. Not all application servers support distributed transactions, and some that provide support do not do it properly.

Listing 7-2 shows the Spring configuration for using JTA transaction management. It will work with the JTA transaction manager to start and end JTA transactions.

Listing 7-2. *Setting Up Transaction Management via JTA in Spring*

```
<beans>
  <bean id="dataSource" class="org.springframework.jndi.JndiObjectFactoryBean">
    <property name="jndiName" value="java:env/jdbc/myDataSource"/>
  </bean>

  <bean id="transactionManager"
        class="org.springframework.jta.JtaTransactionManager"/>
</beans>
```

When working with the JTA transaction manager of an application server, you must use a `DataSource` object that was obtained via JNDI from the same application server. As you can see in Listing 7-2, `JtaTransactionManager` needs no special configuration. This is because the JTA transaction manager in the application server will automatically start and end the transactions on `Connection` objects that were obtained from the JNDI `DataSource` object.

■**Note** The configuration in Listing 7-2 assumes you are deploying your applications as WAR or EAR files in an application server. Some application servers also allow the use of JTA transaction management remotely. This usage scenario is allowed by the Java EE specifications (although some claim it is not officially supported).

Although the underlying transaction management uses JTA, the end result for your applications will be the same. Just pass the `DataSource` object to `JdbcTemplate`. `JtaTransactionManager` will transparently steer transaction management for JDBC, iBATIS, and all the ORM frameworks and APIs with which Spring integrates. The only requirement is to use the Spring template classes in your data-access code.

■**Note** Data-access code that uses Hibernate or JPA can work with Spring's transaction management without using the respective Spring template classes. Some restrictions apply. See Chapter 9 of the Spring reference manual for details.

Transaction Demarcation in Spring

Once you have configured a transaction manager, the next step is to decide on which points in the application flow transactions will start and end. We call this *transaction demarcation* (introduced in Chapter 5). In the remainder of this chapter, we will look at six different ways of setting up transaction demarcation in your application. The first three ways have been supported since Spring 1.0; the fourth one since Spring 1.2; and the last two are new additions to Spring 2.0.

The Spring 2.0 approaches to configuring transaction demarcation build on top of the mechanisms we'll introduce in discussing the Spring 1.0 and 1.2 techniques. Additionally, all forms of transaction demarcation we'll discuss use Spring AOP. This means it's imperative to understand the concepts discussed in Chapters 3 and 4.

Transaction Demarcation Introduced in Spring 1.0

In this section, we'll cover those forms of transaction demarcation that were part of the Spring 1.0 release. Later Spring releases added other forms, most notably Spring 2.0. However, all-round Spring developers should be aware of these older forms, as they have been in common use for many years. Also, other transaction-demarcation mechanisms reuse the components that are introduced here.

TransactionInterceptor and Proxy Creation

The core AOP component in all forms of transaction demarcation is the org.springframework.transaction.interceptor.TransactionInterceptor class. It's an around advice that implements the MethodInterceptor interface (see Chapter 3).

TransactionInterceptor is a thread-safe class that starts a transaction before a method is executed and ends it after the method execution exits. Listing 7-3 shows the configuration of TransactionInterceptor in a Spring XML file.

Listing 7-3. *Configuring TransactionInterceptor*

```
<beans>
  <bean id="dataSource" class="org.apache.commons.dbcp.BasicDataSource"
        destroy-method="close">
    <property name="driverClassName" value="${jdbc.driverClassName}"/>
    <property name="url" value="${jdbc.url}"/>
    <property name="username" value="${jdbc.username}"/>
    <property name="password" value="${jdbc.password}"/>
  </bean>

  <bean class="org.springframework.beans.factory.config. ➥
PropertyPlaceholderConfigurer">
    <property name="location" value="classpath:jdbc.properties"/>
  </bean>

  <bean id="transactionManager"
        class="org.springframework.jdbc.datasource. ➥
DataSourceTransactionManager">
    <property name="dataSource" ref="dataSource"/>
  </bean>

  <bean id="transactionInterceptor"
        class="org.springframework.transaction.interceptor.TransactionInterceptor">
    <property name="transactionManager" ref="transactionManager"/>
    <property name="transactionAttributes">
      <props>
        <prop key="endMatch">PROPAGATION_REQUIRED</prop>
      </props>
    </property>
  </bean>
</beans>
```

The transactionInterceptor bean in Listing 7-3 is an around advice configured to use the DataSourceTransactionManager. The other property, named transactionAttributes, sets the transaction configuration per method. Transactions will be started and ended only for method names that have been configured in transactionAttributes.

We'll look at how to configure the creation of a proxy object that uses the transactionInterceptor around advice with a target object next. The transactionAttributes configuration means that although the transactionInterceptor bean can intercept other methods, it will manage only transactions for the endMatch() method. No transaction management will happen for all other methods that are intercepted by TransactionInterceptor.

The PROPAGATION_REQUIRED keyword in the configuration of the transactionAttributes property in Listing 7-3 indicates the behavior of transaction management. PROPAGATION_REQUIRED means that a new transaction is created *if required* (no transaction will be created if one is already active). A PROPAGATION_* keyword is required, and PROPAGATION_REQUIRED is the most appropriate for almost all cases. Other behavior is available; see *Pro Spring* (Apress, 2005) for details.

Listing 7-4 shows how org.springframework.aop.framework.ProxyFactoryBean has been configured to create a proxy object with the transactionInterceptor around advice bean. Its target object is a DefaultTournamentMatchManager bean (see Chapters 1 through 3).

Listing 7-4. *Configuring ProxyFactoryBean with the transactionInterceptor Around Advice Bean*

```
<beans>
  <bean id="dataSource" class="org.apache.commons.dbcp.BasicDataSource"
        destroy-method="close">
    <property name="driverClassName" value="${jdbc.driverClassName}"/>
    <property name="url" value="${jdbc.url}"/>
    <property name="username" value="${jdbc.username}"/>
    <property name="password" value="${jdbc.password}"/>
  </bean>

  <bean class="org.springframework.beans.factory.config. ➡
PropertyPlaceholderConfigurer">
    <property name="location" value="classpath:jdbc.properties"/>
  </bean>

  <bean id="transactionManager"
        class=" org.springframework.jdbc.datasource.DataSourceTransactionManager">
    <property name="dataSource" ref="dataSource"/>
  </bean>

  <bean id="transactionInterceptor"
        class="org.springframework.transaction.interceptor.TransactionInterceptor">
    <property name="transactionManager"
            ref="transactionManager"/>
    <property name="transactionAttributes">
      <props>
        <prop key="endMatch">PROPAGATION_REQUIRED</prop>
      </props>
    </property>
  </bean>

  <bean id="tournamentMatchManager"
        class="org.springframework.aop.framework.ProxyFactoryBean">
    <property name="target">
      <bean class="com.apress.springbook.chapter07.DefaultTournamentMatchManager">
        <!--other properties omitted -->
      </bean>
    </property>
    <property name="interceptorNames">
      <list>
```

```
                <idref bean="transactionInterceptor"/>
            </list>
        </property>
        <property name="proxyTargetClass" value="false"/>
    </bean>
</beans>
```

Let's review the configuration in Listing 7-4 and how it demarcates transactions:

- `ProxyFactoryBean` creates a proxy object for the `DefaultTournamentMatchManager` bean. It's configured with the `transactionInterceptor` around advice bean that performs transaction management for the `endMatch()` method (see Chapter 3).

- The `transactionInterceptor` around advice bean uses `DataSourceTransactionManager`, which manages transactions on the JDBC `Connection` interface. Before the `endMatch()` method is executed on the target object, the `transactionInterceptor` around advice bean will delegate to this transaction manager to start a new transaction. `DataSource TransactionManager` will obtain a `Connection` object from the `DataSource` object, start a new transaction, and attach the `Connection` object to the current thread.

- This `Connection` object will remain available during the execution of the `endMatch()` method on the target object. This means that whenever a method is executed on `JdbcTemplate`, the `Connection` object will automatically be reused (see Chapter 5).

- After the execution of the `endMatch()` method on the target object ends, the `transaction Interceptor` around advice bean will delegate to the transaction manager to end the active transaction. `DataSourceTransactionManager` will obtain and remove the `Connection` object from the current thread, end the active transaction, and close the `Connection` object.

As you can see, the XML configuration in Listing 7-4 is quite elaborate. Spring 1.0 provides alternative means of configuration that require fewer lines of XML. However, before we discuss these alternatives, we need to take a closer look at how `TransactionInterceptor` handles commit-ting and rolling back exceptions.

■**Note** `TransactionInterceptor` is reused by all other forms of transaction demarcation in Spring. Sometimes this reuse happens behind the scenes. Read carefully through this and the next section to understand how `TransactionInterceptor` handles transaction demarcation. You'll need this understanding when we discuss the other forms of transaction demarcation.

Commit and Rollback with TransactionInterceptor

In the previous section, we said that `TransactionInterceptor` is responsible for starting and ending transactions *around* methods. It delegates the actual starting and ending of transactions to the `PlatformTransactionManager` interface. However, `PlatformTransactionManager` has two methods for ending transactions: `commit()` and `rollback()`. Which one will `TransactionInterceptor` call?

The default behavior for ending transactions of the `TransactionInterceptor` around advice is that of the EJB specifications:

- When methods exit normally or throw a checked exception, the active transaction will be committed.

- When methods throw an unchecked exception—those exceptions that are type-compatible with java.lang.Error or java.lang.RuntimeException—the active transaction will be rolled back.

- When an active transaction has programmatically been marked for rollback, it will also be rolled back. (See Chapter 9 of the Spring 2.0 reference manual for details.)

This behavior is a sensible default, and it mimics the behavior of EJB containers with which many developers are familiar. However, while this is the default behavior, TransactionInterceptor can be configured to behave differently.

The Spring developers have recognized that it would be useful to also allow the rollback of transactions when specific checked exceptions are thrown. For example, say we want to roll back transactions when the endMatch() method throws *any* exception. Listing 7-5 shows the configuration for the transactionInterceptor around advice bean.

Listing 7-5. *Configuring Rollback on Any Exception*

```
<bean id="transactionInterceptor"
      class="org.springframework.transaction.interceptor.TransactionInterceptor">
  <property name="transactionManager"
            ref="transactionManager"/>
  <property name="transactionAttributes">
    <props>
      <prop key="endMatch">PROPAGATION_REQUIRED,-Throwable</prop>
    </props>
  </property>
</bean>
```

We've added the -Throwable clause to the transaction attributes for the endMatch() method. When an exception is thrown by this method, TransactionInterceptor will check if the class name of the exception type contains the string Throwable. If necessary, the entire parent hierarchy of the exception type that was thrown will be traversed to find a match.

Since all exceptions and errors in Java extend the java.lang.Throwable class, the –Throwable rule will cause a rollback for any exception that is thrown by the endMatch() method. If no exception is thrown, the active transaction will be committed (unless the active transaction was programmatically marked for rollback). We can add more exception names to the transaction attributes by providing a comma-separated list where the names are always prefixed with the minus (-) symbol. The class names of the exception that is thrown, and optionally those of all its parents, will be matched against the names in the transaction attribute configuration to decide if a rollback is required.

TransactionInterceptor and Auto-Proxy Creation

In the previous two sections, we've introduced TransactionInterceptor, the core of transaction demarcation in Spring AOP. We've configured proxy creation on a target bean with ProxyFactory Bean, but we've found this approach requires too much XML. Specifically, it requires too many lines of XML per target bean.

The alternative approach we discuss here uses auto-proxy creation. We've already discussed this way of creating proxy objects in the Spring container in Chapter 4, when we covered Spring AOP 2.0. However, auto-proxy creation has been available since the Spring 1.0 release, even though it was not widely used until Spring 2.0. It certainly offers the convenience of creating proxy objects with less XML configuration.

Listing 7-6 shows the Spring configuration for setting up `TransactionInterceptor` with the transaction attributes we've discussed earlier in combination with auto-proxy creation.

Listing 7-6. *Setting Up TransactionInterceptor with Auto-Proxy Creation*

```
<beans>
  <bean id="dataSource" class="org.apache.commons.dbcp.BasicDataSource"
        destroy-method="close">
    <property name="driverClassName" value="${jdbc.driverClassName}"/>
    <property name="url" value="${jdbc.url}"/>
    <property name="username" value="${jdbc.username}"/>
    <property name="password" value="${jdbc.password}"/>
  </bean>

  <bean class="org.springframework.beans.factory.config. ➥
PropertyPlaceholderConfigurer">
    <property name="location" value="classpath:jdbc.properties"/>
  </bean>

  <bean id="transactionManager"
        class=" org.springframework.jdbc.datasource.DataSourceTransactionManager">
    <property name="dataSource" ref="dataSource"/>
  </bean>

  <bean id="transactionInterceptor"
        class="org.springframework.transaction.interceptor.TransactionInterceptor">
    <property name="transactionManager"
              ref="transactionManager"/>
    <property name="transactionAttributes">
      <props>
        <prop key="*">PROPAGATION_REQUIRED,-Throwable</prop>
      </props>
    </property>
  </bean>

  <bean class="org.springframework.aop.framework.autoproxy. ➥
BeanNameAutoProxyCreator">
    <property name="beanNames">
      <list>
        <idref bean="tournamentMatchManager"/>
        <idref bean="otherBean"/>
        <idref bean="anotherBean"/>
      </list>
    </property>
    <property name="interceptorNames">
      <list>
        <idref bean="transactionInterceptor"/>
      </list>
    </property>
    <property name="proxyTargetClass" value="false"/>
  </bean>

  <bean name="tournamentMatchManager"
        class="com.apress.springbook.chapter07.DefaultTournamentMatchManager">
    <!-- other properties omitted -->
  </bean>
```

```
<bean name="otherBean" class="…"/>

<bean name="anotherBean" class="…"/>
</beans>
```

Listing 7-6 uses the `org.springframework.aop.framework.autoproxy.BeanNameAutoProxyCreator` class, which performs the auto-proxy creation. In its bean definition, we define a list of bean names—the `beanNames` property—for which a proxy object with the `transactionInterceptor` around advice bean must be created.

As you'll remember from Chapter 4, auto-proxy creation hooks into the bean life cycle of the Spring container to intercept bean creation and replace beans with proxy objects. In the configuration in Listing 7-6, only those beans whose names have been configured in the `beanNames` property of `BeanNameAutoProxyCreator` will be affected.

Auto-proxy creation reduces the amount of XML. Instead of needing to configure proxy creation for each bean separately, we now add one `BeanNameAutoProxyCreator` bean definition that affects those beans we want to configure for transaction demarcation.

Notice the transaction attribute configuration of the `transactionInterceptor` bean. We've configured transaction demarcation for all (*) methods. This is a sensible default, since in most cases, you want all methods on the target beans to have transaction management. However, as with all sensible defaults, you should carefully check if it applies to your situation.

You're probably better off using `TransactionProxyFactoryBean` (which we'll discuss next) if you want to configure specific methods for transaction demarcation on a few beans. You can still use auto-proxy creation and transaction demarcation for all methods for other beans.

TransactionProxyFactoryBean

The most popular transaction demarcation approach prior to Spring 2.0 was undoubtedly `TransactionProxyFactoryBean`. Listing 7-7 shows a typical `TransactionProxyFactoryBean` configuration. You'll find that it resembles `ProxyFactoryBean` and `TransactionInterceptor` in one bean definition.

Listing 7-7. *Typical TransactionProxyFactoryBean Configuration*

```
<beans>
  <bean id="dataSource" class="org.apache.commons.dbcp.BasicDataSource"
      destroy-method="close">
    <property name="driverClassName" value="${jdbc.driverClassName}"/>
    <property name="url" value="${jdbc.url}"/>
    <property name="username" value="${jdbc.username}"/>
    <property name="password" value="${jdbc.password}"/>
  </bean>

  <bean class="org.springframework.beans.factory.config. ➥
PropertyPlaceholderConfigurer">
    <property name="location" value="classpath:jdbc.properties"/>
  </bean>

  <bean id="tournamentMatchManager"
      class=" org.springframework.jdbc.datasource.DataSourceTransactionManager">
    <property name="dataSource" ref="dataSource"/>
  </bean>

  <bean id="transactionInterceptor"
      class="org.springframework.transaction.interceptor. ➥
TransactionProxyFactoryBean">
```

```
    <property name="transactionManager" ref="transactionManager"/>
    <property name="transactionAttributes">
      <props>
        <prop key="endMatch">PROPAGATION_REQUIRED,-Throwable</prop>
      </props>
    </property>
    <property name="proxyTargetClass" value="false"/>
    <property name="target">
      <bean class="com.apress.springbook.chapter07.DefaultTournamentMatchManager">
        <!--other properties omitted -->
      </bean>
    </property>
  </bean>
</beans>
```

As you can see in Listing 7-7, TransactionProxyFactoryBean requires a configuration per target bean. This is less flexible than auto-proxy creation, yet requires a little less configuration than the separate ProxyFactoryBean and TransactionInterceptor bean definitions.

On many projects, the amount of XML involved in using TransactionProxyFactoryBean is further reduced by using parent bean definitions (see Chapter 2), as shown in Listing 7-8.

Listing 7-8. *Reducing the Amount of XML Required for Configuring TransactionProxyFactoryBean*

```
<beans>
  <bean id="dataSource" class="org.apache.commons.dbcp.BasicDataSource"
        destroy-method="close">
    <property name="driverClassName" value="${jdbc.driverClassName}"/>
    <property name="url" value="${jdbc.url}"/>
    <property name="username" value="${jdbc.username}"/>
    <property name="password" value="${jdbc.password}"/>
  </bean>

  <bean class="org.springframework.beans.factory.config. ➥
PropertyPlaceholderConfigurer">
    <property name="location" value="classpath:jdbc.properties"/>
  </bean>

  <bean id="transactionManager"
        class=" org.springframework.jdbc.datasource.DataSourceTransactionManager">
    <property name="dataSource" ref="dataSource"/>
  </bean>

  <bean id="transactionTemplate"
        class="org.springframework.transaction.interceptor. ➥
  TransactionProxyFactoryBean"
        abstract="true">
    <property name="transactionManager" ref="transactionManager"/>
    <property name="transactionAttributes">
      <props>
        <prop key="*">PROPAGATION_REQUIRED</prop>
      </props>
    </property>
    <property name="proxyTargetClass" value="false"/>
  </bean>
```

```xml
<bean id="tournamentMatchManager" parent="transactionTemplate">
  <property name="target">
    <bean class="com.apress.springbook.chapter07.DefaultTournamentMatchManager">
      <!--other properties omitted -->
    </bean>
  </property>
  <property name="transactionAttributes">
    <props>
      <prop key="endMatch">PROPAGATION_REQUIRED,-Throwable</prop>
    </props>
  </property>
</bean>

<bean id="otherBean" parent="transactionTemplate">
  <property name="target">
    <bean class="…"/>
  </property>
</bean>

<bean id="anotherBean" parent="transactionTemplate">
  <property name="target">
    <bean class="…"/>
  </property>
</bean>
</beans>
```

In Listing 7-8, notice that the transactionTemplate bean definition has all the elements of a typical TransactionProxyFactoryBean configuration, except the target property. Its configuration for the transactionAttributes property takes the sensible default of configuring transaction demarcation for all methods on target beans. Because this bean definition is abstract, the Spring container won't create a bean for it.

The tournamentMatchManager, otherBean, and anotherBean bean definitions all declare transactionTemplate as a parent bean definition. Their own configuration and that of the transactionTemplate bean definition will be merged into one bean definition.

Notice that the tournamentMatchManager bean definition provides its own definition of the transactionAttributes property, thereby overriding the definition of the parent for that property.

When using TransactionProxyFactoryBean, an abstract parent bean definition reduces the amount of XML and offers good flexibility. However, as we'll discuss next, even more flexible options are available.

Transaction Demarcation Introduced in Spring 1.2

At the time of the Spring 1.2 release (May 2005), Java 5 had been released, and with it came an increasing demand for new annotations. The Spring developers introduced the @Transactional annotation to mark methods and entire classes for transaction demarcation. Although this approach requires Java 5, it is a viable alternative for the XML configuration presented in the previous section.

Transaction demarcation is a configuration that is closely related to the source code of applications. You'll typically know in advance where you want to demarcate transactions in your code. And if you learn about new points in the flow of the application where transaction demarcation is required, you can easily modify the source code to add @Transactional annotations. However, the @Transactional annotation does have some limitations, which you'll learn about shortly.

@Transactional Java 5 Annotation

Spring's @Transactional annotation is used to mark methods in your application for transaction demarcation. However, these methods won't just magically be demarcated. You must rely on Spring AOP to do that for you. So the @Transactional annotation serves as an indicator of where you want transaction demarcation and which behavior you want.

The @Transactional annotation can be declared in four locations to configure methods for transaction demarcation: on interfaces, on methods declared in interfaces, in classes, and on public and protected methods declared in classes.

Declaring @Transactional on interfaces will mark all methods that are declared in those interfaces for transaction demarcation. Listing 7-9 shows an example.

Listing 7-9. *Declaring @Transactional on an Interface*

```
package com.apress.springbook.chapter07;

import org.springframework.transaction.annotation.Transactional;

@Transactional
public interface TournamentMatchManager {
  public void endMatch(Match match) throws
      UnknownMatchException, MatchIsFinishedException,
      MatchCannotBePlayedException, PreviousMatchesNotFinishedException;

  // other methods omitted
}
```

Declaring @Transactional on methods declared in interfaces will mark those methods for transaction demarcation. The @Transactional declaration on the interface (if present) will become invisible for these methods. Listing 7-10 shows an example.

Listing 7-10. *Declaring @Transactional on a Method Declared in an Interface*

```
package com.apress.springbook.chapter07;

import org.springframework.transaction.annotation.Transactional;

public interface TournamentMatchManager {
  @Transactional
  public void endMatch(Match match) throws
      UnknownMatchException, MatchIsFinishedException,
      MatchCannotBePlayedException, PreviousMatchesNotFinishedException;

  // other methods omitted
}
```

Declaring @Transactional on classes will mark all public and protected methods declared on those classes for transaction demarcation. The @Transactional declarations on interfaces and methods on interfaces (if present) will become invisible for these methods. Listing 7-11 shows an example.

Listing 7-11. *Declaring @Transactional on a Class*

```
package com.apress.springbook.chapter07;

import org.springframework.transaction.annotation.Transactional;
```

```
@Transactional
public class DefaultTournamentMatchManager
    implements TournamentMatchManager {
  public void endMatch(Match match) throws
        UnknownMatchException, MatchIsFinishedException,
        MatchCannotBePlayedException, PreviousMatchesNotFinishedException {
    // implementation omitted
  }

  // other methods omitted
}
```

Finally, declaring @Transactional on public and protected methods declared in classes will mark those methods for transaction demarcation. The @Transactional declarations on interfaces, methods on interfaces (if present), and classes will become invisible for these methods. Listing 7-12 shows an example.

Listing 7-12. *Declaring @Transactional on a Method Declared in a Class*

```
package com.apress.springbook.chapter07;

import org.springframework.transaction.annotation.Transactional;

public class DefaultTournamentMatchManager
    implements TournamentMatchManager {
  @Transactional
  public void endMatch(Match match) throws
        UnknownMatchException, MatchIsFinishedException,
        MatchCannotBePlayedException, PreviousMatchesNotFinishedException {
    // implementation omitted
  }

  // other methods omitted
}
```

Where you declare the @Transactional annotation is largely up to you. If you want to configure only certain methods for transaction demarcation, it makes sense to declare @Transactional only on those methods. Otherwise, if you want to configure all methods of a class or an interface, you can place @Transactional on the class or interface declaration. This still allows you to add @Transactional on methods to overwrite the transaction demarcation configuration per method.

Whether you should declare @Transactional on a class or the interface it implements is less obvious. You could argue that if transaction management is an obvious requirement for certain use cases, it makes sense to declare @Transactional in the interface that declares those use cases. On the other hand, this does tie your interfaces to the Spring Framework. For this reason, you could argue that it makes more sense to declare @Transactional on classes that implement the interfaces. Whatever approach you choose, we advise you to stick to a sensible convention within your team to avoid inconsistency across your code.

■**Caution** There is more to this story if you use CGLIB proxy objects. Any @Transactional annotations on interfaces will be ignored by Spring if you use this method of creating proxies. We'll talk more about this in the "Limitations of @Transactional" section.

When carrying out operations on a database within transactions, it is usually a good idea to roll back a transaction if your code throws an exception while working on those operations. Listing 7-13 shows how to configure the exceptions that require a rollback on the @Transactional annotation.

Listing 7-13. *Configuring the Exceptions That Require a Rollback*

```
package com.apress.springbook.chapter07;

import org.springframework.transaction.annotation.Transactional;

@Transactional(
  rollbackFor = {
        UnknownMatchException.class,
        MatchIsFinishedException.class,
        MatchCannotBePlayedException.class,
        PreviousMatchesNotFinishedException.class
  }
)

public interface TournamentMatchManager {
  public void endMatch(Match match) throws
        UnknownMatchException, MatchIsFinishedException,
        MatchCannotBePlayedException, PreviousMatchesNotFinishedException;

  // other methods omitted
}
```

Notice that in Listing 7-13 and the previous examples, we didn't declare the propagation behavior (similar to the PROPAGATION_REQUIRED keyword). The @Transactional annotation has required as the default propagation. You can set the propagation behavior yourself, as shown in Listing 7-14.

Listing 7-14. *Declaring @Transactional with Propagation Behavior*

```
package com.apress.springbook.chapter07;

import org.springframework.transaction.annotation.Transactional;
import org.springframework.transaction.annotation.Propagation;

@Transactional(
  rollbackFor = {
        UnknownMatchException.class,
        MatchIsFinishedException.class,
        MatchCannotBePlayedException.class,
        PreviousMatchesNotFinishedException.class
  }
  propagation = Propagation.REQUIRED
)

public interface TournamentMatchManager {
  public void endMatch(Match match) throws
        UnknownMatchException, MatchIsFinishedException,
        MatchCannotBePlayedException, PreviousMatchesNotFinishedException;

  // other methods omitted
}
```

The @Transactional annotation is a convenient mechanism for declaring transaction demarcation in your application code. However, it can't be used in environments that use Java 1.4 or earlier. Also, if you're concerned about adding this kind of configuration detail in your source code, we recommend that you consider the XML solutions provided by Spring 2.0.

Shortly, we'll demonstrate how to configure auto-proxy creation for methods that are marked for transaction demarcation by @Transactional, but first we need to discuss the limitations of @Transactional.

Limitations of @Transactional

You should be aware of two limitations of @Transactional before deciding if this approach can be useful for your applications. The first limitation isn't directly related to the @Transactional annotation, but to Spring AOP. The second limitation is related to the incomplete inheritance model of annotations in Java 5.

Remember from Chapters 3 and 4 that Spring AOP supports only method executions as join points. However, that is not the only limitation of Spring AOP. In Chapter 4, we discussed that in order to invoke advice—in this case, TransactionInterceptor—callers need to execute methods on proxy objects instead of the target objects.

This limitation is pretty straightforward: when using Spring AOP for transaction demarcation, you can't just expect that the execution of *any* method that's marked by @Transactional will actually start and end transactions. Instead, you need to make sure callers of these methods always use a proxy object. As we've discussed throughout this book, proxy objects can be easily passed to callers by using dependency injection in the Spring container.

■Tip The problem of needing to use a proxy object can be solved by using AspectJ for transaction demarcation instead of Spring AOP. You can find the org.springframework.transaction.aspectj. AnnotationTransactionAspect in spring-aspects.jar that is part of the Spring 2.0 distribution. This aspect can also be used with Spring 1.2 releases. You can add this aspect to your aop.xml file and configure the AspectJ load-time weaver. Alternatively, you can choose to compile the aspect with ajc. Whatever approach you choose, all methods that declared @Transactional and all methods in classes and interfaces that declared @Transactional will automatically have transaction demarcation. See the section "Using @Transactional with AspectJ" in the Spring 2.0 reference manual for more details.

The second limitation is more complicated than the one imposed by Spring AOP. This limitation is caused by the limited and incomplete inheritance model of Java 5 annotations. The @Transactional annotation is inherited by subclasses, but only when it's declared on the class declaration of the base class. This means that classes do not inherit annotations that are declared on the interfaces they implement, and concrete implementations of methods do not inherit the @Transactional annotation (if present) of the corresponding method declarations in interfaces. @Transactional *is* inherited from base classes that declare it on their class declarations. On the other hand, if @Transactional is declared on a method in a base class (not an interface), it will not be inherited when this method is overwritten.

Spring's support for the @Transactional annotation can only partially solve this problem. The situation as it stands in the Spring 1.2.9 and 2.0 releases is as follows:

- If you use JDK proxy objects (not CGLIB), Spring *will* detect @Transactional declarations on interfaces and methods on interfaces for any method. This assumes there are no @Transactional declarations on the class that implements the method, the method itself, any base class, or the same method in any base class.

- If you use CGLIB proxy objects, Spring *will not* look at any interfaces implemented by the declaring class for any method. This means @Transactional declarations on interfaces will be silently ignored after you force the use of CGLIB proxy objects in your configuration. It may be surprising when transaction management suddenly stops working, and it may go unnoticed that the actual cause of the problem is switching the proxy type.

Although there are some limitations to the use of @Transactional, you'll find that they won't pose a problem in almost all cases. However, it is important to be aware of these issues.

@Transactional and Auto-Proxy Creation

In this section, we'll configure auto-proxy creation in the Spring container for transaction demarcation based on @Transactional. You'll see that you can combine transaction demarcation with @Transactional and XML in your application without restrictions.

Listing 7-15 shows the configuration you need to add to enable transaction demarcation based on @Transactional. Any bean created by the Spring container that has the @Transactional annotation declared will be replaced by a proxy object. Through this proxy object, the methods that are affected by @Transactional will get transaction demarcation by using TransactionInterceptor behind the scenes.

Listing 7-15. *Configuring @Transactional Transaction Demarcation in the Spring Container for Spring 1.2*

```
<beans>
  <bean id="dataSource" class="org.apache.commons.dbcp.BasicDataSource"
       destroy-method="close">
    <property name="driverClassName" value="${jdbc.driverClassName}"/>
    <property name="url" value="${jdbc.url}"/>
    <property name="username" value="${jdbc.username}"/>
    <property name="password" value="${jdbc.password}"/>
  </bean>

  <bean class="org.springframework.beans.factory.config. ➥
PropertyPlaceholderConfigurer">
    <property name="location" value="classpath:jdbc.properties"/>
  </bean>

  <bean id="transactionManager"
       class=" org.springframework.jdbc.datasource.DataSourceTransactionManager">
    <property name="dataSource" ref="dataSource"/>
  </bean>

  <bean class="org.springframework.aop.framework.autoproxy. ➥
DefaultAdvisorAutoProxyCreator">
    <property name="proxyTargetClass" value="false"/>
  </bean>

  <bean class="org.springframework.transaction.interceptor. ➥
TransactionAttributeSourceAdvisor">
    <constructor-arg>
      <bean class="org.springframework.transaction.interceptor. ➥
TransactionInterceptor">
        <property name="transactionManager"/>
        <property name="transactionAttributeSource">
          <bean class="org.springframework.transaction. ➥
```

```
annotation.AnnotationTransactionAttributeSource"/>
      </property>
    </bean>
  </constructor-arg>
</bean>

<bean id="tournamentMatchManagerWithAtTransactional"
    class="com.apress.springbook.chapter07.DefaultTournamentMatchManager">
  <!-other properties omitted -->
</bean>

<bean id="otherBeanWithAtTransactional" class="…"/>

<bean id="anotherBean WithAtTransactional" class="…"/>
</beans>
```

The DefaultAdvisorAutoProxyCreator bean definition is responsible for enabling auto-proxy creation in the Spring container. It will automatically pass every bean created by the Spring container to the TransactionAttributeSourceAdvisor bean. This bean has been configured with a TransactionInterceptor around advice bean, which in turn has been configured with an AnnotationTransactionAttributeSource bean.

The TransactionAttributeSourceAdvisor bean will use the AnnotationTransactionAttribute Source bean to determine if beans created by the Spring container have declared the @Transactional annotation. For all beans where this is the case, proxy objects will replace them. These proxy objects will use the configured TransactionInterceptor to do the actual transaction demarcation.

Transaction Demarcation Introduced in Spring 2.0

Spring 2.0 offers two new ways of configuring transaction demarcation. You will find that the Spring 2.0 options for setting up transaction demarcation are the easiest to configure. Both new configuration mechanisms use the simplified, custom XML Schema support of Spring 2.0.

The first approach is one XML tag that replaces the rather elaborate XML configuration that was required in Spring 1.2 to set up transaction demarcation with @Transactional. The second approach replaces the even more elaborate configuration of ProxyFactoryBean and Transaction Interceptor. This approach uses the <aop:advisor> XML tag combined with custom XML tags to configure a TransactionInterceptor bean definition.

Both new approaches to configuring transaction demarcation build on top of the mechanisms that were introduced in Spring 1.0 and 1.2, which were explained in the previous sections.

@Transactional and Auto-Proxy Creation

In the previous sections on @Transactional, you learned how to set up auto-proxy creation in the Spring container. In Spring 2.0, you can use one XML tag, as shown in Listing 7-16.

Listing 7-16. *Configuring @Transactional Transaction Demarcation in Spring 2.0*

```
<?xml version="1.0" encoding="UTF-8"?>
<beans xmlns="http://www.springframework.org/schema/beans"
    xmlns:xsi="http://www.w3.org/2001/XMLSchema-instance"
    xmlns:tx="http://www.springframework.org/schema/tx"
    xsi:schemaLocation="http://www.springframework.org/schema/beans
  http://www.springframework.org/schema/beans/spring-beans.xsd
  http://www.springframework.org/schema/tx
  http://www.springframework.org/schema/tx/spring-tx.xsd">
```

```
    <bean id="dataSource" class="org.apache.commons.dbcp.BasicDataSource"
        destroy-method="close">
    <property name="driverClassName" value="${jdbc.driverClassName}"/>
    <property name="url" value="${jdbc.url}"/>
    <property name="username" value="${jdbc.username}"/>
    <property name="password" value="${jdbc.password}"/>
    </bean>

    <bean class="org.springframework.beans.factory.config. ➥
PropertyPlaceholderConfigurer">
        <property name="location" value="classpath:jdbc.properties"/>
    </bean>

    <bean id="transactionManager"
        class="org.springframework.jdbc.datasource. ➥
DataSourceTransactionManager">
        <property name="dataSource" ref="dataSource"/>
    </bean>

    <tx:annotation-driven transaction-manager="transactionManager"
                          proxy-target-class="false"/>

    <bean id="tournamentMatchManagerWithAtTransactional"
        class="com.apress.springbook.chapter07.DefaultTournamentMatchManager">
    <!--other properties omitted -->
    </bean>

    <bean id="otherBeanWithAtTransactional" class="…"/>

    <bean id="anotherBean WithAtTransactional" class="…"/>
</beans>
```

The <tx:annotation-driven> XML tag in Listing 7-16 takes the transaction-manager attribute, where we provide the bean definition name of the DataSourceTransactionManager. As you can see, setting up transaction demarcation with @Transactional becomes a lot easier with Spring 2.0.

By adding the <tx:annotation-driven> custom XML tag, the bean definitions that are marked in bold in Listing 7-15 will be added for you. So <tx:annotation-driven> is a convenient configuration mechanism to enable transaction demarcation for @Transactional more than anything else. The restrictions of @Transactional we discussed previously remain.

Configuring TransactionInterceptor and its transaction attributes has become easier as well, as you'll see next.

Convenient Transaction Advice Configuration

You can use custom XML tags to configure transaction attributes. These attributes are similar to those that we configured on TransactionInterceptor and TransactionProxyFactoryBean earlier in this chapter. In fact, their XML tags will create a TransactionInterceptor bean definition behind the scenes.

Next, use the <aop:advisor> XML tag (see Chapter 4) to select to which methods on beans in the Spring container this TransactionInterceptor will be applied, as shown in Listing 7-17.

Listing 7-17. *Configuring Transaction Attributes in Spring 2.0*

```xml
<?xml version="1.0" encoding="UTF-8"?>
<beans xmlns="http://www.springframework.org/schema/beans"
       xmlns:xsi="http://www.w3.org/2001/XMLSchema-instance"
       xmlns:aop="http://www.springframework.org/schema/aop"
       xmlns:tx="http://www.springframework.org/schema/tx"
       xsi:schemaLocation="http://www.springframework.org/schema/beans
   http://www.springframework.org/schema/beans/spring-beans.xsd
   http://www.springframework.org/schema/aop
   http://www.springframework.org/schema/aop/spring-aop.xsd
   http://www.springframework.org/schema/tx
   http://www.springframework.org/schema/tx/spring-tx.xsd">


  <bean id="dataSource" class="org.apache.commons.dbcp.BasicDataSource"
        destroy-method="close">
    <property name="driverClassName" value="${jdbc.driverClassName}"/>
    <property name="url" value="${jdbc.url}"/>
    <property name="username" value="${jdbc.username}"/>
    <property name="password" value="${jdbc.password}"/>
  </bean>

  <bean class="org.springframework.beans.factory.config. ➥
PropertyPlaceholderConfigurer">
    <property name="location" value="classpath:jdbc.properties"/>
  </bean>

  <bean id="transactionManager"
        class=" org.springframework.jdbc.datasource.DataSourceTransactionManager">
    <property name="dataSource" ref="dataSource"/>
  </bean>

  <tx:advice id="transactionInterceptor" transaction-manager="transactionManager">
    <tx:attributes>
      <tx:method name="endMatch"
                 rollback-for="Throwable/>"
    </tx:attributes>
  </tx:advice>

  <aop:config proxy-target-class="false">
    <aop:advisor pointcut="within(*..TournamentMatchManager+)"/>
                 advice-ref="transactionInterceptor"/>
  </aop:config>

  <bean id="tournamentMatchManager"
        class="com.apress.springbook.chapter07.DefaultTournamentMatchManager">
    <!—other properties omitted -->
  </bean>
</beans>
```

To learn more about transaction management in Spring, see *Pro Spring* (Apress, 2005). Also, check out the Spring 1.2 and 2.0 reference manuals. They are a great source of information on the topic.

Summary

The Spring transaction-management framework solves a problem developers have been struggling with for years: how to transparently blend transaction management with data-access code.

Spring integrates with at least eight transaction-management APIs in Java as well as the JTA. It abstracts the differences between them without losing any of their features. Spring also offers six ways of configuring transaction demarcation. You end up with at least 54 possible combinations for the transaction-management API and transaction demarcation.

All the options are available without needing to change your application logic. Transaction management with Spring is a matter of configuration, flexibility, and choice. When it comes to data access and transaction management, no alternative to Spring offers the same amount of choice and flexibility.

In the next chapter, we move from the data layer into the presentation layer and look at Spring MVC.

CHAPTER 8

■■■

Spring MVC

Welcome to Chapter 8, where you will apply what you've learned about the Spring Framework to building high-quality web applications with the Spring MVC web application framework. This chapter, as an introduction and tour of Spring MVC, certainly does not stand on its own. Before diving into this chapter, we recommend that you have a good understanding of the following:

- The `ApplicationContext` and its configuration files
- Dependency injection
- Data access, such as `JdbcTemplate`
- Transaction management
- Spring AOP

In other words, if you've skipped directly to this chapter and are new to Spring, take a few moments to investigate the previous chapters of this book. They lay the groundwork that is crucial to getting the most out of this chapter. However, if you still have some questions about the core elements of the Spring Framework, such as the `ApplicationContext`, this chapter should help fill in any gaps you might have. This chapter is about putting together a Spring web application as much as it is about Spring MVC.

This chapter assumes you have a good understanding of the Servlet API, along with minimal JSP exposure. You should know what a servlet is, what the `web.xml` file is used for, and generally how Java web applications are constructed. If you are completely new to programming web applications with Java, we recommend you first read *Head First Servlets and JSP* (O'Reilly, 2004). Because Spring MVC is built on top of the Servlet API, all that you know about servlets is applicable to Spring MVC.

You don't need to be an expert in either the Spring Framework or Java servlets to learn how to write web applications with Spring MVC. As you'll see in this chapter, the Spring Framework, with its dedicated Spring MVC web framework, helps to abstract and remove all the technological concerns so that you may focus on the real goal of building business logic. By the time you are finished with this chapter, and the rest of this book, you'll be creating Spring MVC web applications with ease.

■**Note** This book's appendix explains how to configure and use the Eclipse IDE with Spring MVC to ease the development process. If you don't use an IDE and you develop Java applications, run, don't walk, to download one.

Spring MVC is a very large part of the overall Spring Framework. To cover all of Spring MVC in detail takes an entire book (and indeed, one has been written: *Expert Spring MVC and Web Flow*, Apress, 2006). In an effort to get you up and running quickly and with confidence, we will pick and choose the elements of Spring MVC that are most important for new users of the framework.

This chapter will cover the following topics:

- Best practices for Java web application design and architecture
- First-class Spring MVC components, such as the `DispatcherServlet`, controllers, and views
- Spring MVC web application configuration
- Validation techniques
- JSP as a view technology (Chapter 9 covers all of the different view options; JSP is only one choice)
- Implementations of common use cases and user experiences

Web Application Architecture

If we were to choose one word that describes successful web application architectures, it would be *decoupled*. Flexible software is built as a web of dependencies between components. Each component (in Java, each *class*) is responsible for one part in the application and is sufficiently specific to be isolated from other components.

This isolation is typically achieved by abstracting the internal implementation details of a class from other classes. The best way to achieve this abstraction is by using interfaces and the polymorphism they make possible. Two kinds of dependencies in a class can benefit from polymorphism:

- Arguments of methods or constructors
- Static or instance fields

The Spring container can inject objects in arguments of instance and static methods, and constructors via dependency injection. Classes can assign these arguments to fields.

Classes in loosely coupled applications are aware of only interfaces on which they depend. They are not aware of how implementation classes work. This means that a class can change the way it performs its tasks without affecting other classes. This does not mean each and every class in an application must implement an interface. Interfaces are required only for the following:

- Dependencies where the *implementation is likely to change over time*. See Chapter 5 for a discussion on data-access code and change.
- Dependencies where *multiple implementation classes exist*, each one implementing a specific behavior. Spring MVC has many such dependencies.

The goal is to create an application where the implementation details are hidden, so that they may change over time without affecting the application as a whole. The design goals when developing web applications are no different, and care must be taken to keep each area of concern inside well-designated boundaries.

You will find that web applications built on top of Java EE Servlet engines (such as Tomcat) typically have a very conservative setup. This has very little to do with Tomcat or the Servlet specifications. Instead, over the years, one template for web applications has become so popular that it's rooted in the minds of developers. Web applications typically consist of the following areas:

Domain model: Stateful objects that typically, but not always, represent records in the database. These classes can implement business rules. See Chapter 5 for more information about domain classes.

Services: Coarse-grained interfaces provide simple integration points between the application logic and its callers. The implementation classes are stateless, meaning they don't hold data that is related to individual method executions.

Data access: Applications need to integrate with relational databases (see Chapter 5), in order to save and retrieve data that lives longer than HTTP requests or HTTP sessions.

Web request handling: HTTP requests are handled, managed, and routed to the correct controllers.

User interface: The XHTML or other representation of the result of an HTTP request.

Each of these areas, or concerns, represents an entirely separate set of functionality. The challenge is to construct the application such that you, as the developer, can change the underlying details of each area without affecting any other area. By *affecting*, we mean that if one area changes, the other areas will not require modification or recompiling. This loose coupling of layers is the hallmark of a flexible application.

So which areas can depend on others? The domain model is the one constant across the entire system. The other areas align themselves in *layers*, one on top of another. This represents who depends on whom. Take a look at Figure 8-1. Notice how data-access code is at the bottom, and moving up the layers you see services, web request handling, and finally the user interface (UI). By looking at the diagram, you can see that only the service layer depends on the data-access layer.

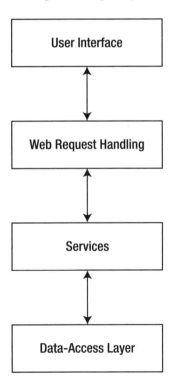

Figure 8-1. *Layers of a web application*

The service layer depends on the data-access layer, but it is still unaware of any implementation details for that layer. By programming to interfaces, you can ensure that clients of your code (or layer) remain unaware of specific implementation details. This helps you to keep a decoupled software design.

Let's take a closer look at each concern. You will see how each of the following areas and principles are actually implemented in the sample application later in the chapter.

The Domain Model

The role of the domain model is to provide a concrete model of the problem domain to the application and its developers. Through this model, the other classes in the application can work with application-specific data from the database. To this end, the classes of the domain model are very often used as data carriers. They typically somehow represent records in the database (see Chapter 5). The domain model objects are converted to and from records in the database by data-access code.

The role of the domain model in applications is under constant discussion in the developer community, with some advocating a more complex domain model. We acknowledge, however, that there remains a class of applications that benefits from a simple domain model that is saved to and restored from the database. The same goes for certain areas of big applications. Here, we focus on using the classes of the domain model to interact with the database, not on putting business logic in the classes of the domain model.

The domain model should not be concerned with, for instance, handling web requests. It should not have any dependencies on the other areas of the system, such as the web request handlers or data access. However, as you'll see shortly, it is acceptable and often required that the other areas depend on the domain model.

The Spring Framework, and thus Spring MVC, does not provide any framework classes for the domain model specifically. This is because the Spring Framework exists to augment and support a domain model by providing nonbusiness logic-specific services such as transaction management, AOP, and dependency injection.

The Data-Access Layer

Typically, web applications need to integrate with a relational database in order to store and retrieve objects. Relational databases are not the only repository types available, but they are certainly the most common.

The Spring Framework encourages a decoupling between the domain model and the data-access layer (see the discussion on the repository adapter in Chapter 5). Given the single responsibility principle (also discussed in Chapter 5), we clearly see that data-access code and application logic are two separate responsibilities.

The Spring Framework assists with this decoupling because it promotes the use of dependency injection. Therefore, you can separate the concerns of application logic and data access in the system architecture, yet combine these separate classes easily at runtime using dependency injection. If you follow this approach, you'll find that the Spring Framework can help you wire up the application in very flexible ways.

Web Request Routing

Most of the Spring MVC code you will write will be to handle and route incoming HTTP requests. This concern is focused on accepting a new request, deciding which business logic should handle it, and mapping any output to the UI. It is not responsible for implementing any of the business logic itself.

The web request routing layer of the application is the glue between the domain model and the Web. It delegates all real functionality down to the model, and because of this, the layer is typically very thin and lightweight.

Spring MVC expresses this layer as a single servlet named `DispatcherServlet` and a set of controller classes. `DispatcherServlet` implements the *front controller*, which Martin Fowler defines as "A controller that handles all requests for a Web site" (`http://www.martinfowler.com/eaaCatalog/frontController.html`).

The controller classes, of which there are many in Spring MVC, are the specific request handlers of the system. A controller acts as a *page controller*, which Fowler defines as "An object that handles a request for a specific page or action on a Web site" (http://www.martinfowler.com/eaaCatalog/pageController.html). These controllers, which you will be responsible for creating, sit behind the DispatcherServlet. These components are discussed in more detail shortly, in the section about Spring MVC's architecture.

User Interface

Rendering the UI for a web application is a separate concern from handling web requests, and thus is considered a separate layer of the system. The controllers are responsible for delegating to the domain model, collecting the results, and then delegating to the UI (or view) for actual rendering of the response.

The controller does not actually render the view because of the single responsibility principle (see Chapter 5). Handling web requests and rendering views are two separate responsibilities, and a controller class would need to change if the API of the business logic changes *and* if the rendering of the view changes. This is one responsibility too many, which is why controllers in Spring MVC are designed to delegate to a view for rendering the UI.

UIs for the Web are primarily encoded in XHTML with CSS, but there are many other options available. Depending on the situation, users may expect Excel spreadsheets, Portable Document Format (PDF) files, graphics, or simple text files. Spring MVC supports all these UI options with ease, along with many different options for rendering XHTML, including JSP, Velocity, and FreeMarker. In typical Spring Framework style, there is no one preferred method for rendering the view. Instead, it makes integration with a wide variety of toolkits available in order to give you the greatest set of choices.

Spring MVC Architecture

Spring MVC is composed of many different moving parts, all configured and managed by the DispatcherServlet servlet. Here, we'll provide an overview of the components of the Spring MVC architecture and how they work.

MVC Components

In this section, we will enumerate the elements of Spring MVC so that you will have a good picture of what functionality is available to you.

DispatcherServlet

As mentioned previously, DispatcherServlet is the front controller for a Spring MVC application. All requests pass through this servlet, as it manages all of the different elements that have a chance to process the request. DispatcherServlet is not meant for subclassing; instead, it is simply declared and configured by you, just like a normal servlet inside a web application. All of the real work is performed by delegates.

Controllers

The job of handling individual page requests is given to controllers. Spring MVC provides a rich collection of controller types, from simple handlers with no workflow to full-featured, form-handling, life-cycle controllers. The following are some of the controllers provided by Spring MVC:

- Simple servlet-like controllers
- Controllers to manage an XHTML form life cycle
- Wizard controllers to manage a simple ordered process
- WebWork-like one-off (disposable) controllers
- Flexible, multiaction controllers, able to handle many different requests

You can easily extend the provided controllers if you don't find one that meets your exact needs.

Controllers are responsible only for accepting a new request, delegating to the domain model, and collecting the result. The controller then creates a model in order to pass it along to the view. The controller does not manage view rendering, but it usually performs view selection.

Typically, controllers are stateless. This means that each controller handles multiple requests concurrently. Therefore, you should not store state during processing of a request in instance properties of the controller.

HandlerMapping Interface

The job of analyzing a request to determine which controller is called is given to the HandlerMapping interface. Typically, the URI is the determining factor, but the HandlerMapping interface is well abstracted. You may choose to map to controllers based on cookies, session variables, time of day, or some combination. It's even possible to declare and configure multiple HandlerMapping instances in order to accommodate multiple resolution strategies. You may even specify the order in which the HandlerMapping instances are consulted.

Model

The model is a collection of objects intended to be rendered by the view. It can contain the results of operations performed by the domain model or objects custom to the view layer. The model is implemented as a simple Map, with String names as keys.

Note In the context of Spring MVC, the *model* and the *domain model* are two different concepts.

Spring MVC combines the model and the view to be rendered into a ModelAndView class. Controllers are responsible for creating and populating an instance of ModelAndView before completing their work. The view and the model are combined like this simply because the controller needs to return both objects when finished processing.

You are not restricted to what you place into the model, as long as your view knows how to render it.

View

Rendering the UI is the job of the view. Spring MVC comes bundled with many different view implementations, all abstracted to work the same way. The following are some of your choices:

- JSP and JSP Standard Tag Library (JSTL)
- Velocity
- FreeMarker
- PDF

- Excel
- Extensible Stylesheet Language Transformations (XSLT)
- JasperReports

You can easily mix and match these different view types within the same web application for ultimate flexibility. Spring MVC even includes useful macros for JSP, Velocity, and FreeMarker to ease the task of building and displaying XHTML forms.

Spring MVC maps views to view names, allowing for complete decoupling of view and controller. The ViewResolver interface is responsible for resolving view names to a particular view instance. You may specify one or more ViewResolvers and chain them together if you require more than one view-resolution strategy.

■**Note** To keep coupling low, the view is typically specified with a logical name. Therefore, the controller is unaware of how the view is implemented.

Locale Resolvers

Spring MVC applications can easily support internationalization (i18n) and localization (l10n) by using Java's native i18n facilities plus helpers from the Spring Framework. These techniques are useful if you wish to serve the same application to multiple cultures, locales, and languages. (See http://en.wikipedia.org/wiki/Internationalization for more details on i18n and i10n.)

Each request is serviced by an instance of LocaleResolver, whose job it is to determine the locale of the request and make it available throughout the request. Locales can be set in many different ways, including reading HTTP headers sent by browsers (the default) or explicit selection by end users. Locale resolution is pluggable, allowing you to create your own scheme for locale selection.

The web application then uses the locale when displaying text messages, so that the message will be translated into the correct language. Any error messages generated by validation can also be translated. The locale is also useful when rendering items such as currency or numbers.

File Uploads

All web frameworks allow for file uploads, and Spring MVC is no different with its Multipart Resolver interface. Like all good things Spring, the framework doesn't actually implement file-upload handling directly. It instead delegates to one of two libraries: Jakarta Commons FileUpload (http://jakarta.apache.org/commons/fileupload/) or Jason Hunter's COS library (http://servlets.com/cos/). We recommend Commons FileUpload, as it is actively maintained.

Any request can contain an uploaded file, and the parsing and management of the file is transparently handled for you by the framework. You can even choose to have the contents of the uploaded file available to you as a File object, a byte[], or a String.

Exception Handling

Errors can occur at any point during the request-handling life cycle, so Spring MVC provides a flexible and configurable exception-handling mechanism. The HandlerExceptionResolver interface maps exceptions to views. Spring MVC provides different resolution strategies, and it is easy to implement this interface in order to use custom logic.

DispatcherServlet and Request Handling

As previously mentioned, the DispatcherServlet servlet handles all incoming requests, as it acts as the application's front controller. DispatcherServlet merely coordinates the activities of many sub-components, routing the request along until processing is finished. You've been introduced to some of the components of the request-processing pipeline: HandlerMapping, ViewResolver, and Handler ExceptionResolver. Each plays its own part in the larger processing pipeline.

Table 8-1 lists all of the interfaces used as delegates by DispatcherServlet. Each has a rich set of implementations, and they are easy to extend so you can create your own.

■**Note** This chapter does not cover all of the components in the processing pipeline. For a complete review of all the available functionality, consult *Expert Spring MVC and Web Flow* (Apress, 2006).

Table 8-1. *Delegate Components of DispatcherServlet*

Class	Purpose
org.springframework.web.multipart.MultipartResolver	Parse an HTTP request that includes a file upload and expose the upload for later processing
org.springframework.web.servlet.LocaleResolver	Determine the locale of the current request and make it available during the request
org.springframework.web.servlet.ThemeResolver	Determine the theme, or UI context, for a request; you can use the theme to modularize the UI, similar to skins
org.springframework.web.servlet.HandlerMapping	Map an HTTP request to a controller
org.springframework.web.servlet.HandlerExceptionResolver	Map exceptions thrown during request processing to error views
org.springframework.web.servlet.RequestToViewNameTranslator	Strategy to determine the view name for a request if none is specified by the controller
org.springframework.web.servlet.ViewResolver	Resolve a logical view name to a view instance

Not all of the components listed in Table 8-1 are mandatory, and many have sensible defaults, as listed in Table 8-2. For most simple cases, the defaults are sufficient. If the component is listed in Table 8-2, DispatcherServlet will create and initialize a bean of the type if no bean of that type can be found in the configuration. If the component is not listed in Table 8-2, there is no default implementation, and you must declare one in the DispatcherServlet's configuration if you wish to use it.

Table 8-2. *Processing Pipeline Components Defaults*

Short Class Name	Default	Behavior
LocaleResolver	org.springframework.web.servlet. i18n.AcceptHeaderLocaleResolver	Reads the Accept-Language header from the HTTP request. This header is normally sent by the browser.
ThemeResolver	org.springframework.web.servlet. theme.FixedThemeResolver	Returns a theme name of theme.
HandlerMapping	org.springframework.web.servlet. handler.BeanNameUrlHandlerMapping	Finds beans in the Spring XML configuration with names beginning with /. The bean name is then used to match against the request URI. Bean names can contain wildcards.
RequestToViewNameTranslator	org.springframework.web.servlet. view.DefaultRequestToViewName Translator	Strips the leading slash and the trailing extension from the request URI to generate the view name.
ViewResolver	org.springframework.web.servlet. view.InternalResourceViewResolver	Maps view names to internal resources that can be called via the RequestDispatcher, such as JSPs and servlets.

To summarize, the default behavior of a Spring MVC web application includes the following:

- i18n is based on the Accept-Language header sent by the browser, a very sensible default.

- Controllers are mapped to URLs with the bean name from the XML configuration file. We will take advantage of this in our sample application.

- View names are generated by looking at the request URI. This means if you do not specify a view name, DispatcherServlet will look for a view matching a portion of the URI. We will use this in our sample application.

- Views are referenced as JSP files, and the names must match the path to the JSP file completely. We will not use the default in our sample application.

In those cases where you're satisfied with one or more of these default classes, you don't need to specify them in your Spring MVC configuration. You can always go back and add bean definitions to change the default behaviors of DispatcherServlet. For full descriptions of what each default component type provides, we suggest reading the Javadoc for each class.

DispatcherServlet has the ability to order and chain multiple implementations of the same component, for selecting component types. For instance, this comes in very handy if you need to support multiple ways to map requests to controllers. Table 8-3 lists the component type and if it supports multiple implementations. If a type is chainable, that means you may specify multiple instances of the type in the XML configuration for the DispatcherServlet. The servlet will then order them, based on their order number, and give each a chance to operate on the request. (Classes that can be chained and ordered implement the `org.springframework.core.Ordered` interface.) The first instance that can successfully answer the request wins.

Table 8-3. *Components and Chainability*

Short Class Name	Chainable?
MultipartResolver	No
LocaleResolver	No
ThemeResolver	No
HandlerMapping	Yes
HandlerExceptionResolver	Yes
RequestToViewNameTranslator	No
ViewResolver	Yes

As you can see, `DispatcherServlet` manages a lot of components during the request life cycle. Figure 8-2 illustrates how a request flows through `DispatcherServlet`.

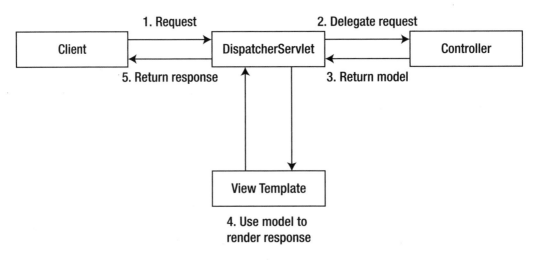

Figure 8-2. *Flow of requests through DispatcherServlet*

Spring MVC Configuration

Configuring your web application to use Spring MVC is very simple if you rely on the defaults. But even if you don't, you'll find that the configuration elements are consistent and easy to use. In this section, we will configure a Java web application to use Spring MVC in preparation for implementing a simple application.

A Spring MVC application typically requires three XML configuration files. The first configuration file is the standard `web.xml`. Each of the other two files defines an `ApplicationContext`: one for the global servlet container's application context and one for the servlet context.

Writing web.xml

All Java web applications are configured the same way, and Spring MVC is no exception. The first thing you must do is configure the web.xml file inside the WEB-INF directory of your web application. You must declare two elements: DispatcherServlet and ContextLoaderListener.

We introduced ContextLoaderListener in Chapter 2. It is responsible for loading the global, or parent, WebApplicationContext, which should contain all of the services on which the web application will be built. A WebApplicationContext is a specialization of an ApplicationContext that is aware of the servlet environment. It must be loaded before DispatcherServlet initializes, ensuring that all of the global application services are available to the web application-specific objects. ContextLoaderListener implements javax.servlet.ServletContextListener, allowing it to respond to initialization and shut down events for the web application. The configuration element inside the web.xml looks like this:

```
<context-param>
  <param-name>contextConfigLocation</param-name>
  <param-value>
    WEB-INF/applicationContext.xml,WEB-INF/propertyPlaceholderForWeb.xml
  </param-value>
</context-param>

<listener>
  <listener-class>
    org.springframework.web.context.ContextLoaderListener
  </listener-class>
</listener>
```

Notice that two main elements are listed: <listener> and <context-param>. The <context-param> element declares a list of XML files that will be combined to define a single WebApplicationContext. The files are located inside the WEB-INF directory for security purposes, as any file inside that directory is hidden from clients. You can also see that the paths to the files are relative to the web application root.

Along with the applicationContext.xml file, we have listed the propertyPlaceholderForWeb.xml file, which contains the mechanism by which properties such as database connections are specified (as you'll see later in the "Configuring the Sample Application" section). We've extracted those properties and values to make testing easy. It is important to note that the ContextLoaderListener will, by default, look for a /WEB-INF/applicationContext.xml file if you do not specify a <context-param> named contextConfigLocation.

The configuration for DispatcherServlet should look familiar if you have ever configured a servlet in a web.xml file:

```
<servlet>
  <servlet-name>spring</servlet-name>
  <servlet-class>
    org.springframework.web.servlet.DispatcherServlet
  </servlet-class>
</servlet>

<servlet-mapping>
  <servlet-name>spring</servlet-name>
  <url-pattern>/app/*</url-pattern>
</servlet-mapping>
```

What you don't see is how DispatcherServlet knows how to configure itself. We are using the default values to decrease the amount of configuration required. When possible, we recommend you do the same.

By default, DispatcherServlet will look for a file named WEB-INF/<servlet-name>-servlet.xml, where <servlet-name> is replaced with the value from the <servlet-name></servlet-name> element. In this case, because the servlet's name is spring, the configuration for DispatcherServlet is found in WEB-INF/spring-servlet.xml. The spring-servlet.xml file, as you will see in the next section, is the definition for the WebApplicationContext created by DispatcherServlet.

> ■**Tip** If you want to use a name other than the default for the DispatcherServlet's XML configuration, simply declare a servlet <init-param> of name contextConfigLocation.

Putting the whole thing together, a typical web.xml for a Spring MVC application will look like Listing 8-1.

Listing 8-1. *A web.xml File with ContextLoadListener and DispatcherServlet Declarations*

```xml
<?xml version="1.0" encoding="UTF-8"?>
<web-app version="2.4" xmlns="http://java.sun.com/xml/ns/j2ee"
  xmlns:xsi="http://www.w3.org/2001/XMLSchema-instance"
  xsi:schemaLocation="http://java.sun.com/xml/ns/j2ee
                      http://java.sun.com/xml/ns/j2ee/web-app_2_4.xsd">

<display-name>Tennis Club</display-name>

<context-param>
  <param-name>contextConfigLocation</param-name>
  <param-value>
    WEB-INF/applicationContext.xml,WEB-INF/propertyPlaceholderForWeb.xml
  </param-value>
</context-param>

<listener>
  <listener-class>
    org.springframework.web.context.ContextLoaderListener
  </listener-class>
</listener>

<servlet>
  <servlet-name>spring</servlet-name>
  <servlet-class>
    org.springframework.web.servlet.DispatcherServlet
  </servlet-class>
</servlet>

<servlet-mapping>
  <servlet-name>spring</servlet-name>
  <url-pattern>/app/*</url-pattern>
</servlet-mapping>

</web-app>
```

Creating ApplicationContexts

A well-designed Spring MVC application contains two ApplicationContexts. The first resides in the servlet container's application scope and is called the global ApplicationContext. The second is scoped to DispatcherServlet, residing in the servlet context. Both are implemented as instances of WebApplicationContext.

Global ApplicationContext

The global ApplicationContext contains the main services of the application, minus anything web-related. You would typically find the DataSource, PlatformTransactionManager, any domain model services, and supporting services here.

In the web.xml file in Listing 8-1, we used two XML files to define the global Application Context: /WEB-INF/applicationContext.xml and /WEB-INF/propertyPlaceholderForWeb.xml. This is an implementation detail, as there is a one-to-many relationship between an instantiated ApplicationContext and its XML definitions. If you require only one definition file, simply name it applicationContext.xml and place it inside the WEB-INF directory. If you follow this convention, it will automatically be detected if you do not specify the contextConfigLocation parameter.

DispatcherServlet spring-servlet.xml

We will register all our web-specific beans, such as Controllers and ViewResolvers, into the spring-servlet.xml file. This creates an ApplicationContext for the DispatcherServlet and its servlet context. It will be nested below the global ApplicationContext, therefore able to resolve all beans from its parent context.

As mentioned previously, the name spring-servlet.xml is generated by using the <servlet-name> value from the web.xml and appending -servlet.xml. This is the default, preferred way to configure the DispatcherServlet. If you require multiple XML definitions, or a different filename, you must set the contextConfigLocation property of the servlet as an <init-param> element. You can add more than one DispatcherServlet to the web.xml file. Each servlet will have a unique name.

Reviewing the Web Application Startup Process

Let's review what happens when a Spring MVC application starts up. Some of the initialization is common to any Java web application, while what happens during those stages is specific to Spring MVC.

■**Note** The following procedure is specific to Spring MVC-related objects. We are ignoring other listeners or servlets also registered with the servlet container.

---

1. The servlet container initializes the web application and then fires the contextInitialized event.

2. ContextLoaderListener receives the contextInitialized event and creates the global (parent) WebApplicationContext. This ApplicationContext is placed into a well-known location inside the ServletContext for easy access.

3. DispatcherServlet is initialized, creating its own WebApplicationContext and nesting it inside the global WebApplicationContext.

4. `DispatcherServlet` searches for components such as `ViewResolvers` and `HandlerMappings`. If a component is found, it will be initialized; otherwise, the default class for the component is instantiated (see Table 8-2).

5. The web application is ready to serve requests.

You now have enough information to dive right into a fully functioning sample application. Let's take what you have learned and build a Spring MVC website.

A Sample Spring MVC Application

So what exactly are we going to build? Keeping with the theme of tennis, we will construct a web application for managing the members of a tennis club. We will focus on three key use cases that highlight common tasks with Spring MVC:

List all members: The application must simply list all of the members of the tennis club, which means displaying the members' names, ages, and addresses. The list must paginate across multiple web pages. The user must be able to sort the list on any of the columns of the list. This use case will highlight how to construct pages that have dynamic information, but don't accept form submissions. You will also learn one way to create paginated lists.

Search for a member: A user may search for a particular member or members with a single search string. The search must be by both first name and last name, as a wildcard. The results are to be listed in the same format as the list all members use case. This use case will show you how to work with a simple XHTML form.

Register a new member: A user may register a new member with the tennis club. The registration requires the following data fields: sex, name, age, address, and one or more phone numbers. It will display a "Thank You" page if registration is complete and validate all the required fields; only line 2 of the address is not required. If there is a validation problem, it will redisplay the form and display the errors. This use case demonstrates many aspects of advanced XHTML form processing inside Spring MVC. It will cover `SimpleFormController`, validation, registering `PropertyEditors`, i18n messages, mapping a form to a class, and even some simple JavaScript for dynamic form manipulation.

The sample application has a simple domain model, but it's rich enough to highlight some issues when using similar elements in a Spring MVC application. We will consider the DAOs, the services, and the model classes as the domain model.

Configuring the Sample Application

In the `web.xml` file in Listing 8-1, we declared a global `ApplicationContext` defined by the file `/WEB-INF/applicationContext.xml`, which is shown in Listing 8-2. This file was created before any lines of Spring MVC code were written, as it is focused on the core services for the application.

Listing 8-2. *The applicationContext.xml File, Which Defines the Global Application Context*

```
<?xml version="1.0"?>
<!DOCTYPE beans PUBLIC
    "-//SPRING//DTD BEAN//EN"
    "http://www.springframework.org/dtd/spring-beans.dtd">
<?xml version="1.0" encoding="UTF-8"?>
<beans xmlns="http://www.springframework.org/schema/beans"
    xmlns:xsi="http://www.w3.org/2001/XMLSchema-instance"
    xmlns:tx="http://www.springframework.org/schema/tx"
```

```
        xsi:schemaLocation="http://www.springframework.org/schema/beans
  http://www.springframework.org/schema/beans/spring-beans.xsd
  http://www.springframework.org/schema/tx
  http://www.springframework.org/schema/tx/spring-tx.xsd">

<bean id="dataSource" class="org.apache.commons.dbcp.BasicDataSource"
        destroy-method="close">
  <property name="driverClassName" value="${jdbc.driverClassName}"/>
  <property name="url" value="${jdbc.url}"/>
  <property name="username" value="${jdbc.username}"/>
  <property name="password" value="${jdbc.password}"/>
</bean>

<bean id="transactionManager"
        class="org.springframework.jdbc.datasource.DataSourceTransactionManager">
  <property name="dataSource" ref="dataSource"/>
</bean>

<bean id="memberDao"
        class="com.apress.springbook.chapter08.domain.MemberDaoImpl">
  <property name="dataSource" ref="dataSource" />
  <property name="phoneNumberDao">
    <bean class="com.apress.springbook.chapter08.domain.PhoneNumberDaoImpl">
      <property name="dataSource" ref="dataSource" />
    </bean>
  </property>
</bean>

<bean id="membershipService"
        class="com.apress.springbook.chapter08.domain.MembershipServiceImpl">
  <property name="memberDao" ref="memberDao" />
</bean>

<tx:annotation-driven/>
</beans>
```

■**Note** We've used the Spring 2.0 `<tx:annotation-driven>` custom XML tag in Listing 8-2 to enable support for `@Transactional` in the Spring container. If necessary, you can switch back to Spring 1.2, as described in Chapter 7.

Now we need to configure the DataSource and transaction manager.

Configuring the DataSource

We are creating our own DataSource instead of relying on one provided by the servlet container. This technique creates a more portable web application, as the configuration for the DataSource is included with the application.

Notice the use of placeholders, such as ${jdbc.username}, inside the definition for the DataSource in Listing 8-2. This is a common way to externalize the configuration elements of a bean, so that it is easy to change them for testing, or even at deployment time. Those placeholders are filled in with values by a PropertyPlaceholderConfigurer, which is defined in the second configuration file for the global ApplicationContext, /WEB-INF/propertyPlaceholderForWeb.xml. Listing 8-3 shows the full contents of that file.

Listing 8-3. *The propertyPlaceholderForWeb.xml File Contains the Location of the JDBC Properties*

```
<?xml version="1.0"?>
<!DOCTYPE beans PUBLIC
    "-//SPRING//DTD BEAN//EN"
    "http://www.springframework.org/dtd/spring-beans.dtd">
<beans>

  <bean id="propertyConfigurer"
        class="org.springframework.beans.factory.config. ➥
PropertyPlaceholderConfigurer">
    <property name="locations">
      <list>
        <value>WEB-INF/jdbc.properties</value>
      </list>
    </property>
  </bean>

</beans>
```

PropertyPlaceholderConfigurer references a properties file for the actual values of the property placeholders. Listing 8-4 shows the contents of jdbc.properties.

Listing 8-4. *The jdbc.properties File with Defined JDBC Properties*

```
jdbc.driverClassName=org.hsqldb.jdbcDriver
jdbc.url=jdbc:hsqldb:hsql://localhost/tennis
jdbc.username=sa
jdbc.password=
```

As you can see, for the sample application, we are using HSQL DB (http://www.hsqldb.org/), an embeddable Java database. For production systems, you would use a full-featured RDBMS instead, but HSQL DB is perfect for testing and demos.

Configuring the Transaction Manager

The transaction management is configured with help from AnnotationTransactionAttributeSource, which reads JDK 5 @Transactional annotations for transaction demarcation. The transaction manager itself, DataSourceTransactionManager, simply manages the JDBC transaction, as there is only one DataSource in use here.

The DefaultAdvisorAutoProxyCreator works with the TransactionAttributeSourceAdvisor to automatically locate beans with @Transactional annotations and transparently create AOP wrapped beans. The aspect, in this case, is transaction management. This technique keeps all transaction-management code out of the implementations. Because MembershipServiceImpl is the only bean with @Transactional annotations, it is the only one that will become transactional.

Scaling This Configuration

The configuration in Listing 8-2 is ideal for web applications that require only one database. For anything other than a demo application, you should certainly use a full RDBMS. However, the DataSource and transaction-management configurations are perfectly suitable for small to medium-sized applications. You may need to tweak DataSource configurations for the pool of database connections as usage grows, however. Another alternative is to use a JNDI DataSource.

As your needs grow, you might find it necessary to change the implementations of either the DataSource or the transaction manager. For example, your application server might provide DataSources that have greater failover capabilities. Doing so should not affect the initial

assumptions you've made, as Spring hides those implementation details very well behind interfaces. The benefits of this configuration are that you can scale your solution by changing only bean
implementations. The wiring and configuration remain the same.

   We've kept any web-related beans out of the global ApplicationContext. Let's now look at how
to build a web application on top of the main MembershipService, which integrates the web application with the data-access layer.

Implementing the List All Members Use Case

Let's begin our Spring MVC programming with the task of displaying all members in the tennis
club. We know this use case is a simple read-only dynamic page; therefore, we will subclass org.
springframework.web.servlet.mvc.AbstractController to create an AllMembersController controller. AbstractController is a good solution when you don't need complex form handling or any
predefined workflow.

Creating the Controller

Like all good controllers, AllMembersController will act as the middleman between the service
(MembershipService in this case) and the view. Listing 8-5 contains the source code for AllMembers
Controller.

Listing 8-5. *The AllMembersController Links the Service and the View*

```
package com.apress.springbook.chapter08.web;

import java.util.List;

import javax.servlet.http.HttpServletRequest;
import javax.servlet.http.HttpServletResponse;

import org.springframework.web.servlet.ModelAndView;

import org.springframework.web.servlet.mvc.AbstractController;

import com.apress.springbook.chapter08.domain.Member;
import com.apress.springbook.chapter08.domain.MembershipService;

public class AllMembersController extends AbstractController {

  private MembershipService membership;

  public AllMembersController() {
    setSupportedMethods(new String[]{"GET"});
  }

  public void setMembershipService(MembershipService membership) {
    this.membership = membership;
  }

  @Override
  protected ModelAndView handleRequestInternal(HttpServletRequest request,
      HttpServletResponse response) throws Exception {
    List<Member> members = membership.getAllMembers();
    return new ModelAndView().addObject(members);
  }
}
```

▪Note We'll cover the Member class in the "Implementing the Register a New Member Use Case," where we consider complex web forms and how they are related to domain model classes.

The bean definition for the controller can be found in the spring-servlet.xml file, which defines all web-related beans for the DispatcherServlet. Listing 8-6 shows the AllMembers Controller bean definition.

Listing 8-6. *AllMembersController Bean Definition in spring-servlet.xml*

```
<bean id="allMembersController"
      class="com.apress.springbook.chapter08.web.AllMembersController">
  <property name="membershipService" ref="membershipService" />
</bean>
```

Let's now take a close look at the controller's source code (Listing 8-5). Inside the constructor, the setSupportedMethods() method configures the controller to allow only the GET HTTP method to be invoked. If a client attempts another method, for instance POST, it will receive an error. We restrict the methods on a controller in order to enforce the usage and semantics of the interaction with the controller. With a read-only page such as this one, it makes no sense to POST to this controller. Therefore, by restricting the methods allowed, we enforce correct usage.

▪Tip The semantics for each HTTP method are clearly defined. By using each method correctly, you are helping to create strong, web-friendly architectures. You should restrict the HTTP methods on a controller to only those that make sense for each instance.

The setMembershipService() method is provided so that dependency injection is able to inject the MembershipService.

Finally, the handleRequestInternal() method (an abstract method of AbstractController) is invoked for every HTTP request. Here, the real work is done as the membership.getAllMembers() method is called. The result is placed into an instance of ModelAndView, which is returned at the end of the method.

▪Note Remember that controllers are singletons; therefore, they are able to handle multiple requests concurrently. Do not change the state in member variables when handling individual requests.

After handleRequestInternal() is finished, DispatcherServlet determines the view to be rendered and provides it with all objects from the model. As you can see, the view was not specified in ModelAndView here. We are letting the convention defaults determine the view name, in order to minimize the configuration required. By default, the convention for view-name generation is to use the URI without the context path of the WAR file (if any) and the extension (if any). Table 8-4 shows examples of context paths, servlet mappings, request URIs, and resulting view names.

Table 8-4. *Examples of Generated View Names*

Context Path	Servlet URL Mapping	Request URI	Generated View Name
/test	*.html	/test/members.html	members
/	*.html	/members.html	members
/test	g	/test/app/members.html	app/members
/test	/app/*	/test/app/members	app/members
/	/app/*	/app/members	app/members
/	*.html	/index.html	index

But how is the URI of controllers chosen? The convention is to use the short name of the controller's class. In this case, the class name is AllMembersController. By default, the Controller suffix is removed, and the remaining string is made lowercase. We are left with allmembers. As you'll recall, DispatcherServlet is mapped to /app/*, so we can now access AllMembersController with http://example.org/servletcontext/app/allmembers. If DispatcherServlet is mapped to *.html in web.xml, we can access AllMembersController with http://example.org/servletcontext/app/allmembers.html.

To utilize this convention in your application, you must declare a ControllerClassNameHandler Mapping bean in your spring-servlet.xml file. This is because the convention of taking the controller's class name to build the URI mapping is not the default. Fortunately, it's very easy to declare. Simply add Listing 8-7 to your spring-servlet.xml file.

Listing 8-7. *ControllerClassNameHandlerMapping in spring-servlet.xml*

```
<bean id="controllerNameHandlerMapper"
      class="org.springframework.web.servlet.mvc.ControllerClassNameHandlerMapping"
 />
```

Getting back to how the view is chosen, if the URI ends with /app/allmembers, the last element is allmembers. The view name therefore is allmembers. Of course, if we specified the view name in ModelAndView, that would take precedence over this default view name.

■**Caution** This convention of automatic view-name generation is new with Spring MVC 2.0. It does not work with releases prior to 2.0.

So to which view does allmembers map? For this sample application, we are using JSP pages as the view technology and we have placed all JSP pages into the /WEB-INF/jsp directory. Therefore, we need to resolve the allmembers logical view name into a filename for the JSP.

Creating the View Resolver

We will create a ViewResolver for this task, specifically an InternalResourceViewResolver. Internal resources are items able to be dispatched to via the Servlet API's RequestDispatcher. This includes JSP pages, servlets, and even other controllers.

InternalResourceViewResolvers are nice because they can be configured with a prefix and suffix that can be added to the logical view name in order to create the full path to the view file. In this case, the view name is allmembers, the prefix is /WEB-INF/jsp/, and the suffix is .jsp. Therefore, the InternalResourceViewResolver can resolve allmembers into /WEB-INF/jsp/allmembers.jsp.

Listing 8-8 shows the bean definition for the ViewResolver, which can be found in spring-servlet.xml.

Listing 8-8. *Bean Definition for InternalResourceViewResolver in spring-servlet.xml*

```
<bean id="viewResolver"
      class="org.springframework.web.servlet.view.InternalResourceViewResolver">
  <property name="viewClass"
            value="org.springframework.web.servlet.view.JstlView" />
  <property name="prefix" value="/WEB-INF/jsp/"/>
  <property name="suffix" value=".jsp"/>
</bean>
```

Moving on to the view itself, Listing 8-9 contains the source for allmembers.jsp.

Listing 8-9. *The allmembers.jsp File*

```
<?xml version="1.0" encoding="ISO-8859-1" ?>
<%@ page language="java" contentType="text/html; charset=ISO-8859-1"
    pageEncoding="ISO-8859-1"%>
<%@ taglib prefix="c" uri="http://java.sun.com/jsp/jstl/core" %>
<!DOCTYPE html PUBLIC "-//W3C//DTD XHTML 1.0 Strict//EN"
  "http://www.w3.org/TR/xhtml1/DTD/xhtml1-strict.dtd">
<html xmlns="http://www.w3.org/1999/xhtml">
  <head>
    <meta http-equiv="Content-Type" content="text/html; charset=ISO-8859-1" />
    <title>List Members</title>
  </head>

  <body>
    <h1>List Members</h1>

    <c:if test="${empty memberList}">
      <p>No members found.</p>
    </c:if>

    <table>
      <thead>
        <tr>
          <th>Name</th>
          <th>Age</th>
          <th>Address</th>
        </tr>
      </thead>

      <tbody>
        <c:forEach items="${memberList}" var="member">
          <tr>
            <td>${member.name.last}, ${member.name.first}</td>
            <td>${member.age}</td>
            <td>${member.address}</td>
          </tr>
        </c:forEach>
      </tbody>
    </table>
  </body>
</html>
```

There's nothing Spring-specific in this JSP page. It iterates through the list of members (identified by `memberList`) and prints out the details for each member.

You might have noticed something strange in Listing 8-9. Where did the name `memberList` come from? This is another convention of Spring MVC 2.0. The names of the objects placed into the model are dynamically generated if no name is provided, based on the short class name of the object (name of the class with package name). In the case of collections, the string `List` is appended to the short class name. Table 8-5 shows object types and the generated names in the model.

Table 8-5. *Generated Model Names for Object Types*

Type	Generated Name
my.package.OrderItem	orderItem
Array of my.package.OrderItem	orderItemList
Collection where first element is my.package.OrderItem type	orderItemList

---

■**Caution** Generating a model name will fail if a `Collection`, `Set`, or `List` object is empty. If this is possible, it's best to provide a model name yourself by calling the `org.springframework.web.servlet.ModelAnd View#addObject(String, Object)` method.

Going back to `handleInternalRequest()`, you saw that we placed a `List<Member>` into `ModelAnd View`. It received the name `memberList`, due to the rules specified in the previous paragraph. The name is then used to reference the object from inside the view.

Paginating the Members List

We've built the simple listing of all members, but the original use case wants the list to be paginated. This simply means the list of results should be spread across multiple pages, instead of being one long list on a single page. Paginated lists are a bit more work to create than single lists, but the user experience is much better.

A single long list overwhelms the user with information, as well as the database system, as it's asked to pull the entire list for every request. Paginated lists, on the other hand, provide a slice of the full list, with navigational elements such as previous and next links to aid the user in moving through the full list.

You can accomplish pagination in at least three ways:

- Load the entire list for every page and create a sublist in the controller. This is inefficient, because there's no need to load the entire list if you only need to display, say, ten items.

- Load the entire list on the first page, and keep the list around in the HTTP session. This avoids having to load the entire list on every request, but then places a burden on memory usage as you are storing the whole list in the session.

- Rely on the database to do the sorting and limiting. This is the most optimized method, as it retrieves only the sublist for each request. We will use this approach for our sample application.

We will build on what you learned from `AllMembersController` to build a `PaginatedAllMembers` `Controller` controller. It becomes more complex now, because we need to track the following:

- How many items to display on each page
- How many total items are in the list
- What page we are currently viewing
- The sort order, either ascending or descending
- What, if anything, the user is sorting on

We are going to delegate the sorting and sublist generation to the database. The job of `PaginatedAllMembersController` is to get the pagination parameters down to the service layer.

We will delegate the rendering of the paginated list to a handy JSP tag library (taglib) called DisplayTag (`http://displaytag.sourceforge.net/11/`). This taglib helps render and manage XHTML tables, including those displaying paginated lists.

In order to allow DisplayTag to efficiently render the paginated list, we will wrap the list results in `PaginatedList`, a class provided by DisplayTag. `PaginatedList` provides metadata methods to a `List` that specifies which page this `List` represents and how many total items there are in the full `List`, among other things. DisplayTag uses this `PaginatedList` in order to render the correct UI elements, such as next and previous buttons.

Because we are delegating the hard work to the database, the only real trick with the `Paginated` `AllMembersController` is to handle two different request scenarios. The first request might be for the beginning of the list, or the first page. This request will not provide any parameters, so we will have to use defaults. The second type of request will be for any other page of the list, and it will contain parameters dictating which sublist to display.

Listing 8-10 contains the full source code for `PaginatedAllMembersController`.

Listing 8-10. *PaginatedAllMembersController Handles Two Different Request Scenarios*

```java
package com.apress.springbook.chapter08.web;

import java.util.List;

import javax.servlet.http.HttpServletRequest;
import javax.servlet.http.HttpServletResponse;

import org.springframework.web.bind.ServletRequestUtils;

import org.springframework.web.servlet.ModelAndView;

import org.springframework.web.servlet.mvc.AbstractController;

import org.displaytag.pagination.PaginatedList;

import org.displaytag.properties.SortOrderEnum;

import com.apress.springbook.chapter08.domain.Member;
import com.apress.springbook.chapter08.domain.MembershipService;

public class PaginatedAllMembersController extends AbstractController {

  private MembershipService membership;
  private static final int PAGE_LENGTH = 5;
  private int pageLength = PAGE_LENGTH;
```

```
public PaginatedAllMembersController() {
  setSupportedMethods(new String[]{"GET"});
}

public void setPageLength(int pageLength) {
  this.pageLength = pageLength;
}

public void setMembershipService(MembershipService membershipService) {
  this.membership = membershipService;
}

@Override
protected ModelAndView handleRequestInternal(HttpServletRequest request,
          HttpServletResponse response) throws Exception {
  final int pageNumber = ServletRequestUtils.getIntParameter(request, "page", 1);
  final String sortOrder =
    ServletRequestUtils.getStringParameter(request, "dir", "asc");
  final String sortCriterion =
    ServletRequestUtils.getStringParameter(request, "sort", null);

  final List<Member> members = membership.getAllMembers(
            (pageNumber-1)*pageLength,
            pageLength, sortOrder, sortCriterion);
  final int numberMembers = membership.getNumberMembers();

  ModelAndView mav = new ModelAndView();
  mav.addObject("memberList", new PaginatedList() {

    public List getList() {
      return members;
    }

    public int getPageNumber() {
      return pageNumber;
    }

    public int getObjectsPerPage() {
      return pageLength;
    }

    public int getFullListSize() {
      return numberMembers;
    }

    public String getSortCriterion() {
      return sortCriterion;
    }

    public SortOrderEnum getSortDirection() {
      return sortOrder.equals("asc") ? SortOrderEnum.ASCENDING :
        SortOrderEnum.DESCENDING;
    }

    public String getSearchId() {
      return null;
    }
```

```
    });
    return mav;
  }
}
```

Listing 8-11 shows the bean definition for PaginatedAllMembersController.

Listing 8-11. *PaginatedAllMembersController Bean Definition in spring-servlet.xml*

```
<bean id="paginatedAllMembersController"
      class="com.apress.springbook.chapter08.web.PaginatedAllMembersController">
  <property name="membershipService" ref="membershipService" />
</bean>
```

PaginatedAllMembersController uses Spring's org.springframework.web.bind.ServletRequest
Utils class to convert parameter values and to use default values. ServletRequestUtils is a convenient class that you can use anytime you want to convert the String value of HTTP parameters
to specific Java types in your controllers. When working with complex forms, Spring MVC offers a
more intuitive way of working, yet ServletRequestUtils is handy when you only need to get a number of parameters and you're not working in the context of a form.

There's also a pageLength property, which allows you to overwrite the default page length by
adding a property to the bean definition in spring-servlet.xml.

As with AllMembersController, we are relying on the convention of generating the view name
from the URI, and mapping the URI to the short class name for the controller.

Two things of note are going on inside the handleRequestInternal() method. The first is the
reading of the parameters from the request in order to determine which sublist the user would like,
and the delegation of the request to the MembershipService. The second is how the results are
wrapped inside a PaginatedList anonymous inner class.

How do we display this sublist, with the appropriate next, previous, first, and last links? This is
where DisplayTag comes in. Listing 8-12 shows how to use this taglib with a PaginatedList.

Listing 8-12. *The paginatedallmembers.jsp File*

```jsp
<?xml version="1.0" encoding="ISO-8859-1" ?>
<%@ page language="java" contentType="text/html; charset=ISO-8859-1"
    pageEncoding="ISO-8859-1"%>
<%@ taglib prefix="c" uri="http://java.sun.com/jsp/jstl/core" %>
<%@ taglib prefix="dt" uri="http://displaytag.sf.net" %>
<!DOCTYPE html PUBLIC "-//W3C//DTD XHTML 1.0 Strict//EN"
  "http://www.w3.org/TR/xhtml1/DTD/xhtml1-strict.dtd">
<html xmlns="http://www.w3.org/1999/xhtml">
  <head>
    <meta http-equiv="Content-Type" content="text/html; charset=ISO-8859-1" />
    <title>List Members - Paginated</title>
  </head>

  <body>
    <h1>List Members - Paginated</h1>

    <dt:table name="memberList" id="member" sort="external" defaultsort="1"
            requestURI="/app/paginatedallmembers">
      <dt:column title="First Name" sortable="true" sortName="name_first">
        ${member.name.first}
      </dt:column>
      <dt:column title="Last Name" sortable="true" sortName="name_last">
        ${member.name.last}
```

```
    </dt:column>
  </dt:table>

</body>
</html>
```

As you can see, there are no previous or next links in the JSP file. They are added by the `<dt:table>` tag at runtime. In fact, DisplayTag sorts the columns and renders the XHTML `<table>` and even the correct message to display if the list is empty. Best of all, the `<table>` that is rendered is styled completely through CSS. For a full explanation of DisplayTag and its options, visit `http://displaytag.sourceforge.net/11/`.

Implementing the Search for a Member Use Case

Let's move on to something a little more interesting: handling simple forms. Because Spring MVC embraces and exposes the Servlet API, you should feel very comfortable handling simple form submissions. The use case of searching for a member demonstrates simple form handling, in preparation for the main event: full form handling.

As you'll see when we implement the register a new member use case, Spring MVC provides the `SimpleFormController` controller for handling full form workflow—displaying a form, binding the form submission to an object, validating it, displaying any possible errors, and handling the submission. While it manages the full form life cycle, sometimes you don't need all of it. For example, a simple search box often doesn't require validation. When you need to handle a simple one-field form that doesn't result in an object changing on the back-end, you can use the `Abstract Controller`.

For this example, we will add a search box to the list all members page, from the first use case. It will allow a user to search for one or more members using a wildcard that will match against both the first and last names of members.

The form itself is quite simple, requiring only one field. There is nothing Spring MVC-specific contained in the markup. Listing 8-13 contains the XHTML for the form.

Listing 8-13. *Search for Members Form*

```
<form action="searchformembers" method="get">
  <p>
    <label for="q">First or Last Name:</label>
    <input type="text" name="q" value="${param.q}"/>
    <input type="submit" value="Search" />
  </p>
</form>
```

You'll notice that this form uses `method="get"`. Because this form is read-only (that is, it does not change any object state), we chose the GET method. Using GET, we can easily tie into web architecture elements such as caching. To save future bandwidth and CPU time, we can inform browsers and intermediate caches that the results from the search can be stored for a short amount of time (say, two minutes). Therefore, if someone attempts the exact same search again before the cache expires, that user will see the cached version.

■**Note** Of course, caching only makes sense when the information in the page does not need to be real time, or changes infrequently. However, efficient use of caching can save bandwidth and CPU cycles, so make sure to use it if you can.

The form has a single field with a name of q, short for query. This name is arbitrary; you should pick a name that has meaning to you. Notice how the value of the input field can be populated with the request parameter itself. This is a nice UI touch, as it will display the search criteria on the result page (as you will see shortly).

The action attribute points to searchformembers, which matches the name of SearchForMembers Controller.

The controller itself is very simple, as it delegates the actual searching to the service layer. We will even reuse allmembers.jsp from the list all members use case, as the search results display the same information. Listing 8-14 contains the code for SearchForMembersController.

Listing 8-14. *SearchForMembersController Delegates the Search to the Service Layer*

```
package com.apress.springbook.chapter08.web;

import java.util.List;

import javax.servlet.http.HttpServletRequest;
import javax.servlet.http.HttpServletResponse;

import org.springframework.web.servlet.ModelAndView;

import org.springframework.web.servlet.mvc.AbstractController;

import com.apress.springbook.chapter08.domain.Member;
import com.apress.springbook.chapter08.domain.MembershipService;

public class SearchForMembersController extends AbstractController {

  private MembershipService membership;
  private String searchForMemberResultViewName = "allmembers";

  public void setMembershipService(MembershipService membership) {
    this.membership = membership;
  }

  @Override
  protected ModelAndView handleRequestInternal(HttpServletRequest request,
          HttpServletResponse response) throws Exception {
    List<Member> members =
      membership.findMembersByFirstOrLastName(request.getParameter("q"));
    ModelAndView mav = new ModelAndView(searchForMemberResultViewName);
    mav.addObject(members);
    return mav;
  }
}
```

Handling a simple search form is as easy as grabbing the request parameter and sending it on through the service layer.

Of course, you must be wary of passing request parameters into the service layer, where they will eventually interact with the DAOs, because a malicious attacker might be attempting to perform a SQL injection attack.

■Note A SQL injection attack is an attack that attempts to coerce the SQL query into selecting, updating, or deleting more than intended. To learn how to prevent SQL injection attacks, see `http://en.wikipedia.org/wiki/SQL_injection`.

The bottom line is that you must use `PreparedStatements` when dealing with queries using information coming from untrusted sources.

Implementing the Register a New Member Use Case

The register a new member use case illustrates how Spring MVC handles complex forms. We will build the workflow for registering (or creating) a new `Member` with the tennis club. A full `Member` has many properties, which have been selected to show you a wide variety of situations you will encounter while using Spring MVC.

`Member` contains the following information, all of which must be captured by the form:

- Name, including first, middle, and last
- Address, including street, city, state, and ZIP code
- Sex, male or female
- Age
- One or more phone numbers

Once a fully populated `Member` class is created, it will be saved into the database and a success message will be displayed.

While implementing this use case, we will show you how to do the following:

- Handle properties of types other than `Strings`
- Handle nested objects (for example, a `Member` has a nested `Name` object)
- Enforce acceptable ranges for values through validation
- Handle collections of items, such as `Lists`

In contrast to the previous simple form use case, a full form submission life cycle has many steps and states, including the following:

1. Display the form.
2. User submits the form.
3. The form data is bound to an object.
4. The object is validated, and errors are collected.
5. If there are errors, the form is redisplayed with the original data.
6. User fixes all errors, and then resubmits the form.
7. Steps 3 through 5 are repeated.
8. The object is sent to the service layer for processing.
9. A confirmation page is displayed.

To help you manage this process, Spring MVC provides `SimpleFormController`. It gets its name from making this nine-step process simple and easy to implement.

`SimpleFormController` brings a lot of functionality, essentially masking the direct interaction you would have with the Servlet API. Instead of working with request parameters directly, you work with objects. This is accomplished through form binding.

Form Binding

Binding a form to an object is preferable to simply manually interacting with request parameters for many reasons. For instance, handling a form with many fields is cumbersome and verbose, requiring code that can mask the true intent of the operation. Type-checking of the parameter values by the compiler is not possible, as every value is a `String`. If you require that a parameter is of a different type (such as an `int` or a `boolean`), the manual conversion process is repetitive and error-prone.

A better scenario for manipulating forms is to encapsulate the parameters into one or more objects. This command bean, populated from the form parameters, is strongly typed, validatable, and easily processed by the rest of the system. *Form binding* is the act of binding form request parameters to a command bean, and is supported by Spring MVC.

To understand form binding, you must understand the general rules defining JavaBeans. Anyone who has written JSP files, especially with the JSTL, will find these ideas familiar. As you probably know, the JavaBean specification says that a class has a property if the class has both a getter and setter method for that property. Spring MVC makes use of the JavaBean property naming convention to perform its form binding. It will match form request parameter names to class property names. Therefore, if your XHTML form has a field named `firstName`, on submission, the value from that field will be placed into the command object with the `setFirstName(String)` method.

Spring MVC doesn't stop at populating simple command objects with `String` values. Your command objects can have properties of type `int`, `boolean`, or even custom classes. A `PropertyEditor`, another object for standard JavaBean support, can be used to do the type conversion. Spring MVC also supports binding to nested command objects, which you'll see an example of shortly. In other words, you are able to encapsulate form-submission data in rich, nested command beans. Don't feel constrained to use only flat objects with `String` properties.

Validating Data

As data is entering your system from the untrusted outside world, validation is an important part of your Spring MVC application. Validation is performed in dedicated validators, which apply validation-specific logic to command beans before they enter your service layer. If there are errors, they are generated during validation, and the command bean is rejected.

Spring MVC's validators are tightly coupled to Spring MVC's error message system. It's very easy to create modular validators, allowing you to mix and match validation logic as easily as your command beans can be nested and composed.

Validators can be dependency-injected like any other bean in the system; therefore, your validation logic can contain simple logic such as "is required" or "max length," as well as logic that requires calls into your service layer. We'll use a custom validator called `MemberValidator` to check the details of new members.

Using Domain Model Classes

To begin working on this use case, let's look at the `Member` class. This class started life inside the domain model, yet its design reflects our intentions to use it as a command bean in Spring MVC. These decisions promote an overall integrated design, in contrast to designing layers in isolation, which would result in a system that is difficult to integrate.

By using domain model classes as command beans in the web layer, we avoid creating classes specifically for form submissions. If your form mirrors a domain model object, you should use the object from your domain model as the command bean. As you'll see, it becomes very easy to bind the form to the object, validate it, and send it straight into your service layer.

Listing 8-15 contains the code for the Member class.

Listing 8-15. *Member Class*

```java
package  com.apress.springbook.chapter08.domain;

import java.util.List;
import java.util.ArrayList;
import java.util.Collections;

public class Member {

  private Integer id;
  private Name name = new Name();
  private Integer age;
  private Sex sex;
  private Address address = new Address();
  private List<PhoneNumber> phoneNumbers = new ArrayList<PhoneNumber>();

  public Member() { }

  public Member(String firstName, String lastName) {
    this.getName().setFirst(firstName);
    this.getName().setLast(lastName);
  }

  void setId(Integer id) {
    this.id = id;
  }

  public Integer getId() {
    return id;
  }

  public Address getAddress() {
    return address;
  }

  public Integer getAge() {
    return age;
  }

  public void setAge(Integer age) {
    this.age = age;
  }

  public Name getName() {
    return name;
  }

  public List<PhoneNumber> getPhoneNumbers() {
    return Collections.unmodifiableList(phoneNumbers);
  }
```

```
public void addPhoneNumber(PhoneNumber phoneNumber) {
  this.phoneNumbers.add(phoneNumber);
}

public void removePhoneNumber(PhoneNumber phoneNumber) {
  this.phoneNumbers.remove(phoneNumber);
}

public void removePhoneNumber(int index) {
  this.phoneNumbers.remove(index);
}

public Sex getSex() {
  return sex;
}

public void setSex(Sex sex) {
  this.sex = sex;
}

}
```

Let's look at the contents of the Member class. First, you'll notice that it has a lot of getter and setter methods. As discussed earlier, any property that will be mapped to a form field should be exposed via a getter and setter.

The second important aspect of this class implementation is the initialization of any nested objects. For instance, name, address, and phoneNumbers are initialized upon object instantiation. This is essentially required if the object is to be used as a command bean.

■**Caution** Initialize any nested object of a command bean before attempting to bind it to a form. Otherwise, you will get NullPointerExceptions.

For the full picture, Listings 8-16 through 8-19 show the Name class, the Sex enum, the Phone Number class, and the Address class.

Listing 8-16. *Name Class*

```
package  com.apress.springbook.chapter08.domain;

public class Name {

  private String first;
  private String middle;
  private String last;

  public String getFirst() {
    return first;
  }
  public void setFirst(String first) {
    this.first = first;
  }
  public String getLast() {
    return last;
  }
}
```

```java
  public void setLast(String last) {
    this.last = last;
  }
  public String getMiddle() {
    return middle;
  }
  public void setMiddle(String middle) {
    this.middle = middle;
  }
}
```

Listing 8-17. *Sex Enum*

```java
package   com.apress.springbook.chapter08.domain;

public enum Sex {
  MALE, FEMALE
}
```

Listing 8-18. *PhoneNumber Class*

```java
public class PhoneNumber {

  public enum Type { HOME, WORK, CELL };

  private Integer id;
  private String areaCode;
  private String number;
  private Type type;
  private Member player;

  public Type getType() {
    return type;
  }
  public void setType(Type type) {
    this.type = type;
  }
  public String getAreaCode() {
    return areaCode;
  }
  public void setAreaCode(String areaCode) {
    this.areaCode = areaCode;
  }
  public String getNumber() {
    return number;
  }
  public void setNumber(String number) {
    this.number = number;
  }
  public Integer getId() {
    return id;
  }
  void setId(Integer id) {
    this.id = id;
  }
  public void setMember(Member player) {
```

```java
      this.player = player;
    }
    public Member getMember() {
      return player;
    }
}
```

Listing 8-19. *Address Class*

```java
package  com.apress.springbook.chapter08.domain;

import org.apache.commons.lang.StringUtils;

public class Address {

  private String line1;
  private String line2;
  private String city;
  private String state;
  private String zip;

  public String getCity() {
    return city;
  }
  public void setCity(String city) {
    this.city = city;
  }
  public String getLine1() {
    return line1;
  }
  public void setLine1(String line1) {
    this.line1 = line1;
  }
  public String getLine2() {
    return line2;
  }
  public void setLine2(String line2) {
    this.line2 = line2;
  }
  public String getState() {
    return state;
  }
  public void setState(String state) {
    this.state = state;
  }
  public String getZip() {
    return zip;
  }
  public void setZip(String zip) {
    this.zip = zip;
  }

  public String toString() {
    StringBuilder addr = new StringBuilder();
    addr.append(line1);
    if (StringUtils.isNotEmpty(line2)) {
```

```
        addr.append(" ");
        addr.append(line2);
    }
    addr.append(" ");
    addr.append(city);
    addr.append(", ");
    addr.append(state);
    addr.append(" ");
    addr.append(zip);
    return addr.toString();
  }
}
```

Creating the Member Form and XHTML Page

Now let's look at the form used to create and register a new Member. Listing 8-20 contains the full XHTML page with the Member form, called registerMember.jsp.

Listing 8-20. *Member Form and XHTML Page (registerMember.jsp)*

```
<?xml version="1.0" encoding="ISO-8859-1" ?>
<%@ page language="java" contentType="text/html; charset=ISO-8859-1"
    pageEncoding="ISO-8859-1"%>
<%@ taglib prefix="form" uri="http://www.springframework.org/tags/form" %>
<%@ taglib prefix="spring" uri="http://www.springframework.org/tags" %>
<%@ taglib prefix="c" uri="http://java.sun.com/jsp/jstl/core" %>
<!DOCTYPE html PUBLIC "-//W3C//DTD XHTML 1.0 Strict//EN"
  "http://www.w3.org/TR/xhtml1/DTD/xhtml1-strict.dtd">
<html xmlns="http://www.w3.org/1999/xhtml">
  <head>
    <meta http-equiv="Content-Type" content="text/html; charset=ISO-8859-1" />
    <title>Register a New Member</title>
  </head>

  <body>
    <h1>Register a New Member</h1>

    <form:form commandName="member">
      <form:errors path="*"/>

      <table>
        <tbody>
          <tr>
            <td class="form-label"><label for="sex">Sex:</label></td>
            <td class="form-field">
              <form:select path="sex">
                <form:option value="FEMALE" />
                <form:option value="MALE" />
              </form:select>
            </td>
          </tr>
          <spring:nestedPath path="name">
            <tr>
              <td class="form-label">
                <form:label for="first">First Name:</label>
              </td>
```

```
        <td class="form-field"><form:input path="first"/></td>
      </tr>
      <tr>
        <td class="form-label">
          <form:label for="last">Last Name:</label>
        </td>
        <td class="form-field"><form:input path="last"/></td>
      </tr>
    </spring:nestedPath>
    <tr>
      <td class="form-label"><form:label for="age">Age:</label></td>
      <td class="form-field"><form:input path="age"/></td>
    </tr>
    <spring:nestedPath path="address">
      <tr>
        <td class="form-label"><form:label for="line1">Line 1</label></td>
        <td class="form-field"><form:input path="line1" /></td>
      </tr>
      <tr>
        <td class="form-label"><form:label for="line2">Line 2</label></td>
        <td class="form-field"><form:input path="line2" /></td>
      </tr>
      <tr>
        <td class="form-label"><form:label for="city">City</label></td>
        <td class="form-field"><form:input path="city" /></td>
      </tr>
      <tr>
        <td class="form-label"><form:label for="state">State</label></td>
        <td class="form-field"><form:input path="state" /></td>
      </tr>
      <tr>
        <td class="form-label"><form:label for="zip">Zip</label></td>
        <td class="form-field"><form:input path="zip" /></td>
      </tr>
    </spring:nestedPath>
    <tr>
      <td style="vertical-align:top"><label>Phone Number(s):</label></td>
      <td>
        <c:forEach items="${member.phoneNumbers}"
                   var="phoneNumber"
                   varStatus="loop">
          <div id="phone-number-fields">
            <form:input path="phoneNumbers[${loop.index}].areaCode" />
            <form:input path="phoneNumbers[${loop.index}].number" />
            <form:select path="phoneNumbers[${loop.index}].type"
                         items="${phoneNumberTypes}" />
            <input type="submit" name="action_removePhoneNumber_${loop.index}"
                   value="Remove Phone Number" />
          </div>
        </c:forEach>

        <input type="submit" name="action_addPhoneNumber"
               value="Add Phone Number" />
      </td>
    </tr>
```

```
      <tr>
        <td />
        <td><input type="submit" value="Register" /></td>
      </tr>
    </tbody>
  </table>
  </form:form>
  </body>
</html>
```

That's a large XHTML page, so let's cover each important aspect one by one, beginning with Spring MVC's form taglibs.

Taglibs and Form Tags

Because we're using JSP as the template system for the application, we will be using taglibs. Notice the three taglib declarations at the top of Listing 8-20. We've included the Spring core tags (spring prefix), the Spring XHTML form tags (form prefix), and the JSTL core tags (c prefix).

■Tip The JSTL core tags provide useful and base functionality required by most dynamic JSP pages. For instance, you can use them to loop through collections or provide conditional rendering. If you're not already using these tags for your JSP pages, you'll be pleasantly surprised to discover just how much they offer. Take the time to learn about the JSTL tags if you haven't already. For more information, we recommend *JSTL in Action* (Manning, 2002).

We use the Spring core tags primarily for the spring:nestedPath tag. There are other tags in this set, but you'll find yourself using the Spring form tags more often. These tags help you write XHTML forms that are easier to read, as they make the binding process simpler and more explicit.

You can see we make heavy use of the form tags whenever we need to render XHTML form <input> elements. These tags map the properties from the command object to the form field.

We'll start at the beginning, with the <form:form> tag:

```
<form:form commandName="member">
...
</form:form>
```

This tag is the root for all form tags, and is responsible for declaring the command bean as well as rendering the XHTML <form> element. Notice we don't set an action attribute on the form taglib. If we don't set the action attribute, the taglib will automatically generate the URI of the controller that generated the view. This is because SimpleFormController handles both the viewing of the form and the form submission. You can, of course, always dictate the action specifically.

The second attribute, commandName="member", binds the form itself to the command bean named member. This command bean is bound to the form, such that all of the form's fields have corresponding properties on the command bean. SimpleFormController is responsible for creating an instance of the Member class and making sure it is available to the JSP page.

Now that we have established the command bean as the context for the form and its fields, let's take a closer look at the XHTML form itself. Here are the fields that represent a Member's Name:

```
<spring:nestedPath path="name">
  <tr>
    <td class="form-label"><label for="name.first">First Name:</label></td>
    <td class="form-field"><form:input path="first"/></td>
  </tr>
  <tr>
```

```
      <td class="form-label"><label for="name.last">Last Name:</label></td>
      <td class="form-field"><form:input path="last"/></td>
    </tr>
  </spring:nestedPath>
```

To review, the Member class has a nested Name object, which has both first and last properties. This relationship is reflected in Listing 8-15.

First, <spring:nestedPath> sets the nesting to the Name object through path="name". The root implicit object throughout the form is an instance of Member, so <spring:nestedPath path="name"> is equivalent to member.getName(). All of the tags inside the <spring:nestedPath> tag are local to the Name object. Once <spring:nestedPath> closes, the implicit context is back to the Member object.

We set the name instance to be the current object so that path="first" resolves correctly. Remember that Name, not Member, has getFirst(). So the <form:input form="first" /> tag must be relative to Name.

Translating the combination of <spring:nestedPath path="name"> and <form:input path="first" />, the equivalent Java code is member.getName().getFirst(). We know getName(). getFirst() belongs to the member command bean because the <form:form> tag is bound to member.

You can see now why providing getters and setters for properties you would like to bind to form fields is so important. The names of the properties from your command bean match the names of the fields in the form. Those properties are accessed via the getters and setters on form display and submission.

Lists of Objects

One of the trickiest issues that new developers face when working with Spring MVC is handling Lists of objects in their command bean. It becomes an issue when a form attempts to render an element of the List that hasn't been populated with items. The trick is to ensure that a List contains all of the items before you display their properties. To do this effectively requires a slight extension to SimpleFormController plus two more submit buttons. We'll begin by looking at the XHTML required for handling Lists, and then move on to the controller itself.

As you learned in the previous section, the form fields are bound to properties on the command bean. Of course, for this to work, the command bean must not be null, although the raw property values themselves can be null. This is because the command bean is constantly queried for the property value, through calls such as member.getSex().

Slightly more complicated is the member.getName() example. We know that Name is a nested object with both first and last properties. When binding to a form, we need to reference the first property, through member.getName().getFirst(). As you can see, neither member nor name can be null in this context; otherwise, there will be a NullPointerException when getFirst() is called. Therefore, all objects up to but not including the last property must never be null. Spring MVC will not simply create an object on the fly for you to replace a null instance.

When handling Lists, you must be aware of what can be null and what can't be null. The List itself must not be null, *and the object inside the List must not be null*. However, the properties of the objects inside the List can be null, assuming they are the binding target. Let's put this into concrete terms.

Looking at Listing 8-20, you can see how the List of PhoneNumbers is displayed. This code is as follows:

```
<c:forEach items="${member.phoneNumbers}" var="phoneNumber" varStatus="loop">
  <div id="phone-number-fields">
    <form:input path="phoneNumbers[${loop.index}].areaCode" />
    <form:input path="phoneNumbers[${loop.index}].number" />
    <form:select path="phoneNumbers[${loop.index}].type"
                 items="${phoneNumberTypes}" />
    <input type="submit" name="action_removePhoneNumber_${loop.index}"
```

```
            value="Remove Phone Number" />
    </div>
</c:forEach>
<input type="submit" name="action_addPhoneNumber" value="Add Phone Number" />
```

Because there can be more than one PhoneNumber, we loop through them using the `<c:forEach>` tag. Each PhoneNumber has a type (HOME, CELL, or WORK), so we loop through those using `<form:select>`.

Each PhoneNumber instance is identified by its location in the List. The [ ] notation is used to indicate the index of the item in the List. For example, phoneNumbers[0].areaCode is the equivalent of member.getPhoneNumbers().get(0).getAreaCode(). Again, you can see why it's important to ensure the items inside the List are not null; otherwise, getAreaCode() would generate a Null PointerException.

This situation exposes a mini-workflow, which the form-handling logic must take into account. Upon the display of a new form, there must be at least one PhoneNumber in the List. As the user adds more PhoneNumbers via the UI, the List must be updated. The List must also remove any Phone Numbers the user wishes to delete. As you can see, the contents of the List must be kept in perfect sync with the form elements. If the form needs to display three PhoneNumbers, there must be three PhoneNumbers in the List.

To keep the backing List in sync, we've added two submit buttons. One button, named action_addPhoneNumber, allows the user to add a new PhoneNumber to the form. The action_remove PhoneNumber_${loop.index} button exists for every PhoneNumber in the List, allowing the user to safely remove the PhoneNumber. These two buttons do not trigger a formal form submission; instead, they trigger only the addition and removal of items from the List.

With much of the XHTML explained, including some of the background for the workflows involved, let's finish painting the picture by looking at RegisterMemberController.

Creating the RegisterMemberController Class

To fully understand the RegisterMemberController controller, we will review the different possible workflows it manages. This single controller handles many different paths through its logic. RegisterMemberController is responsible for the following:

- Displaying the XHTML form on the initial request
- Creating a new Member object upon the initial request and storing it in the HttpSession
- Detecting if either the Add Phone Number or Remove Phone Number button is clicked
- Detecting if the formal form submit button is clicked
- Delegating the processing of the new Member to the MembershipService
- Coordinating validation and displaying the XHTML form if there are errors

It's important to keep in mind that much of the decision logic is handled in SimpleForm Controller and its superclasses. Therefore, it won't be apparent if you look at only RegisterNew MemberController. This is a strength of SimpleFormController, as it encapsulates the form-handling logic very well and provides for well-defined extension points.

Listing 8-21 contains the full source code for RegisterNewMemberController.

Listing 8-21. *RegisterNewMemberController*

```
package com.apress.springbook.chapter08.web;

import java.util.Map;
import java.util.HashMap;
```

```java
import java.util.Enumeration;

import javax.servlet.http.HttpServletRequest;
import javax.servlet.http.HttpServletResponse;

import org.springframework.beans.propertyeditors.CustomNumberEditor;

import org.springframework.web.bind.ServletRequestDataBinder;

import org.springframework.web.servlet.ModelAndView;

import org.springframework.web.servlet.mvc.SimpleFormController;

import com.apress.springbook.chapter08.domain.Member;
import com.apress.springbook.chapter08.domain.PhoneNumber;
import com.apress.springbook.chapter08.domain.MembershipService;

public class RegisterMemberController extends SimpleFormController {

  private MembershipService membership;

  public RegisterMemberController() {
    setCommandClass(Member.class);
    setCommandName("member");
    setValidator(new MemberValidator());
    setSessionForm(true);
    setFormView("registerMember");
    setSuccessView("redirect:successRegisterMember");
  }

  public void setMembershipService(MembershipService membership) {
    this.membership = membership;
  }

  @Override
  protected void initBinder(HttpServletRequest request,
          ServletRequestDataBinder binder) throws Exception {
    binder.registerCustomEditor(Integer.class,
                                new CustomNumberEditor(Integer.class, true));
  }

  @Override
  protected boolean isFormChangeRequest(HttpServletRequest request) {
      return isAddPhoneNumberRequest(request) ||
             isRemovePhoneNumberRequest(request);
  }

  private Integer getPhoneNumberIndex(HttpServletRequest request) {
    Integer index = null;
    for (Enumeration e = request.getParameterNames(); e.hasMoreElements(); ) {
      String paramName = (String) e.nextElement();
      if (paramName.startsWith("action_removePhoneNumber_")) {
        index = Integer.valueOf(paramName.substring(
                      "action_removePhoneNumber_".length()));
      }
    }
```

```
        return index;
    }

    private boolean isRemovePhoneNumberRequest(HttpServletRequest request) {
        return (getPhoneNumberIndex(request) != null);
    }

    private boolean isAddPhoneNumberRequest(HttpServletRequest request) {
        return (request.getParameter("action_addPhoneNumber") != null);
    }

    @Override
    protected Object formBackingObject (HttpServletRequest request)
            throws Exception {
        Member member = new Member();
        member.addPhoneNumber(new PhoneNumber());
        return member;
    }

    @Override
    protected void onFormChange(HttpServletRequest request,
            HttpServletResponse response, Object command) throws Exception {
        Member member = (Member) command;
        if (isAddPhoneNumberRequest(request)) {
            member.addPhoneNumber(new PhoneNumber());
        } else if (isRemovePhoneNumberRequest(request)) {
            member.removePhoneNumber(getPhoneNumberIndex(request));
        }
    }

    @SuppressWarnings("unchecked")
    @Override
    protected Map referenceData(HttpServletRequest request) throws Exception {
        Map data = new HashMap();
        data.put("phoneNumberTypes", PhoneNumber.Type.values());
        return data;
    }

    @Override
    protected ModelAndView onSubmit(Object command) throws Exception {
        Member member = (Member) command;
        membership.saveMember(member);
        ModelAndView mav = new ModelAndView(getSuccessView());
        mav.addObject("memberName", member.getName().getFirst());
        mav.addObject("memberId", member.getId());
        return mav;
    }
}
```

We'll start with the constructor, which declares the command bean class (Member.class), the validator (if any), that the command bean should be stored inside the session, and the names of the views for the XHTML form and the success page.

As you saw earlier, in the <form:form> tag, the commandName attribute matches the value for setCommandName(). These names must match to ensure proper usage of the form tags.

The initBinder() call is where all PropertyEditors are registered and configured. As mentioned previously, PropertyEditors are used to convert strings into other types, such as integers or Booleans. The Spring Framework registers many default PropertyEditors, but you will often need to customize their configurations or provide custom implementations.

In our case, we are declaring and configuring a CustomNumberEditor that will convert strings into integers. This is actually a default PropertyEditor, so normally we do not need to declare this class. However, we are setting allowEmpty to true in CustomerNumberEditor's constructor, which says that if the String is null, don't complain. Otherwise, the default behavior is to create an error if the String is null. We'll let our validator handle the null case, so we will silently ignore it when binding.

The next interesting method is isFormChangeRequest(), which asks the question, "Is this request intended to change the form?" A form-change request is not the final form submission, which is an important distinction. You should return true from this method when you want to modify the form without submitting it. In our case, because we are handling the addition and removal of PhoneNumbers, which changes the form, we override isFormChangeRequest() with custom logic.

■Note SimpleFormController makes a distinction between form submission and form modification. Use isFormChangeRequest() to detect the intent of the user's request.

The method formBackingObject() creates and returns a new Member object. After this object is returned from this method, it will be stored in the session so this method is called only on the first request for the form.

Skipping to referenceData(), many forms require a set of dynamic, but default, objects to help display the form. We use this method to return the list of all possible PhoneNumber.Type objects. Objects returned from this method are not to be modified by the form-submission process, but rather are read-only. A typical use case for this method is collecting all of the elements for an XHTML select list (as we have done here). This method will be called whenever the form is displayed.

We now reach the last two methods of interest: onFormChange() and onSubmit(). As their names indicate, they are event handlers for form-change requests and form-submission requests, respectively. These two methods are mutually exclusive; one or the other can be called during the same request, but not both.

When isFormChangeRequest() returns true, onFormChange() is eventually called. This method is responsible for modifying the command bean object, with the intent of redisplaying the form and its command bean. This makes it the perfect place to implement the addition or removal of Phone Numbers from the Member's List of numbers.

The last method to be called is onSubmit(), which handles the case of form submission. If the code reaches this method, it is assumed that the command bean was successfully populated with form field values, was fully validated, and is ready to be processed by the service layer.

Our implementation of onSubmit() delegates to MembershipService.saveMember(). Once complete, it arranges for the Member's name and new memberId to be displayed on the resulting page. After every form submission, the user should be redirected, not internally forwarded, to the success page. This is a very important user experience and data-integrity concern, so always redirect a user after an HTTP POST request.

On an HTTP redirect, any objects in the model will be appended to the request URI as query parameters. For instance, the user will be redirected to successRegisterMember?memberName=[name_from_form]&memberId=XXX after a successful form submission.

Let's now take a look at how to build validators and generate validation errors.

Building Validators

The validation logic is decoupled from controllers through the org.springframework.validation.
Validator interface. SimpleFormController can be configured with zero to many validators to
ensure that the command bean is populated with correct values. If a validator detects that a value is
not allowed, an error will be created and linked to the property that has the problem. SimpleForm
Controller will then detect that one or more errors were generated and it will redisplay the form.

The Validator interface is very simple, and not tied to Spring MVC or HTTP requests.
Listing 8-22 shows the interface.

Listing 8-22. *Validator Interface*

```
public interface Validator {

  /**
   * Return whether or not this object can validate objects
   * of the given class.
   */
  boolean supports(Class clazz);

  /**
   * Validate an object, which must be of a class for which
   * the supports() method returned true.
   * @param obj  Populated object to validate
   * @param errors  Errors object we're building. May contain
   * errors for this field relating to types.
   */
  void validate(Object obj, Errors errors);

}
```

As you can see, any errors that are found during validation are collected inside the Errors
instance. Each validator is provided the object to validate and its errors (which may be empty if
everything validated successfully).

The Errors interface collects all binding and validation errors for a command bean. Binding
errors occur when a form field's value could not be coerced into the property of the command bean,
usually when a PropertyEditor fails. A validation error occurs when a validator's business rule is
violated.

Errors are divided into two groups: FieldErrors and ObjectErrors. FieldErrors are specific to a
field of a command bean. ObjectErrors are general problems with the command bean. This distinction is important, as it allows queries such as "What errors are on this field?"

It's important to note that Spring MVC does not provide generic validation rule implementations, such as "max length," "required," or "regex match." The actual value checks must be
implemented by your code. However, the rules, if correctly written, are simple and easily bundled
into a utility or validation helper class. We will show you how to correctly create validation rules to
maximize reuse.

The MemberValidator Class

To review, from RegisterMemberFormController, we declared a MemberValidator class to handle
validation tasks. Because the Member class is composed of many smaller classes, such as Name and
Address, MemberValidator delegates the validation of each nested class to a more specific validator.
In this section, we will list the code for all of the validators, and then discuss certain design decisions.

We begin with the MemberValidator class, as shown in Listing 8-23.

Listing 8-23. *MemberValidator*

```
package com.apress.springbook.chapter08.web;

import org.springframework.validation.Validator;
import org.springframework.validation.Errors;

import com.apress.springbook.chapter08.domain.Member;

import static com.apress.springbook.chapter08.web.ValidationUtils.rejectIfEmpty;
import static com.apress.springbook.chapter08.web.ValidationUtils. ➥
rejectIfNotBetweenInclusive;

public class MemberValidator implements Validator {

  private Validator nameValidator = new NameValidator();
  private Validator phoneNumberValidator = new PhoneNumberValidator();
  private Validator addressValidator = new AddressValidator();

  public boolean supports(Class clazz) {
    return Member.class.isAssignableFrom(clazz);
  }

  public void validate(Object obj, Errors errors) {
    Member player = (Member) obj;
    errors.pushNestedPath("name");
    nameValidator.validate(player.getName(), errors);
    errors.popNestedPath();

    for (int i = 0; i < player.getPhoneNumbers().size(); i++) {
      errors.pushNestedPath("phoneNumbers["+i+"]");
      phoneNumberValidator.validate(player.getPhoneNumbers().get(i), errors);
      errors.popNestedPath();
    }

    errors.pushNestedPath("address");
    addressValidator.validate(player.getAddress(), errors);
    errors.popNestedPath();

    if (rejectIfEmpty("age", errors)) {
      rejectIfNotBetweenInclusive(18, 120, "age", errors);
    }
  }
}
```

MemberValidator delegates to three other validators: NameValidator (discussed in the next section), PhoneNumberValidator, and AddressValidator.

> **■Note** Here, we didn't use dependency injection to set the instances of the component validators. This was certainly a judgment call. We felt that these validators would not change their implementations and thus didn't warrant the use of dependency injection. They are considered lightweight objects, because they don't require other dependencies or external resources such as database connections. Therefore, to minimize the configuration required, we simply initialized them inside MemberValidator. However, if a dependent object would be considered heavyweight, or required external resources, you should use dependency injection to manage the dependency.

Inside validate(Object, Errors), MemberValidator is acting as a coordinator for the individual validators by sending only the objects the validators know how to validate. For example, Name Validator knows how to validate only Name objects. Therefore, MemberValidator sets the context for the errors object with the pushNestedPath("name") call, sends player.getName() to NameValidator, and then removes the "name" context from the errors object with errors.popNestedPath().

The methods pushNestedPath() and popNestedPath() act just like the <spring:nestedPath> taglib you saw in Listing 8-20. When working with binding or validating nested objects, the path can become quite nested. The taglib and push and pop methods help to manage the path by setting the context for the object being bound or validated. It's a way to keep NameValidator blissfully unaware that it is within the context of MemberValidator. The rejectIfEmpty() and rejectIfNotBetween Inclusive() methods are defined in the ValidationUtils class, which we'll discuss after the next section on NameValidator.

The NameValidator Class

Let's now look at NameValidator, where some real validation is performed. Listing 8-24 shows the NameValidator class.

Listing 8-24. *NameValidator*

```
package com.apress.springbook.chapter08.web;

import org.springframework.validation.Validator;
import org.springframework.validation.Errors;

import com.apress.springbook.chapter08.domain.Name;

import static com.apress.springbook.chapter08.web.ValidationUtils.rejectIfEmpty;
import static com.apress.springbook.chapter08.web.ValidationUtils. ➥
rejectIfLengthGreaterThan;

public class NameValidator implements Validator {

  public boolean supports(Class clazz) {
    return Name.class.isAssignableFrom(clazz);
  }

  public void validate(Object obj, Errors errors) {
    if (rejectIfEmpty("first", errors)) {
      rejectIfLengthGreaterThan (255, "first", errors);
    }
```

```
    if (rejectIfEmpty("last", errors)) {
      rejectIfLengthGreaterThan(255, "last", errors);
    }
    rejectIfLengthGreaterThan(255, "middle", errors);
  }
}
```

The nice thing about NameValidator is that it is decoupled from any other validator or object; it is focused on validating Name objects only. Designing validators like this keeps your validation system flexible.

Now, how is validation performed? The actual logic for validation is found inside the ValidationUtils object, which is filled with useful, small validation routines. These routines are built to work with any property from any class.

Note Spring MVC ships with a very limited set of built-in validation routines. It is up to you to write more specific validation routines.

The ValidationUtils Class

Because Spring MVC does not ship with many validation routines, we will create a base set for this sample application. The routines themselves are imported into a validator through JDK 5's static import feature. Using the new language feature helps to keep the code clutter to a minimum.

All the routines work approximately the same way. They require the errors object, as it contains the object being validated plus any errors that have occurred. The routine also needs to know the name of the field to validate. To keep the routines flexible, we chose to reference the field names through Strings. The downside to this is that your IDE's refactoring tool won't recognize these field names if you attempt to rename a field. You can fix this by using anonymous inner classes that return the field value to be validated, with the cost of added lines of code.

Any other specific validation routine parameters are included, such as maximum or minimum field lengths.

And what happens if there is an error? Let's look at ValidationUtils.rejectIfEmpty(), in Listing 8-25.

Listing 8-25. *rejectIfEmpty() Validation Routine*

```
public static boolean rejectIfEmpty(String field, Errors errors) {
  Object value = errors.getFieldValue(field);
  if (!StringUtils.hasLength(value.toString())) {
    errors.rejectValue(field, MSG_REQUIRED, new Object[]{
         msr(field,errors)}, "Field " + field + " is required");
    return false;
  }
  return true;
}
```

Note ValidationUtils is a class written specifically for the sample application. You can download it with the rest of the source code from the book's website. It also includes the msr() method, which we'll show later in Listing 8-28.

The actual check, using `org.springframework.util.StringUtils.hasLength(String)`, is straightforward in its intent. However, direct your attention to `errors.rejectValue()`, which has the signature `rejectValue(String field, String errorCode, Object[] errorArgs, String defaultMessage)`. The arguments are as follows:

- `field`: The name of the field that failed the validation.

- `errorCode`: The error message name, such as `errors.required`, which is turned into a full `String` when rendered on the UI.

- `errorArgs`: Arguments to the error message, for instance, the name of the field.

- `defaultMessage`: If a valid translation of the `errorCode` can't be found, the `defaultMessage` is displayed.

The errors and error messages rely on the Spring Framework's ability to perform i18n tasks such as translations. This is why `rejectValue()` requires an `errorCode`, such as `errors.required`, instead of a full error message such as "The field is required."

Requiring translation of error messages is useful for two reasons:

- It forces you to centralize the error messages into a single file (which you'll see very shortly). This has an added benefit of enforcing reuse of error messages.

- It natively handles i18n when you need to provide multiple language support. You might not need it immediately, but you'll be happy it's there when you do.

So where does the `errorArgs` parameter come into play? To answer that, let's look at the error messages themselves. Listing 8-26 shows the `messages_en.properties` file, which contains the English translations for the error messages and supporting messages.

Listing 8-26. *The messages_en.properties File*

```
errors.required={0} is required.
errors.too-long={0} must not be longer than {1} characters.
errors.value-between={0} must be between {1} and {2}.

name.first=First Name
name.middle=Middle Name
name.last=Last Name

areaCode=Area Code
number=Phone Number

address.line1=Line 1
address.line2=Line 2
address.city=City
address.state=State/Province
address.zip=Zip/Postal Code
```

This file is specified inside an `ApplicationContext` as a `ResourceBundleMessageSource` instance. We've declared the bean inside the `spring-servlet.xml` file, as it contains messages specific to the web application. Listing 8-27 shows the bean definition that uses this messages file.

Listing 8-27. *messageSource Bean Definition in spring-servlet.xml*

```
<bean id="messageSource"
      class="org.springframework.context.support. ➥
ReloadableResourceBundleMessageSource">
```

```
    <property name="basenames">
      <list>
        <value>messages</value>
      </list>
    </property>
</bean>
```

Notice how even though the full name of the file is `messages_en.properties`, you declare only its short name: `messages`. This is because the `.properties` extension is assumed, and the language specifier, `_en`, is merely one possible instance of the messages file. You don't specify the full language in the bean definition because it can vary depending on the locale of the client visiting your website.

■**Tip** If you want to externalize your messages, but want to present the same language to all your visitors regardless of their native language, you can add a `messages.properties` file to the classpath. This file will be used to resolve error codes when no specific file is found for the locale of a visitor.

One final configuration note: the `messages_en.properties` file must be found in the root of the classpath, as the class loader will try to load it. The easiest way to do this is to place the file into `WEB-INF/classes`.

Now, back to the messages file itself. You can see, in Listing 8-26, the `errors.required` code and its English translation: `{0} is required`. As you might have guessed, the `{0}` represents an argument to the translation, which is where `errorArgs` from `rejectValue()` comes in. The array elements for `errorArgs` are placed into the translation `String`, matching their index number in the array to the placeholder value. Therefore, the first element in `errorArgs` will fill `{0}` in the translation.

■**Note** The placeholders do not need to appear in numerical order. The translation `{1} should be {0}` is perfectly valid.

The messages file uses the standard Java properties format. In classic Spring Framework style, the developers did not create their own i18n system; instead, they simply integrated the existing Java i18n facilities. Therefore, all of the existing i18n features of Java are available for use here. (To learn more about Java's i18n features, refer to `http://java.sun.com/j2se/1.5.0/docs/guide/intl/index.html`.)

The Spring Framework did improve on one area with Java's i18n, and it explains the last question you should have about the `rejectValue()` call in Listing 8-25. If you look closely, you will see the `errorArgs` parameter set with an array with a single value: `msr(field,errors)`. Looking back at the translation for `errors.required`, `{0} is required`, we know we need to get the name of the field into the first placeholder. The end result for a translated message should be, for example, "First name is required." How do we get from `msr(field,errors)` to "First name"? Here's where Spring improves on Java's i18n facilities.

The `msr()` method (short for `MessageSourceResolvable`) helps build error messages by turning the field name into something that can be translated. If we simply placed the value for the field name into the `errorArgs` parameter, we would end up with a translation of "firstName is required." That's not a friendly error message. We need to translate `first` (the first name property of the `Name` class) into something like "First name" before we can translate the `errorCode errors.required`. This creates a recursive translation requirement, something the Java i18n facilities do not support.

Enter the MessageSourceResolvable interface, provided by Spring to indicate if something can be translated into a proper String. It turns out that before Spring sends the errorCode (errors. required) and its arguments to be turned into a formal translated String, it will look at all the elements of errorArgs to see if any need to be translated. If an element of errorArgs is an instance of MessageSourceResolvable, Spring will translate it before attempting to translate the original error message.

Now, turning something into a MessageSourceResolvable is a verbose (in terms of number of characters) operation, and one that can have an impact on the readability of your code. This is because, among other things, you need to use the DefaultMessageSourceResolvable implementation. That's quite a keyboardful, so to condense things a bit, we now present the msr() method (which, again, is something written for the sample application, but is simple to adapt for your application). Listing 8-28 contains the msr() code.

Listing 8-28. *msr() Convenience Method*

```
private static Object msr(String fieldName, Errors errors) {
  List<String> fieldNames = new ArrayList<String>();
  fieldName = errors.getNestedPath() + fieldName;
  fieldNames.add(fieldName);
  int index = -1;
  while ((index = fieldName.indexOf('.')) > -1) {
    fieldName = fieldName.substring(index+1);
    fieldNames.add(fieldName);
  }
  return new DefaultMessageSourceResolvable(
        fieldNames.toArray(new String[fieldNames.size()]));
}
```

You can tell that the msr() method does more than simply wrap fieldName in a DefaultMessage SourceResolvable. We've made this method able to create very flexible error message arguments based on the fieldName plus the nested path it is in.

Spring's i18n enhancements also include the ability to specify multiple message codes per message. If one message code is not found, the next will be tried until a match is found. This allows you to provide a range of message codes, ranging from very specific to very general.

Let's take the example of the NameValidator, nested inside the MemberValidator, to illustrate multiple message codes. If you remember from Listing 8-23, MemberValidator called errors. pushNestedPath("name") before delegating to NameValidator. At this point, the nestedPath() was set to "name", and the fieldName value was either first or last (depending on what was being validated at the moment).

There are now two possible values for the translated field name code: name.first and first. You can consider the former code, name.first, the fully qualified code, as it includes both the path and the field name. The latter example, first, is the least specific message code.

In any case, we now get to the punch line. Going back to Listing 8-26, we provided a translation for name.first, but if that didn't exist, there should be a translation for first. The msr() method is built to provide all possible message codes for the full path of the field name all the way down to just the field name without any path qualifiers.

When is this useful? It's handy anytime that you have multiple objects of the same type but require slightly different translations for *some* of their fields. For example, suppose you have two Address instances: cityAddress and ruralAddress. You may want to always translate the country property as "Country," but you may want to translate line1 as "City Line 1" or "Rural Line 1," depending on the instance. Luckily, you can now do this with cityAddress.line1 and ruralAddress. line1 translations in your error messages properties file.

Reviewing the Sample Application Implementation

Spring MVC has an incredible amount of functionality, both through its provided implementations and the easy-to-extend interfaces and abstract classes. We've only begun to show you all that you can do, but you should now have a feel for how to use Spring MVC. We hope that you are beginning to see how you can make design choices that help you get the most out of the framework.

To show you the whole picture, Listing 8-29 includes the full source code for the spring-servlet.xml file.

Listing 8-29. *The spring-servlet.xml File*

```xml
<?xml version="1.0"?>
<!DOCTYPE beans PUBLIC
    "-//SPRING//DTD BEAN//EN"
    "http://www.springframework.org/dtd/spring-beans.dtd">
<beans>

  <bean id="messageSource"
      class="org.springframework.context.support. ➥
ReloadableResourceBundleMessageSource">
    <property name="basenames">
      <list>
        <value>messages</value>
      </list>
    </property>
  </bean>

  <bean id="viewResolver"
      class="org.springframework.web.servlet.view.InternalResourceViewResolver">
    <property name="viewClass"
            value="org.springframework.web.servlet.view.JstlView" />
    <property name="prefix" value="/WEB-INF/jsp/"/>
    <property name="suffix" value=".jsp"/>
  </bean>

  <bean id="controllerNameHandlerMapper"
      class="org.springframework.web.servlet.mvc. ➥
ControllerClassNameHandlerMapping" />

  <bean id="beanNameHandlerMapper"
      class="org.springframework.web.servlet.handler.BeanNameUrlHandlerMapping" />

  <bean id="registerMemberController"
      class="com.apress.springbook.chapter08.web.RegisterMemberController">
    <property name="membershipService" ref="membershipService" />
  </bean>

  <bean id="searchForMembersController"
      class="com.apress.springbook.chapter08.web.SearchForMembersController">
    <property name="membershipService" ref="membershipService" />
  </bean>

  <bean id="allMembersController"
      class="com.apress.springbook.chapter08.web.AllMembersController">
    <property name="membershipService" ref="membershipService" />
  </bean>
```

```
<bean id="paginatedAllMembersController"
      class="com.apress.springbook.chapter08.web.PaginatedAllMembersController">
  <property name="membershipService" ref="membershipService" />
</bean>

<bean name="/successRegisterMember"
      class="org.springframework.web.servlet.mvc.UrlFilenameViewController" />

</beans>
```

Summary

This chapter started with a discussion of the layout of a typical well-designed web application, in which domain-specific code, data-access code, and UI code are cleanly separated by means of layers.

Next, we discussed the architecture of Spring MVC as well as the configuration of key components. This chapter is intended as a quick-start introduction. The definitive guide is *Expert Spring MVC and Web Flow* (Apress, 2006). You should also take a look at "The Web" section of the official Spring Framework reference documentation at `http://static.springframework.org/spring/docs/2.0.x/reference/`.

The second half of this chapter looked at three use cases with Spring MVC from the sample application that comes with this book. The screen templates in this chapter are based on JSP and JSTL.

The next chapter covers how to integrate other web view technologies with Spring MVC and your applications. You'll discover how to integrate alternatives to JSP such as Velocity and FreeMarker, and how to send PDF and Excel files to clients. You'll also find examples of these integrations in the sample application.

If you want to start building web applications that use JSP and JSTL with Spring MVC, you've seen everything you need. Before you start and while developing, look back at the sample application and its documentation. Many features that you'll need in your applications have already been implemented in this application.

Good luck with Spring MVC, and don't forget to read the last chapter of this book, which covers testing.

CHAPTER 9

View Technologies

In the previous chapter, you were introduced to the Spring MVC framework. We demonstrated how to use JSP as a view technology to render the data in your model. However, Spring provides support for a number of other view technologies, including FreeMarker and Velocity. It also provides support for document-based views, which allow you to have your web application output Adobe PDF or Microsoft Excel documents.

This chapter details the support Spring provides for working with different view technologies. First, we'll discuss some of the considerations for choosing a view technology. Next, we'll describe how Spring resolves logical view names returned by the controllers to the actual concrete view implementation. Then we'll explain how to use each of the supported view technologies. Finally, we'll introduce some new Spring-provided tags that make it easier to work with forms.

Choosing a View Technology

By using the MVC pattern for building a web application, you clearly separate your presentation logic from the actual representation, the concrete view implementation. Having this separation between logic and presentation enables you to switch view technologies or even combine them. However, choosing the right view technology is not trivial.

When choosing a view technology, you should consider the following:

Expertise: Although using a new technology can be a nice challenge, it usually includes a learning curve. Most Java developers have worked with JSP. Similarly, if you are already familiar with XSLT, you might choose that as the view technology for your web application.

Programming model: Each technology either enables or forces you to work in a certain way. For example, Velocity and FreeMarker do not allow you to write Java code inside your view files. JSP allows you to disable the use of Java code inside your view files. FreeMarker is very strict about the MVC pattern; for instance, it does not allow you access to the request object. Therefore, FreeMarker does not let you change anything inside the model data. Depending on your personal preferences, you may feel as though a particular technology is constraining you by its programming model or is assisting you in working the correct way.

Technology maturity and quality: Because JSP is part of the J2EE specifications, it has a certain amount of maturity. FreeMarker and Velocity are separate, open source projects that are not part of any specification. Being part of a specification generally translates to more tool support. FreeMarker is easy to extend and allows the use of JSP tags in the template files, which means you can reuse existing tag libraries and take advantage of tool support for JSP tags.

Application environment: You should take into account the environment in which the application will be deployed. All servlet containers and application servers allow you to use JSP out of the box. With Velocity and FreeMarker, you need to distribute the required dependencies yourself. This may not be an issue, as both Velocity and FreeMarker may be part of your application already. Both can be used in a wider range of environments to do templating; for instance, either can be used as a templating language for generating dynamic e-mail messages. Also consider the nature of the data your web application is using. For example, if your application consists of mostly XML data, then using XSLT as the view technology is a good choice.

All of these aspects should be considered when choosing a view technology. Depending on your needs, you will probably pick a particular view technology as the primary one for your web application. But, as you will see in the next section, Spring lets you combine different view technologies and therefore leverage the benefits of each technology.

Using View Resolvers

The Spring MVC framework promotes the use of separation between your Java code and the actual representation. The presentation logic is located in a controller, which just needs to be aware of the logical view name it wants to display. This logical view name is then resolved by Spring to the actual view implementation. This can be a JSP page, as demonstrated in the previous chapter, or a different view technology, such as Velocity, FreeMarker, or PDF.

To achieve this, Spring MVC relies heavily on its *view resolution* architecture. If you do not specify a view resolver in your configuration files, Spring provides you with a default view resolver: `InternalResourceViewResolver`. However, you are free to specify in your application context any number of view resolvers, which will take care of resolving the logical view name to the actual view implementation.

Using General-Purpose View Resolvers

Spring provides several general-purpose view resolvers for you to use, which are listed in Table 9-1. Each of the view resolvers in Table 9-1 will be discussed in this chapter.

Table 9-1. *Concrete View Resolvers Provided by Spring*

Tag	Description
`BeanNameViewResolver`	Resolves the logical view name by looking up a bean by its name in the application context. This bean should be an implementation of the `View` interface.
`InternalResourceViewResolver`	Resolves the logical view name by forwarding to a resource in the web application (for instance, a JSP file).
`ResourceBundleViewResolver`	Resolves the logical view name by looking up a view definition using the `ResourceBundle` mechanism and a specified basename.
`XmlViewResolver`	Resolves the logical view name by looking up a view bean definition in a separate bean definitions XML file.

Note that several view technology-specific resolvers are also provided by Spring, which will be discussed in the appropriate sections later in this chapter. Although it is possible, you will rarely, if ever, need to create your own `ViewResolver` implementation.

Combining View Resolvers

As we mentioned earlier, it is also possible to combine view technologies. This is done by combining view resolvers. You could, for instance, use JSP as the primary view technology and use an InternalResourceViewResolver as the view resolver. Or you might decide that you want your web application to output a PDF document, and use the ResourceBundleViewResolver to look up the PDF view file.

But how does Spring know which view resolver to use for which request? This is done by having most view resolvers implement an Ordered interface, which allows you to specify the ordering in which Spring should try to resolve the view. The Ordered interface is used to prioritize the view resolvers, where the lowest number has the highest priority. Listing 9-1 shows a combination of view resolvers with a certain ordering.

Listing 9-1. *An Example of Using Three Ordered View Resolvers*

```
<bean id="beanNameResolver"
      class="org.springframework.web.servlet.view.BeanNameViewResolver">
  <property name="order" value="0"/>
</bean>

<bean id="resourceResolver"
      class="org.springframework.web.servlet.view.ResourceBundleViewResolver">
  <property name="order" value="1"/>
  <property name="basename" value="views"/>
</bean>

<bean id="viewResolver"
      class="org.springframework.web.servlet.view.InternalResourceViewResolver">
  <property name="viewClass" value="org.springframework.web.servlet.view.JstlView"/>
  <property name="prefix" value="/WEB-INF/jsp/"/>
  <property name="suffix" value=".jsp"/>
</bean>
```

The configuration in Listing 9-1 instructs Spring MVC to first look up a logical view name as a bean in the application context. If a bean by the specified name is not found, the name is looked up in the ResourceBundle with the basename views. (For more information about the ResourceBundle mechanism, see http://java.sun.com/j2se/1.4.2/docs/api/java/util/ResourceBundle.html.)

The last view resolver used in Listing 9-1 is InternalResourceViewResolver, which will try to look up the logical view name as a JSP file in the web application. Note that InternalResource ViewResolver does not have its order set. This is because this view resolver does not implement the Ordered interface and will always try to retrieve the internal resource, regardless of whether it actually exists. An HTTP 404 error is returned to the user if the resource does not exist. Therefore, InternalResourceViewResolver should always be last in the ordering of view resolvers.

Using View Technologies

Now we will look at how to use the various view technologies supported by Spring. These include the web view technologies JSP, XSLT, Velocity, and FreeMarker. Additionally, some applications require you to output not only HTML, but also some document-based views. Spring provides support for document views in such a way that you do not need to change any logic in your controller to produce them. You can reuse your existing controllers to generate a PDF version of a certain page or an Excel file, as you'll learn in the sections about those document-based views. Finally, you'll see how to use the JasperReports reporting tool.

JSP

JSP is part of the J2EE specification as an extension of the Java servlet technology, which makes it an out-of-the-box view technology option for all servlet containers and application servers. It is currently the mostly widely used view technology for Java web applications. In the previous chapter, you used JSP as a means of rendering your views. Based on the data in the model, the JSP file took care of rendering the HTML.

Preventing Scriptlet Use

JSP allows you to write scriptlets in your view files; however, you should not use them. Using Java code in your view files increases the risk of including more than just view-related functionality in your view files. This will prevent you from migrating to another view technology at a later stage. You can prevent the use of scriptlets in your view files by adding the JSP property to your `web.xml` file, as follows:

```
<jsp-property-group>
  <url-pattern>*.jsp</url-pattern>
  <scripting-invalid>true</scripting-invalid>
</jsp-property-group>
```

Using an Expression Language and Spring-Provided Tags

As of JSP 2.0, and older versions in combination with JSTL tags, it is also possible to use an expression language to simplify accessing data in your model. You have already seen this expression language at work in the previous chapter. It uses the ${*xxx*} notation to access variables in your model, where *xxx* is the key under which the requested data is in the model.

To help you implement views using JSP pages, Spring provides a number of tags as part of its web framework. These tags help you use the JSP technology in conjunction with the Spring Framework. Table 9-2 lists the most commonly used tags Spring provides.

Table 9-2. *Commonly Used Spring-Provided Tags*

Tag Name	Description
`<spring:bind>`	Evaluates the status of a certain bean or property. The status is bound to the request context in the form of a `BindStatus` instance.
`<spring:transform>`	Allows you to transform a certain value that is not part of your command object in the same way as a property that is part of your command object. This tag can be used only inside a `<spring:bind>` tag.
`<spring:nestedPath>`	Allows you to set a nested path on the command object. This supports working with nested bean properties.
`<spring:hasBindErrors>`	Allows you to bind errors on the command object. Using this tag binds an `Errors` instance in the page scope from which you can get information about errors on the command object.
`<spring:message>`	Allows you to internationalize the contents of your pages. This tag uses Spring's `MessageSource` and locale support to retrieve messages in the correct language.

You can use the tags shown in Table 9-2 to create forms using a Spring `FormController`. Note that the previous chapter used the new form tags provided in Spring 2.0, which will be discussed later in this chapter. Listing 9-2 shows part of the form used to subscribe a member from the previous chapter, but uses the tags listed in Table 9-2.

Listing 9-2. *The Register a New Member Page Using the Spring-Provided Tags*

```
<?xml version="1.0" encoding="ISO-8859-1" ?>
<%@ taglib prefix="spring" uri="http://www.springframework.org/tags" %>
<%@ taglib prefix="c" uri="http://java.sun.com/jsp/jstl/core" %>
<!DOCTYPE html PUBLIC "-//W3C//DTD XHTML 1.0 Strict//EN"
                      "http://www.w3.org/TR/xhtml1/DTD/xhtml1-strict.dtd">

<html xmlns="http://www.w3.org/1999/xhtml">
  <head>
    <title>Register a New Member</title>
  </head>

  <body>
    <h1>Register a New Member</h1>

    <form method="post">
      <table>
        <tbody>
          <tr>
            <spring:bind path="member.sex">
              <td>Sex:</td>
              <td>
                <select name="${status.expression}">
                  <option>FEMALE</option>
                  <option>MALE</option>
                </select>
              </td>
            </spring:bind>
          </tr>
          <spring:nestedPath path="member.name">
            <tr>
              <spring:bind path="name.first">
                <td>First Name:</td>
                <td>
                  <input type="text" name="${status.expression}"
                         value="${status.value}"/>
                </td>
              </spring:bind>
            </tr>
            <tr>
              <spring:bind path="name.last">
                <td>Last Name:</td>
                <td>
                  <input type="text" name="${status.expression}"
                         value="${status.value}"/>
                </td>
              </spring:bind>
            </tr>
          </spring:nestedPath>
          <tr>
            <spring:bind path="member.age">
              <td>Age:</td>
              <td>
                <input type="text" name="${status.expression}"
                       value="${status.value}"/>
```

```
          </td>
      </spring:bind>
    </tr>
  <spring:nestedPath path="member.address">
    <tr>
      <spring:bind path="address.line1">
        <td>Line 1:</td>
        <td>
          <input type="text" name="${status.expression}"
                 value="${status.value}"/>
        </td>
      </spring:bind>
    </tr>
    <tr>
      <spring:bind path="address.line2">
        <td>Line 2:</td>
        <td>
          <input type="text" name="${status.expression}"
                 value="${status.value}"/>
        </td>
      </spring:bind>
    </tr>
    <tr>
      <spring:bind path="address.city">
        <td>City:</td>
        <td>
          <input type="text" name="${status.expression}"
                 value="${status.value}"/>
        </td>
      </spring:bind>
    </tr>
    <tr>
      <spring:bind path="address.state">
        <td>State:</td>
        <td>
          <input type="text" name="${status.expression}"
                 value="${status.value}"/>
        </td>
      </spring:bind>
    </tr>
    <tr>
      <spring:bind path="address.zip">
        <td>Zip:</td>
        <td>
          <input type="text" name="${status.expression}"
                 value="${status.value}"/>
        </td>
      </spring:bind>
    </tr>
  </spring:nestedPath>
```

```
      <tr>
        <td/>
        <td><input type="submit" value="Register" /></td>
      </tr>
    </tbody>
  </table>
  </form>
 </body>
</html>
```

The sample JSP form in Listing 9-2 uses the `<spring:bind>` and `<spring:nestedPath>` tags to render and capture the data that is needed to register a member. Notice the use of the `<spring:nestedPath>` tag to allow all containing `<spring:bind>` tags to emit the `member` command name. Also notice that the `name` and `value` attributes of the fields are set using the `BindStatus` instance, which is set by the `<spring:bind>` tag. You can also use this status object to retrieve the value in case the form is shown twice and some values have already been filled in on the command object.

Velocity

Velocity is a Java-based templating engine that can be used as a view technology for web applications. Velocity uses its own templating engine to render the templates. Using Velocity as a view technology promotes the separation between your Java code and the presentation layer by not allowing you to write Java code inside a template. This enables a clear separation of responsibilities between HTML developers and Java developers.

Setting Up Your Application to Use Velocity

To use Velocity as your view technology, first you need to add a configurer to your servlet application context to configure Velocity. Second, you need to change the view resolver to the one that is specific to Velocity. Setting up your web applications to use Velocity as the view technology is demonstrated in Listing 9-3.

Listing 9-3. *Velocity Configurer and the Corresponding View Resolver Configuration*

```
<bean id="velocityConfigurer"
      class="org.springframework.web.servlet.view.velocity.VelocityConfigurer">
  <property name="resourceLoaderPath" value="/WEB-INF/velocity/"/>
</bean>

<bean id="velocityViewResolver"
      class="org.springframework.web.servlet.view.velocity.VelocityViewResolver">
  <property name="suffix" value=".vm"/>
</bean>
```

Note that the configurer is configured with the path to retrieve the templates, relative to the root of the web application. Be sure to place the template files inside the `WEB-INF` folder so they are not directly accessible to users.

The view resolver is configured with a suffix, just as when JSP is used as the view technology. The `.vm` extension is the default Velocity extension; however, you are free to use any extension for your template files.

Creating Velocity Templates

Now that the web application has been set up to use Velocity as the view technology, you can start to write your view templates. Listing 9-4 shows the list members page rewritten as a Velocity template.

Listing 9-4. *List Members Rewritten As a Velocity Page*

```
<?xml version="1.0" encoding="ISO-8859-1" ?>
<!DOCTYPE html PUBLIC "-//W3C//DTD XHTML 1.0 Strict//EN"
                      "http://www.w3.org/TR/xhtml1/DTD/xhtml1-strict.dtd">

<html xmlns="http://www.w3.org/1999/xhtml">
  <head>
    <title>List Members</title>
  </head>

  <body>
    <h1>List Members</h1>

    <form action="searchformembers" method="get">
      <p>
        <label for="q">First or Last Name:</label>
        <input type="text" name="q" value="$param.q" />
        <input type="submit" value="Search" />
      </p>
    </form>

    #if( $memberList.size() == 0 )
      <p>No members found.</p>
    #end

    <table>
      <thead>
        <tr>
          <th>Name</th>
          <th>Age</th>
          <th>Address</th>
        </tr>
      </thead>
      <tbody>
        #foreach( $member in $memberList )
          <tr>
            <td>$member.name.last, $member.name.first</td>
            <td>$member.age</td>
            <td>$member.address</td>
          </tr>
        #end
      </tbody>
    </table>
  </body>
</html>
```

For more information about Velocity, see *Pro Jakarta Velocity: From Professional to Expert* (Apress, 2004).

FreeMarker

FreeMarker is another template engine that works in a manner similar to Velocity. Like Velocity, it provides a clear separation between the logic and the actual presentation.

Setting Up Your Application to Use FreeMarker

Setting up your web application to use FreeMarker as the view technology is very similar to setting it up to use Velocity, as demonstrated in Listing 9-5.

Listing 9-5. *Freemarker Configurer and the Corresponding View Resolver Configuration*

```
<bean id="freemarkerConfigurer"
      class="org.springframework.web.servlet.view.freemarker.FreemarkerConfigurer">
  <property name="resourceLoaderPath" value="/WEB-INF/freemarker/"/>
</bean>

<bean id="freemarkerViewResolver"
      class="org.springframework.web.servlet.view.freemarker. ➥
FreemarkerViewResolver">
  <property name="suffix" value=":ftl"/>
</bean>
```

In this case, we use a configurer and view resolver specific to FreeMarker, and configure them in a manner similar to the Velocity configuration. For FreeMarker templates, .ftl is the default file-name extension.

Creating FreeMarker Templates

FreeMarker templates are also very similar to Velocity templates. Listing 9-6 shows the list members page rewritten as a FreeMarker template.

Listing 9-6. *List Members Rewritten As a FreeMarker Page*

```
<?xml version="1.0" encoding="ISO-8859-1" ?>
<!DOCTYPE html PUBLIC "-//W3C//DTD XHTML 1.0 Strict//EN"
                      "http://www.w3.org/TR/xhtml1/DTD/xhtml1-strict.dtd">

<html xmlns="http://www.w3.org/1999/xhtml">
  <head>
    <title>List Members</title>
  </head>
  <body>
    <h1>List Members</h1>

    <form action="searchformembers" method="get">
      <p>
        <label for="q">First or Last Name:</label>
        <input type="text" name="q" value="${param.q}" />
        <input type="submit" value="Search" />
      </p>
    </form>
```

```
<#if ${memberList}?size == 0>
  <p>No members found.</p>
</#if>

<table>
  <thead>
    <tr>
      <th>Name</th>
      <th>Age</th>
      <th>Address</th>
    </tr>
  </thead>
  <tbody>
    <#list memberList as member>
      <tr>
        <td>${member.name.last}, ${member.name.first}</td>
        <td>${member.age}</td>
        <td>${member.address}</td>
      </tr>
    </#list>
  </tbody>
</table>
</body>
</html>
```

For more information about FreeMarker, see the FreeMarker project page at SourceForge
(http://freemarker.sourceforge.net).

XSLT

XML has gained significant popularity over the past years as the means to model and store data.
XSLT is a transformation language for XML and allows you to transform XML to, for instance, HTML
using XSL. If you are already familiar with XSLT, and your web application works with data in the
form of XML, this view technology is a good choice.

Implementing an XSLT View

To use XSLT as your view technology, first you need to create your custom implementation of the
AbstractXsltView class. The implementation should implement the createDomNode() method to
provide an XML source to transform. Listing 9-7 demonstrates how to implement the abstract view
class to provide access to a Resource (discussed in Chapter 2), which is available in the model under
the key xmlResource. It uses classes from http://www.jdom.org/.

Listing 9-7. *A Sample Implementation of the AbstractXsltView Class*

```
package com.apress.springbook.chapter09.web.view;

import java.util.Map;

import javax.servlet.http.HttpServletRequest;
import javax.servlet.http.HttpServletResponse;

import org.w3c.dom.Node;
```

```
import org.jdom.Document;
import org.jdom.input.SAXBuilder;

import org.springframework.core.io.Resource;

import org.springframework.web.servlet.view.xslt.AbstractXsltView;

public class XmlView extends AbstractXsltView {

  protected Node createDomNode(Map model,
                               String root,
                               HttpServletRequest request,
                               HttpServletResponse response)
    throws Exception {
    Resource resource = (Resource) model.get("xmlResource");
    Document doc = org.jdom.input.SAXBuilder.build(resource.getInputStream());
    return new org.jdom.output.DOMOutputter().output(doc);
  }
}
```

The view implementation is called with the model containing the data to render, the name of the root element (which defaults to DocRoot), and the request and response. In this case, the Resource that is available in the model is returned as a Node instance.

Creating an XSL File

The next step is to create an XSL file, which will transform the XML resource to HTML. A sample XSL file is shown in Listing 9-8.

Listing 9-8. *A Sample XSL File That Transforms XML to HTML*

```
<?xml version="1.0" encoding="UTF-8"?>
<xsl:stylesheet xmlns:xsl="http://www.w3.org/1999/XSL/Transform" version="2.0">
  <xsl:output method="text/html" omit-xml-declaration="yes"/>

  <xsl:template match="/">
    <html>
      <head><title>List members</title></head>
      <body>
        <h1>List members</h1>
        <xsl:for-each select="memberList/member">
          <xsl:value-of select="."/><br />
        </xsl:for-each>
      </body>
    </html>
  </xsl:template>
</xsl:stylesheet>
```

Note that this is just a simple example that will list all member names contained in the source XML file.

Configuring Your Application to Use XSLT

Now that you have implemented the XSLT view and created the XSL file, you need to configure your web application to use them both. You can do this by changing (or adding) a view resolver to your servlet application context. In this case, you want to access the view as a bean. Spring provides a view resolver implementation that does exactly that: BeanNameViewResolver. As the name suggests, it uses the view name returned by the controller to look up a bean (by name) that will be used as the view to render. Listing 9-9 shows how to configure this view resolver and the XSLT view in your application context.

Listing 9-9. *Configuration for Resolving the XSLT View As a Bean*

```
<bean id="beanNameResolver"
      class="org.springframework.web.servlet.view.BeanNameViewResolver"/>

<bean name="viewName" class="com.apress.springbook.chapter09.web.view.XmlView">
  <property name="stylesheetLocation" value="/WEB-INF/stylesheet.xsl"/>
</bean>
```

Note that you need to configure the XSLT view implementation with the location where it can find the XSL file shown in Listing 9-8. This path should be relative to the web application root and should be within the WEB-INF folder so it is not directly accessible to users.

XSLT is a very powerful language that you can use to perform complex transformations of data in XML format. You can find more information about XSLT in *Beginning XSLT 2.0: From Novice to Professional* (Apress, 2005).

PDF

Adobe PDF is a document format that is widely used to share mainly read-only data. It provides a cross-platform document structure that ensures a consistent layout across these platforms. Spring provides support for creating PDF documents as part of your web application using iText, a library for creating PDF documents.

To demonstrate the ease of adding a PDF view to your application, the following example will generate a PDF version of the list members page of the sample application.

Implementing a PDF View

As with the XSLT view, you need to extend an abstract view class to render the specific view. In this case, you need to extend the AbstractPdfView class. Listing 9-10 shows a sample implementation that assumes a list of members is available in the model data. The members in that list are rendered as a PDF document.

Listing 9-10. *A Sample Implementation of the AbstractPdfView Class*

```
package com.apress.springbook.chapter09.web.view;

import java.util.Map;
import java.util.List;

import javax.servlet.http.HttpServletRequest;
import javax.servlet.http.HttpServletResponse;

import com.lowagie.text.Document;
import com.lowagie.text.Paragraph;
import com.lowagie.text.pdf.PdfWriter;

import org.springframework.web.servlet.view.document.AbstractPdfView;

import com.apress.springbook.chapter09.Member;
```

```
public class MatchPdfView extends AbstractPdfView {

  protected void buildPdfDocument(Map model,
                                  Document document,
                                  PdfWriter writer,
                                  HttpServletRequest request,
                                  HttpServletResponse response)
    throws Exception {
      document.addTitle("Members");
      List<Member> memberList = (List<Member>) model.get("memberList");
      for  (Member member : memberList) {
        document.add(new Paragraph(member.getName().getLast() + ", " +
          member.getName().getFirst()));
      }
    }
  }
}
```

The example in Listing 9-10 extends the `AbstractPdfView` by implementing the abstract `buildPdfDocument()` method. This method accepts several parameters, of which the model and the created document are the most important. The model can be used to retrieve the data you want to render. The document is the main class of iText and can be used to add content and metadata to the document.

Note that Spring takes care of creating, opening, and closing the document for you. This example sets the title of the document and adds the content of the model to the document.

For more information about working with iText to generate PDF documents, visit the iText website: `www.lowagie.com/iText/`.

Configuring Your Application to Use PDF

To use the created PDF view, you need to configure a view resolver to correctly resolve the view. You can use the previously discussed `BeanNameViewResolver` to resolve the view based on its name in the bean container. However, Spring provides an alternative way to resolving views defined as beans. You can use the `ResourceBundleViewResolver`, which uses the Java built-in `ResourceBundle` mechanism to define your views. This view resolver uses one or more properties files to resolve a view name. To use this view resolver, you need to define a properties file and define the created PDF view, as shown in Listing 9-11.

Listing 9-11. *The views.properties Properties File Defining the Created PDF View*

```
# The match pdf view
matchPdfView.class=com.apress.springbook.chapter09.web.view.MatchPdfView
```

Next, you need to define the view resolver and configure it to use the previously created properties file, as shown in Listing 9-12. You configure the view resolver using the name of the file without the extension, as the `ResourceBundle` mechanism will append the extension.

Listing 9-12. *The ResourceBundleViewResolver Configuration*

```
<bean id="resourceViewResolver"
    class="org.springframework.web.servlet.view.ResourceBundleViewResolver">
  <property name="basename" value="views"/>
</bean>
```

Note that you can also specify multiple properties files by using the `basenames` property, which takes a list of names as an argument.

> ■**Caution** The created PDF view will set the content type of the document appropriately. However, not all browsers respect this content type. You should therefore always use the .pdf extension for your PDF views. Be sure to also map the extension to the Spring DispatcherServlet in your web.xml file.

Excel

Spring provides support for creating a Microsoft Excel spreadsheet document as part of your application in a manner similar to its PDF support. However, you can choose to use one of two libraries for generating Excel documents: Jakarta POI (http://jakarta.apache.org/poi) or JExcelApi (www.jexcel.org). Spring includes an abstract view class for each of those libraries, which provide you with an initialized spreadsheet specific to that library. The libraries offer very similar capabilities. However, at the time of this writing, JExcelApi is the only one that offers support for handling images as part of your spreadsheet. Our example uses the JExcelApi library, but the configuration for using Jakarta POI is basically the same.

Implementing an Excel View

To get started creating an Excel view, you need to extend the abstract view base class. Listing 9-13 shows how to create an Excel view that fills a spreadsheet with match data retrieved from the model.

Listing 9-13. *A Sample Implementation of the AbstractJExcelView Class*

```
package com.apress.springbook.chapter09.web.view;

import java.util.Map;

import javax.servlet.http.HttpServletRequest;
import javax.servlet.http.HttpServletResponse;

import jxl.write.WritableWorkbook;
import jxl.write.WritableSheet;
import jxl.write.Label;

import org.springframework.web.servlet.view.document.AbstractJExcelView;

public class MatchExcelView extends AbstractJExcelView {

  protected void buildExcelDocument(Map model,
                                    WritableWorkbook workbook,
                                    HttpServletRequest request,
                                    HttpServletResponse response)
    throws Exception {
    WritableSheet sheet = workbook.createSheet(
            "Sheet 1", workbook.getNumberOfSheets());

    sheet.addCell(new Label(0, 0, "This is a sample label"));
  }
}
```

The example in Listing 9-13 uses the match data obtained from the model to add content to the provided Excel workbook. Note that the creation of the workbook and the writing of the contents to the view are handled by Spring.

Configuring Your Application to Use Excel

To configure your web application to use the created Excel view, add the lines shown in Listing 9-14 to the previously created `views.properties` file (Listing 9-11).

Listing 9-14. *The views.properties Properties File Defining the Created Excel View*

```
# The match excel view
matchExcelView.class=com.apress.springbook.chapter09.web.view.MatchExcelView
```

A nice feature of the Excel view base classes is that they offer you the ability to use an existing Excel file as the template for your Excel views. This allows you to manually create or reuse an existing Excel file containing, for instance, all formulas and charts. In addition, you can have your view implementation insert only the necessary data. For example, to use an existing Excel document named `sample.xls` as the template for your Excel view, add the lines shown in Listing 9-15 to the `views.properties` file.

Listing 9-15. *The views.properties Properties File Defining the Excel View Template*

```
# The template to use for the match excel view
matchExcelView.url=sample
```

Note that Spring will load the existing Excel file and provide it as input to your Excel view implementation. The code inserting the data into the workbook will remain unchanged. Because Spring uses the `ResourceBundle` mechanism to load the existing Excel document, you could also include different Excel templates for different languages.

■**Caution** The created Excel view will set the content type of the document appropriately. However, not all browsers respect this content type. You should therefore always use the `.xls` extension for your Excel views. Be sure to also map the extension to the Spring `DispatcherServlet` in your `web.xml` file.

JasperReports

JasperReports is a powerful, open source reporting tool that allows you to create rich reports in the form of HTML, XLS, PDF, and so on. Spring provides convenient support for using JasperReports to add report-generating capabilities to your web application. As with the PDF and Excel support described in the previous sections, Spring provides view implementations for JasperReports views, as listed in Table 9-3.

Table 9-3. *The JasperReports View Classes Provided by Spring*

View Class	Description
JasperReportsCsvView	Renders a report as comma-separated values (CSV)
JasperReportsHtmlView	Renders a report in HTML
JasperReportsPdfView	Renders a report in PDF
JasperReportsXlsView	Renders a report as an Excel file
JasperReportsMultiFormatView	Allows you to choose the rendering at runtime (demonstrated in Listing 9-16)

JasperReports reports need to be either configured in XML or designed using a graphical editor, such as OpenReports (http://oreports.com) or iReport (http://jasperforge.org/sf/projects/ireport). These reports must also be compiled in order for them to be rendered by JasperReports. When using Spring's JasperReports view classes, you do not need to worry about this. Spring will make sure the report gets compiled if it has not been compiled already.

Implementing a JasperReports View

Listing 9-16 shows how to use JasperReports in your web application. It uses XmlViewResolver, which we introduced earlier. The view resolver looks up the specified view name in an external XML bean definition file. Of course, you do not necessarily need to use this view resolver to work with JasperReports; you can use any of the view resolvers we described earlier.

First, you need to define the views you want to use in a separate XML file—in this case, reports.xml. Listing 9-16 uses the JasperReportsMultiFormatView view implementation. This implementation can be used to choose the format for rendering the report at runtime.

Listing 9-16. *The reports.xml Views Declaration for the XML-Based View Resolver*

```
<?xml version="1.0" encoding="UTF-8"?>
<!DOCTYPE beans PUBLIC "-//SPRING//DTD BEAN//EN"
                       "http://www.springframework.org/dtd/spring-beans.dtd">

<beans>
  <bean id="report"
        class="org.springframework.web.servlet.view.jasperreports. ➥
JasperReportsMultiFormatView"/>
</beans>
```

Configuring Your Application to Use JasperReports

Next, you need to define the correct view resolver in your servlet application context, just as you would any other view resolver you have seen so far, as shown in Listing 9-17.

Listing 9-17. *The Declaration of the XML-Based View Resolver*

```
<bean id="xmlViewResolver"
      class="org.springframework.web.servlet.view.XmlViewResolver">
  <property name="location" value="/WEB-INF/reports.xml"/>
</bean>
```

Note that Spring also provides a view resolver specific to JasperReports: JasperResportsView Resolver. This provides a convenient way to translate a URL to the location of a specific report using a prefix and suffix. It also allows you to set some default properties on each view that is resolved by this view resolver.

Now that you are ready to use the view, there is one thing left to handle. The JasperReports MultiFormatView view implementation chooses the format to render based on a format string available in the model under the key format. You can specify a property on the bean definition to change this default key by using the setFormatKey(String) setter method. However, you still need to have your controller put the format that it should render in the model. The most commonly used feature (and therefore also the default mapping provided by the multiview implementation) is to use the extension of the requested file. This means that if a user requests a report with the extension .pdf, the view implementation renders the report in PDF format. Listing 9-18 demonstrates a sample controller that retrieves the extension from the requested file path and stores it in the model under the format key for retrieval by the JasperReportsMultiFormatView.

Listing 9-18. *The Controller Implementation That Retrieves the Format from the File Extension*

```
protected ModelAndView handleRequestInternal(HttpServletRequest request,
                                             HttpServletResponse response)
throws Exception {
  ModelAndView mav = super.handleRequestInternal(request, response);

  String filePath = request.getRequestURI();
  String format = filePath.substring(filePath.lastIndexOf(".") + 1);
  mav.addObject("format", format);

  return mav;
}
```

Of course, Spring allows you to change the default format mapping through configuration or programmatically by means of the formatMappings property. Table 9-4 lists the default mapping used by the JasperReportsMultiFormatView.

Table 9-4. *The JasperReports View Classes Provided by Spring*

Format Mapping Key	Format	View Class
csv	CSV	JasperReportsCsvView
html	HTML	JasperReportsHtmlView
pdf	PDF	JasperReportsPdfView
xls	Excel	JasperReportsXlsView

You can learn more about JasperReports at the JasperReports project page at SourceForge (http://jasperforge.org/sf/projects/jasperreports).

Introducing New Spring 2.0 Form Tags

As of version 2.0, Spring offers a number of new tags in addition to the ones described earlier. These tags are designed to make it easier to write forms. We used most of these tags in the previous chapter. Table 9-5 lists the new tags provided by Spring.

Table 9-5. *The New Spring Form Tags*

Tag Name	Description
<form:form>	Renders an HTML form element and makes sure the command object specified by the commandName attribute is bound and made available to all inner tags.
<form:input>	Creates an HTML input element of type text for a property on the command object specified by the path attribute.
<form:password>	Generates an HTML input element of type password for a property on the command object specified by the path attribute.
<form:hidden>	Creates an HTML input element of type hidden for a property on the command object specified by the path attribute.
<form:select>	Renders an HTML select element for a property on the command object specified by the path attribute. It should be used in conjunction with the <form:option> and <form:options> tags in order to correctly render the selected value.

Continued

Table 9-5. *Continued*

Tag Name	Description
`<form:option>`	Generates an HTML option element and sets the selected attribute based on the bound value.
`<form:options>`	Generates multiple HTML option elements based on the specified items and sets the selected attribute based on the bound value of the parent `<form:select>` tag.
`<form:radiobutton>`	Creates an HTML input element of type radio for a property on the command object specified by the path attribute.
`<form:checkbox>`	Creates an HTML input element of type checkbox for a property on the command object specified by the path attribute.
`<form:textarea>`	Renders an HTML textarea element for a property in the command object specified by the path attribute.
`<form:errors>`	Renders any field errors inside an HTML span element. Note that you can indicate that you want to either render all errors for a specific property on the command object by specifying the property path as the path attribute or render all errors for the command object by specifying * as the path attribute.

Using these new tags, we can rewrite the register a new member page (Listing 9-5), as shown in Listing 9-19.

Listing 9-19. *The Register a New Member Page Using the New Spring-Provided Tags*

```
<?xml version="1.0" encoding="ISO-8859-1" ?>
<%@ taglib prefix="form" uri="http://www.springframework.org/tags/form" %>
<%@ taglib prefix="c" uri="http://java.sun.com/jsp/jstl/core" %>
<%@ taglib prefix="form" uri="http://www.springframework.org/tags/form" %>
<!DOCTYPE html PUBLIC "-//W3C//DTD XHTML 1.0 Strict//EN"
                      "http://www.w3.org/TR/xhtml1/DTD/xhtml1-strict.dtd">

<html xmlns="http://www.w3.org/1999/xhtml">
  <head>
    <title>Register a New Member</title>
  </head>
  <body>
    <h1>Register a New Member</h1>

    <form:form commandName="member">
      <table>
        <tbody>
          <tr>
            <td>Sex:</td>
            <td>
              <form:select path="sex">
                <form:option value="FEMALE"/>
                <form:option value="MALE"/>
              </form:select>
            </td>
          </tr>
```

```
      <tr>
        <td>First Name:</td>
        <td>
          <form:input path"name.first"/>
        </td>
      </tr>
      <tr>
        <td>Last Name:</td>
        <td>
          <form:input path="name.last"/>
        </td>
      </tr>
      <tr>
        <td>Age:</td>
        <td>
          <form:input path="age"/>
        </td>
      </tr>
      <tr>
        <td>Line 1:</td>
        <td>
          <form:input path="address.line1"/>
        </td>
      </tr>
      <tr>
        <td>Line 2:</td>
        <td>
          <form:input path="address.line2"/>
        </td>
      </tr>
      <tr>
        <td>City:</td>
        <td>
          <form:input path="address.city"/>
        </td>
      </tr>
      <tr>
        <td>State:</td>
        <td>
          <form:input path="address.state"/>
        </td>
      </tr>
      <tr>
        <td>Zip:</td>
        <td>
          <form:input path="address.zip"/>
        </td>
      </tr>
      <tr>
        <td/>
        <td><input type="submit" value="Register" /></td>
      </tr>
    </tbody>
  </table>
  </form>
  </body>
</html>
```

As you can see in Listing 9-19, using these new Spring-provided form tags greatly reduces the length of your forms. More important, your forms are easier to read and maintain. Also note that the `<form:select>` tag will determine the currently selected value when reshowing the form in case of validation errors.

Another advantage of using Spring form tags is that they provide you with a convenient mechanism to display validation errors. You can use the `<form:errors>` tag to display validation errors in your page. Listing 9-20 shows validation error messages for the `firstName` field of a member.

Listing 9-20. *Sample Use of the errors Tag*

```
<tr>
  <td>First Name:</td>
  <td>
    <form:input path="name.first"/>
    <form:errors path="name.first"/>
  </td>
</tr>
```

The path you specify for the `<form:errors>` tag defines which errors are displayed for your form field. Besides showing field-specific errors by specifying their complete name, you can also use wildcards to show any arbitrary number of errors. For instance, you could display all errors by specifying `path="*"`. To see all validation errors for the `name.first` and `name.last` properties, use `path="name.*"`.

Another useful feature is that you can specify several attributes on the form tags, including `cssClass` and `cssStyle`, to customize the appearance. In relation to the previously mentioned `errors` tag, you can specify an attribute on most form tags by the name of `cssErrorClass`, which indicates the CSS class to set on the generated widget in case there are validation errors for the specific field. Spring will handle this transparently for you.

Summary

This chapter introduced Spring's support for different view technologies and provided you with some guidelines for choosing the right technology to fit your needs.

You may start using any one of these technologies for your web applications, or even better, combine them to provide your users with the most sophisticated views on the data within your web application.

The, next and final, chapter discusses the importance of testing, explaining the difference between unit and integration testing. We will show you how to verify that the applications you create actually work as intended. Testing is a major aspect of modern-day software development; therefore, the next chapter is definitely a must-read.

■ ■ ■ ■

Testing

During the course of this book, you have seen how Spring helps you build robust Java applications. This chapter covers testing your applications. We start by discussing two important testing concepts, unit testing and integration testing (also called functional testing), explaining the difference between them. We also talk about test-driven development as a way to develop your software.

Then we introduce JUnit and EasyMock, two frameworks that are the de facto standard when it comes to testing Java applications. We will show you how to use the power of both frameworks to extensively test your application.

Of course, this chapter would not fit in this book if it did not expand on some of the testing features provided by Spring. You will learn how to test your Spring configuration files and the configuration of the objects created by the Spring container. Using the information in this chapter, you will be able to test the configuration of your web applications.

Introducing Testing Approaches

Testing is often considered to be the responsibility of a separate department within a software development organization. This quality assurance (QA) department will take all written code and test it against certain requirements set forth by the client. This form of testing, often referred to as *system testing*, is an important step in developing high-quality software applications. However, software testing should start with the developers. They are the front line when it comes to ensuring the quality of their software prior to handing it off to QA. This chapter focuses on testing performed by developers.

Generally speaking, testing should be used to ensure the following aspects of an application:

Correctness: You want to ensure the correctness of your application. For example, suppose that you have written a `calculate()` method on a `Calculator` class. You want to make sure that certain input for this method results in a correct calculation result.

Completeness: Testing can be used to ensure that your application is complete by verifying that all required operations have been executed. Suppose you have a signup process that includes creating an invoice for newly signed-up members. You want to test whether a member is actually added to the database, and also if an invoice has been created for that user.

Quality: Testing can ensure the quality of your application, and this goes beyond software-quality metrics. A well-tested piece of software creates confidence with developers. When existing code needs to be changed, it's less likely that developers will be afraid of unintentionally breaking the software or reintroducing bugs.

Another major advantage of testing is that it provides you with a harness for your code. This harness enables you to refactor your code at a later stage with more confidence.

As you have probably experienced, most code is not perfect when it is originally written. In many cases, you will revisit the code a couple of times during the development and rewrite parts of it, either to fit new requirements or just to improve its quality.

For example, suppose that when the previously mentioned `Calculator` class is implemented, we have written tests to assert that certain results are returned on certain input. Now let's assume we revisit the code after a couple of weeks and decide our initial implementation needs to be improved. We decide to rewrite our calculation algorithm to calculate the result. Because we have written a set of tests, we will know whether our new implementation works as well as the previous implementation. We can assert this by running the tests we wrote.

Testing efforts can be split into two separate ways of testing applications. Specific parts of an application, called *units*. can be tested in isolation. Those units can also be tested together to assert that they work together as expected. These types are referred to as unit testing and integration testing, respectively.

Unit Testing

A unit in the context of unit testing depicts *a specific piece of functionality* in your code, usually residing in a specific method or constructor in a specific class. Unit testing is the microscale of testing and is typically done by developers who know how such a unit should function.

As you have learned by reading this book, the key to flexible applications is abstractions. As such, it's important to abstract Java code from the environment in which it will operate. We say that this code is unaware of its environment, unless it chooses to become aware of it in a minority of cases.

This so-called plain old Java object (POJO) approach to Java coding, combined with defining interfaces for important parts of your application (see Chapter 8), provides the basis for thorough testing. The Spring Framework promotes exactly this approach (we could also say the Spring Framework makes this approach possible). By separating your code into well-defined interfaces and objects, you have already defined the units that are eligible for unit testing.

One goal of unit testing is to ensure that each unit of an application functions correctly in isolation. Another goal is to define a *framework*, *harness*, or *contract* (all referring to a strict set of rules that must be respected) that must be satisfied by the unit test. As long as the tests can be run successfully, the unit is considered to work properly. (If there are bugs in the test code, the unit will function properly according to this buggy test code.)

Unit testing offers a number of benefits for developers:

Facilitate change: As previously mentioned, having a set of unit tests for a specific piece of code provides confidence in refactoring existing code. The unit tests will ensure the module continues to function correctly according to the available tests as long as the tests succeed. Given there are enough tests for all the code in the application, this promotes and facilitates changing implementation details of units in the application. An important aspect of facilitating change is preventing solved problems or bugs from reentering the code.

Simplify integration: Unit testing provides a bottom-up testing approach, which ensures that low-level units function properly according to their tests. This makes it easier to write integration tests at a later stage. There is no need to have two tests for units. In integration testing, described in the next section, the *interaction* between units can be tested, rather than individual units. This makes integration tests much easier to write because their scope is limited.

Promote well-defined separation: In order for you to be able to completely and efficiently write unit tests, your code needs to be separated into well-defined units. Each unit needs to be tested in isolation and should therefore allow the replacement of dependencies with test-specific ones. Thus, writing unit tests promotes the separation of your application into well-defined units.

Integration Testing

As opposed to unit testing, integration testing is the testing of a number of units and how they work together. Integration testing obviously spans the boundaries of a unit, but can also span across the boundaries of your code. Often, integration testing also includes testing of integration with external systems, such as databases or legacy systems.

Integration testing is just as important as unit testing. While unit testing ensures that all units work properly according to their tests in isolation, integration testing ensures they collaborate as expected.

For example, suppose you have a repository adapter implementation using JDBC to modify the database. Such a class is very hard to unit test, since it's difficult to isolate the data-access code from the database. With integration tests, you can assert the data-access configuration of the application and whether the data-access code and SQL statements are valid for the target database. This is where integration testing comes in. This chapter will show you how Spring helps you to create sophisticated integration tests.

Test-Driven Development

Test-driven development (TDD) is a way of implementing code by writing a unit test before implementing the actual class. This will ensure that you first think about what the implementation should do—what contract it should fulfill. This manner of implementing code is highly emphasized in Extreme Programming. TDD defines the following development cycle:

Write the test: You should always begin with writing a test. In order to be able to write a test, you should have a clear understanding of the specification and the requirements. In order to get those specifications and requirements, you first need to ask questions and get answers. (In Extreme Programming, this question-and-answer interaction with the user translates into use cases and stories.)

Write the code: Next, you should write the code that will make the test pass. The implementation is finished only when the test passes. At this stage, you should look back at your test code to ensure it tests what you are actually trying to implement. It's not uncommon to get better insights in the implementation you are trying to create, which results in correcting or improving your test.

Run the automated tests: The next step is to run the automated test cases and observe if they pass or fail. If they pass, you can be confident that the code meets the test cases as written. If there are failures, the code did not meet the test cases and you should continue to the next step.

■Note It's important to make sure the test fails before the implementation has been written. Otherwise, from a psychological perspective, there would be no difference between writing the test and writing a correct implementation. In other words, a test that only succeeds if the implementation is correct is a reward for the developer.

Refactor: The final step is the refactoring step. This step involves improving the code that actually passed the test. Because you know the code already fulfills the contract, you can refactor here with confidence. The tests are then rerun and observed. Refactoring can happen at any time. It does not need to happen immediately after the first implementation is written, although developers may be more focused at that time.

Repeat: After completing the refactor step, the cycle will then repeat, starting with either adding functionality or fixing any errors.

Using TDD has a number of benefits. First, the tests you start off creating act as the first user of your code. Secondly, it can help you write modular software. Next, it also provides some sort of documentation for your software. Assuming you have written a test for a specific unit, another developer can check the test in order to see how the unit is supposed to be used and works. And lastly, TDD promotes refactoring, on the one hand because it is part of the development cycle, and also because it provides developers with the confidence that is required to refactor code in the first place.

For more information about TDD, see *Test-Driven Development: A J2EE Example* (Apress, 2004).

UNIT TESTS AS DOCUMENTATION?

It's debatable whether unit tests can ever provide all the documentation required for an application. Moreover, writing tests to test application code *and* to serve as documentation unavoidably overloads unit tests with responsibilities. This overload may not always be apparent. However, we've seen cases where unit tests could not be altered to become more efficient in the way they tested the software because developers feared they would not document the code anymore.

We believe that "unit tests that serve as documentation" is a misleading approach to unit testing and that many developers take it too seriously. We can understand that developers welcome any approach that relieves them from having to write documentation. We also believe that this argument has helped to sell TDD books in the past (and probably still does today). But as far as we are concerned, this argument has no strong foundation. Good documentation is much more beneficial to the consumer of an application. And it requires developers to profoundly think about the approaches they are taking.

Writing Unit Tests Using JUnit

JUnit is the de facto standard for unit testing of your Java applications. It is an automated testing framework that allows you to easily create tests for your Java classes. JUnit provides the most commonly used functionality for building robust unit tests. Another advantage of using JUnit is that most IDEs provide support for running JUnit tests. Also, JUnit is supported out of the box by build tools like Ant (http://ant.apache.org) and Maven (http://maven.apache.org).

In this section, we will use JUnit to build a test for a unit of our tennis club application. First, we will need to develop the functionality to meet the requirements.

Establishing the Requirements

We need to calculate the membership fee per member based on a number of factors. These factors can change over time, but currently we use these rules to determine the rate:

- Members younger than 14 years old pay $25 for three months or $90 for a full year membership.

- Members between 14 years and less than 18 years old and members over 50 years old pay $35 for three months or $126 for a full year membership.

- Members over 18 years and less than 50 years old pay $50 for three months or $180 for a full year membership.

- A member's age is his or her age at the date of the invoice.

- All members get a 25% reduction on all the membership rates if they have a membership with the national tennis federation.

We could create an interface that is responsible for calculating the membership fee, like this:

```
package  com.apress.springbook.chapter10;

public interface MembershipFeeCalculator {
  double calculateMembershipFee(Member member);
}
```

The `MembershipFeeCalculator` interface looks adequate for other classes in the sample application to use whenever they need to calculate the membership fee for a member. However, some issues make this interface less than acceptable.

First of all, for now we only need to know the age of a member, the member's payment preference, and whether the member has a membership with the national tennis federation. For this data, there are getter methods on the `Member` class. However, it seems like the `Member` class is too generic for this calculation since it has many other getter methods. Hence, the `MembershipFeeCalculator` doesn't clearly communicate how membership fees are calculated. This may sound like a good abstraction, since callers should not care about how the membership fee is calculated, but if we take a closer look, we'll find that other classes can calculate a membership fee only for the current age of a member. The `MembershipFeeCalculator` can't calculate future membership fees. It also cannot calculate fees for prospective members, since they do not have a `Member` object.

Note We could create a dummy `Member` object, but that goes against the nature of the `Member` class. `Member` represents an active or past member of the tennis club. Using a concrete class for multiple purposes will unavoidably lead to problems and bugs, since developers will need to take all the roles of a class into account when they change it. For the `Member` class, these roles would be real members and prospective members. As you can imagine, a real member has many more properties than a prospective member.

We clearly need a better abstraction mechanism to calculate membership fees. Here is a reworked `MembershipFeeCalculator`:

```
package  com.apress.springbook.chapter10;

public interface MembershipFeeCalculator {
  double calculateMembershipFee(
    int age,
    boolean perTrimesterNotPerAnnum,
    boolean tennisFederationMembership);
}
```

This `MembershipFeeCalculator` is much more specific than the previous version, but unfortunately, it is too specific. Callers now need to know about all the gory details to calculate a membership fee. They must get a member's age, whether the member wants to pay per trimester or per annum, and whether the member has a valid national tennis federation membership at the time of the calculation. This may be exactly what's needed for some callers, but is likely to be painful, complicated, and not cost-effective for other callers. This is especially true if the requirements for calculating the membership fee change. All callers would suddenly have to get other data, and this change would badly affect the application. So this second version of the `MembershipFeeCalculator` is not a good abstraction for our purposes.

Here is yet another reworked version of the `MembershipFeeCalculator`:

```
package com.apress.springbook.chapter10;

public interface MembershipFeeCalculator {
  double calculateMembershipFee(PayingMember payingMember);
}
```

This `MembershipFeeCalculator` version uses the `PayingMember` interface, which is shown in Listing 10-1.

Listing 10-1. *The PayingMember Interface*

```
package com.apress.springbook.chapter10;

public interface PayingMember {
  int getAge();
  boolean isPaymentPerTrimester();
  boolean isMemberOfNationalTennisFederation();
}
```

One possible next step could be to let the `Member` class implement the `PayingMember` interface. Another option is to create an adapter class for `Member` objects, as shown in Listing 10-2.

Listing 10-2. *PayingMember Adapter Class for Member Objects*

```
package com.apress.springbook.chapter10;

import java.util.Date;

public class PayingMemberAdapterForMember {
  private Member member;
  private Date calculationDate;

  public PayingMemberAdapterForMember(Member member, Date calculationDate) {
    this.member = member;
    this.calculationDate = calculationDate;
  }
  public int getAge() {
    // calculate age at calculation date based on member
    // birth date.
  }
  public boolean isPaymentPerTrimester() {
    // get payment option for member and return
  }
  boolean isMemberOfNationalTennisFederation() {
    // get membership details of member at the calculation date
  }
}
```

We can now create as many implementation classes of the `PayingMember` interface as are required. One interesting advantage of this adapter approach is that callers of the `MembershipFee Calculator` interface no longer need to know exactly which details are required to perform the calculation. They just need to pass an instance of the `PayingMember` interface as they see fit.

If the fee calculation changes, and with it the required data changes, we just need to refactor the `PayingMember` interface and its implementation classes. This may affect callers of the `MembershipFeeCalculator` interface, but it will always be possible to keep this impact limited yet maintain flexibility. Membership fee calculation will never change in such a way that our approach would become inflexible.

In order to be able to run the tests at a later stage, we also want to create a default implementation of the `MembershipFeeCalculator` interface. It works best if we start off by creating a default implementation that just throws an `UnsupportedOperationException` for all method invocations. This allows us to run the tests and get an indication of which methods have not yet been implemented. Listing 10-3 shows the initial implementation of the `MembershipFeeCalculator` interface.

Listing 10-3. *Initial Default Implementation of the MembershipFeeCalculator Interface*

```
package com.apress.springbook.chapter10;

public class RegularMembershipFeeCalculator implements MembershipFeeCalculator {
  public double calculateMembershipFee (PayingMember member) {
    throw new UnsupportedOperationException("not implemented yet!");
  }
}
```

SHOULD WE ACT DUMB?

Extreme Programming and some related methodologies do not encourage you to deliberate on your interfaces during the first iteration. You are encouraged to go through this kind of deliberation only when the need to find a better abstraction becomes imminent. We can't agree with such a dogma.

We believe that encouraging developers to act "dumb" when it comes to creating flexible applications is the wrong approach. We do agree that very often requirements can't be known in advance, but not all requirements are equal. Some requirements, like calculating a membership fee, are sufficiently limited in scope. It's fairly straightforward to come up with working abstractions, and it's easy to prove how they can adapt to potential changes. As such, it's also easy to prove these abstractions can save time and money, and many small profits can make a big whole.

If you encounter comparable cases where some brainstorming can lead to good abstractions, we advise you to embrace the flexibility of your application and go for it. There's a risk in acting dumb, in that you may not be able to improve your applications if there's no urgent need.

Writing the Test

Taking the TDD approach, we now want to create our test to define the contract for our MembershipFeeCalculator implementation. We're ready to write a unit test. Listing 10-4 shows the RegularMembershipFeeCalculatorTests class.

Listing 10-4. *RegularMembershipFeeCalculatorTests Class*

```
package com.apress.springbook.chapter10;

import junit.framework.TestCase;

public class RegularMembershipFeeCalculatorTests
    extends TestCase {

  public void testLessThan14YearsOldPerTrimesterNoNTFMember() {
    MembershipFeeCalculator mfc = new RegularMembershipFeeCalculator();

    PayingMember payingMember = new TestPayingMember(13, true, false);

    double result = mfc.calculateMembershipFee(payingMember);

    assertEquals((double)25, result);
  }
```

```java
  public void testLessThan14YearsOldPerAnnumNoNTFMember() {
    MembershipFeeCalculator mfc = new RegularMembershipFeeCalculator();

    PayingMember payingMember = new TestPayingMember(13, false, false);

    double result = mfc.calculateMembershipFee(payingMember);

    assertEquals((double)90, result);
  }

  public void testLessThan14YearsOldPerTrimesterNTFMember() {
    MembershipFeeCalculator mfc = new RegularMembershipFeeCalculator();

    PayingMember payingMember = new TestPayingMember(13, true, true);

    double result = mfc.calculateMembershipFee(payingMember);

    assertEquals((double)25 * 0.75, result);
  }

  public void testLessThan14YearsOldPerAnnumNTFMember() {
    MembershipFeeCalculator mfc = new RegularMembershipFeeCalculator();

    PayingMember payingMember = new TestPayingMember(13, false, true);

    double result = mfc.calculateMembershipFee(payingMember);

    assertEquals((double)90 * 0.75, result);
  }

  private class TestPayingMember implements PayingMember {
    private int age;
    private boolean paymentPerTrimester;
    private boolean memberOfNationalTennisFederation;

    private TestPayingMember(
            int age,
            boolean paymentPerTrimester,
            boolean memberOfNationalTennisFederation) {
      this.age = age;
      this.paymentPerTrimester = paymentPerTrimester;
      this.memberOfNationalTennisFederation = memberOfNationalTennisFederation;
    }

    public int getAge() {
      return age;
    }

    public boolean isPaymentPerTrimester() {
      return paymentPerTrimester;
    }

    public boolean isMemberOfNationalTennisFederation() {
      return memberOfNationalTennisFederation;
    }
  }
}
```

Notice that we used the name of the class we're testing and appended Tests to it. This is not a requirement for JUnit, but is considered a best practice, and the Tests extension is often used to determine which classes should be executed as tests. Furthermore, our test extends the JUnit TestCase base class. This class provides the base functionality for building tests.

If you take a closer look at the test*() methods, you should notice the use of the assert Equals() method, which is made available by the TestCase superclass. This method does exactly what its name suggests: it asserts whether the first and second argument are equal.

TestCase provides many methods for you to assert results and influence the outcome of the test. Table 10-1 lists the most commonly used methods of the JUnit TestCase base class. Each of those methods also has a version that allows you to specify a message for when the test fails, which might help when you're debugging failing test methods.

Table 10-1. *Commonly Used Methods of the JUnit TestCase Base Class*

Method	Description
assertEquals	Asserts that two objects are equal. Along with checking two Object instances for equality, a number of convenience versions exist. These take as input primitives or regularly used objects, such as long, int, double, String, and so on.
assertTrue	Asserts that a Boolean condition evaluates to true.
assertFalse	Asserts that a Boolean condition evaluates to false.
assertNull	Asserts that an object is null.
assertNotNull	Asserts that an object is not null.
assertSame	Asserts that two objects refer to the same instance.
assertNotSame	Asserts that two objects do not refer to the same instance.
fail	Explicitly makes a test fail.

Definining a Test Suite

JUnit normally executes all methods that contain test as part of the name. You can override this behavior, as well as temporarily disable it or exclude certain test methods, by defining a *test suite*. Using JUnit, this is fairly simple—you just need to add a static method to your test class called suite, which returns a TestSuite instance.

Listing 10-5 shows a sample test suite, which makes sure only the first three test methods are executed.

Listing 10-5. *A Sample Test Suite Definition for the RegularMembershipFeeCalculatorTests Class*

```
public static TestSuite suite() {
  TestSuite suite = new TestSuite();
  suite.addTest(new RegularMembershipFeeCalculatorTests(
    "testLessThan14YearsOldPerTrimesterNoNTFMember"
  ));
  suite.addTest(new RegularMembershipFeeCalculatorTests(
    "testLessThan14YearsOldPerAnnumNoNTFMember"
  ));
  suite.addTest(new RegularMembershipFeeCalculatorTests(
    "testLessThan14YearsOldPerTrimesterNTFMember"
  ));
  return suite;
}
```

Now that we have created fully functional tests, we can run them (for instance, in an IDE). Of course, the tests will all fail because they are not yet implemented.

Next, we need to finish the `RegularMembershipFeeCalculator` class, as shown in Listing 10-6.

Listing 10-6. *The Implementation of the RegularMembershipFeeCalculator Class*

```
package com.apress.springbook.chapter10;

public class RegularMembershipFeeCalculator implements MembershipFeeCalculator {
  public double calculateMembershipFee (PayingMember member) {
    double fee = 0;

    int age = member.getAge();

    // Member is under 14
    if (age < 14) {
      if (member.isPaymentPerTrimester()) {
        fee = 25;
      } else {
        fee = 90;
      }
    }

    // Member is a between 14 and 18, or is over 50
    if ((age >= 14 && age < 18) || age > 50) {
      if (member.isPaymentPerTrimester()) {
        fee = 35;
      } else {
        fee = 126;
      }
    }

    // Member is between 18 and 50
    if (age >= 18 && age <= 50) {
      if (member.isPaymentPerTrimester()) {
        fee = 50;
      } else {
        fee = 180;
      }
    }

    // Reduce the fee if they are a member of the national federation
    if (member.isMemberOfNationalTennisFederation()) {
      fee = fee * 0.75;
    }

    return fee;
  }
}
```

You can find more information about JUnit at the JUnit website (http://www.junit.org).

Creating Mock Implementations with EasyMock

The previous section demonstrated how to write unit tests for your classes using JUnit. For the membership calculator example, this works fine, but now let's consider testing a class with a number of dependencies. Suppose we have a currency converter object that converts amounts in one currency to the appropriate amounts in another currency. In this case, the currency converter class has a dependency: an exchange rate service that can be queried for the current exchange rates. We'll use this example to demonstrate the use of EasyMock.

EasyMock (http://www.easymock.org/) is an open source library that allows you to easily create mock implementations of interfaces (or even classes for that matter). You can use EasyMock to dynamically create mock objects for interfaces of dependencies (also called *collaborators*). EasyMock is not the only mock object framework for Java, but it is considered one of the best.

Remember that unit testing is defined as testing classes or methods in isolation. Using the approach of unit testing described in the previous section does not work when testing classes that depend on collaborators. In order to test a class that depends on collaborators, you need to be able to eliminate the testing of the collaborators (they are tested by their own unit tests). This is where mock objects come in. A *mock object* is a dummy interface or class where you define the dummy output for a certain method call. In the case of the currency converter, we need to define a mock version of the exchange rate service to be able to truly unit test the converter. You could create mock objects by hand for each collaborator and have them return certain values. However, using a library for this makes your life much easier and gives you some added functionality, as you will see in this example.

Defining and Implementing the Interface

For this example, we will use the interface for the currency converter shown in Listing 10-7 and the default implementation for it shown in Listing 10-8.

Listing 10-7. *The CurrencyConverter Interface*

```
package com.apress.springbook.chapter10;

public interface CurrencyConverter {
  double convert(double amount, String fromCurrency, String toCurrency)
    throws UnknownCurrencyException;
}
```

Listing 10-8. *The Default Implementation of the CurrencyConverter Interface*

```
package com.apress.springbook.chapter10;

public class DefaultCurrencyConverter implements CurrencyConverter {
  private ExchangeRateService exchangeRateService;

  public void setExchangeRateService(ExchangeRateService exchangeRateService) {
    this.exchangeRateService = exchangeRateService;
  }

  public double convert(double amount, String fromCurrency, String toCurrency)
    throws UnknownCurrencyException {
    // get the current exchange rate for the specified currencies
```

```
    double exchangeRate =
      exchangeRateService.getExchangeRate(fromCurrency, toCurrency);
    // return the amount multiplied with the exchange rate
    return amount * exchangeRate;
  }
}
```

The default implementation of the CurrencyConverter has a collaborator defined by an interface, ExchangeRateService, shown in Listing 10-9.

Listing 10-9. *The ExchangeRateService Interface*

```
package com.apress.springbook.chapter10;

public interface ExchangeRateService {
  double getExchangeRate(String fromCurrency, String toCurrency)
    throws UnknownCurrencyException;
}
```

Notice the getExchangeRate() method, which takes the two currencies as arguments and returns the exchange rate as a double. This is the method that is used by our default implementation of the CurrencyConverter interface.

Creating a Mock Object

Now we want to unit test our currency converter. We would probably start out the same as we did in the previous section, by defining a test class and implementing a number of test methods on it. Listing 10-10 shows the test skeleton using EasyMock to create a mock object for the collaborators of the converter.

Listing 10-10. *The Test Skeleton for the DefaultCurrencyConverter Class*

```
package com.apress.springbook.chapter10;

import junit.framework.TestCase;

import org.easymock.EasyMock;

public class DefaultCurrencyConverterTests extends TestCase {
    private DefaultCurrencyConverter converter;

    private ExchangeRateService exchangeRateService;

    public DefaultCurrencyConverterTests(String name) {
        super(name);
    }

    protected void setUp() throws Exception {
        converter = new DefaultCurrencyConverter();

        exchangeRateService = EasyMock.createMock(ExchangeRateService.class);
        converter.setExchangeRateService(exchangeRateService);
    }

    // tests go here ...
}
```

Note that the setUp() method is overridden in order to create and assign the class under testing. However, the converter relies on an implementation of the ExchangeRateService interface. We could also instantiate and assign an actual implementation for this interface, but that would mean that our test would also test the inner workings of that class. This would result in this test no longer being a real unit test, as unit tests are supposed to test units in isolation.

Instead of using an actual implementation of the collaborator interface, Listing 10-10 uses EasyMock to dynamically create a mock object for the interface. As you can see, it takes only one line of code to create a mock object for an interface. We use the static createMock() method on the EasyMock class and provide it with the interface for which we want it to create a mock object. The return value is a mock implementation of the provided interface, which we can directly set as a collaborator on the converter instance.

Note EasyMock also supports the creation of mock objects for existing classes instead of just interfaces by using the EasyMock class extensions.

Testing with EasyMock

As mentioned earlier, using EasyMock offers much more functionality than just creating dynamic mock objects. It also allows you to test which methods are called on the collaborators by the class under testing. You can specify which methods you expect to be called by your implementation. For methods that have a return value, you can also specify which value the method call should return. It is also possible to have the method throw an exception in order to verify the exception handling of the class under testing.

Listing 10-11 shows a simple test method of the DefaultCurrencyConverterTests, which tests the convert() method with valid input and asserts the result.

Listing 10-11. *A Simple Test Method of the DefaultCurrencyConverterTests Class*

```
public void testConvertWithValidInput() throws UnknownCurrencyException {
  EasyMock.expect(exchangeRateService.getExchangeRate("EUR", "USD"))
        .andReturn(1.2).times(2);

  EasyMock.replay(exchangeRateService);

  assertEquals(12.0, converter.convert(10.0, "EUR", "USD"));
  assertEquals(24.0, converter.convert(20.0, "EUR", "USD"));

  EasyMock.verify(exchangeRateService);
}
```

The first line of the test method tells EasyMock to expect a method call to the getExchange Rate() method on the mock ExchangeRateService with "EUR" and "USD" as arguments. By calling the andReturn() method, you can specify the value the mock object should return. The last part of the first line of code specifies the number of times we expect this method to be called. In this case, it expects the method to be called twice because the convert() method is called twice with different amounts, so the getExchangeRate() should also be called twice: once for each convert() invocation.

EasyMock mock objects have state: they are either in record or replay mode. When they are first created, they are in record mode. This allows you to specify the expected behavior of the mock object as just demonstrated. However, in order to use the mock object for testing, you need to inform EasyMock that the specified behavior should be replayed. You do this by calling the static replay() method on the EasyMock class with the mock object to replay as an argument. If you do not put the mock object in replay mode, EasyMock will not replay the behavior and will not inform you of unexpected method calls.

After making sure the mock object is in replay mode, you test the class. In this case, the convert() method is called twice, and the result is asserted to be correct. Note that the correct result is based on the return value that was specified for the exchange rate service. If the return value specified in the first line of code were changed to, for instance, 1.3, the correct return values for assertion would be 13.0 and 26.0, respectively.

Finally, you should inform EasyMock that testing has finished. This is done by calling the static verify() method on the EasyMock class, again with the mock object as the argument. Informing EasyMock that testing has finished is not required, but it gives you the added value that EasyMock will verify that all specified expected method calls have actually been called. So if the test in Listing 10-11 calls the convert() method just once, the verify() method will throw an exception, because the expected method call is done only once.

You also will want to have your tests check whether exception handling is correctly implemented. In this case, we want to make sure that the UnknownCurrencyException thrown by the exchange rate service is correctly handled (in this example, just thrown and not handled by the implementation). To have the mock object throw an exception, you can just specify which exception to throw instead of specifying a return value, as demonstrated in Listing 10-12.

Listing 10-12. *Using EasyMock for Testing Exception Handling*

```
public void testConvertWithUnknownCurrency() throws UnknownCurrencyException {
  EasyMock.expect(exchangeRateService.getExchangeRate(
        (String)EasyMock.isA(String.class), (String)EasyMock.isA(String.class)))
      .andThrow(new UnknownCurrencyException()).times(2);

  EasyMock.replay(exchangeRateService);

  try {
    converter.convert(10.0, "EUR", "-UNKNOWN-");
    fail("an unknown currency exception was expected");
  } catch (UnknownCurrencyException e) {
    // do nothing, was expected
  }

  try {
    converter.convert(10.0, "-UNKNOWN-", "EUR");
    fail("an unknown currency exception was expected");
  } catch (UnknownCurrencyException e) {
    // do nothing, was expected
  }

  EasyMock.verify(exchangeRateService);
}
```

First, notice the replacement of the andReturn() invocation with the andThrow() invocation, which has an instance of the UnknownCurrencyException as an argument. The rest of the test is much of the same, except that this test method tests for the exceptions actually being thrown.

Also notice that the currency arguments are switched for the second convert() invocation in order to fully test the method. In the previous test method, the currency arguments were fixed. This allowed us to specify expected arguments to the expected method call. In this case, however, we can't specify arguments, because the value is different for both invocations. To help us, EasyMock allows for an argument matcher to be specified for each argument. You can either implement your own argument matcher or use one of the default argument matchers provided by EasyMock, which are listed in Table 10-2. Note that when using argument matchers, you need to use an argument matcher for all arguments.

Table 10-2. *Argument Matchers Provided by EasyMock*

Argument Matcher	Description
eq(X value)	Matches if the actual value is equal to the expected value. Available for all primitive types and for objects.
anyBoolean(), anyByte(), anyChar(), anyDouble(), anyFloat(), anyInt(), anyLong(), anyObject(), anyShort()	Match any value of a specific type. Available for all primitive types and for objects.
eq(X value, X delta)	Matches if the actual value is equal to the given value allowing the given delta. Available for float and double.
aryEq(X value)	Matches if the actual value is equal to the given value according to Arrays.equals(). Available for primitive and object arrays.
isNull()	Matches if the actual value is null. Available for objects.
notNull()	Matches if the actual value is not null. Available for objects.
same(X value)	Matches if the actual value is the same as the given value. Available for objects.
isA(Class clazz)	Matches if the actual value is an instance of the given class, or if it is an instance of a class that extends or implements the given class. Available for objects.
lt(X value), leq(X value), geq(X value), gt(X value)	Match if the actual value is less than/less or equal/greater or equal/greater than the given value. Available for all numeric primitive types.

To review, the most important aspect of EasyMock is that it dynamically generates mock objects for your interfaces. In addition, EasyMock allows you to verify that only expected methods are called, that they are actually being called, the number of times they are called, and the arguments that are provided to the methods. Also, EasyMock makes it easy to have the methods return values or throw exceptions without having to code all that yourself. For more information, about EasyMock see the EasyMock project page (http://www.easymock.org/).

Using Spring Support for Integration Testing

When working with Spring for building your applications, you will typically use one or more XML configuration files for defining your application context. These configuration files are not Java files and will therefore not be compiled. Of course, if you include the Spring DTD or use Spring's namespace support, some aspects of your configuration files will be validated. But issues such as defining a nonexisting class as the class for a bean in your application context or setting a nonexisting property on a bean definition are discovered only when you actually load the application context at runtime. This is where integration testing comes into the picture.

The goal of integration testing is to test how the individually tested units of your application collaborate with each other. When working with Spring, you wire those dependencies together using Spring's configuration files. In order to test part of your whole application, you typically want to load the Spring application context and test one or more beans configured in that application context. Fortunately, Spring provides convenient support for this. In order to use these features, you need to add `spring-mock.jar` to your classpath.

Spring provides three convenient test base classes for integration testing of your Spring applications: `AbstractDependencyInjectionSpringContextTests`, `AbstractTransactionalSpring ContextTests`, and `AbstractTransactionalDataSourceSpringContextTests`. These classes are discussed in the following sections.

Testing Without Transactions

The `org.springframework.test.AbstractDependencyInjectionSpringContextTests` base class is the test class you will typically use when testing parts of your application that do not require access to a database or any other transactional support. You should extend this class by first implementing the `getConfigLocations()` method, which should return an array of application context locations to be loaded by the test. When the test is executed, the specified configurations will be loaded as an application context.

The major advantage of using this base class is that the application context will be loaded only once for each test method. If you were to load the application yourself in the `setUp()` method of a test, the application context would be reloaded for every test method. This is especially useful when loading configurations that require a lot of initialization, such as a Hibernate session factory. Another advantage of using this base class is that you can define fields for this test that are populated automatically by Spring based on your application context.

Assume we have a Spring configuration file that defines the default implementation of the currency converter we created earlier. The configuration file, named `applicationContext.xml`, also contains all required dependencies—in this case, only the exchange rate service. We can just add a field of type `CurrencyConverter`, and it will get injected into our test on creation. The property is then available to our test methods for testing the converter. Listing 10-13 shows this configuration file.

Listing 10-13. *A Sample Application Context for Integration Testing*

```xml
<?xml version="1.0" encoding="UTF-8"?>
<!DOCTYPE beans PUBLIC
    "-//SPRING//DTD BEAN//EN"
    "http://www.springframework.org/dtd/spring-beans.dtd">

<beans>

    <bean id="currencyConverter"
        class="com.apress.springbook.chapter10.DefaultCurrencyConverter">
      <property name="exchangeRateService" ref="exchangeRateService"/>
    </bean>

    <bean id="exchangeRateService"
        class="com.apress.springbook.chapter10.DefaultExchangeRateService"/>

</beans>
```

The next step is to create an integration test class for testing the currency converter using Spring's test support. Listing 10-14 shows this integration test, which extends the `Abstract DependencyInjectionSpringContextTests` base class.

Listing 10-14. *An Integration Test for the Currency Converter Using Spring's Test Support*

```
package com.apress.springbook.chapter10;

import org.springframework.test.AbstractDependencyInjectionSpringContextTests;

public class CurrencyConverterIntegrationTests
  extends AbstractDependencyInjectionSpringContextTests {

  private CurrencyConverter currencyConverter;

  public void setCurrencyConverter(CurrencyConverter currencyConverter) {
    this.currencyConverter = currencyConverter;
  }

  protected String[] getConfigLocations() {
    return new String[] { "classpath:/applicationContext.xml" };
  }

  public void testWithValidInput() {
    try {
      assertEquals(12.234, currencyConverter.convert(10.0, "EUR", "USD"));
    } catch (UnknownCurrencyException e) {
      fail("something went wrong in testWithValidInput()");
    }
  }

  public void testConvertWithUnknownCurrency() {
    try {
      currencyConverter.convert(10.0, "EUR", "-UNKNOWN-");
      fail("an unknown currency exception was expected");
    } catch (UnknownCurrencyException e) {
      // do nothing, was expected
    }
  }
}
```

As you can see, the getConfigLocations() method is implemented to return the previously created application context. This application context contains the currency converter, which is automatically injected by Spring. This injection is done in one of two ways:

- Through setter injection—creating setter methods for the dependencies you want to have injected. They will be satisfied by autowiring by type.

- Through field injection—declaring protected variables of the required type that match named beans in the context. This is autowiring by name, rather than type.

By default, all dependencies are injected using setter injection. You need to set the populateProtectedVariables property to true in the constructor of the test to switch on field injection.

Note that the test methods in the test class in Listing 10-14 perform an integration test, because they also include the exchange rate service dependency of the currency converter.

Testing with Transactions

Another convenient test base class is org.springframework.test.AbstractTransactionalSpring
ContextTests, which builds on top of the functionality offered by the AbstractDependency
InjectionSpringContextTests test base class. Each test method that is executed by a subclass of
this base class will automatically participate in a transaction. Because the default is to roll back
the transaction after each test method execution, no actual modifications will be made to any
transactional resources. This makes it the perfect choice for performing integration tests using
a transactional data source.

Using this base class allows you to integration test functionality that will make modifications
to the database without having to worry about the changes affecting any other test methods. It also
allows you test code that requires a transactional context. And you can write data to the database
without worrying about cleaning it up afterwards.

As mentioned, all modifications to the database are rolled back at the end of each test method
execution. In order to override this behavior, you have two alternative approaches:

- Set the defaultRollback property to false, to make the transaction not roll back by default
  after each test method execution.

- Call setComplete() in a test method in order to inform the test not to roll back the transaction after the test methods complete.

Testing with a DataSource

A third convenient test base class is org.springframework.test.AbstractTransactionalDataSource
SpringContextTests, which builds on top of the functionality provided by AbstractTransactional
SpringContextTests. In order to use this base class, you need to include a DataSource definition in
the application context loaded by this test. The data source is automatically injected, as explained
earlier.

The main feature offered by this base class is that it provides you with a JdbcTemplate as a
protected field, which you can use to modify the data source, within the transactional context. You
could, for instance, insert some data that the test needs in order to succeed. Because the statements
to the JdbcTemplate are also executed within the transactional context, you do not need to worry
about cleaning up the database or modifying the existing data.

Using Spring Mock Classes

So far, you have seen how Spring helps you integration test the beans defined in your application
context and provides support for testing code that actually modifies the database. Spring also
provides support for testing your J2EE-specific application code. Because much of your web application code is very much tied to J2EE classes, it is hard to test. For instance, testing a servlet or a
Spring controller implementation requires you to somehow mock the HttpServletRequest and
HttpServletResponse classes. You could use EasyMock to do this, but there is a much easier alternative: Spring's web mock classes.

Table 10-3 lists the web mock classes provided by Spring to help you test your web application
code.

Table 10-3. *Web Mock Classes Provided by Spring*

Class	Description
MockHttpServletRequest	Mock implementation of the HttpServletRequest interface. Can be used to test servlets and controllers.
MockHttpServletResponse	Mock implementation of the HttpServletResponse interface. Can be used to test servlets and controllers.
MockHttpSession	Mock implementation of the HttpSession interface. Can be used to test code that requires a session in order to function.
MockFilterConfig	Mock implementation of the FilterConfig interface. Can be used to test filter implementations.
MockServletConfig	Mock implementation of the ServletConfig interface. Can be used to test servlets.
MockServletContext	Mock implementation of the ServletContext interface. Can be used to test servlets.
MockRequestDispatcher	Mock implementation of the RequestDispatcher interface. Can be used to test servlets and controllers.
MockPageContext	Mock implementation of the PageContext abstract class. Can be used to test JSP tag implementations.
MockExpressionEvaluator	Mock implementation of the ExpressionEvaluator abstract class. Can be used to test JSP tag implementations.

Along with these web-specific mock objects, Spring also provides mock objects for a number of other hard-to-mock J2EE interfaces and classes. Currently, it provides mock objects mainly for working with JNDI, such as the SimpleNamingContext, which provides a mock object for the Context interface.

Summary

This chapter started with an overview of testing, including unit testing, integration testing, and TDD. We then introduced JUnit as a framework for writing tests, and EasyMock to mock the dependencies your classes may have. Finally, you saw how Spring provides a number of convenient base test classes and mock objects to perform integration testing and test your web application code.

■ ■ ■

Installing the Eclipse Web Tools Platform

No longer is it acceptable to run through a long and cumbersome series of steps just to see if a simple change worked. The modern way to create web applications is to embrace integrated development environments (IDEs) and the benefits they offer. Two leading Java IDEs—Eclipse (`http://www.eclipse.org`) and IntelliJ IDEA (`http://www.jetbrains.com/idea/`)—allow you to work quickly and efficiently, avoiding painful and delayed deployment.

In this appendix, we will show you how to set up and configure Eclipse with its Web Tools Platform (WTP). We are providing instructions for the Eclipse WTP because it is free and easily available. Both the Eclipse and IntelliJ IDEA IDEs are excellent, and there is no bias for one over the other. We recommend that after you get started, you try them both to see which you prefer. It's worth the effort to find your favorite IDE—even if it costs money—if you make your living developing web applications.

So what is the Eclipse WTP, and what does it bring to the standard Eclipse IDE? To quote the Eclipse WTP home page (`http://www.eclipse.org/webtools/main.php`):

> *The Eclipse Web Tools Platform (WTP) Project provides APIs for J2EE and Web-centric application development. It includes both source and graphical editors for a variety of languages, wizards and built-in applications to simplify Web Service development, and tools and APIs to support deploying, running, and testing apps.*

In other words, it brings editors and wizards for common web application development tasks into the Eclipse IDE. With the WTP, you'll have editors for HTML, JSP, XML, and other files.

But most important is the fact that the WTP allows you to run a servlet container, such as Tomcat, inside Eclipse. This means that you can deploy and debug web applications directly inside your IDE with a single click. This also means that you don't need to recompile and redeploy your web application while developing. It's now possible to make changes to your application, including both JSP files and your Java classes, and see those changes reflected in your server live. This is a huge time-saver, and the core reason why we are recommending that you use a modern IDE.

We are assuming you have some knowledge of Eclipse, or that you have used Java IDEs before. What follows is not a generic Eclipse tutorial. For more information on Eclipse, we recommend *Eclipse in Action* (Manning, 2003).

Installing Tomcat

Even though the Eclipse WTP includes servlet container integration for many of the top containers, it does not include an actual servlet container. You can choose from many excellent and mature servlet containers, but we recommend the Tomcat server from the Apache Group. Tomcat is free and open source, and the WTP integrates with it very well. Before you download and install the WTP, take the time to download the latest version of Tomcat 5.5 from `http://tomcat.apache.org/`.

You must use Tomcat 5.5.*x* or later to run the examples in this book, because we take advantage of JSP 2.0 and Servlet 2.4 specifications. However, Spring MVC applications do not require a Servlet 2.4-compliant container (but we do recommend using the latest versions and specifications, if possible). Tomcat 5.5 requires Java 5 or later.

Follow these steps to download Tomcat:

1. Go to `http://tomcat.apache.org/download-55.cgi`.

2. Choose the latest version of the Core distribution. Select the zip or tar/gz download, whichever one you prefer. Don't download the Windows executable.

Note Tomcat comes in a Windows installer download and a platform-independent download. We recommend that you download the platform-independent version, even if you're running on Windows. There's really nothing to install—it's just a matter of configuring Tomcat in the Eclipse WTP—and this download allows you to extract Tomcat wherever you want.

---

3. Extract the archive to a location on your drive. You'll need to point to the directory containing the Tomcat distribution when configuring Tomcat in the WTP.

There is no configuration of Tomcat required, as the WTP will manage the server and your web application.

Installing Eclipse

The current version of Eclipse is 3.2 and is part of the Callisto project. Once Eclipse is downloaded and running, you can download and install the WTP through the built-in update manager. We'll run through all the steps required to get Eclipse and the WTP working, so that you can start creating web applications with the Spring Framework and Spring MVC.

Do you already have an Eclipse installation? That's not a problem, as you can point multiple Eclipse installations to the same workspace. That way, you won't interfere with your existing Eclipse installation, and you'll get the benefits of a simple, stand-alone web application development IDE.

Note You must have a Java Development Kit (JDK), version 5 or greater, downloaded and installed before attempting to run Eclipse.

Follow these steps to download and run Eclipse:

1. Go to `http://www.eclipse.org/downloads/`. This page will display the download for your platform (Windows, Mac OSX, or Linux).

2. Choose a mirror close to you.

3. Download and unzip the file into an easy-to-remember directory.

4. Browse to the directory you unzipped the file into and run the `eclipse` command (`eclipse.exe` for the Windows platform).

5. Accept the default workspace location if you haven't run Eclipse before. If you have used Eclipse before, the suggested location will be your existing workspace. You can choose another workspace location if you want to create a new one, but you can just reuse your current one.

■**Note** If you're already using Eclipse, any additional plugins you may have installed will not be available in Eclipse 3.2, which means you will need to reinstall them.

Congratulations, you now have Eclipse installed and working, and are ready to install the WTP.

Installing WTP

The Eclipse WTP and other plugins that are part of the Callisto project can be downloaded and installed from the Callisto update site via the built-in update manager. Here are the steps to install the WTP:

1. Open the Eclipse update manager by selecting Help ➤ Software Updates ➤ Find and Install, as shown in Figure A-1.

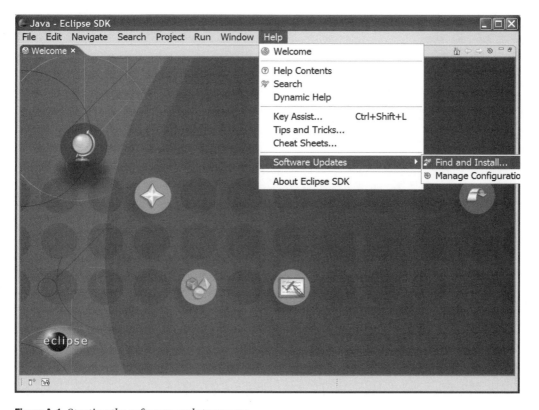

Figure A-1. *Starting the software update process*

2. The Install/Update screen will be displayed, as shown in Figure A-2. Select the second option, "Search for new features to install," and click Next.

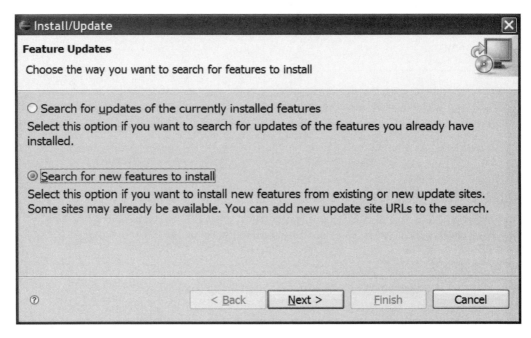

Figure A-2. *Choosing to search for new features*

3. Click the check box next to Callisto Discovery Site to select it. Make sure it is the only site selected, as shown as Figure A-3. Click Finish.

4. Select an update site close to your location from the Update Site Mirrors list, as shown in Figure A-4. Click OK to continue.

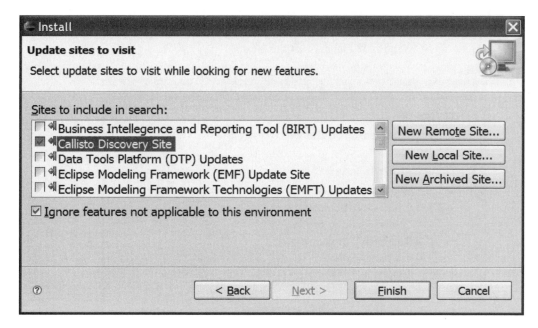

Figure A-3. *Selecting the Callisto Discovery Site*

Figure A-4. *Choosing an update site*

5. In the list of features to install, check the Web and J2EE Development option. You will get a warning message saying dependencies are missing. Click the Select Required button to resolve these, as shown in Figure A-5. Click Next.

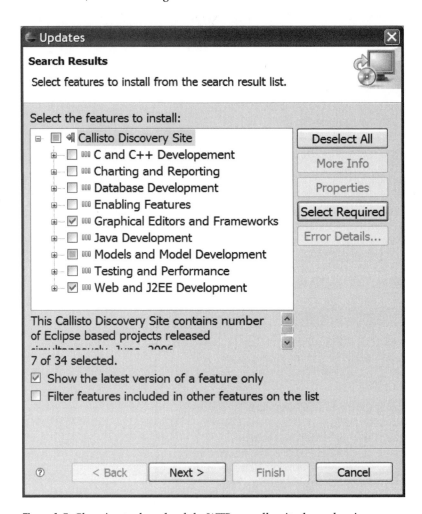

Figure A-5. *Choosing to download the WTP, as well as its dependencies*

5. Select "I accept the terms in the license agreements" and click Next.

6. Accept the default location for installing the WTP (shown in Figure A-6) and its dependencies by clicking Finish. The plugins will now be downloaded.

Figure A-6. *Completing the WTP installation*

7. Surprisingly, some of the downloaded plugins may not be properly signed, as shown in Figure A-7. Click Install or Install All to approve their installation.

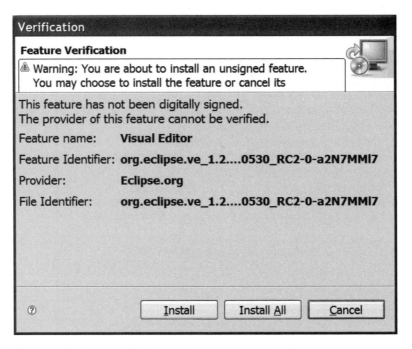

Figure A-7. *Details of a plugin that is not properly signed*

8. After all plugins have been installed, click Yes to restart Eclipse with the WTP.

With the WTP installed, you're ready to create a new web project.

Starting a New Web Project

The WTP includes a new project type, the Dynamic Web Project. This project type is what you'll use whenever you create a servlet-based (and thus Spring MVC) application. The Dynamic Web Project type includes and integrates all of the helpful wizards and editors that are useful when developing a web application. We will now show you how to create a new, blank Dynamic Web Project.

Note The following instructions are valid for at least Eclipse 3.2 and the WTP. Different versions of this product might require different steps.

1. Select File ➤ New ➤ Project to start the New Project wizard.

2. Open the Web folder and choose Dynamic Web Project, as shown in Figure A-8. Then click Next.

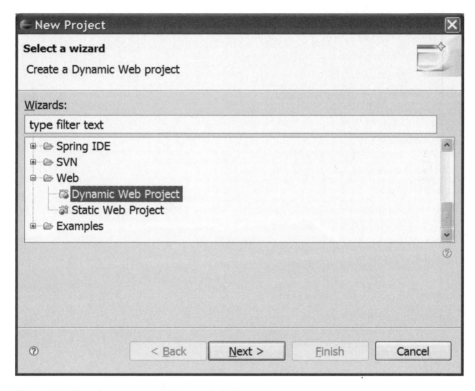

Figure A-8. *Choosing to create a Dynamic Web Project*

3. Choose a meaningful name for the project. Figure A-9 shows an example. You next need to configure a target runtime. This is the servlet container in which the application will run during development. Click the New button to create a new server runtime.

Figure A-9. *Setting up a Dynamic Web Project*

4. Select your server runtime environment. For the examples in this book, we are using Tomcat 5.5. Open the Apache folder and choose Apache Tomcat v5.5, as shown in Figure A-10. Then click Next.

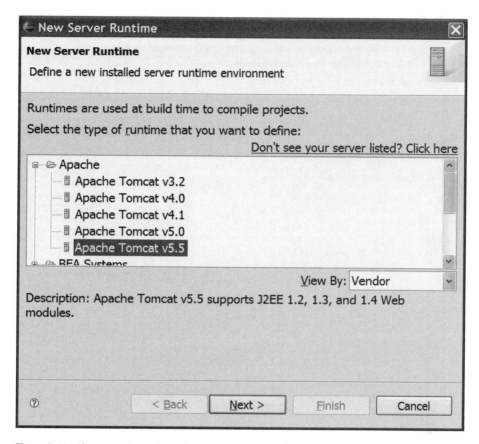

Figure A-10. *Choosing Tomcat as the target runtime*

5. Now it's time to point to the directory where you extracted the Tomcat download. Click the Browse button and locate the Tomcat installation directory, as shown in Figure A-11. It's a good idea to double-check that you are using Java Development Kit (JDK) 5 for this web project. You can use the New Server Runtime dialog box to choose JDK 5. Click the Finish button.

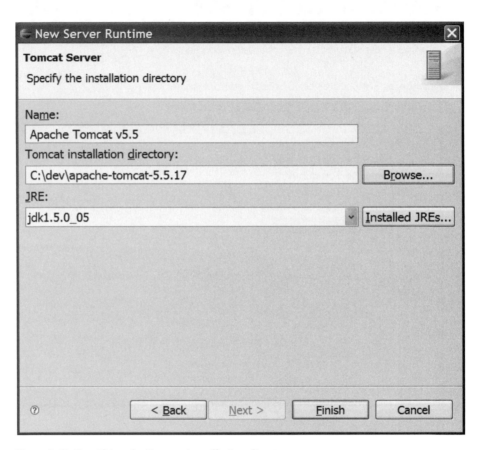

Figure A-11. *Specifying the Tomcat installation directory*

6. The New Dynamic Web Project dialog box now displays your selected target runtime, as shown in Figure A-12. Click the Finish button to complete the wizard.

Figure A-12. *Completing the Dynamic Web Project setup*

7. At this point, you might see a License Agreement dialog box, as shown in Figure A-13. You are seeing this because the WTP is downloading and caching the XML Schema for the web.xml file in order to perform validation. Review the agreement, and if you agree, click the I Agree button.

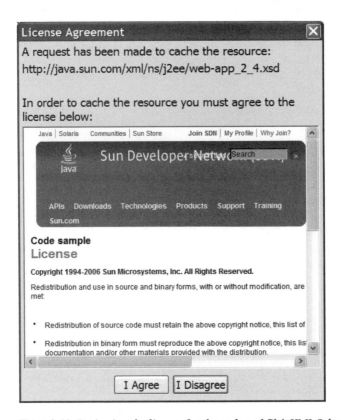

Figure A-13. *Reviewing the license for the web.xml file's XML Schema*

8. You are now finished creating a new Dynamic Web Project. Eclipse will suggest that you switch to the J2EE perspective, as shown in Figure A-14. Click Yes to do so.

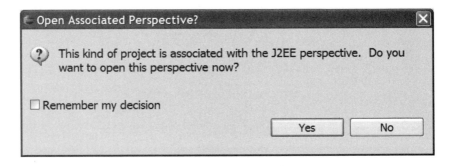

Figure A-14. *Switching to the J2EE perspective*

Back in the Project Explorer view, if you open all the folders, you will see the file layout shown in Figure A-15.

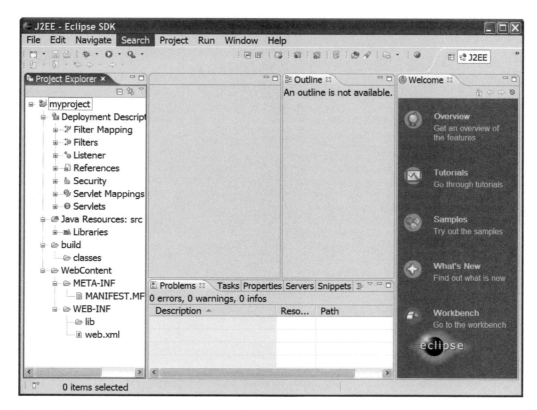

Figure A-15. *The file layout in the Dynamic Web Project*

You're now ready to get your hands dirty with Spring MVC, which is covered in Chapters 8 and 9.

Index

Find it faster at http://superindex.apress.com/

You Need the Companion eBook

Your purchase of this book entitles you to buy the companion PDF-version eBook for only $10. Take the weightless companion with you anywhere.

We believe this Apress title will prove so indispensable that you'll want to carry it with you everywhere, which is why we are offering the companion eBook (in PDF format) for $10 to customers who purchase this book now. Convenient and fully searchable, the PDF version of any content-rich, page-heavy Apress book makes a valuable addition to your programming library. You can easily find and copy code—or perform examples by quickly toggling between instructions and the application. Even simultaneously tackling a donut, diet soda, and complex code becomes simplified with hands-free eBooks!

Once you purchase your book, getting the $10 companion eBook is simple:

1. Visit **www.apress.com/promo/tendollars/**.

2. Complete a basic registration form to receive a randomly generated question about this title.

3. Answer the question correctly in 60 seconds, and you will receive a promotional code to redeem for the $10.00 eBook.

THE EXPERT'S VOICE™

2855 TELEGRAPH AVENUE | SUITE 600 | BERKELEY, CA 94705

Offer valid through 2/27/08.